The Force of Culture:
Unionist Identities in Twentieth-Century Ireland

The Force of Culture:
Unionist Identities in
Twentieth-Century Ireland

CORK UNIVERSITY PRESS

First published in 1999 by
Cork University Press
University College
Cork
Ireland

British Library Cataloguing in Publication Data
A CIP catalogue record for this book is available from
the British Library

ISBN   1 85918 204 6   hardcover
       1 85918 205 4   paperback

Typeset by Tower Books, Ballincollig, Co. Cork
Printed by ColourBooks, Baldoyle, Co. Dublin

For Brendan

Contents

Acknowledgements

Scholarships from the British Academy and the Foreign and Commonwealth Office allowed me to pursue my doctoral research, and I register my thanks for that support here. Additionally, I owe thanks to the following libraries and research centres: the Public Record Office of Northern Ireland; Belfast Central Library; the Linen Hall Library; the Library of Queen's University, Belfast; BBC's Written Archive Centre, Cavesham; the Ulster Folk and Transport Museum; and the National Museums and Galleries of Northern Ireland (Ulster Museum). For permission to quote from their archives I would like to thank the Deputy Keeper of the Records, the Public Record Office of Northern Ireland and BBC's Written Archives Centre, Cavesham. I would also like to thank Fergus and Angélique Bell for their permission to examine Sam Hanna Bell's papers, and their encouragement and hospitality while I did so. Thanks also to David Higham Associates, representatives of the estate of Louis MacNeice. I am grateful to Fergus Bell for permission to quote from the work of Sam Hanna Bell, and to Lucy Cohen for permission to quote from the work of W.R. Rodgers. Thanks are also due to Blackstaff Press and the John Hewitt estate for permission to quote from the work of John Hewitt. Although every effort has been made, I apologise to the owners of copyright whom I have been unable to contact, or whom I have inadvertently overlooked.

Professor Alvin Jackson supervised the doctoral research on which this book is based. During that research period and since, he has provided me with constant encouragement and much sound advice, which I continue to appreciate. My Master's research, under the supervision of Professor Tom Dunne, set me on the path of unionist culture. I am grateful for the guidance he gave me then and his support which I have benefitted from since. I have also benefitted from the support of colleagues and friends in the School of Modern History and School of English, and in the Institute of Irish Studies, QUB, Belfast. Beyond those realms, two friends who deserve particular mention are Tom Clyde and Dr Maura Cronin; both share the great combined qualities of enthusiasm and patience, not only for their own, but for the work of others. Given the pressure of their individual scholarly endeavours I appreciate the time they gave to reading early drafts of this work, and the many conversations with them which have helped me to clarify my thoughts. Finally, thanks are due to Cork University Press' readers, anonymous guides who stimulated and encouraged me to review and reconsider aspects of the text. My family have always kept me rooted in the most important things in life. They are included in the book's dedication with love.

Abbreviations

AC:	Minutes of the Arts Council of Northern Ireland.
BBCNI:	British Broadcasting Corporation in Northern Ireland.
CAB:	Cabinet papers.
CEMA	Council for the Encouragement of Music and the Arts.
COM:	Ministry of commerce papers.
FIN:	Ministry of finance papers.
FOB:	Festival of Britain.
FOBCNI:	Festival of Britain Committee Northern Ireland.
FOBNI:	Festival of Britain in Northern Ireland.
GPFSC:	General Purposes and Finance Sub Committee.
HA:	Ministry of home affairs papers.
JS:	Jubilee supplement.
LA:	Local authorities papers.
PRONI:	Public Records Office of Northern Ireland.
RH:	Diary of Ruby Hewitt.
SHB:	Sam Hanna Bell.
SHBP:	Sam Hanna Bell's papers.

Introduction

Culture is not a power, something to which social events, behaviours, institutions or processes can be casually attributed; it is a context, something within which they can be intelligibly – that is, thickly – described.[1]

Clifford Geertz

Between 1920 and 1960, in both literature and ceremony, the identity, image and character of Northern Ireland and the Northern Irish were dominated by unionist historians, biographers, journalists, government officials, and (following the Second World War) creative writers. In constructing their identity, unionists drew on an exclusively protestant ethos and a history rich in myth and tradition. The foundation histories of the 1920s and the monumental histories of the 1930s and 1940s, which celebrated the state's founding fathers Carson and Craig, drew on this protestant past to legitimise the actions of unionists in the present and to endorse the state in general.[2]

From its foundation, unionists' overriding concern was the survival of the Northern Irish state. An examination of unionism's relationship with both Britain and the southern Irish state is important to any consideration of the evolution of unionist identity.[3] Throughout this period unionists perceived, and reacted to, a series of threats to the state from a variety of sources; from Éire (and the declaration of the republic in 1948), from Westminster (and its negotiations with Éire to end partition in order to gain the use of the Treaty ports in 1940) and from within unionist ranks themselves. These developments influenced and at times acted as the catalyst for unionist ceremonies and literature.

A number of themes recur throughout this period: the need for unity in order to maintain the state; loyalty; betrayal; sacrifice. Stereotypes of unionists and nationalists, established in the period of the first home rule crisis, were endorsed and publicised in the new state. The colour and drama of unionist demonstrations in the period 1885–1922 has already been established.[4] This theatricality and rich symbolism continued to find expression in the new Northern Irish state, particularly in the ceremonies surrounding the erection of the statue to the state's founding father, Edward Carson, in the

1

Festival of Britain in Northern Ireland in 1951, and in the numerous royal visits which culminated in the triumphal coronation visit of Elizabeth II in 1953. These large-scale public demonstrations and the political culture associated with them were an integral part of unionism, allowing the movement to appeal to and incorporate a diverse protestant community, gathering it into a coherent unit, defining its role in the union, and creating a particular identity for the Northern Irish state.

A recurring focus of this book is the visits of royalty to Northern Ireland. Unionists saw these events as occasions of affirmation for the state, and an endorsement of their culture and their rule in Northern Ireland. The way the protestant community planned and celebrated these royal rituals reflected the priorities of unionists and the tensions and strains within the state. While the royal visits were clearly an embodiment of shared consensus among protestants and unionists, they were also 'an attempt to make authoritative a certain way of looking at society by invoking people's loyalties towards a particular symbolic representation of the social order'.[5] Of course, there were sections of the society, in particular the catholic community, who were hostile to these occasions, and this was particularly evident during the coronation visit in 1953. But, as Patrick Buckland has argued, the unionist government sought to maintain the loyalty of its supporters through an informal style of government and by discrimination in favour of protestants and unionists 'in respect of education and representation, and to a lesser extent, governmental employment and law and order'.[6]

There is an absence of literature exploring the culture and writings of this period. Both Terence Brown in *Ireland: a social and cultural history, 1922–85*, and Arthur Marwick in *Culture in Britain since 1945*, have left Northern Ireland out; while Jonathon Bardon in his *History of Ulster* neglects to mention culture in the state almost entirely.[7] This leads to a general assumption that unionism had no active culture of its own, and gives the impression of a colourless and inactive time in which little happened. As this present study suggests, this was far from the truth. Contrary to the argument of some commentators, unionist visions of their history and their expressions of their culture, in common with their nationalist counterparts, were neither lacking in emotional range, nor in complexity.[8] Seeking to restore the balance, this book explores the culture and literature of unionism over a thirty-five-year period, a period marked by rich political theatre and broad literary expression – from the early unionist foundation histories to the effusive poetry of W.R. Rodgers. Of necessity, this work does not deal with unionist culture exhaustively. Extensive work has already been done on the history of unionism and Northern Ireland, its high politics, high-profile political figures, and political theory from the first home rule crisis to the present day.[9] More specifically, Alvin Jackson, A.T.Q. Stewart and Peter Gibbon have contributed significantly to an understanding of unionism's popular culture at the turn of the century.[10] Dennis Kennedy's *A widening gulf*, which examined the state through contemporary newspaper sources, was a welcome and illuminating addition to this body of literature. This book has also benefited from the work of authors whose interests lie in different (but related) fields – in particular, the work on public rituals by David Cannadine and David Chaney, and that on the cultural and social dimensions of broadcasting by Paddy Scannell, David Cardiff and James Curran. These authors, in conjunction with more standard cultural theorists such as Raymond Williams and Clifford Geertz, have inspired what I hope is an innovative and refreshing approach to unionist history.

Culture is a description of a particular way of life which expresses certain meanings and values, not only in art and learning, but also in institutions and ordinary behaviour.[11] Unionist literature and ceremonies were made up of unique features which provide an opportunity to explore the identity of the society in which they took place.[12] These creations and performances feed into one another, and with each event reference is made implicitly to the previous occasion while future rituals are predicted. In addition, it is possible to read through the documentary and textual forms which unionists left behind to 'reconstitute . . . the "structure of feeling" – the patterned ways of thinking, feeling and living shared by individuals living in similar circumstances – which originally lay behind or supported such forms'.[13] The cultural diversity of Northern Ireland was problematic for unionists who were promoting an image of the state and its people as a homogenous unit. The unionist political culture and literature which emerged in this period focused on the unique identity of unionists in Ulster, their historic separateness from the rest of Ireland, and their bond with Britain rooted in the plantations and reinforced in the modern age through two world wars. In the stereotypes which they rehearsed, unionists argued for their separateness, and were critical of both the southern state and the British. The developing unionist identity was therefore complex and full of contradictions. Unionist culture and literature were élitist, professedly loyal to the crown and empire, and at times openly anglophobic.

Geared towards the survival of the state, unionism was almost continually in a defensive mode. Officially, Northern Ireland was a united and homogenous protestant state; unofficially, it was a diverse state, made up of catholics as well as a variety of protestant sects, and full of tension and disharmony. Diversity was problematic for the unionist government who saw unity among protestants – even when that was merely superficial – as the only way in which the state could survive; at the same time that very diversity was a rich source for creative writers and BBC producers. Catholic consciousness and identity were not considered, or considered only when they intruded upon unionist consciousness: of more importance for the unionist hierarchy throughout this period was the maintenance of protestant unity, and the glossing-over of fissures within the unionist rank and file. Unionism was exclusionist and officially had a narrow vision of what constituted being Northern Irish. But Britain, the Irish republic and dissident forces within their own borders constantly impinged upon unionist visions of the state. Yet the majority of unionists failed to reconcile themselves to the often conflicting factors which made up the state. It was not until the post-war period that the complex identity and image of Northern Ireland came to be debated by figures such as John Hewitt and Sam Hanna Bell.

This book then provides an analysis of the discourse of unionist self-identification, traced through the efforts of various protestant élites to influence public representations, manifestations and perceptions of an ideal 'Ulster' collective identity. One commentator has argued that the 'debate over the *status* of Ulster Protestant identity has tended to deflect attention away from its *substance*'.[14] The pages that follow will hopefully provide some of that substance.

Notes and References

1   'Understanding a people's culture exposes their normalness without reducing their particularity . . . It renders them accessible: setting them in the frame of their own banalities, it dissolves their opacity', Clifford Geertz, *The interpretation of cultures: selected essays* (New York, 1973), p. 14.

2   'In short, the person of the present learns from monumental history that "the greatness that once existed was in any event once possible and may be thus again"'. See Kathleen Nutt, 'Irish identity and the writing of history', *Éire-Ireland*, vol. xxix, no. 2, Summer 1994.

3   Culture and literature are social facts which can only be 'fully understood within the material world in which they come to life'. Terence Brown, *A social and cultural history of Ireland, 1922–85* (London, 1985), p. 9. 'Culture can be seen as a map by means of which the nature of changes can be explored.' Raymond Williams, *Culture and society* (London, 1961), p. 16.

4   In addition to the references in note 9, see my 'Politics as theatre: the popular culture of Ulster unionism', unpublished MA, University College Cork, Sept., 1992.

5   Elizabeth Hammerton and David Cannadine, 'Conflict and consensus on a ceremonial occasion: the Diamond Jubilee in Cambridge in 1897', *The Historical Journal*, vol. 24, no. I (1981), p. 113.

6   Patrick Buckland, *The factory of grievances: devolved government in Northern Ireland, 1921–39* (Dublin, 1979), p. 6.

7   Terence Brown, *Ireland: a social and cultural history, 1922–85*, Arthur Marwick, *Culture in Britain since 1945* (London, 1991), Jonathon Bardon, *A history of Ulster* (Belfast, 1992).

8   'That [protestant] imagination is one that in modern times (at least since 1886) had recourse to a vision of the protestant community's history which is starkly simple in outline and depressingly lacking in emotional range and complexity', Terence Brown, *The whole protestant community: the making of a historical myth* (Derry, 1985), p. 5.

9   See in particular Alvin Jackson, *Edward Carson* (Dundalk, 1993), *The Ulster Party: Irish unionists in the House of Commons, 1884–1911* (Oxford, 1989). John Harbinson, *The Ulster Unionist Party 1882–1973: its development and organisation* (Belfast, 1973). Patrick Buckland, *Irish unionism II* (Dublin, 1973), *The factory of grievances: devolved government in Northern Ireland, 1921–39* (Dublin, 1979), *James Craig* (Dublin, 1980). More recently see Bryan Follis, *A state under siege: the establishment of Northern Ireland, 1920–25* (Oxford, 1995) and James Loughlin, *Ulster unionism and British identity* (London, 1995).

10   Alvin Jackson, 'Unionist politics and protestant society in Edwardian Ireland', *The Historical Journal*, 33, (1990), 'Unionist myths, 1912–85', *Past and Present* (Aug. 1992), 'Irish unionism', *The making of modern Irish history*

(London, 1996), 'Irish unionism and the empire', in Keith Jeffery (ed.), *An Irish empire?' Aspects of Ireland and the British empire* (Manchester, 1996). A.T.Q. Stewart, *The Ulster crisis* (London, 1967), *The narrow ground* (London, 1977), *Edward Carson* (Dublin, 1981). Peter Gibbon, *The origins of Ulster unionism, the formation of popular protestant politics and ideology in nineteenth century Ireland* (Manchester, 1975).

11 Raymond Williams, 'The analysis of culture', in T. Bennett, G. Martin, C. Mercer, J. Woolacott (eds.), *Culture, ideology and social process* (London, 1981), p. 41.

12 Clifford Geertz argues that human beings are animals suspended in webs of significance which they themselves have spun: 'culture is those webs, and the analysis of it is an interpretive process in search of meaning'. Clifford Geertz, *The interpretation of cultures: selected essays* (New York, 1973), p. 5, p. 14.

13 Raymond Williams, 'The analysis of culture', p. 40.

14 Ian MacBride, 'Ulster and the British problem', in Richard English and Graham Walker (eds.), *Unionism in Modern Ireland* (Dublin, 1996), p. 7.

1. The Seamless Fabric of History:
unionist histories and the Northern Irish state

St John Ervine, in the preface to his 1949 biography of Craigavon, explained that his purpose in writing the book was 'to try to translate my countrymen, the Ulster people, into such terms that those who misunderstand and misinterpret them, shall at least perceive that we have reasons for our attitude towards our fellow-countrymen'.[1] Writing in the early twentieth century, unionist authors explained, by means of an historical narrative, the contemporary position of northern protestants in Ireland, and the position of the Northern Irish state itself. In this way, much as it was for nationalist writers, history was written by unionists to 'serve a legitimising function for present commitment'.[2] The political developments of the first two decades of the century (the third home rule crisis, the Easter Rising and the Battle of the Somme, the British negotiations with Irish nationalists post-1916 and so on) strongly influenced what was written. Indeed, in some cases, such events initiated that writing. Authors such as Lord Ernest Hamilton, James Logan, D.A. Chart, Cyril Falls, W.A. Phillips[3] and others wrote their various interpretations of the past in order to legitimise the current political position, or as an explanation for contemporary events and feelings, or to show that in the seamless fabric of history a specific happening was just one more strand. The work of these authors was a response to political crisis and change, and indicated unionist perceptions of ongoing political developments.

Throughout the first thirty years of the state's existence, this was to remain the case; in the 1930s, unionist demonstrations, such as that to honour Edward Carson, were orchestrated in response to the unionist leadership's fears about unity within the unionist rank and file; throughout the history of the BBC in the state successive unionist governments reacted strongly to programmes which they believed brought into question the protestant/British identity of Northern Ireland (which they promoted as the *sole* identity of the state); later protestant authors (such as John Blake, St John Ervine and John Hewitt) all responded through their writing to the pressures and tensions within the state and within the unionist community.

This chapter will focus on unionist authors such as Hamilton, Chart, Logan and Falls, who established modern stereotypes of 'Ulstermen' and

'Southerners', of 'native Irish' and the 'planters', and through their writing wove significant 'sacred' protestant dates, such as 1641 and 1798, into the modern psyche of Ulster protestants. They created the template which subsequent protestant Northern Irish writers inherited and often echoed; in particular writers who repeated (or reacted to) stereotypes of 'Ulstermen' and 'Southerners'. Their texts also provided the ideological backbone for unionism's civic rituals in the 1930s and the later 1940s. The work of these authors is therefore crucial as a means of exploring some key dimensions in unionist psyche and identity in the period when the Northern Irish state was being founded. As Benedetto Croce wrote, 'history pinpoints the problems of its own times more fully even than those of the era about which it is supposed to be concerned'.[4]

Throughout the 1930s and '40s the relationship between unionists and the British government was complex and often fraught. This is borne out by unionist and, more broadly, protestant literature of the era where a constant sniping at, and criticism of, the British can be found. Unionist anxieties over the reliability of the British, in terms of protecting their interests, had its roots in the nineteenth century, and echoed through the foundation histories of the 1920s. The tone of unionist authors when referring to the British administration was generally admonishing; the notable exception being D.A. Chart who, perhaps because of his civil-service status, pragmatically avoided this quagmire by merely avoiding any discussion of what he termed 'recent controversies' and 'painful memories'.[5] By way of contrast, in 1926 W.A. Phillips condemned the British administration in bold terms:

> It is a tragic history – as nearly all Irish history has been, and the tragedy lies not so much in the bloodshed and terror of these years as in the igno-rances, the misconceptions, the want of clear guiding principle, which made the terror and the bloodshed inevitable. It lies, in short, in the bankruptcy of British statesmanship.[6]

Such unionist feelings of betrayal had their roots as far back as the first home rule crisis of 1886, but they were resurrected in 1911 with the third home rule bill. Then unionists had looked for the support of a major British politician and found it in the shape of Andrew Bonar Law, the son of an Ulster-Scots emigrant to Canada. The loss of two consecutive elections under Arthur Balfour had caused British conservatives and unionists great frustration. Bonar Law and the conservatives turned to the Ulster stage, as Randolph Churchill had in 1886 (the year after Salisbury's minority tory government fell), and Arthur Balfour had in 1893 (a year after the tories had lost the general election in Britain). The desire to be associated with Ulster unionists had, in George Dangerfield's words, 'very little to do with Ireland: it had a great deal to do with beating the Liberal Party into an irremediable mess of political blood and brains'.[7] Although political opportunism held sway, many British conservatives had a genuine sympathy for the unionists' cause. However, despite an instinctive identification with Ulster unionism, their anti-home rule cause was to pose Bonar Law and the conservatives with some difficult problems. While many tories wished to protect Ulster and were opposed to home rule, they were divided on how far their opposition should go, particularly 'whether or not they could support rebellion against the government'.[8] The British League for Support of Ulster and the Union, which first came to the public's notice in March 1913, epitomised the tory dilemma. The league was formed by Richard Grenville Verney, 19th Lord Willoughby de Broke, who was, according to Rodner, unusual among tories in 'his unabashed willingness to consider the use of force'.[9] When Verney and Alfred Milner (a former high commissioner to South Africa) orchestrated a parallel British Covenant to that held in Ulster in 1912, moderates like Cecil and Austen Chamberlain signed it only after Verney had weakened its language so as to make it practically meaningless. They signed it to maintain an appearance of party unity, and to increase the pressure on the liberals by the public spectacle of so many people signing.[10] The British Covenant highlighted the gap in political terms between tory rhetoric and policy – a gap which Ulster unionists refused to recognise.[11]

The adoption by the tories of violent rhetoric and the qualified endorsement by some of extra-parliamentary behaviour reflected their belief that the formation of a government, and the subsequent removal of the House of Lords' veto as a preliminary to a third home rule bill, was an illegitimate use of a parliamentary majority by the liberals, in alliance with the nationalists. To quote Bonar Law in 1912: 'We can imagine nothing which the Unionists in Ireland can do [in] which they will not be justified against a trick of this kind.'[12] The destruction of the Lords' veto allowed for the triumph of constitutional nationalism, while at the same time forcing Ulster unionists (the crown's most loyal subjects) into extra-parliamentary and often illegal activity.[13] The tories' rhetorical justification for the Ulster unionists' proposed resistance to the democratically elected government of Britain was largely motivated by their desire to force an election, through which they hoped to regain power. For unionists, it was a different matter: the conspiracy theory was incorporated into their historically based self-image which charted the occasions when treacherous Irish catholics had attempted to destroy them and when, in more recent times (for instance, when Gladstone had declared for home rule in 1886), the British government had been willing to abandon them to their 'enemies'. As D.W. Miller has noted, however, conspiracy or not, by the very fact that they established the Ulster Volunteer Force to resist attempts to establish home rule in Ulster, Ulster unionists indicated that they were not willing to allow their fate to be decided by the British parliament or electorate.[14] That resistance brought them to the brink of civil war in 1914. 'For the first time in a period of more than one hundred years', wrote the leader of the *Weekly Northern Whig* in January 1914,

> we have the prospect of war – and that in its worst form of civil-war – in our land . . . It is not to subdue rebels against our sovereign or enemies to the safety and prosperity of the Empire and the Kingdom . . . we actually find that war may be waged by the Government against a great community simply because of loyalty to the Throne and the Empire.[15]

By the summer of 1914 unionists were not alone in expecting civil-war; the British administration was equally aware of the possibility. Trouble in Europe that year, when it came, according to Paul Fussell, was 'expected to be domestic and embarrassing rather than savage and incomprehensible'.[16] The arena for conflict in the summer of 1914 was to be the Western Front, not Ulster. The war began in August 1914, and came to act for those involved and commentators as a simplifier of life's complexities; it witnessed the 'death of ambiguity'.[17] The war years were marked by the use of simple oppositions: those who could be trusted and those who could not; the honourable and the dishonourable; those who were right and those who were wrong. This reflected traits apparent in the rhetoric of unionists in the pre-war period, and it continued to be a characteristic in the decade that followed.[18] In a new differentiation between the British government and the British Empire, the 'empire' became an abstract image which unionists could support without experiencing a crisis in their position. While hostility to the British government was intensified by proposals for Irish conscription and the reintroduction of home rule, the *Northern Whig* editorialised in July 1918:

> Allegiance [to empire] is not affected by the fact that it has earned us more rebuffs than gratitude – at least from the politicians; and indeed we do not know what better proof of sincerity of Ulster's feelings could be given than their survival of the treatment she has received. But brooding over injuries we leave to others. Nothing can alter Ulster's attitude towards the Empire but the driving of her out of it.[19]

The Battle of the Somme, particularly, came to be seen by unionists as the stage for their ultimate sacrifice for the empire and their subsequent betrayal by the British administration, and was ultimately incorporated into unionist myth and history.

Out of government in the first half of 1886, in 1892 and 1912, British tories were not associated with the liberal policies of home rule. During the First World War, however, British tories did control the reins of power, in coalition with the liberals, and with Asquith as prime minister until December 1916. The actions of the coalition government, dominated by men whom the Ulster unionists had presumed to be their allies, proved no more favourable to the unionists' cause than the liberals had been, and created a great deal of resentment among unionists. The creation of their own 'Ulster' division and its destruction, the Easter Rising and its contrast with the Battle of the Somme in 1916, and the anti-conscription campaign in 1918 established a heightened psychological framework for their political position. The rhetoric which formulated an exclusively Ulster protestant identity had been developed through three home rule crises, and focused on the fears of aggressive catholic nationalism and the threat which home rule posed to unionists' social, religious and economic position within the country and the empire. The importance of these rhetorical themes was superseded by the development of a new hostility to a British government which was perceived by unionists, by 1918, as having betrayed their interests. This added resentment was reflected in the tone adopted by Hamilton, Falls, and Phillips towards the British government and already highlighted in their texts. The unionist experience of the First World War reinforced existing attitudes, and made the post-war period for them, as for many others, one of great complexity and difficulty.

Once war was declared in 1914, unionists and nationalists alike lost little time in volunteering to fight. Theoretically both did so for the empire; in reality leaders of both political organisations sought to influence British policy by volunteering their followers. Ultimately, unionist politicians hoped to prevent the implementation of the British government's home rule proposals through their actions in the war. In this, unionists were subscribing to the Allies' war philosophy, sharing in its static sense of history, and preparedness to fight for the preservation of the *status quo*. The First World War took place in a 'static world, where the values appeared stable', in a period where one saw a 'seamless, purposeful history'.[20] Unionists could easily identify with the Allies' war motives; history and a pride in the past provided the substance for French and British identities as it did for Ulster protestants. Speaking to the unionist faithful at the Balmoral demonstration of 1912, Edward Carson reminded his audience that home rule was an issue which went to the very root of their lives. 'It is', he stressed, 'a question which is to secure for us those civil and religious liberties which our forefathers won, and which we are going to maintain'.[21] In this the unionist leader pre-empted the Allied war psyche; to quote a letter from a British soldier at the front in October 1914: 'We are just at the beginning of the struggle I'm afraid, and every hour we should remind ourselves that it is our great privilege to save traditions of all the centuries behind us.'[22]

Cyril Falls believed that the achievements of the 36th Ulster Division were as a result of a 'racial spirit possessing already in amplitude the seeds of endurance and of valour'.[23] Similarly, for James Logan, the war threw into relief all that was best in the 'Ulsterman': 'Under no compulsion, but willingly, with the courage of their forefathers and with lion-hearted bravery, they heard the call of duty and obeyed.'[24] Yet, there was an overt element of opportunism in the unionist response to the war. Speaking at a meeting of the Ulster Unionist Council in September 1914, Carson said: 'England's difficulty is not Ulster's opportunity. However we are treated, and however others act, let us act rightly. We do not seek to purchase terms by selling our patriotism.'[25] However, this is precisely what unionist, and indeed nationalist, leaders expected to gain through their efforts in the war for the empire. In a letter to Carson one unionist wrote: 'It must indeed be a matter of great pride to Ulster that her Volunteers, trained and equipped, have hurried to the defence of the Empire they love so well: and that the Empire will justly appreciate the value of their services, recognising their self-sacrifice and the suppression of injured feelings.'[26] In addition, unionists feared that the British government would negotiate a swift settlement of the home rule issue with nationalists in order to secure the home front, Redmond having threatened that he would not be able to 'hold Ireland' if the bill was not placed on the statute books. 'There is some unease locally', noted the leader in the *Belfast Evening Telegraph*, 'that the Government will yield to Nationalist pressure, knowing that Loyal Ulster will not take advantage of the Empire's trouble.'[27]

Thus, unionists looked on the war as an opportunity to demonstrate and reinforce publicly their commitment to imperial values, an image nurtured by them and one which had played a pivotal role in their propaganda up to this point. There was, of course, also an element of principle in the unionist war effort. In this regard, their ideological stance required little adjusting, and, in their public presentation of events, home rule and German aggression came to embody parallel threats to the empire which they had been vociferously claiming to defend since 1886.[28] Edward Carson's rhetoric about, and attitude towards, the empire (which epitomised that of unionists generally), like Redmond's, was complex, being both sincere and manipulative. Both political camps expected the gratitude of the British administration for their willingness to sacrifice themselves, and the rank and file of their parties. Neither foresaw that in the First World War all special interests would be expendable.

War enthusiasm in Ireland generally mirrored that across Europe but, as elsewhere, it had particular local effects. In the south of Ireland it united unionists and nationalists in a joint war effort, with both groups volunteering for the same regiments. Unionist Ulster remained aloof from the rest of the country; the desire for separateness was particularly clear when unionists sought and were granted their own division, the 36th 'Ulster' Division. Nationalists failed to have a separate army division created for southern recruits; although the 16th Division was made up predominantly of southern catholics, they were refused any distinctively Irish insignia or identity. James Craig, however, persuaded Lord Kitchener that the Ulster Volunteer Force (UVF) should form the nucleus of the 36th Division of the British army. The 'Curragh Mutiny' had illustrated the sympathy and bias of many British army officers towards the unionist cause. In addition, many officers in the Ulster Volunteer Force had served in the British army previously, and empathised with the army's function in Ireland, welcoming it 'as a bulwark against separation and republicanism'.[29] With this in mind and with the general antipathy and distrust within higher British army circles towards Irish nationalists and catholics, the creation of a specifically Ulster protestant division was not surprising. For Cyril Falls and Ernest Hamilton, celebrating the achievements of the 36th Division was in its own way a celebration of the Ulster Volunteer Force, infused as they felt it was with a distinctly 'Ulster' culture and identity. Pride in the UVF, difficult for these authors to express following the Easter Rising, was thus transferred to the 36th 'Ulster' Division.

As Edward Carson announced the creation of the 36th Division to the Ulster Unionist Council, few could have missed the obvious irony of the unionists' position; only a few months previously they had imported German arms to oppose British government measures and now they were volunteering in huge numbers to fight for that same government against the Germans. The *Northern Whig*'s editorial saw no irony in the unionist position: 'It may be that the Government will have good reason to be thankful for the establishment of the Ulster Volunteer Force. There is not a man in that force who would not gladly give his life for the defence of the national flag.'[30] On another level it was the same cause for unionists, an extension of their long-running provincial drama. As one unionist paper put it in 1916, referring to those who had signed the Solemn League and Covenant in September 1912: 'The Ulster Division is a unique unit of the British Army. It is composed of Covenanters who had bound themselves together with the object of resisting attacks on their hard-won liberties'.[31] Again, their perception of the seamless fabric of history connected the provincial politics of Ulster with the wider politics of the European war. The 36th was certainly unique, being overwhelmingly protestant and unionist in nature and the mass enlistment of Ulster Volunteers created a division that 'truly represented Unionist Ulster'.[32] According to Lord Plumer, its achievements were the result of the character of 'a people brought up in great traditions and inspired with a fervent spirit of loyalty'.[33] The makeshift uniforms of the UVF were replaced by the standard British army uniform of tin hat and puttees. To this regular uniform the 36th were granted permission to add the red hand badge of Ulster, a significant public concession to their separate identity by the British administration.[34]

The experience of the First World War, in particular that of the Somme in July 1916, was to mark Ulster protestant opinion and self-perception irrevocably. To quote Keith Jeffery: 'It marks the Union sealed with blood. It stands for the ultimate test of Ulster's loyalty; a blood-sacrifice to match any made by Irish Nationalists.'[35] In later years the Battle of the Somme came to be seen by unionists as the stage for their betrayal by the British administration. The importance invested in the war had been evident from the beginning in the almost devotional reaction of unionists to the creation of the 36th Division in 1914; its subsequent destruction at the Somme was traumatic and this is evident in its enduring place, to the present day, in unionist history, mythology and iconography. The editorial of the *Weekly Northern Whig*, following the division's losses at the Somme, placed the force in traditional historical context:

> The same feelings which inspired Cromwell's Ironsiders animated all ranks and gave to the Division an unconquerable spirit . . . they fear God and nothing else. The ordeal by fire, gas, and poison through which they passed proved that they were made of pure metal. Ulster's old watchword 'No Surrender' which was on the lips of those gallant fellows as they rushed into the valley of death, will have a new and an even nobler meaning for most of us in the days to come.[36]

The actions of the 36th thus attained mythical proportions, and a level of meaning which bore no relation to the reality of their situation. As one veteran of the battle told the *Belfast Telegraph* in 1966: 'Nothing was further from my mind than the Boyne on the Somme.'[37] In writing about the Battle of the Somme neither Ernest Hamilton, James Logan or Cyril Falls could disguise the enormous loss of life suffered by Ulster recruits and the Ulster community.[38] 'Hardly a family', wrote Logan, 'but suffered, directly or indirectly, the havoc of war, and on the 1st July, 1916, when more than five thousand Ulstermen stepped out of the trenches, never to return, the hills of home quivered to their foundations.'[39] Equally, however, they were not keen to focus overly on the more negative aspects of the war. Lord Plumer, for instance, was positively upbeat in his preface to Cyril Falls's book: 'all who read', he wrote, 'will realise that in the great struggle which convulsed Europe for more than four years the men of Ulster did not fail'.[40] All those who wrote of the war were aware of the sensitive nature of the subject they dealt with. Falls, therefore, presented an image of the 36th Division which, even though it had suffered serious losses in a disastrous battle, shone in the adverse circumstances: 'Of the deeds of heroism that day accomplished, it is not possible to enumerate one-hundredth.' Falls presents a slightly fanciful picture to his readers, an image more to do with wishful thinking than reality: as the survivors of the battle returned from the Front, he wrote:

> Officers and men wore marigolds in caps to honour the day; the bands played 'King William's March'. The least practised eye could tell that to these men confidence was returning; that the worst of the horror they had endured had been shaken from their shoulders. They marched like victors as was their right.[41]

Lord Plumer believed that 'young men approaching manhood and young women approaching womanhood' should read Falls's book and 'ponder over the example their predecessors had set them'.[42]

The fact that the 36th 'Ulster' Division manifested distinct elements of Ulster culture and projected a distinctly Ulster protestant identity, although not political Unionism specifically, exacerbated the grief of the Ulster community at its loss. To quote a newspaper editorial after the Somme: 'it typifies us in all that we cherish and stand for, and in all that we are in the eyes of the rest of the nation whatever view they take of us.'[43] Organised on a regional basis, as the Ulster Volunteer Force had been, it was infused with a deep sense of family and community. This was in keeping with the armies of the First World War which were, in general, people's armies, 'composed of men who joined together from the same town, the same street, the same office, or factory, or coal mine'.[44] Ulster had possessed its own people's army since 1912, thus enhancing this pattern. The 'Ulster' division was not loosely based on the already existing Volunteer force. Instead, individual UVF battalions were formed directly into the 36th's battalions, and even retained their individual names unofficially. When listing the war dead many unionist papers included not only the soldier's rank and regiment, but the Volunteer corps to which he had belonged. Such intensity of feeling made the horrors of war excruciating for the 36th's recruits and combined to exacerbate them, as they did for many recruits from across Europe who had joined the local army unit with their neighbours and friends. 'What was so appalling for the soldiers was that they were watching friends, relations and neighbours dying beside them, not just other troops. The closely terri-torial – almost tribal – bonding of the UVF saw to that'.[45] Although Cyril Falls cautioned his readers that 'it behoves those who were eye-witnesses to depict [the war] in all its aspects, not to shrink from discovering its horror, indeed, but not to pretend that it had not a better side', from those experiences, he concluded, 'many men have emerged happy and strong'.[46]

The 36th did not cross to training grounds in Sussex until 1915, training in the intervening period in camps located across the province. This enhanced the new recruits' strong, and already well-established, identification with Ulster. Less than seven months later they played a central role in what Paul Fussell has termed the most 'egregious ironic action of the whole war', the Battle of the Somme.[47] Of the 100,000 recruits involved in the attack in July 1916, 60,000 were wounded or killed. The 36th suffered 5,000 casualties, almost half their number. Owing to war censorship, which became particularly stringent after the Somme (reflecting the extent of the carnage), little of the battle's human tragedy was reflected in the press commentaries. It is in the lists of the war dead in the press that the impact of the Somme becomes apparent. The *Belfast Newsletter*'s daily column, 'Ulster and the War', went from an average of two columns to five, and the headlines in the press told their own story; for days after the Somme they read 'Ulster's Sacrifice' and 'Ulster's Sacrifice for Empire'. The division's short life and tragic destruction ensured it a place in unionist mythology; later and retrospectively its perceived betrayal by the British government guaranteed its status as a 'vibrant symbol of Unionist Ulster's martyrdom'.[48] The losses at the Somme drew Ulster's unionist community together in its grief. Two hundred years previously Ulster protestants had fought another battle by another river and the symbolic parallel was not lost on the public; 'from the Boyne to the Ancre the thread of history seemed to run clearly'.[49] 'The men of the 36th Division', noted the editorial in the *Northern Whig*, 'were only putting into practice the ideals and traditions of their race. Ulstermen may be destroyed, but they will never yield when they know their cause is just.'[50] Their ancestors had endured great suffering and had been victorious at the Battle of the Boyne (which had not been a decisive victory in fact and which was in itself, therefore, a myth), and now they clung to the hope that out of the carnage of the Somme some victory would be secured. The 36th had in fact succeeded in carrying out its battle orders. Having achieved its objective, which was to lead an attack through a specific section of the German trenches, it was ordered to retreat by Allied commanders owing to the lack of reserves available to support it. The battle's main aim had been to distract the enemy while the Allies advanced elsewhere on the front line. The realisation in retrospect that the 36th Division's achievements had been fruitless, the fact that they had been merely decoys sacrificed for a broader objective, exacerbated the bitterness of those involved in the event and those at home.

In Ulster, following the Somme, the war itself became an abstraction with the 'covenanting' soldiers of the 36th sacrificing themselves for their people in Ulster, depicted by the press and other commentators as following in the footsteps of their ancestors at the Boyne. The memory of the Boyne, according to Falls, was of 'very special significance' to the soldiers of the 36th Division: 'A stirring in their blood bore witness to the silent call of their ancestors. There seemed to them a predestination in the affair'.[51] Thus the province's protestant combatants were mythologised, transformed into historic figures from the past as the war became a version of the Battle of the Boyne, transferred to a time (and a past) which bore no resemblance to the reality of the First World War. In post-war Europe 'faced with the horrendous possibility that the war might not have been worth the effort people simply buried the thought for a time'.[52] Barbara Tuchman points out that the motivation for the war's soldiers had been the hope of a 'better' world: 'nothing less could give dignity or sense to monstrous offensives in which thousands and hundreds of thousands were killed to gain the yards and exchange one wet-bottomed trench for another'.[53] In Ulster the unionist experience of war was sanitised by transforming it into something familiar which they could deal with without too much distress. It was transformed therefore into another plank with which to shore up their political claims and grievances; its reality was in this way glossed over. Ernest Hamilton and Cyril Falls commemorated Ulster's war dead with one regimental and two divisional histories between them, but these histories had a broader message for the reader than the mere actions of the soldiers in the war.[54] The message was that Ulster had taken part and sacrificed much for the empire in the First World War, and in this context, having suffered huge losses, it deserved reciprocal loyalty from the British government. Some benefit, it was felt, had to come from their losses in the form of political compensation, to be gleaned from a British administration vulnerable to accusations of having sacrificed the 36th to advance the Allied front in another quarter. 'Their devotion', commented the *Belfast Newsletter*'s editorial, 'deserves the gratitude of the Empire'.[55] The Battle of the Somme could, therefore, be used to tie Ulster more closely to Britain. But within weeks of the battle, it became obvious to unionist observers that they would gain little political favour in return for their losses. While their rank and file were dying for the Allied cause, unionists in Ulster watched as the British government negotiated with those who had proven their disloyalty, according to unionists, the previous April in the Easter Rising.

The proximity of the rising and the Somme meant that the two would be forever united in the collective mind of unionist Ulster; the former the epitome of treachery, the other the price of loyalty.[56] The rising in Phillips's rhetoric was full of the 'brutal murders' of unarmed policemen, of 'seething mobs' who issued from slums, of mob violence and the terror of fire.[57] 'On the 24th April 1916', wrote Cyril Falls, 'in the midst of the Battle of Verdun and of the preparations for that of the Somme, another rebellion broke out.'[58] In his 1953 school text Hugh Shearman continued the same pattern of juxtaposing the rising and the Somme; 'It so happened', he wrote, 'that the year 1916, which saw the Dublin rising, also saw the most severe Ulster casualties in the war . . . . Thus the year 1916 saw men prepared to die for their convictions on both sides of the Irish controversy.'[59] Even in 1960, in his book *The First World War*, Cyril Falls set the Battle of the Somme in the context of the rising.[60]

Easter 1916 would, for unionist writers, always be the backdrop to the drama of the first war and fit into the established unionist paradigm, which traced in Irish history a pattern of 'native' Irish rebellions. The impact of the Somme on the psyche and self-image of Ulster unionists was reinforced by their response three months earlier to the events in Dublin in Easter 1916. In the unionist press reports that followed the battle, the rising was referred to bitterly:

> It was intense loyalty to the Empire that thrilled the heart and strengthened the arm of the Ulster Division as it wrote a new and brilliant chapter in Britain's book of fame; it is disloyalty that has revived the Home Rule controversy and diverted the attention of the nation from that one subject on which it ought to be concentrated – the war.[61]

Unionists, in their war rhetoric, regularly focused on the union and its maintenance rather than on the war itself; separatists, meanwhile, used a different aspect of the same tactic, concentrating on the opportunity the war provided to stage a rebellion. For both, the war provided a useful diversion. From a unionist perspective Ulster protestants had shown themselves loyal and constant to the British Empire, willing to die for its cause, and the Battle of the Somme was a particularly gory manifestation of this.

The joint effect of the rising and the Battle of the Somme on Ulster unionists' self-image was intensified by the reaction of the British administration to developments in Ireland. It became clear that Westminster's attitude towards Ulster unionism had altered in the context of war. British sympathy in pre-war days gave way to frustration and a feeling, according to A.T.Q. Stewart, that 'Ulstermen had all along thwarted a settlement in Ireland'.[62] British unionists now concentrated their complete attention on the European conflict. Gone were the days when leaders like Randolph Churchill, in 1886, and Bonar Law, in the period 1912 to 1914, had sought to gain support and publicity on an Ulster stage by aligning themselves with the Ulster unionist cause. They were now willing to accept home rule, with the exclusion of the six north-eastern counties, on 'a point of expediency rather than on a point of principle'.[63] Britain's concern with Ireland had been dictated largely by the extent to which Irish affairs could enhance or secure Britain's position domestically and internationally. As Michael Laffan points out, the third home rule bill was 'intended to be a concession large enough to keep Ireland quiet and remove her from the centre of British public life'.[64] In time of war it would be of no benefit to the British administration to have the majority of Irishmen antagonistic towards them, their relationship with Westminster unstable and volatile. Thus, in the wake of the rising where unionists had expected firm government action against nationalists they were faced instead by Westminster's attempts at conciliation.

The Twelfth of July celebrations following the end of the war reflected the atmosphere which the war had helped to generate among Ulster unionists. New arches covered in images of gallant Ulstermen fighting for the empire and angelic nurses ministering to the wounded were erected. They invited the people to 'Remember our fallen heroes of the 36th Ulster Division'. The war was added to protestant mythology as a paradigm and enshrined in books such as Falls's. In the same way that banners had portrayed the gallant men and women of Derry who had endured great suffering in the siege of 1689 but had through their own resolve survived, contemporary banners in 1919 portrayed the new heroes of protestant Ulster, the men who had given their lives for the empire's cause and had, subsequently, been betrayed by their allies. Britain took on the role of Lundy in this scenario, deserting the unionists and negotiating with nationalists to save themselves. The dead of the 36th 'Ulster' Division retrospectively had not died for the Allied war effort but for the freedom of the protestants of Ulster; as much as the leaders of the 1916 rising, they became martyrs. This is reflected in Carson's bitter rhetoric at the commemoration of the Twelfth of July in Belfast in 1919: 'While the Orange Institution points with melancholy to the records of Thiepval and Messines, those against whose designs they armed in 1912 exult over the records of Easter Week, 1916, in Dublin'.[65] National-ists' abandonment of the First World War's legacy, despite the very large number of casualties they had suffered, made it easier for unionists to portray the years of conflict in this way. For them, the treachery displayed by the rebels in 1916 and the nationalists generally in 1918 overshadowed the reality of the south's contribution to the Allied victory.

In general in the post-war period, Irish nationalists abandoned the history and symbolism of the war, incapable of reconciling it with the new forces at play in post-rising society. The anti-conscription campaign of 1918 ensured that their memories of the war would be permeated with a bitter-ness which allowed no room for war nostalgia. There could be no reconciliation of their role as soldiers in the British army during the war and the rising which was portrayed by nationalists subsequently as having set Ireland free from that very colonial power. As that much quoted lament from Tom Kettle has it, the rebels of 1916 would go down in history as heroes and martyrs while he would go down (if at all) as a 'bloody British officer'.[66] Ulster unionists found no such conflict, and took sole possession of Ireland's contribution to the conflict. Their rhetoric throughout the war geared them for such a position; throughout the war years they had claimed that theirs was the greatest contribution in Ireland to Britain's war effort, and their suspicions of the inherent disloyalty of nationalists were vindi-cated in their eyes through the rising. This and the nationalists' anti-conscription campaign reinforced their belief that nationalists were not only disloyal but treasonable – their actions in unionist eyes being engi-neered to undermine Allied efforts to win the war. While Lord Ernest Hamilton's *The first seven divisions* responded to a public hungry for infor-mation in the midst of the war, books such as Cyril Falls's acted as reminders to the British administration that its debt to Ulster unionists was not forgotten and that its continued support of the Northern Irish state was the price of that debt. For many unionist writers the events of the Somme could not be spoken of without the introduction of the Easter Rising in Dublin in 1916. Thus in a unionist government publication in 1951 Hugh Shearman wrote:

a small rebellion in Dublin in 1916 and the clear evidence which the war
provided of the willingness of the Ulster community to share the gravest
burdens as well as claim the advantages of their British citizenship and
nationhood caused the separate treatment of Ulster to become an
accepted principle for the United Kingdom Government when the war
was over.[67]

And so the thread of history ran on.

In the aftermath of the war Ulster unionists felt their isolation more than
ever. The world for them had become divided in two and this is reflected in
the writings of unionist historians: those whom they knew and trusted and
those whom they knew and distrusted. This mentality, which had manifested itself as a unionist trait prior to the war, was intensified by their
experience in the conflict; their post-war legacy was a habit of simple
distinction, and opposition. To quote Paul Fussell, 'If truth is the main casu-
alty in war, ambiguity is another'.[68] Protestants in Ulster saw themselves
surrounded by enemies – the nationalists whom they had always perceived
as disloyal and of course, more powerfully, the British government, which
they had long suspected was unreliable and which they now believed,
following its actions during the war, was also treacherous. Confident,
however, that they held the moral high ground, having as they claimed
contributed so much to the Allied victory, and having accepted home rule
and partition under duress to aid the British war effort, they were equally
confident that they would not be coerced into an all-Ireland parliament.

The war exacerbated an existing isolationist identity, and combined with
their traditional self-image to alienate them effectively from both nationalist
Ireland and from the politicians at Westminster. 'War', Jeffery says, 'like any
serious disease, is a difficult thing to shake off.'[69] Irish problems may have
taken second place to the post-war peace negotiations but in the year following the armistice, as Westminster allowed its Irish policy (insofar as they had
one) to drift, Ulster unionists determined to impose their own solution. They
emerged from the war years with a sense of identity which had been sharp-
ened and hardened by the experience and which was now encapsulated in
several foundation histories. Unionist histories sought to legitimise, praise
and blame, and articulate the progressive destruction of unionist faith in the
British government, and give vent to unionist bitterness at the position they
found themselves in. To quote Modris Eksteins: 'The faith was gone and along
with it the fixity'.[70] Through their writings, these authors manifested the
need of unionism to establish a common narrative identity, and historic
vindication, for the citizens of the embryonic Northern Irish state. In the
decade after the war Ulster unionists struggled to create their own fixity, with
their own state, whose barriers neither nationalists nor Westminster could
penetrate. In the years which followed, unionist collectivity, articulated
through their foundation histories, was reinforced through other means.

A number of themes run through these foundation histories and recur
throughout the next thirty years, manifested in broadcasting, ritual, and
literature: the Irish 'natives' and their relationship with the Ulster
'colonists'; the nature of these two stereotyped groups; the relationship of

'colonists' to the British government; the significance of 'sacred' dates in protestant history; and the broader themes of loyalty, betrayal, sacrifice and the need for protestant unity in the face of recurring threats (or perceived threats) to their position.[71] These authors drew their terms of reference, and their conceits, from an historical heritage rich in myth and tradition. As the nationalist historian A.S. Green wrote, 'the far past and the far future' are 'part of the eternal present, the very condition of thought, the furniture', without which, the mind is bare.[72]

In his preface to *The Irish rebellion of 1641* (written in 1920, a year before the Northern Irish state was established), Ernest Hamilton argued that the events of the past, and in particular the 1641 rebellion, had 'shaped the destinies of the province'.[73] An amateur historian, Hamilton was read nevertheless by the professional historians who followed him.[74] Hamilton's formative political period had been that of the first two home rule crises, when he was a unionist MP for Tyrone and the rhetoric of that period echoes through his writing.[75] Author of several books, Hamilton set a framework for the writing of Ulster history around the 'magic' protestant numbers 1641, 1690, 1914 and so on; *The first seven divisions* (1916) commemorated the Ulster soldiers in the First World War, *The Irish rebellion of 1641* (1920) addressed, as its title suggests, the 'massacre' of Planters by the 'native' Irish, and *Elizabethan Ulster* (1922) told the story of the plantation of Ulster in the seventeenth century. His subject matter provided the inspiration for many unionist writers subsequently; D.A. Chart, for instance, wrote a history of Northern Ireland from pre-history to the present (although his synopsis of Northern Irish history from the First World War up to the establishment of the state was brief); Cyril Falls wrote *The history of the 36th (Ulster) Division* in 1922, *The Royal Irish Rifles* in 1925, and *The birth of Ulster* in 1936; and James Logan picked up on the characterisation of the 'Ulsterman' in his 1923 book *Ulster in the x-rays*.

Other unionists, such as W.A. Phillips, professor of modern history at Trinity College Dublin, and Ronald McNeill, consciously or not, echoed much of Hamilton's rhetoric. Hamilton's *The soul of Ulster* (1917) covered the history of protestants in Ulster to 1917, and also acted to establish the 'Ulsterman' as a 'type'. By then Ulster unionists had realised that unity was essential to achieve their political aims; only as protestants could they stand united, despite their other differences of class and religious sect, against the perceived threat of Irish nationalism. These authors contributed to this process of unity through their writing – articulating a common protestant history – and to the creation of a common narrative identity. In this scenario, both the 1641 'massacres' and the Battle of the Boyne came to act as paradigms for the position in which they found themselves in the early decades of the twentieth century with the renewed threat of home rule.[76] After 1916 the Easter Rising and the Battle of the Somme were added to the list of perilous situations which unionists had faced. These 'historical' events were the beacon buoys for unionists, marking the rocks on which Ulster protestants had almost foundered in the past but which they had overcome through their own tenacity.

The characterisation of the 'Ulsterman', which had its roots in the nine-teenth century, was a part of this process of unity. The 'Ulsterman' was a stereotype which unionists could readily identify and feel a common bond with. Indeed the 'Ulsterman' portrayed by unionist writers in the late nine-teenth century was not radically different from the image presented by Ernest Hamilton; his 'Ulstermen' were farmers and traders, men whose 'ways were for peace'.[77] His 'Ireland' was a stereotyped, two-dimensional world; one divided into 'settlers' and 'natives' between whom, he suggested, 'harmony is no more possible than it is between the dog with the bone and the dog without it'. The 'Ulsterman' was a member, Hamilton contended, of 'a strong race, brave and true, and with a clean conscience'.[78] In James Logan's *Ulster in the x-rays*, for which Hamilton provided a preface, this same pattern was followed. However, for Logan the 'Ulsterman's' virtues went further: 'modest as the primrose peeping beneath the thorn', he wrote, 'they are content to delight in diligence and duty'.[79] 'Ulstermen', he contin-ued, were individuals of 'commonsense' and 'excellent men to have as friends'. Aimed at an expatriate Ulster protestant audience, Logan's book reveals some interesting stereotypes not touched on by Hamilton; for him 'Northmen are the hewers of wood and drawers of water in Ireland; people in the South shelter under the motto "Shure it'll do"'.[80] Epitomising the best qualities of the 'Ulsterman', for James Logan, were the 'Islandmen', the Belfast shipyard workers who would be celebrated by the novelist and BBC producer Sam Hanna Bell in the late 1940s.[81] 'The "Islandmen" are rough and ready', Logan wrote, 'staunch and determined, loyal and enthusiastic, hardworking and industrious.'[82] These were traits which Logan had lauded in 1922; then according to him Northern Ireland enjoyed prosperity through its people's grit and determination.[83] In the 1940s and 1950s Hugh Shear-man, a moderate apologist for the unionist government, also presented readers with an image of Northern Ireland as a centre of culture and progression and modernity, an indication that the unionist writers in the early years of the Northern Irish state continued to be a significant influ-ence on later writers.

The use of stereotyped imagery was not something original to either Ernest Hamilton or James Logan. In the home rule crises of the late nine-teenth century Ulster unionists had utilised identifiably 'Irish' imagery and identity in their public demonstrations.[84] Unionists in this period rejected not what was 'Irish' in their heritage, but rather what they believed would diminish their position within the empire and undermine the British element of their traditions. Ian MacBride cites the case of an unidentified Stormont minister, who as late as 1956, 'admitted the "sentimental appeal" of a common Irish identity but lamented the fact that it had become incom-patible with "being at the same time British"'.[85] This was to develop into a complex fear, and at times a rejection, of Ulster local culture in the 1940s, prompted by a belief on the part of unionists that local culture was the 'Trojan horse' for an Irish national culture.[86] By 1917, however, Irish language and imagery were already problematic; they had become an intrin-sic part of Irish nationalism, and could no longer be used by unionists. Some unionist authors did delve into the past to accredit 'Ulster' with an 'Irish' identity, but this was largely in response to the nationalist jibe that northerners were not 'real Irishmen' and had, therefore, no say in the island's political future. In his 1927 history of Northern Ireland, D.A. Chart noted that before the plantations 'the North was strongly Celtic and independent'; by making Northern Ireland the most 'Irish' of places Chart could simultaneously argue for a Northern Ireland entirely distinctive from the rest of the island (whose character had been, he argued, more affected by the plantations), and which was therefore deserving of different treatment in contemporary times.[87] Hugh Shearman in his 1953 school textbook significantly echoed Chart's work: 'the area which was most purely Irish and least affected by the invaders was Ulster . . . Behind its geographical frontiers Ulster had served as the last fortress of old Irish life and customs.'[88]

This creation within unionism of a strong provincial and political identity developed under similar influences and by similar means to parallel trends among nationalists in the south, but operated to different ends. For example, while notions of distinctiveness were common to both ideologies, they developed in ways that polarised identity. As Oliver MacDonagh has observed, the mental habits of both nationalists and unionists tend to converge: 'their rhythms, their ultimate world-views, are extraordinarily similar'.[89] As a corollary to the creation of the stereotypical 'Ulsterman', Ernest Hamilton and James Logan established a particular image of the 'Southern Irish' and the 'native Irish'. A.S. Green, writing in 1912, believed that the 'native Irish' were marked by 'chivalry, learning, patriotism [and] poetry'.[90] On the contrary Hamilton believed that the 'curse of Ireland' was 'and always [had] been, lack of moral courage'.[91] Hamilton's remarks, written a year after the Easter Rising and the Battle of the Somme, appear all the more pointed in the light of the general unionist belief that the southern Irish had shirked their war duty in the First World War and had, with the actions of the rebels in 1916, betrayed the empire at a time when Ulstermen were dying at the Somme. Above all, Hamilton's thesis ran, the 'native Irish' had a history of savage and uncivilised behaviour, which had resurfaced with the Easter Rising. Both Hamilton and Chart endorsed the thesis that the 'native Irish' were incapable of (or at best just not very good at) governing themselves, an argument familiar in the colonial history of the twentieth century.[92] W.A. Phillips developed this theme; the 'native Irish' were incapable of ruling themselves, he explained, because of the 'characteristic qualities of the Irish, which were – and largely still are – those of the clansmen . . . the Celtic race, by virtue of its inherent qualities, is incapable of developing unaided a high type of civilisation'.[93] The 'inherent qualities' he spoke of were a combination of savagery, insincerity, surface charm, and childlike backwardness. These qualities were repeated in Hugh Shearman's work some twenty years later; in April 1949, for instance, he remarked upon the 'grave condition of social backwardness and economic stagnation' in Éire.[94] 'It comes about', wrote Hamilton in 1920, 'that the native, or Celtic, Irish, from their earliest childhood are fed on legends in which their ancestors are depicted as the inoffensive victims of English tyranny. These legends are taken seriously and are believed.'[95] Six years later W.A. Phillips concurred with Hamilton; 'the memory of the Irish peasant is very long; he has no sense of historical perspective; and the wrongs suffered by his ancestors centuries ago are to him as things of yesterday'. Phillips's remark is more than a little ironic given that in 1920 Hamilton made an analogy between the reprisals taken by the English forces against the 'native Irish' in the aftermath of the 1641 rebellion and the armistice negotiated in the aftermath of the war against the Germans. These stereotypes of the southern Irish betray a contradiction in the mentality of unionist history writers who when dealing with their own past felt that it had shaped their present and was therefore relevant to contemporary life: on the other hand when the 'native Irish' remembered their past (in as selective a way as their 'settler' counterparts) they were deemed to be childlike for not understanding that the past was the past and should be left there.

There was often consensus between unionist historians over the past, but this was not uniformly the case. D.A. Chart viewed the 'massacre' in 1641 as premeditated but, referring to the 'bitterness of the dispossessed' natives, acknowledged that there was motivation for it; Hamilton saw none at all.[96] 'Without any provocation', he wrote, 'and equally without any warning, the native Irish, who for thirty-two years had given no sign of hostility, rose at a preconceived signal, fell upon the isolated colonists, and stripped them literally to the skin'.[97] W.A. Phillips concurred with Hamilton's theory of a preconceived and motiveless revolt;

> the Catholic Gaels seized the opportunity, and the rising of 1641 rapidly developed into a war of extermination between the rival races and creeds, which has left bitter memories to this day . . . The Protestant "planters" were expelled from their holdings with every circumstance of barbarous cruelty, many of them being tortured and massacred.[98]

What is striking about Phillips's interpretation of the 1641 'massacre' is its similarities to contemporary unionist press reports in the early 1920s that dealt with the violence in the south of Ireland. Following the establishment of both states in 1921 a civil war began in the Irish Free State. Attacks against southern protestants were represented by the unionist press in terms of a pogrom; the *Belfast Newsletter* headed a story of violence against a southern protestant farmer as being a 'War on Protestants'.[99] Northern unionist politicians followed a similar line in their rhetoric. H.M. Pollock told the Presbyterian General Assembly that there was 'overwhelming evidence that there have been many cases of persecution of Protestants in the South. It is well known that this is going on and that one of the objects of the rebels is to drive the Protestants from their districts'.[100] The attacks were presented in terms of the seamless fabric of protestant history, one in which their past and present-day experiences became one. Thus, according to the *Northern Whig* in May 1922: 'The murders [in the south] are only the last in a long series which began as far back as 1641'.[101] The *Belfast Newsletter* highlighted the violence in similar terms: 'The systematic persecution of Protestants which is going on all over the South and West of Ireland . . .

never since the rebellion of 1641 have the minority been in greater danger'.[102] Phillips's writing would appear to have been coloured by these developments and influenced by this unionist rhetoric. Returning to the 'massacre', Ernest Hamilton thought the actions of the rebels in 1641 'too revolting for reproduction', before showing how revolting they were by reproducing them in detail.[103] Chart, typically, suggested that 'long private vengeance and national and religious animosity' had motivated the 'natives'.[104] Hugh Shearman, whose 1953 *Modern Ireland* was strongly influenced by Chart's 1927 publication, also made the connection between what he termed the 'changes in land-ownership' which had 'caused great disturbance and hardship' for the Irish and the 1641 rebellion 'where the new colonists suffered severely at the hands of the Irish'.[105] However, the most interesting treatment of 1641 is Ernest Hamilton's in 1920. Hamilton adopted a contemporary analogy for the massacre: 'the 1641 massacres are no greater slur on the Irish nation than the Reign of Terror is on the French or Bolshevism on Russia as a whole. All three represent the temporary ascendancy of the brute element'.[106] He engaged in an extraordinary contemporary analogy between the 1641 rebellion and the First World War (which had concluded two years before Hamilton's *The Irish rebellion of 1641* was published). The English army's reprisals following the 1641 rebellion, Hamilton wrote:

> Have been graven in stone, as memorials of British cruelty to the Irish, as they unquestionably would have been had the massacres not preceded them. In the light of the massacres, however, they merely appear as acts of just retribution . . . Three hundred years hence the peace terms of 1919 would read as cruel and tyrannous were the previous deeds of Germany deliberately suppressed.[107]

And so, the rebellious 'native' Irish of 1641 became latter-day Germans, reminding readers at the same time of the unionists' belief that the Irish rebels in 1916 were working with the Germans to undermine the empire.

Other areas of the past were also problematic for unionist authors, notably the 1798 rebellion and the Ulster Volunteer Force. With regard to the former, Hamilton and others went to some lengths to explain the involvement of Ulster protestants (established by these authors as exemplars of ultimate loyalty) in the 1798 rising. And that, moreover, 'the people of Ulster, however, were by no means united in support of the rebels, and many assisted the government by serving the yeomanry corps'.[108] Although initially motivated by the desire that 'persons of every creed' be granted political rights, Chart explained that as 'the (United Irish) society fell . . . into the hands of extremists' the population of Ulster became disassociated from it.[109] This was the standard explanation for this 'aberration' in the behaviour of the most loyal of the empire's citizens, and was echoed by Hugh Shearman in 1953: 'If revolutionary ideas inspired the small group of Protestant rebels in Ulster, the Wexford rising was a passionate one, inspired by feelings rather than ideas, and it had much less connexion [*sic*] with the original programme and aims of the United Irishmen.'[110] Ernest Hamilton, on the other hand, embraced the theory of a premeditated conspiracy of the 'natives' to destroy the planters, familiar from his treatment of the 1641 'massacre': 'No sooner, however, was the rebellion on the apparent high-road to success, than the mask was thrown off, a holy war was proclaimed, priests assumed the command of the rebel army, and the extermination of the Protestants became the avowed aim of the victorious insurgents.'[111] His assessment found W.A. Phillips's support in 1926.[112] Moreover, Phillips used 1798 as an example of why a united Ireland in contemporary times would never work: 'thus ended in a welter of blood and sectarian hate, the short-lived experiment of uniting the Irish sects in a single nation'.[113] Finally, Cyril Falls, the son of a prominent Fermanagh unionist, whilst acknowledging that 'Ulster's feet' had 'wavered' for a moment, reassured his readers that, after 1798, Ulster's feet were 'set upon the path they . . . steadfastly followed ever since'.[114] The United Irish rebellion was thus presented as the result of 'popish bigotry' and a return to the 'massacres' of 1641, and where protestant involvement was acknowledged it was claimed as a momentary aberration.[115] Interestingly, the *Northern Whig*, in the 1880s, with supreme paradox, had adopted the imagery of the United Irish rebellion to illustrate to the British administration the strength of their anti-home rule stance.

> The muskets of '98 have been beaten into ploughshares and the pikes into pruning hooks, and the cursed arts of civil war have been abandoned for the blessed industries of peace . . . But, sir, reverse all this – force a Dublin parliament on Ulstermen anew, and so re-establish a more ignorant and intolerant ascendancy, and it will soon be seen that the spirit of the sires yet lives in the sons, and that Ulstermen have still in them the stuff of rebels.[116]

After 1916 unionist writers were not keen to emphasise that unionists had within them 'the stuff of rebels'; it was no longer a politically expedient image. In this context, then, the issue of the Ulster Volunteer Force was yet another complex topic for Ernest Hamilton and other unionist writers. The difficulty lay in presenting unionism's armed resistance to the British government as a positive achievement for the movement (which the majority of unionists believed it had been) while at the same time condemning the actions of the rebels in Dublin in 1916 and presenting unionists who took part in the First World War as supreme loyalists.[117] For Ernest Hamilton and D.A. Chart the solution was simply to ignore that episode of unionism's recent history, or refer to the period selectively. One could, however, read the divisional histories penned by Ernest Hamilton and Cyril Falls as surreptitious celebrations of the UVF, given the close links of the 36th Division to the Volunteers. In any event, it would be for later unionist historians to celebrate publicly the Ulster Volunteer Force's contribution to the development of twentieth-century unionism.[118]

Unionists used the past to effective contemporary political effect. For instance, rather than criticising the contemporary British administration in Ireland, some unionist authors drew the British administration's responsibility for Irish affairs (and in particular the position Ulster found itself in) back to the seventeenth century, and the policy of plantation. Ernest Hamilton considered the antagonism between northern protestants and the rest of the island's inhabitants to have germinated in the process of the Ulster plantations.[119] While the dispossession of the 'natives' had created the foundations of contemporary troubles, Hamilton argued that the colonists were not to blame, they 'were neither pirates nor marauders. Their deportation was not even of their own doing. By a state measure they were – willy-nilly – taken from their own surroundings and dropped down in a strange land'.[120] His work represented a strand in what was the complex colonial basis to Ulster unionism. 'If', he continued, 'the title of the Government was faulty, then the immorality of transfer lies at the door of the Government, not of the unhappy transferees.'[121]

In the context of the time in which the book was being written, the message seems to be that the British administration was responsible for the state of Ireland then as now, and had a duty to rectify the situation. Here, Hamilton was echoing the belief of Thomas MacKnight, an earlier unionist author, who in 1896 claimed that the British government's chief responsibility was to those settlers and their descendants: 'When the Ulster settlements were made, there was an implied compact that they who crossed the Irish sea, on what was believed to be a great colonising and civilising mission should not in themselves, nor in their descendants, be abandoned to those who regarded them as intruders, and as enemies'.[122] It was a point endorsed by the grand master of the Orange Lodge in Belfast in April 1912: 'England planted their forefathers in Ulster to keep the country, and nobly they kept their trust', said Colonel Wallace: 'Their descendants had done their best to do the same, and was England now going to throw over men who had been holding the fort for her to the domination of her hereditary enemies?'[123] However, for D.A. Chart, the root of the island's difficulties lay not in the seventeenth century, but in the nineteenth – in relation to Catholic Emancipation he believed that the actions of the British government had exhibited a 'deplorable want of knowledge, imagination and sympathy'.[124] Later, the unionist press would use the same rhetoric to explain the British government's handling of the renewed home rule threat and the Easter Rising. Chart believed that the British administration had failed to grant Catholic Emancipation until threatened with 'a palpable menace' in the form of O'Connell and the Catholic Association. As a result he believed Irish nationalists had drawn 'the obvious conclusion' that the threat of force would sway the British government; 'the rebellious spirit which with tactful handling might have died out in Ireland after 1798 was fostered and kept alive by thirty years of fierce political contention . . . The spirit of antagonism still survives and still works many evils'.[125] Again, Chart was writing before the third home rule crisis had gained its full momentum, and before the Easter Rising and the First World War, in what Boyce has termed one of Irish history's 'long wary truces'.[126] Ironically, O'Connell's influence can be seen in the actions of Ulster unionists in their 1912–14 campaign; they had learned the lesson long before the rebels of 1916 that the threat of force could be an effective influence on the British administration.

The need to apportion blame and responsibility lay in the realisation by unionists that they were essentially dependent upon Westminster for their political survival, and therefore needed to remind the British administration continually of its responsibility to the descendants of the seventeenth-century colonists. In this context unionists were faced with a dilemma – a lack of confidence in the British government coupled with a continuing reliance on them for political survival and a continuing need to appeal to British public opinion for support. This led to their vocal opposition to the policies of the British administration being combined with public protestations of loyalism. To quote the leader in the *Belfast Weekly Telegraph* in June 1912:

> We know our destiny lies in the hands of England, and we have confidence in her ultimate justice; their generous instincts through want of knowledge of the facts and conditions may be temporarily misled, but they are bound to discover the evils of a disintegrating policy that would split the Empire at its very heart.[127]

The work of unionist writers like Hamilton, Falls and Phillips represented a world vision structured by opposites: where the 'wicked, uncivilised, tyrannical and "rough" people outside the walls confront the good civilised, freedom loving "religious" people within'.[128] It was a perspective common to the majority of unionists and reinforced annually by Ulster protestants' re-enactment of both the Battle of the Boyne and the Siege of Derry. These unionist historians represented Ulster protestants as colonial settlers, with a distinct air of separateness and historic difference which clearly distinguished them from the 'native' Irish. Hamilton and Phillips were typical of unionist writers who denied that any responsibility for Ireland's political problems lay at the door of the original planters or their descendants. For Falls the planters were to be celebrated for the qualities they had brought to the country and bequeathed to their descendants. He lamented in *The birth of Ulster* (1936) that there was 'hardly even legend where [the colonists] were concerned'; the 'great events' at the opening of the reign of William of Orange had, he believed, 'obscured in the popular mind those which went before, the Plantation as much as the Rebellion of 1641'.[129] This is interesting for two reasons; the Battle of the Boyne in fact received only passing attention from any of these unionist authors. For W.A. Phillips, for instance, it marked the beginning of a hundred years of undisputed protestant ascendancy.[130] Ernest Hamilton introduced contemporary tones by linking the Battle of the Boyne with the Ulster crisis of 1912–14; William III was, according to him, 'the first lawful king, and organised resistance without treason was now for the first time possible'.[131] Chart, writing in 1927, gave the Boyne more contemporary significance. In an obvious attempt to remind the reader of the contribution of Ulster recruits to the Allied cause in the First World War he wrote: 'Enniskillen furnished to King William's army regiments of horse and foot which helped to win the victory at the Boyne, and have ever since maintained their places as units of the British Army'.[132] This was in a government publication which was keen to remind British observers of that role.

According to Hamilton, before the plantation, Ulster had been 'a land torn by internal strife, saturated with its own blood shed by itself, idle, ragged and wretched'.[133] Following the plantation of English and Scots colonists (individuals of a more solid and stable race according to Hamilton), 'peace and prosperity took the place of rapine and misery, and before the first quarter of the seventeenth century was passed the justification of the Ulster Plantation seemed beyond dispute'.[134] In his narrative Phillips acknowledged that 'to the natives it was small consolation that the colonists introduced greatly improved methods of farming' or that 'other peoples have found political salvation as a result of foreign conquest'.[135] Chart also engaged in this area of debate, but suggested that 'possibly if, in the execution of the scheme, more attention had been paid to the rights of the native occupier of the soil, the project would have been successful'. This was a line of argument familiar from his book on Catholic Emancipation. Indeed, for a unionist-approved school text, Chart's version of the Ulster plantation seems far too heavily weighted on the side of the dispossessed natives. 'The leaderless natives', he wrote:

> mostly poor or broken men, received little except freedom to depart with their goods and chattels into any other part of the realm they pleased. Most of them did not do so, but, with characteristic Celtic love of the native place, stayed in their own districts occupying the less fertile land of mountain or bog which had been excluded from the plantation. From this harsh soil they wrested a scanty subsistence, full of bitter memories and confronted daily with the sight of those whom they regarded as their supplanters.[136]

All these authors believed however that the experience of the plantation had once and for all marked Ulster off as a distinctive place from the rest of the island. This 'solid block of Protestant Englishmen and Scotsmen' had maintained their distinctiveness by resisting absorption into the Gaelic population, according to Phillips.[137] By way of contrast Hamilton noted that this had not been the case in the other three provinces where experience had proven that 'the effect of mixing the two races [was] not always elevating but rather the reverse'. 'A standing testimony to the stern resistance of the colonists to the allurements of the native girls' was, Hamilton believed, 'to be found in the present-day Ulster's 800,000 Protestants, all of whom would to-day be profitable members of the Church of Rome, had their forebears at any time through the centuries yielded to the charms of the native daughters of Erin.'[138]

In contrast to the seventeenth and eighteenth centuries, these unionist authors looked to the nineteenth century as a positive period for Ireland, north and south; it was a century which did not leave 'so large a legacy of bitter memories as the eighteenth century' had.[139] Their arguments about the union can be read as arguments for the rejection of home rule. According to Cyril Falls, Ulster in the nineteenth century was characterised by the spread 'of an intense loyalty', a loyalty 'which has been the subject of praise and derision, of comfort to England in time of trouble and of inconvenience to her more compromising statesmen in time of bargaining.'[140] Falls was referring to any number of unionist beacon buoys, but almost certainly to the Ulster crisis of 1912–14.

The cause of this happy century was of course the Act of Union, and its beneficial policies. Unsurprisingly these unionists believed that the union had aided 'the purification and improvement of the Irish administration'. Chart argued that 'the new authorities were not immersed in the storms of Irish controversy, nor were they carried away by the vehement prejudices and minorities which so often lead men of Irish birth into excess'.[141] W.A. Phillips felt that the union had saved the country from itself:

> With the perceptions of the deep traditional cleavages in Irish life, with its bitter racial and religious antagonisms, came the conviction that it was only the fact that Ireland was embraced in a wider unity that kept her united, and that, left to herself, she would become prey to cruel civil strife and ultimately suffer disruption. This has proved to be the case.[142]

Writing in 1926, Phillips is undoubtedly referring to the civil war, but is also rehearsing a long-held unionist belief that the Irish were incapable of governing themselves because of their inherently unpolitical and uncivilised natures. Ulster, according to Chart, had flourished under the union, while in contrast the rest of the country was rife with disorder.[143] Writing in 1910, he hoped that the 'accumulated grievances and sorrows of six centuries' were being removed by Britain's statesmen; 'perhaps', he continued, 'we are not far from the day when Ireland will be a prosperous and peaceful country like her many sister lands of the British Empire'.[144] Such rhetoric is reflective of British government policy at the time; in the early years of the twentieth century, when home rule tensions appeared to have subsided, tories had hoped to 'kill home rule with kindness'. The policy created mixed feelings among unionists, but for some it played into the hands of those who wished, through home rule, to destroy the empire and thus undermine the security of Ulster protestants. Chart's sentiments have an added poignancy given the events which were to follow in the next decade. W.A. Phillips concurred with Chart on the benefits of the union; as a direct result Ireland (and particularly Ulster) had enjoyed speedy growth of wealth and 'the contentment that comes with it.'[145] This was a traditional unionist argument for maintenance of the union, rehearsed through three home rule crises. Of course the nineteenth century looked all the rosier for authors such as Phillips in the light of the Ulster crisis of 1912–14, the Easter Rising, the First World War and the subsequent Anglo-Irish treaty.

Chart, in measured tones, saw the nationalist move for home rule as a marker in Irish history; it signified a 'divergence of view between Ulster, broadly speaking, and the rest of Ireland, and it became evident that a settlement on the basis of a single parliament for all Ireland was impractical'.[146] No such moderation is to be found in Ernest Hamilton's writing: 'in Ulster the cry "Ireland for the Irish" is not the mere innocent expression of a laudable patriotism', he declared, 'it has a deeper and a far more sinister meaning. It means the expulsion from Ireland of the Protestant colonists, and is so understood clearly by both sections of the population. There are no sentimental illusions in Ulster, whatever there may be in England.'[147] Writing before the establishment of the two Irish states, Hamilton saw the nationalist desire for home rule, in traditional unionist terms, as the age-old desire of the 'native' Irish – 'the hope that it will provide the machinery by which the British colonists can be got rid of and Irish soil revert once more to the Irish'.[148] Hamilton was writing before what Phillips referred to as the 'surrender', that is the Anglo-Irish Treaty, but he had been politically active through the first two home rule bills. The passing of the home rule bill in 1914 was viewed by Ronald McNeill in *Ulster's stand for union* as an act of treachery by the British government, a view which reflected the rhetoric of the unionist press at the time.[149] 'In an eloquent peroration', wrote the *Belfast Newsletter*, '[Carson] affirmed that it was never a manly part to submit to betrayal, and he described the action of the Government in Irish affairs as a great betrayal of the foulest character.'[150] In turn, the treaty of 1921 was perceived in these traditional terms of treachery and betrayal by the majority of Ulster unionists; they viewed it as a reward by the British administration to Irish nationalists for the treachery of Easter 1916; in contrast, they felt, the Ulster protestants had been model citizens of the empire by sacrificing themselves in the First World War and they had been forced to accept a policy (home rule) that they had in fact mobilised against in 1912. The subsequent unionist distrust of the British administration was articulated in the work of unionist writers. Writing in 1936, Falls sounded a bitter note which was directed against Westminster: '[Ulster protestants]', he wrote, 'denied that any nation had the right to cast off children who loved her in order to hand them over to a rule which they abhorred'.[151]

Ulster unionists had campaigned against three home rule bills – in effect campaigning against the British government – in an attempt to preserve the union. Their attempt had created an exclusive politics in which there was no room for diversity and where diversity within unionist ranks was obsessively glossed over. This became a feature of unionist literature and unionist rituals over the following decades, and was to find its ultimate expression in the Festival of Britain in Northern Ireland in 1951. Unionists had themselves undermined the whole basis of the union and the empire which united, by its very nature, many disparate groups under the rule of the mother country – thus the most loyal of the empire's subjects, in opposing the will of the mother parliament, came perilously close to subverting that which they proclaimed vehemently they wished to preserve. The outbreak of the First World War gave them the opportunity to emphasise their loyalty to the empire and their willingness to sacrifice themselves for it, rather than to remind the British that they had been arming themselves with German guns to engage in conflict with the crown's forces. The *Northern Whig* argued at the outbreak of war: 'Though the enemy has changed the challenge is the same, and England enters the lists not as a defender of selfish interests, but as champion for civilisation'.[152] The Allies presented the war with Germany as a 'struggle to preserve social values . . . notions of justice, dignity, civility, restraint, and a "progress" governed by a respect for law'.[153] Unionist anti-home rule rhetoric had been filled with such sentiments for over three decades. Thus unionist and British opinion, in their different ways, looked to the war to preserve or restore the world they knew. However, as three anti-home rule campaigns to oppose British government measures had illustrated, the world which the British and that which the unionists wished to preserve were not necessarily the same, something which the following decades would highlight further.

Notes and References

1   St John Ervine, preface to *Craigavon: Ulsterman* (London, 1949), p. xviii.
2   R.F. Foster, 'History and the Irish Question', *Transactions of the Royal Historical Society*, 5th Series, vol. 33 (1983), p. 170.
3   W.A. Phillips although not an Ulster unionist is included because of his influence as a southern unionist author on unionist writers in general.
4   Cited in Marc Ferro, *The use and abuse of history: or how the past is taught* (London, 1981), p. viii.
5   D.A. Chart, *A history of Northern Ireland* (Belfast, 1927), p. 24.
6   W.A. Phillips, *The revolution in Ireland, 1906–23*, p. 1. Again, this attitude was repeated in Hugh Shearman's biography of Craig; referring to Craig's early years as premier of the new northern state, Shearman wrote: 'the first care was the very existence of the State. He had learnt that British sympathy was not to be relied on in this respect'. Hugh Shearman, *Not an Inch* (London, 1942), p. 168.
7   George Dangerfield, *The strange death of Liberal England* (London, 1936), p. 84.
8   D.G. Boyce, *Nineteenth century Ireland: the search for stability* (Dublin, 1990), p. 235.
9   W.S. Rodner, 'Leaguers, Covenanters, Moderates: British support for Ulster, 1913–1914', *Éire-Ireland*, vol. xvii, no. 3, 1982, p. 71.
10   Walter Long, a senior British conservative, claimed that by 1914 two million people in Britain had signed the pledge.
11   'Historians who complacently celebrate the smooth transition from aristocratic to democratic government in Britain perhaps overlook the Ulster crisis as the moment of truth for a politically emasculated governing class, resisting the implications of representative government', Peter Clarke, *Hope and Glory. Britain 1900–1990* (London, 1996) p. 68.
12   Quoted in W.S. Armour, *Armour of Ballymoney* (London, 1934), p. xii.
13   Although Alvin Jackson makes the point that there was no 'systematic' rejection of Westminster by Ulster unionists, the 'relative significance of parliament was being reduced through the more intensive local political activity of Unionist politicians'. This he argues occurred not just as a consequence of the 1912–14 crisis in Ulster, but also in the earlier Edwardian period. Alvin Jackson, *The Ulster Party: Irish Unionists in the House of Commons, 1884–1911* (Oxford, 1989), p. 309.
14   D.W. Miller, *Queen's rebels: Ulster loyalism in historical perspective* (Dublin, 1978), p. 162.
15   *WNW,* 3 Jan. 1914.
16   Paul Fussell, *The Great War and modern memory* (Oxford, 1975), p. 24.
17   ibid., p. 79.
18   James Craig noted in July 1907 'that the entire democracy of Ireland is divided into two, and only two, camps – one dumb-driven by the priest and the agitator, the other free men politically and spiritually', *Manchester Guardian,* 2 July 1907.
19   *NW,* 12 July 1918.

20   Paul Fussell, *The Great War and modern memory*, p. 21.

21   Edward Carson, *NW,* 10 Apr. 1912.

22   Quoted in Modris Eksteins, *The rites of spring: the Great War and the birth of the modern age* (London, 1990), p. 171.

23   Cyril Falls, *The history of the 36th (Ulster) Division* (Belfast, 1922), p. 301.

24   James Logan, *Ulster in the x-rays* (London, 1923), p. 170.

25   Edward Carson, cited in A.T.Q. Stewart, *Edward Carson* (Dublin, 1981), p. 94.

26   Letter to Edward Carson, author unknown, 25 Sept. 1914, D1496/6, PRONI.

27   *BET,* 6 Aug. 1914.

28   'Our loyalty is of no recent date', noted the *BET* in August 1914, 'but has been the very foundation and groundwork of all our political action and the motive power of our sacrifice to maintain our position in the United Kingdom.'

29   P. Callan, 'Voluntary recruiting for the British Army in Ireland during the First World War', unpublished PhD, University College Dublin, 1984, p. 136.

30   *NW,* 5 Aug. 1914.

31   *WNW,* 15 July 1916.

32   D.G. Boyce, *Nineteenth century Ireland*, p. 246.

33   Lord Plumer preface to Cyril Falls, *The history of the 36th (Ulster) Division*, p. ix.

34   The ability to credit them with such distinctively Ulster protestant achievements would have been impossible if the recruits had found themselves incorporated in a regular British army division.

35   Keith Jeffery, *TLS*, quoted on the dust-jacket of the Faber & Faber edition of Frank McGuinness, *Observe the sons of Ulster marching towards the Somme* (London, 1986).

36   *WNW,* 15 July 1916.

37   *BT,* 30 June 1966.

38   Given that Hamilton's book was written while the conflict was still in progress, this was a particularly sensitive issue for him.

39   James Logan, *Ulster in the x-rays*, p. 176. Logan also notes the contribution of southern recruits and their friendly relations with Ulster soldiers.

40   Lord Plumer, preface to Cyril Falls, *The history of the 36th (Ulster) Division*, p. xi. The book in addition was under the patronage of Edward Carson and Sir James Craig.

41   Cyril Falls, ibid., pp. 60–3.

42   Lord Plumer preface to Cyril Falls, *ibid.*, p. xi.

43   *BNL,* 8 July 1916.

44   D.G. Boyce, *Nineteenth century Ireland*, p. 244.

45   Phillip Orr, *The road to the Somme: men of the Ulster Division tell their story* (Belfast, 1987), p. 169.

46   Cyril Falls, *The history of the 36th (Ulster) Division*, pp. xv–xvi.

47   Paul Fussell, *The Great War and modern memory*, p. 12.

48   P. Callan, 'Voluntary recruiting for the British Army in Ireland during the First World War', p. 155.

49   Phillip Orr, *The road to the Somme*, p. 161.

50   *NW,* 8 Aug. 1916.

51   'When we commemorate that great corporation of men which was the 36th (Ulster) Division, our minds should embrace the whole company of dead and living, for they are of one brotherhood'. Cyril Falls, *The history of the 36th (Ulster) Division*, p. 51, p. 301.

52   Modris Eksteins, *The rites of spring*, p. 341.

53   Barbara Tuchman, *August 1914* (London, 1962), p. 426.

54   Lord Ernest Hamilton's *The first seven divisions* (1917), and Cyril Falls's *The history of the 36th (Ulster) Division* (1922), and *The Royal Irish Rifles* (1928).

55   *BNL*, 7 July 1916.

56   Ronald McNeill, dealing with the rising, wrote: 'The strongest sentiment was one of horror at the treacherous blow dealt to the Empire, while engaged in a life-and-death struggle with a foreign enemy', *Ulster's stand for union* (London, 1922), p. 244.

57   W.A. Phillips, *The revolution in Ireland, 1906–23* (London, 1923), pp. 98–9.

58   Cyril Falls, *The birth of Ulster* (London, 1936), p. 247.

59   Hugh Shearman, *Modern Ireland* (London, 1952), p. 141.

60   Cyril Falls, *The First World War* (London, 1960), p. 165.

61   *NW*, 8 July 1916.

62   A.T.Q. Stewart, *Edward Carson*, p. 118.

63   D.G. Boyce, *Englishmen and Irish troubles* (London, 1972), p. 36.

64   Michael Laffan, *The partition of Ireland, 1911–25* (Dublin, 1983), p. 25.

65   *NW*, 12 July 1919.

66   Tom Kettle, National Volunteer, killed in 1916 at the Western Front. J.B. Lyons, *The enigma of Tom Kettle: Irish patriot, essayist, poet, British soldier, 1880–1916* (Dublin, 1983), p. 293.

67   Hugh Shearman, *How Northern Ireland is governed* (HMSO, 1951), p. 12.

68   Paul Fussell, *The Great War and modern memory*, p. 79.

69   Keith Jeffery, *The British army and the crisis of empire, 1918–22* (Manchester, 1984), p. 155.

70   Modris Eksteins, *The rites of spring*, p. 350.

71   The glaring gap in this literature is the lack of any celebration of the UVF and the actions of the unionist leaders in the 1912–14 Ulster crisis. Ronald McNeill does address this period of unionist history but in the period in question it was no doubt considered impolitic to bring attention to Ulster unionism's defiance of the British government, particularly when unionist commentators were using the Easter Rising as a stick to beat Irish nationalists.

72   A.S. Green, *The old Irish world* (Dublin, 1912), p. 1.

73   Lord Ernest Hamilton, *The Irish rebellion of 1641* (London, 1920), p. v.

74   Both D.A. Chart and Cyril Falls acknowledged his importance to their area of interest.

75   In addition, Hamilton took a 'leading role', according to James Loughlin, in the British Fascists. See Loughlin's 'Northern Ireland and British fascism in the inter-war years', *IHS*, vol. xxix, no. 116 (Nov. 1995) p. 539. See chapter two below for more on fascism and communism in Northern Ireland in the 1930s.

76   In the home rule crises of the 1880s and 1890s the Siege of Derry rather than the 1641 'massacre' was the paradigm in use.

77   Lord Ernest Hamilton, *The soul of Ulster* (London, 1917), p. 157.

78   ibid., p. 195. The leader of the *Belfast Weekly Telegraph* of 6 February 1886 noted that 'there may be some confidence entertained that, in any event, the Protestants of Ulster, like their forefathers, will be able to protect themselves'. Perhaps given that this is the political rhetoric which Hamilton had dealt with over a twenty-five year period the tone of his books is more understandable.

79   James Logan, *Ulster in the x-rays*, p. 53.

80   ibid., p. 62.

81   Bell in his miscellany of Ulster, published in 1972, spoke of the 'Islandmen' in respectful tones; 'in a shipyard, boys do the work of men and men do the work of giants'. Sam Hanna Bell, *Within our province* (Belfast, 1972), p. 85.

82   James Logan, *Ulster in the x-rays*, p. 45.

83   This is echoed by Cyril Falls writing in 1936: 'Whatever its [Ulster's] fate, it will not perish because its defensive virtues of constancy and tenacity have gone to rust', *The birth of Ulster* (London, 1936), p. 254. Ian McBride argues that

unionists, 'eager to distinguish themselves from the native stock of the degenerate south, depicted the archetypal Ulsterman as an Anglo-Saxon, the embodiment of the industrious virtues celebrated in the Victorian literature of self-help', Ian McBride, 'Ulster and the British problem', p. 9, in Richard English (ed.), *Unionism in Modern Ireland: new perspectives on politics and culture* (Dublin 1996).

84 The 1892 convention for instance with its use of shamrock and harp imagery and the use of Irish over the entrance to the pavilion. Again, the Solemn League and Covenant signed by Carson was rich with Celtic design.

85 See Breandan Ó Buachalla, *I mBeal Feirste cois cuain* (Dublin, 1968). Ian MacBride, 'Ulster and the British problem', p. 11.

86 Edna Longley, 'Progressive bookmen: politics and northern Protestant writers since the 1930s', *The Irish Review*, no. 1 (1986), p. 56.

87 D.A. Chart, *A history of Northern Ireland* (Belfast, 1927), p. 15. D.A. Chart was the first deputy keeper of the PRONI in 1924. A Dublin Castle civil servant and southern protestant, he moved to Belfast following partition. The author of several books (on medieval Dublin and the archaeology of Northern Ireland), he was to write this first school history text for the new Northern Irish State in 1927, supported by the permanent secretary, Bonaparte-Wyse. 'For I had dreams of being a political writer of the same style as Denis [sic] Ireland, but on the other side . . . but nobody seemed to want to hear the views of a juvenile Unionist living in Cork', D.A. Chart, 'Two kinds of storytelling', chairman's address to Belfast PEN, 5 Jan. 1946, D1246/2B. See Chart's obituary by Kenneth Darwin in *Archives*, vol. v, no. 25, 1961.

88 Hugh Shearman, *Modern Ireland*, pp. 13–14.

89 Oliver MacDonagh, *States of mind* (London, 1983) p. 14.

90 A.S. Green, *The old Irish world*, p. 61. A.S. Green (1847–1929), born Kells, Co. Meath. Author of *Henry II* (1888), *Town life in the Fifteenth Century* (1894), *The making of modern Ireland and its undoing* (1908), *Irish nationality* (1911) which was dedicated to the Irish dead, and *A history of the Irish state to 1014* (1925).

91 Lord Ernest Hamilton, *The soul of Ulster*, p. 149.

92 'The main proof', writes J.J Lee, 'offered of their unfitness was their opposition to English rule, the logical conclusion of this train of thought being that the natives could demonstrate their fitness for self-government only by explicitly avowing their unfitness for it', 'Some aspects of modern Irish history' in E. Schulin (ed.), *Gedenkischrift Martin Göhring: Studien zur Europäischen Geschichte* (Wiesbaden, 1968) p. 434.

93 W.A. Phillips, *The revolution in Ireland, 1906–23* (London, 1926), p. 13. The overall argument of this book was that by analysing Irish history one could deduce that a united Ireland was never a viable proposition. See Phillips, ibid., p. 16.

94 Hugh Shearman, 'Recent developments in Anglo-Irish Relations', *World Affairs* (Apr. 1949).

95 Lord Ernest Hamilton, *The Irish rebellion of 1641*, p. vi.

96 D.A. Chart, *A history of Northern Ireland*, p. 19.

97 Lord Ernest Hamilton, op. cit., p. 36.

98 W.A. Phillips, *The revolution in Ireland, 1906–23*, pp. 14–15.

99 Quoted in Dennis Kennedy, *The widening gulf: northern attitudes to the independent Irish state, 1919–49* (Belfast, 1988), p. 50.

100 *BNL*, 11 June 1921.

101 *NW*, 1 May 1922.

102 *BNL*, 9 May 1922.

103 Lord Ernest Hamilton, *The soul of Ulster*, p. 45.

104   D.A. Chart, A *history of Northern Ireland*, p. 20.

105   Hugh Shearman, *Modern Ireland*, p. 15.

106   Lord Ernest Hamilton, *The Irish Rebellion of 1641* p. vi.

107   Lord Ernest Hamilton, *The Irish rebellion of 1641*, pp. vii–viii.

108   D.A. Chart, *A history of Northern Ireland*, p. 23.

109   D.A. Chart, *Ulster Yearbook* (1926), p. 9.

110   Hugh Shearman, *Modern Ireland*, p. 60. This echoes the unionist belief that the 'Ulsterman' was logical and full of common sense and that the 'native' Irish were by contrast victims to their emotions.

111   Lord Ernest Hamilton, *The soul of Ulster*, p. 102.

112   See W.A. Phillips, *The revolution in Ireland, 1906–23*, p. 24.

113   W.A. Phillips, ibid., p. 24.

114   Cyril Falls, *The birth of Ulster*, p. 243.

115   Oliver MacDonagh, *States of mind*, p. 4.

116   *NW*, 5 Nov. 1888.

117   Ronald McNeill does celebrate this episode in unionist history but both Hamilton and Chart avoid it. Hugh Shearman, in *Modern Ireland* (1953), refers to it very briefly, and really only mentions the Larne gun-running episode.

118   See Alvin Jackson's 'Irish unionism', in D.G. Boyce and Alan O'Day (eds.), *The making of modern Irish history: revisionism and the revisionist controversy* (London, 1996), for a discussion of the unionist literature which covers this area.

119   'The ethics of the Ulster question', Ernest Hamilton wrote, 'are fast bound up in the general ethics of colonization. Is colonization to be classed as an act of piracy, or is it a necessary part of the gradual reclamation of the world?', *The soul of Ulster*, p. 3.

120   Lord Ernest Hamilton, *The soul of Ulster*, p. 123.

121   ibid., p. 194.

122   Thomas MacKnight, *Ulster as it is* (London, 1896), p. 379.

123   Colonel Wallace quoted in the *NW*, 10 Apr. 1912.

124   D.A. Chart, *Ireland from Union to Catholic Emancipation* (London, 1910), p. 306.

125   ibid., p. 17.

126   D.G. Boyce, *Nineteenth century Ireland*, p. 241.

127   *BWT*, 22 June 1912.

128   A.D. Buckley, *History and ethnicity* (London, 1989), p. 186.

129   Falls acknowledged Lord Ernest Hamilton's books *Elizabethan Ulster* and *The Irish rebellion of 1641*, texts which celebrated the planters and their influence on Ulster, and his observation was therefore not universally true. Cyril Falls, *Birth of Ulster*, p. ix.

130   W.A. Phillips, *The revolution in Ireland, 1903–26*, p. 16.

131   Lord Ernest Hamilton, *The soul of Ulster*, p. 79.

132   D.A. Chart, *Ulster Yearbook* (1926).

133   Lord Ernest Hamilton *The fall of Ulster*, p. 24.

134   ibid., p. 34.

135   W.A. Phillips, *The revolution in Ireland, 1906–26*, p. 6.

136   D.A. Chart, *A history of Northern Ireland* (Belfast, 1927), p. 19. This has parallels, ironically, with M. Hayden and G. Moonan's version of the plantation in their nationalist school text of 1921, *A short history of the Irish people* (London, 1921): 'The Ulster Plantation produced amongst the native Irish a burning sense of injustice, and a desire for revenge. It was probably one of the chief causes of the great insurrection of 1641', p. 275. Again compare this to Chart's entry to the *Ulster Year Book* of 1926 where he noted that the colonists were 'regarded with all the odium attaching to supplanters' and suggested this as the root cause of the 1641 rebellion.

137 W.A. Phillips, *The revolution in Ireland, 1906–23*, p. 12.
138 Lord Ernest Hamilton, *The soul of Ulster*, p. 71.
139 D.A. Chart, *A history of Northern Ireland*, p. 304. For example, Chart felt that the traumas suffered by the protestants of Ulster in 1798 had made them fearful of accepting Catholic Emancipation.
140 Cyril Falls, *Birth of Ulster*, p. 245.
141 D.A. Chart, *Ireland from Union to Catholic Emancipation*, p. 303.
142 W.A. Phillips, *The revolution in Ireland, 1906–26*, p. xi.
143 D.A. Chart, *Ireland from Union to Catholic Emancipation*, p. 308.
144 ibid., p. 308.
145 'How this process was stopped, and Ireland turned from a state of pastoral peace into one of anarchy and bloodshed, it is the purpose of the following pages to tell', introduction to W.A. Phillips, *The revolution in Ireland, 1906–26*, pp. 43–4.
146 D.A. Chart, *Ulster Yearbook* (1926).
147 Lord Ernest Hamilton, *The soul of Ulster*, pp. 118–19.
148 op. cit., p. 112.
149 Ronald McNeill, *Ulster's stand for Union*, p. 235.
150 *BNL,* 25 Sept. 1911.
151 Cyril Falls, *The birth of Ulster*, p. 246. This has echoes of Edward Carson in 1911: 'I know that force has been used to compel retention of a Government against the will of the people, but a precedent has yet to be created to drive out by force loyal and contented citizens from a community to which by birth they belong', cited in St John Ervine, *Sir Edward Carson and the Ulster movement* (Dublin, 1915) p. 191.
152 *NW,* 5 Aug.1914.
153 Modris Eksteins, *The rites of spring*, p. 245.

2. Symbolic Mirrors:
unionist commemorations in the 1930s*

The 1930s in Northern Ireland was a period of rituals, performed for the population at large. The colour and drama of these ceremonies were forcefully conveyed through the pages of the main unionist papers, the *Belfast Newsletter*, the *Northern Whig*, and the *Belfast Telegraph*. The attention given these rituals in the press in Northern Ireland is important because through the press these often élitist events were made accessible to the public. Through press coverage, which was as comprehensive as it was dramatic, the masses were given a sense that they were participating in the collective life of their community. The major ceremonial festivals of this decade, all ritually performed, were the opening of the Stormont parliament, the unveiling of the statue honouring Edward Carson in 1933, the silver jubilee celebrations of George V in Belfast in 1935, the funeral of Carson in October of the same year, and finally the coronation visit of King George VI and Queen Elizabeth in 1937. In addition, the state's and unionism's founding father, Edward Carson, was honoured in an impressive three-volume biography, which inherited much of its style from previous unionist histories. Manifest in this decade's rituals were symbols of the Northern Irish state as a homogenous community.[1] They were the major events in the history of Northern Ireland, following the boundary commission, bringing together the unionist leadership, unionist politicians, the state's protestant religious leaders, and other members of Northern Ireland's establishment. Through the medium of these occasions many unionist certitudes were affirmed in a manner which combined 'inducing awe in the audience with sentimental involvement'.[2] They were also expressions of state building. Ultimately, such rituals made the abstract Northern Irish state, its place in the union, and its unionist identity tangible to the unionist community and to onlookers.

This was a period in which unionism was trying to rally its faithful in a show of strength; their state rituals made a high-profile point that unionist

---

* See my 'Symbolic mirrors: commemorations of Edward Carson in the 1930s', *IHS*, forthcoming, Nov. 2000.

collectivity was not only possible, but was a reality. The unionist commemorations of the 1930s were marked by distinctive ceremonial settings,
formal speeches and, often, spectacular dress.[3] This goes some way to
explaining why the press described the ceremonies in such theatrical
terms.[4] These events aimed at reinforcing the state and formally proscribing
any doubts and tensions within the unionist camp.[5] In addition they gave
the Northern Irish state physical endorsement. To call these unionist ceremonies staged or manufactured is not to suggest that they were generated
cynically, merely to note that they were consciously organised, staged and
publicised. They were, moreover, overtly political in nature. They were
rituals which spoke primarily, although not exclusively, to a unionist audience. Their elaborate ceremonies took a traditional unionist form, and were
organised by an easily identifiable narrative full of references to a protestant and unionist past. The unveiling of the Carson statue, in particular, was
so imbued with significance and unionist sentiment that as a ritual it spoke
for itself, needing very little interpretation. It presented unionists with the
opportunity to exercise nostalgia over a romanticised unionist past, as well
as indicating their aspirations (and fears) for the future of their state.[6] The
visits of British royalty to the state allowed for a more long-term historic
perspective, assessing unionism in terms of the wider empire. Indeed, Alvin
Jackson in his 'Irish Unionism and the empire, 1880–1920' argues for the
varied nature of unionist attitudes towards the empire:

> Popular imperialism in Ulster, therefore, had little to do with the objec-
> tive condition of the empire, and a great deal to do with popular political
> morale: popular imperialism reflected more directly the relationship
> between Unionism and the British crown and the relationship between
> Unionism and the rest of Irish politics.[7]

In general, in a period of economic depression and social unrest within the
state, combined with de Valera's alterations to the Free State's constitution,
these ceremonies enabled unionism to appeal to and incorporate a diverse
protestant population.[8] In this way they regrouped unionism into a coherent
political movement, defining its role in the shifting political environment
and reinforcing its own particular ethos.

The Northern Irish state was affirmed for unionists by the creation and
opening of the Stormont parliament in November 1932. 'The Northern
Parliament', wrote the editor of the *Northern Whig*, 'is the symbol and guarantee of Ulster's status as a province of the United Kingdom: from that
position there can be no receding'.[9] The Government of Ireland Act had
created a six-county state, assuring unionists an overall majority, although
there was no unionist majority in two of the counties, Fermanagh and
Tyrone. Thus, as Mansergh has argued, there was 'a Protestant parliament
but for more than a Protestant people'.[10] Northern Ireland's parliament had
held its initial sessions in Belfast city hall and then in the Presbyterian
Assembly college, and the king and queen paid a brief visit to the state in
1921 to open its initial sessions. By 1932 the construction of the new

parliament building was completed in the grounds of Stormont castle and the Prince of Wales was engaged to perform its official opening.

The construction of the building was not without its problems.[11] In August 1921 Craigavon wrote to the Earl of Crawford and Balcarres (the first commissioner of works, David Lindsay) to tell him that Stormont castle had been selected as the location for the new parliament building.[12] In an aside he requested that furniture from Dublin castle be taken for the new building:

> It has occurred to me that during the truce would be a favourable time to have such furniture got out of Dublin – a matter of utter impossibility if hostilities are recommenced . . . As Dail Eiran [sic] meets on the 16th, and the result of such meeting may be a breakdown, there is not a moment to lose.[13]

The issue of the furniture aside, the earl wrote tersely to James Craig in August 1921 saying he was disturbed that the Stormont castle estate had been bought without consultation with him: 'I hope that my technical advisors may be able to show my fears to be exaggerated, for I shall be embarrassed if they report that land ill-suited for our special object has been acquired without my knowledge'.[14] St John Ervine recorded the Prince of Wales' 1932 visit in *Craigavon: Ulsterman*; famously the prince was not keen to perform the opening, a fact which Ervine put down to the influence of a man in the prince's circle with 'pro-Southern Irish sympathies', who had 'filled his head with stuff and nonsense about the North'. Despite this, wrote Ervine:

> Great crowds of one of the warmest hearted peoples in the world stood for hours in the streets to welcome him and were presented with an unsmiling face and glum and sulky looks. But Ulster people are not easily discouraged from their loyalty, even by princes.[15]

Casting a slightly different hue on the event, Henry Maxwell, author of *Ulster was right*, saw a deep significance in the prince's presence:

> His words to those who stood within its precincts came not only as the gracious accents of the King's representative fulfilling with charming accord an agreeable incident of Royal duty, but with the deep spiritual significance of Royal Assent to a second, an unwritten, but nevertheless in every particle as solemn a covenant as the Act of Settlement.[16]

Reflecting the worldwide economic depression of the period, the Prince of Wales was anxious that 'not one penny more' than was 'absolutely essential' was to be spent on his visit to the state; in a letter to the Duke of Abercorn he wrote:

> It is obvious that the fact of my going to Belfast to open the new Parliament Buildings must to a certain degree remind those thousands who are unfortunately unemployed and almost starving, that, since the War, an enormous amount of money has been expended on bricks and mortar, and they naturally reason that this money would have been better spent

on the great commercial enterprise which, in better times, provided these unfortunate people with a livelihood – as for instance the great shipbuilding industry of Belfast.

'I shall not', the prince concluded, 'measure my welcome by elaborate decorations or any other form of outward display.'[17] The day of the parliament's opening was declared a public holiday and the route the prince was to follow was lined with enthusiastic supporters.[18] So that all present could feel involved, the ceremonial proceedings were relayed to those inside and outside the Stormont building through loudspeakers. Those outside the building were made up of invited guests; tickets for the event were provided for members of the police force and their wives, a hundred tickets went to each MP and senator, as well as an allocation of tickets to the girl guides, boy scouts and boys' brigade.[19] In addition the guest list for the reception for the prince at the Ulster Hall, which followed the ceremony, was drawn up by the lord mayor of Belfast and Craigavon.[20] The policing of the grounds was carried out by 5,000 orangemen wearing special badges embodying the Prince of Wales's feathers.[21] In a letter to R.E. Thornley, at the ministry of finance, one correspondent reflected on the opening: 'The staff work of the ceremonial, the really effective pageantry, and all the incidentals such as the traffic arrangements seemed to me (if I may add my humble tribute) magnificent.' The writer went on to remark that the opening of the Australian Commonwealth Parliament had been like the opening of a 'village bazaar' compared to the Northern Irish 'show'.[22]

Memories of the king's visit to the province eleven years previously were recalled and the prince's speech echoed that of his father. The creation of Stormont, and the construction of the building was advertised in the press as 'the gift of the British parliament to the Ulster people'.[23] The very building, in both its triumphalist architecture and what it symbolised for unionists, was a striking manifestation of the mentality of those who controlled the new state. Craigavon, for his part, was in no doubt as to what it symbolised: 'It is indeed', he said, 'a noble building, and will stand on its base of granite from the Mountains of Mourne, as a symbol of the link between Great Britain and Northern Ireland.'[24] Moreover, and in line with unionist concerns about unity within their rank and file, Craigavon thanked the Office of Works for employing local labour; Stormont, he argued, would stand 'as a memorial not only to the distinguished Architect but also to the enterprise and skill of the Ulster working man'.[25]

In Stormont unionists gained not only a place to hold their assemblies but the symbolic and public endorsement of their state from those forces vital to its continued survival.[26]

To-day the most momentous and significant event in Ulster history was enacted in the opening with state pomp and ceremonial of the Parliamentary and Administrative Building of Northern Ireland at Stormont, Belfast, the ceremony, stately in setting, rich in all the colours of pageantry, and impressive to the last degree, being performed by His Royal Highness the Prince of Wales, K.G., K.P., on behalf of his Gracious Majesty the King.[27]

A poem sent to the prime minister, in honour of the prince's visit, high-lighted unionist concerns for their state's security, and their need for unity, at this time:

> Arise ye Sons of Ulster, whose principles are pure.
> And give Our Prince a Welcome when he lands on Ireland's shore.
> Heed not the treacherous foxy tongues, who work in darkest night,
> But close your ranks and trust in God, and all things will come right.[28]

In many ways, the Stormont parliament was built to convince unionists and others that 'not only had they arrived but that they would remain'.[29] The prince noted in his speech that:

> The responsibility of those who are entrusted with government and the making of laws can never be a light one. Heavy indeed is the burden that lies upon those who have to build upon new foundations. It is a matter for rejoicing that so many of those who have carried through this difficult task with such conspicuous success are still with you to give counsel and guidance in the difficulties which lie ahead.[30]

The unionist need to represent their political position within the union as permanent and immutable was given physical manifestation in the construction of 'this grandiose shell'.[31] That they should have placed so much importance in a building is not surprising when one considers their long tradition of political demonstrations in impressive, carefully selected, settings. From a temporary but impressive wooden pavilion used to house the 1892 Ulster Unionist Convention, unionists had progressed to an impressive granite building: 'The beautiful white buildings, as yet unstained by the smoke or rain of generations, towered in their impressive dignity, and if anything looked more stately for their baptismal day.'[32]

The Stormont parliament was thus in an established unionist tradition of symbolic structures. It was also a grand stage for unionists to recall the past and portray their unity, echoing the pattern of politics-as-theatre which had dominated unionism prior to the First World War. In Stormont Carson's first biographer, Edward Marjoribanks, saw Edward Carson's 'personal achieve-ment and monument':

> He undertook the most arduous political leadership of recent times, that politics became his first interest, and only held him till, his task, as he thought, achieved, he returned to his first love, the Law, on the founda-tion of the Ulster Parliament.[33]

Again Ian Colvin (who became Carson's biographer on Marjoribanks's death) in the third, and final, volume of the biography, spoke of the Stormont parliament as the conclusion of Carson's political work.[34] The new parlia-ment can, therefore, be seen as the original unionist monument honouring Edward Carson – completed the year before the imposing statue of the former unionist leader was unveiled in the grounds of Stormont – as well as being a monument to the endurance of unionism.[35] Yet, despite the tangible reassurance of the Stormont parliament, threats to the unionist state were seen by unionists as coming throughout the 1930s, from both the Free State, and from within their own borders. 'There are signs', wrote the *Belfast Weekly Newsletter* in the summer of 1932, 'which it would be a profound mistake to ignore, that we may have to face criminal conspiracies from inside and outside our borders to stir up trouble, upon which to base a demand for another settlement of the Irish problem.'[36]

The Thirty-First International Eucharistic Conference was held in the Free State's capital in June 1932 and, as a high-profile expression of self-confident catholicism, embodied part of the perceived threat to unionism. The Northern Ireland parliament opened at Stormont against the background of the Eucharistic Congress. The catholic faithful from Northern Ireland made the trip to Dublin for the spectacle of the papal legate leading the southern state's catholics in religious devotion. Members of the Northern Irish parliament, Joseph Devlin, Cahir Healy, Senator T.J. Campbell and T. McLoughlin, attended as canopy bearers: 'The Catholic members of the Belfast Corporation wore their municipal robes. Every parish in the Six Counties sent a contingent; almost every Catholic family an envoy, every sodality and confraternity a majority of their members.'[37] Some of the Northern Irish delegates were attacked on their journey home, as their trains passed through Larne, Ballymena and into Belfast.[38] In a letter to the prime minister, a civil servant at the Ministry of Home Affairs referred to those who had been arrested in connection with the 'disturbances' in Belfast and Ballymena who, he claimed, were of 'good character'. His letter linked the incidents to the opening of the new parliament, and indicated the attitude of some within the Northern Irish government towards the Free State:

> I do not want when the new Parliament House is opened or when, on the other hand, we might be engaged in very violent disturbances in connection with the Free State, to have the Government handicapped by having 70 or 80 young fellows in gaol.[39]

The director of organisation for the Eucharistic Congress, F. O'Reilly, had written to invite members of the Northern Irish senate and parliament to attend the congress. The official response was brief: 'On submitting it to the Minister he was of the opinion that in all the circumstances the best thing to do is to completely ignore the invitation.'[40] This was clearly not the policy of the unionist press. The *Belfast Weekly Telegraph* reported fully on the congress, and with the odd touch of irony:

> Yesterday the Papal Legate was received in Dublin by the Lord Mayor, Alderman A. Byrne, wearing the Papal colours and a chain of gold presented to the city by William of Orange. The paradox has probably no parallel in history. It was a memorable demonstration in pomp, pageantry and enthusiasm.[41]

The reporter was clearly caught up in the ceremony: 'it was easy to visualise the supreme beauty of this spectacle', he wrote having described the 'saffron and St Patrick's blue' uniforms of Cardinal Lauri's guard of honour, and the 'ostrich blue' of the four officers of the guard. A week later the congress was still an item of interest in the press; summing up its climax the *Belfast Weekly Telegraph*'s reporter wrote:

> Viewed as a spectacle it was transcendent in its universality and unique complexion; viewed as a picture it was both beautiful and brilliant; viewed as a demonstration of spiritual expression it was without a parallel in the whole Catholic history of Ireland.[42]

The penultimate moment of the congress was the pontifical mass celebrated in the Phoenix Park: 'With the Cardinal's robes, the jewelled crosses, diamonds that sparkled in the sunshine, and the mingling of races and raiment – the scene was a never-forgettable one'.[43] John McCormack, the Irish tenor, sang at the service which was heard not only by those who attended the Phoenix Park but by a wider audience throughout the country who received the radio broadcast of the ceremony.[44]

The Eucharistic Congress, taken together with the 1929 celebration of the centenary of Catholic Emancipation, increased the identification of the Irish Free State with catholicism, emphasised the widening gap between the two jurisdictions, and threw the Northern Irish state's protestant identity into sharper relief. Craigavon's remark at the Twelfth of July celebration in 1932 that 'ours is a Protestant Government and I am an Orangeman', and his statement in early 1933 that he was an Orangeman first and a politician second, that they were a protestant parliament and a protestant state was in direct response,[45] Craigavon claimed, to the frequent boast that the Free State was a catholic state, and de Valera's remark in 1931 at the Fianna Fáil Ard Fheis that he was 'a Catholic first'.[46] As Dennis Kennedy has noted, de Valera had no hesitation in declaring Ireland a catholic nation: 'In a St Patrick's Day broadcast in 1935 he said that since St Patrick, Ireland had been a Christian and Catholic nation. All attempts through the centuries to force her from this allegiance had not shaken her faith – "She remains a Catholic nation".'[47] Remarks such as these were widely noted in Northern Ireland by unionist politicians and press. With this in mind, it is worth considering James Craig's statement, in the run-up to the Craigavon demonstration of 1911: 'We hold that Orangeism in the North was only organised resistance against Fenianism in the South, and that our Protestantism, not aggressive but defensive, is no more militant than the Roman Catholic Church has made necessary.'[48] The unionist demonstrations of the 1930s thus found inspiration in the colourful and flamboyant catholic pageantry of the Eucharistic Congress, while simultaneously reacting against what it symbolised about the nature of the Free State.[49]

In 1933 Edward Carson came to symbolise much about the nature of the Northern Irish state, embodying that recent past when unionists had fought to remain in the union and had succeeded.[50] In 1935, the editor of the *Belfast Weekly Newsletter* offered an explanation of unionism's need to commemorate the past: 'They recall the past, not in a spirit of boastfulness, but as an inspiration to them of what men will dare and suffer for a cause in which they believe'.[51] Having visited the statue of Edward Carson in the grounds of Stormont, R.J. Lynn wrote: 'What a flood of memories it brought back – hard work, dangers, anxieties but every task made light by the sympathy, guidance and courage of our incomparable Chief.'[52] The statue by L.S. Merrifield would serve to remind those who looked on it, Craigavon suggested, that Carson 'at times of greatest danger' had saved unionists and saved 'the Province'.[53] In his speech, Sir Edward Archdale, chairman of the Ulster Unionist Council, drew contemporary relevance from Carson's achievements:

> We understand how much we are indebted to our late leader for all his work on that behalf. Notwithstanding the bribes offered us of green pillar-boxes – (laughter) – heavy taxes and great smuggling across the border we are resolved to stick to the British Empire and the Union Jack.[54]

'The people of Ulster', wrote Ian Colvin, 'never forgot what they owed to Edward Carson, and took a pride in erecting such a monument as would testify their gratitude to all time'.[55] As Alvin Jackson has noted, Carson articulated the belligerence of Ulster unionism between 1912 and 1914.[56] It was this unionist identity and this image of the past which unionists wished to hark back to, and associated with the Carson monument. The signing of the Solemn League and Covenant was, therefore, referred to continually by commentators throughout this period.[57] A central image of that time was of Edward Carson, with James Craig close at hand, signing the covenant at the city hall surrounded by the unionist hierarchy. This image of Carson with Craig at his shoulder became a constant in unionist iconography and in the countless newspaper reports which covered the two men at unionist demonstrations and rallies. In 1933 it was re-enacted at the unveiling. 'James Craig and I were two of the biggest rebels that ever stood in London', said Carson at the ceremony: 'Yes, I admit we were rebels. We were rebels to those who were rebels to the King and nothing could drive it out of our bones and marrow what we had inherited and what we were determined to maintain.'[58]

Both Carson and Craig had offered their domestic audience traits with which it could identify and in which it could have confidence. But in the 1930s it was Carson who was cast as the saviour of unionism; Craigavon would never be celebrated to the same extent. Alvin Jackson has identified reasons behind the differing treatment which Carson and Craigavon received from the unionist faithful; Carson, he argues, 'was deified by Ulster Unionists, but this was precisely because he was an outsider, above, and not within, the northern Protestant community. James Craig, by way of contrast, was a prophet in his own land, uncharismatic because familiar, undervalued because accessible.'[59] The day of the unveiling, according to St John Ervine, was cold and drizzling 'but the weather did not deter a crowd from coming to cheer their old commander, now old and nearly done'.[60] Although Edward Carson was, by 1933, frail and elderly he had become the embodiment of this recent and glorious unionist past, a period full of drama and tangible unionist strength.[61]

Lord Londonderry, presenting Lady Carson with a smaller replica of the larger statue, spoke of Edward Carson as the embodiment of the strengths of the 'Ulsterman' (ironic given that he was a Dubliner) as well as the ideal unionist:

> What had Lord Carson been? He had been the upholder of the cause and theory upon which, he believed, the greatness of Great Britain and the Empire had always depended – steadfastness and loyalty to duty and tradition, and the carrying out of the behests which their forefathers laid on their shoulders for developing the heritage which had been handed down to them. That was what Edward Carson did.[62]

'One might almost say', Henry Maxwell wrote, 'that he was the incarnation of principle'.[63] 'Steadfastness', 'loyalty to duty and tradition', the heritage of their forefathers – all the major tenets of the unionist ideology, familiar from their pre-war rhetoric, echoed throughout their legitimising histories of the early 1920s, and were easily recognisable as such by the unionist faithful witnessing this ceremony. As outlined in chapter one, throughout the 1920s Cyril Falls, Ernest Hamilton and W.A. Phillips had created a body of literature which provided historical legitimisation for the infant Northern Irish state.

The Observer in its coverage of the unveiling ceremony spoke of the statue's 'bold' conception and 'firm line' which gave, its reporter argued, 'a vivid idea of Lord Carson's striking personality'.[64] The statue was certainly spectacular: 'The total height of the monument from the ground to the head is 32ft 8in., the figure, which is of bronze, being 12ft high. The monument will be illuminated at night with floodlights concealed beneath the monument'.[65] Newspaper photographs showed Carson right arm aloft and noted that he had, during a speech full of his 'old vigour', dropped into 'the characteristic attitude' the statue depicted: 'In the centre towered the great bronze figure, vivid and impelling, of the man whom they had come to honour. And below, a dark figure on the platform was the man himself'.[66] The line separating Edward Carson the man and Edward Carson the monument was very thin indeed, and this can be seen as the beginning of a process of mythologising the former unionist leader and the unionist past he had come to signify. The statue was unveiled on 8 July, but the ceremony was outlined in the unionist press days in advance.[67] The *Northern Whig*, for example, informed its readers on 29 June that the religious leaders of the anglican, presbyterian and methodist churches would officiate at the religious ceremony which would precede the unveiling. In addition, 'Orangemen from all parts of Northern Ireland will be present as well as representatives of the various unionist Associations and prominent personages closely identified with political, commercial, and industrial life of the community'.[68] The prime minister, the *Belfast Newsletter*'s report continued, 'said he appreciated more highly than he could say the honour of unveiling the statue in the presence of the cream of the people of Ulster and of that veteran statesman and saviour of Ulster'.[69] The *Belfast Telegraph* informed its readers that the hymn associated with Carson's campaigns in the past, 'O God, Our help in ages past', would launch proceedings. The 'historic' duty of unveiling, it continued, would be performed by the prime minister of Northern Ireland 'who so worthily took up the reins of office from Lord Carson'.[70] The public were forewarned of the large crowds expected by the organisers (the idea and image of a large supporting crowd was thus established for unionists prior to its becoming a reality); the *Belfast Newsletter* noted that loudspeakers had been installed to enable 'those standing at a distance to follow the proceedings as if they were close to the pedestal'.[71] The event was, therefore, affirmed by the presence of 'thousands of Ulster men and women', who in themselves as onlookers were 'as essential for the success of the spectacle' as the more 'starring performers'.[72]

On the day of the unveiling the scenes were 'reminiscent of the days of the fight against Home Rule', according to one English newspaper, with an estimated 20,000 loyalists present at what the *Belfast Newsletter* noted was an 'historic ceremony'.[73] The ceremony harked back, perhaps deliberately, to those pre-war unionist demonstrations. The *Northern Whig* noted the presence of 'all ranks and classes', 'and a great band of colour in the foreground showed that the Orangemen of the province had turned out in force'.[74] This reporting of unionist 'unity' crossing class boundaries had been a feature in reports of unionist demonstrations throughout the home rule crises prior to the First World War. For example, at the Balmoral demonstration of 1911, the *Belfast Newsletter* noted the 'men of all professions' in the audience, 'what a significance there was in the oneness of mind in the common purpose that had drawn them all together'.[75]

This renewed focus on class unity in 1933 followed the Outdoor Relief Riots of October and November 1932. In Northern Ireland in the 1930s having no job 'meant often having no income, or at most to have less money than was needed to survive'.[76] Demanding an increase in the relief provided for the unemployed, outdoor relief workers went on strike in October 1932. Craigavon claimed, in his Twelfth of July speech in 1933, that strikers in the state were attempting to undermine it.[77] In this context the emphasis throughout the unionist ceremonies of 1933 on the need for protestant unity is not surprising, as the Craig government worked to sublimate the social aspirations of their constituency in the rhetoric of community solidarity. In addition, given the economic slough that unionists found themselves in, there was also undoubtedly a need to project a more united image of the state's work force to potential foreign investors. In 1933, as he had in 1911, Edward Carson provided unionists with a central figure around whom they could unite, across class. As president of the Ulster Unionist Council and of the Ulster Unionist Labour Association 'which strongly represented the workmen of the shipbuilding yards, the foundries and the factories', 'He spoke, indeed for all classes of that united community, which clung together in that north-eastern corner of Ireland like a little Greek State of old time between mountain and sea.'[78]

In addition to these domestic disturbances the stability of the Northern Irish state was also seen by unionists to be under threat from the evolution of de Valera's overtly catholic state (Fianna Fáil had come to power in February

1932). In this context, then, the Carson statue was a rallying point for beleaguered unionism. In 1933 the *Belfast Telegraph* reminded its readers that unionism could only be 'assailed by the enemy with any hope of success' when there was 'weakness and dissension in the garrison inside'.[79] *The Observer*, in its coverage, acknowledged the obvious symbolism of the ceremony:

> The statue is in the centre of the Processional-road and it is fitting that it should find a resting place at Stormont, a noble pile of buildings which will for all time mark the consummation of Lord Carson's great struggle to prevent Northern Ireland being included in the jurisdiction of a Parliament in Dublin.[80]

Around the base of the statue, apart from Carson's name, were panels representing unionism's most recent 'sacred dates': the signing of the Solemn League and Covenant at Belfast City Hall in 1912, a review of the Ulster Volunteers by Lieut-General Sir George Richardson, and Carson addressing a crowd outside the Ulster Hall. It was this period of unionist history, the third home rule crisis, which the newspapers recalled: 'In many respects, the scene at Stormont on Saturday was reminiscent of the great demonstrations of 1912–14, which made it clear to the world that if need be the loyalists of Ulster would fight for their birthright'.[81] Craigavon reminded the audience that in any future struggle, if at any time attacks were made on 'Ulster's liberties', there would be Ulstermen and Ulsterwomen throughout the dominions willing to come to her aid.[82] But, this was mere rhetoric; unionism was no longer in a position to mount a military resistance to its enemies, as it had been in 1914, and, in any case, its enemies had become too diverse and intangible for simple opposition.

Unionists looked to an increasingly mythologised past for strength. The speeches at the unveiling were filled with images of protestant deliverance from the hands of the enemy through the ministrations of Edward Carson. 'Today', said Craigavon:

> We are moved by a deep emotion and we reflect upon what might have happened to our beloved country had not Lord Carson shouldered the burden of meeting and defeating our enemies . . . there is no change in our intention to remain firmly part and parcel of Great Britain and the Empire.[83]

Again, Lord Londonderry's speech recalled unionist days of glory:

> When in the old days the Province resounded to the tramp of armed men, when they were called rebels across the water, and throughout the world, what was it they did? They stood steadfast to their principles and loyal to their traditions and everything they said and did, and everything that their great leader commanded them to do had been vindicated by every single thing that had happened since that time.[84]

The speeches of the main speakers were reminiscent, commented the *Belfast Newsletter*'s reporter, of the 'old days when one of Ulster's slogans was "Ulster will fight, and Ulster will be right".'[85] Surpassing the 1641

'massacres' and the Battle of the Boyne, the signing of the Solemn League
and Covenant, the Ulster Volunteer Force and the establishment of the
Northern Irish state were now the paradigms for the position unionists
found themselves in. Viewed as triumphs through the power of unionist
collectivity, these events were added to unionist mythology, the most recent
beacon buoys marking the dangers they had overcome, through their own
resourcefulness, to remain within the empire.

The silver jubilee of King George V fell in 1935 and provided an opportunity for unionists to display their loyalty to the crown in a high-profile way,
and to reaffirm their wider political position in terms of empire.[86] This
editorial of the *Northern Whig* assessed the situation:

> The North is Unionist, Protestant, loyal; the South is separatist, Catholic,
> disloyal. The North honours the King; the South repudiates him. The
> North stands for religious liberty; the South for ecclesiastical tyranny.
> The North is determined to retain its place in the British Common-
> wealth; the South is heading for secession and a republic.[87]

W.S. Armour, a former editor of the *Northern Whig*, interpreted the situation
somewhat differently: 'For over a century Ulster's part in the development of
Ireland has been negative, and for about fifteen years she has been in the
position of a beleaguered garrison'.[88] Above all, their part in the jubilee
marked the fact that the Northern Irish state had survived as part of the
union.[89] Craigavon was in no doubt as to the importance of the ceremonies;
in a letter to the British Secretary of State, Sir John Gilmour, he wrote of his
'deep appreciation of all that was done to give Ulster a "place" in the pageant
and accompanying festivities. I am *extremely* grateful.'[90] The jubilee was
exhaustively covered in the unionist press. A special jubilee supplement
provided by the *Belfast Newsletter* in May 1935 contained, for example, an
article on 'Ireland during the King's reign'. In it Ian Colvin, Lord Carson's
biographer, reflected on the period of the third home rule crisis referring to
the displays of defiant unionism – to Winston Churchill's visit to Belfast in
1912, 'the formation of the Ulster Volunteers, the signing of the Covenant,
the affair of the Curragh, and the gun-running at Larne'.[91] The visit of Bonar
Law and the signing of the Solemn League and Covenant were noted as the
'outstanding events' of 1912. Colvin continued:

> The four years before the opening of the Great War were marked in the
> North by a political enthusiasm and unity without parallel in the story of
> the island – depth of feeling was shown by a steadily-growing devotion to
> Sir Edward Carson and implicit confidence in his leadership.[92]

In common with the unionist histories of the '20s this article made much of
Ulster's contribution to the First World War, juxtaposing it, in now tradi-
tional fashion, with the Easter Rising of 1916. The achievements of the 36th
'Ulster' Division were discussed; it had, wrote Colvin,

> upheld the highest traditions of the Province at the opening of the Battle
> of the Somme on 1st July 1916, the capture of Messines Ridge on 7th

June, 1917, the Battle of Langemarck in August, 1917, the Battle of Cambrai towards the close of the same year, the great German offensive of March, 1918, and, under Major-General Clifford Coffin, V.C., the advance to the final victory.[93]

This reminder of the bond which the war had created between Ulster and the rest of the empire was set alongside the British prime minister's 'betrayal' of Ulster, 'violating his pledged word'.[94]

The celebration of the royal jubilee provided the first opportunity since the opening of the Stormont parliament in 1932 for the Northern Irish state to proclaim, with some ceremony, its loyalty to the crown. The opportunity for a display of public loyalty echoed throughout its rhetoric. The Duke of Abercorn, as governor of Northern Ireland, invited Prince George to visit the 'people of Ulster' in his jubilee year but the response from his private secretary was that the king and queen wished all their family to be with them in St Paul's Cathedral for the thanksgiving service on 6 May.[95] The Duke of Gloucester, therefore, acted as the royal representative to Northern Ireland. A service of thanksgiving was held in St Anne's Cathedral in Belfast, on 12 May 1935, with the moderator of the presbyterian church, the president of the methodist church and the lord primate of Ireland as the celebrants. The public celebration of the jubilee took a traditional unionist form; the streets were strewn with bunting and a demonstration was organised at the Balmoral showgrounds on 11 May.[96] The official programme described some of the events:

> The Girl Guides – Irish Dancing, A Display of Irish Country Dancing, in Costume, by 84 Guides, representing the Four Divisions of Belfast, and the counties of Antrim, Down, and Armagh. The Dance to be performed is the Fairy Reel, a traditional Irish dance for six people, to music supplied by the RUC Band.[97]

The event – where a traditional 'Irish' dance was accompanied by the band of the Royal Ulster Constabulary – exemplifies the contradiction inherent within unionist image-making. Also advertised in the press was the Royal Silver Jubilee Year Show from 29 May until 1 June 1935, 'a Great Exhibition dealing with every phase of the Country's Principal Industry'.[98] However, beneath the surface of these celebrations there was a strain of tension. The boy scouts in Great Britain planned to light a series of bonfires or beacons throughout the country to mark the occasion. In a letter to Oscar Henderson, C.H. Blackmore, the cabinet secretary for Northern Ireland, noted that the prime minister felt that 'in lieu of bonfires, which might raise difficulties on "party" lines, it might be better to arrange for fireworks . . . As you will appreciate we do not want to encourage anything at the time of the celebrations which would be likely to cause trouble'.[99] The 'beacon chain' was eventually allowed to go ahead, but the concerns expressed in Blackmore's letter highlight the volatile atmosphere in the northern state at the time. Tensions were running high enough for Craigavon's government to ban all marches from 18 June, although this decision was reversed following representations from Sir Joseph Davison, the grand master of the Orange Lodge in Belfast. Despite the use of troops and the imposition of a curfew, however, rioting flared, and disturbances continued throughout the summer. Belfast's lord mayor, Crawford McCullagh, was reported in the press asking that people adopt the motto 'Peace and goodwill to all men'.[100] Nationalists boycotted the jubilee celebrations, leading some commentators to lay the blame for the disturbances at their door; 'the Nationalist members of the Ulster parliament must bear a share of responsibility', wrote the *Belfast Weekly Newsletter*'s editor:

> In an ill-advised and provocative manifesto these gentlemen, who have taken an oath of allegiance to the Crown, referred to the King as 'King George of England', with the celebrations of whose Jubilee they disassociated themselves, and after referring to 'Black and Tan barbarity' and the 'dismemberment of the nation', represented Roman Catholics as the victims of 'a cruel policy of boycott and extermination'.[101]

By the end of August, as a result of disturbances, thirteen people were dead. Asked about the Belfast disturbances, when he visited London at the end of July, Craigavon assured reporters that the disorder was 'dying down'. 'It has never', he said, 'been so serious as has been made out'.[102] But it had been serious enough for a curfew to be imposed prior to the Duke of Gloucester's visit. 'A curfew was one possible way of casting a calm veneer over the city to please the Royal gaze . . . The curfew had the desired effect. The Duke's visit passed without incident and the curfew was lifted on 14 May'.[103]

In October 1935, 'Ulster's Grand Old Man' died. 'I have no doubt', observed the reporter in the *Belfast Telegraph*, 'that during his last hours he must have experienced consolation in the knowledge that the North was safe, and as determined as ever to maintain the position his efforts secured for her.'[104] Craigavon made the announcement of Carson's death in the Northern Irish House of Commons; referring to Carson as one of unionism's 'securities', he said: 'I would close by saying that Lord Carson and I were like David and Jonathan throughout our political lives and we never had one word to say except for the good of Ulster'.[105] Carson was buried in St Anne's Cathedral in Belfast; 'Ulster', Craigavon said in his appreciation of Carson broadcast on the BBC, 'will thus be able to care tenderly for the body of her old leader . . . who lived a perfect life and died a national hero'.[106] As with other unionist ceremonies, provisional arrangements for Carson's funeral had been made months in advance. At a cabinet meeting in June 1935, Craigavon had informed the Northern Irish cabinet that Carson was seriously ill with bronchial pneumonia, and that, given his age, 'there appeared to be grave doubts as to the possibility of his recovery':

> The Prime Minister thought it advisable, therefore, that tentative plans should be made for Lord Carson's funeral, plans which would in any case have to be made at some period even if death did not immediately intervene on this occasion.[107]

The dean of St Anne's wondered whether, for reasons of hygiene, Carson's body could be cremated before being interred, but Craigavon was offended by the suggestion, and the matter was dropped.[108] In death Carson became even more of an embodiment of ideal unionism and the ideal unionist.[109] 'He was the apostle of their patriotic faith', Craigavon said in an interview with the *Daily Mail*, 'the incarnation of that profound loyalty to King and country which burns more fiercely in Northern Ireland than in other parts of the United Kingdom.'[110]

Predictably, Carson's funeral ceremony was rich with symbolism; soil from each of the six counties was taken from a silver bowl, presented by the Northern Ireland cabinet, and placed on his coffin, while the grave was lined with green moss 'gathered from the hills of Down'.[111] Interestingly, The Revd John MacNeice (the poet Louis MacNeice's father) who conducted the funeral service would not allow the coffin to be draped with the Union Jack.[112] Orangemen lined the route the coffin took through Belfast:

> The Six Counties were hushed and silent for the Leader's State funeral. Belfast was a city of sorrow. Half-a-million people from all parts of Northern Ireland and many Loyalists from the Irish Free State poured into the Ulster capital.[113]

The mourners, the *Belfast Telegraph* noted, were 'deeply moved' when the congregation sang 'O God, our help in ages past', 'the hymn which Lord Carson had always insisted should be sung at the opening of his campaign meetings'.[114] The unionist faithful rallied to their old leader in death, as they had in life, taking to heart his last message to them at the Twelfth of July in 1935: 'My advice to you is, trust your Government and close up your ranks, and then Ulster will be as unconquerable as ever. Always the same – No Surrender!'[115] This display of devotion, although engineered, was a genuine expression of affection for a man who had come to represent the glory years of unionism.[116] However, for nationalists Carson represented the means by which the island had been partitioned. When the House of Commons came to debate paying the treasury £1,270 to defer the cost of Carson's funeral, nationalist MPs objected. Speaking against the vote T.J. Campbell argued:

> You say that Lord Carson rendered signal service to your party. We on our side say he rendered disservice to our people, and our people have been forced into political and economic thraldom as a result of his efforts. Yet you ask us to share this Vote and to pay a share of the expenses of the funeral. I can only say that the proposition bespeaks a degree of complacency in regard to our natural feelings equal to your attitude in other respects to our people.[117]

Campbell concluded his argument by saying that their leader, Joe Devlin, was a man equal to Carson, but had never been honoured in a similar way; finally, Patrick O'Neill suggested that the money for the funeral should come from unionist party funds.[118]

Lord Carson had possessed 'magnanimity of greatness', according to his second biographer, Ian Colvin.[119] Unionism's glory years and those of the

man most associated with them were celebrated, between 1932 and 1936, in
an impressive three, volume biography. As with the ceremonies for the
opening of Stormont, and the unveiling of the Carson statue, this biography
played an important role in the collectivisation of unionism. To quote
Edward Homberger: 'The broad appeal of biography is reassuring. It suggests
that in our interest in the lives of others there is at least the possibility, the
link of a surviving common culture'.[120] In addition to the unifying figure of
Carson, the biography rehearsed protestant history in a familiar form for the
reader, thus projecting a reassuring common heritage for unionists. The
biography's advertising had all the drama of the decade's ceremonies; the
dust jacket of volume two, for instance, read:

> But Ulster is the heart and centre of the story: and when, after finishing
> the book, one considers what might have happened had not the shot
> been fired at Sarajevo, one feels that here is a book the historical impor-
> tance of which is impossible to exaggerate.[121]

Edward Marjoribanks, the author of the first biography, committed suicide
in 1932.[122] He was in the midst of what, according to one reviewer, 'must
have been a masterpiece'.[123] Volume one covered Carson's early career as a
lawyer. It was imbued with the language of drama; one review noted that: 'in
Mr Marjoribanks' descriptions these half-forgotten trials live as vividly as the
trials that hold us spellbound in the theatre'.[124] In a letter to Carson,
Marjoribanks outlined how he saw the writing of the biography progressing:

> What I should really want would be your narrative of events and of
> people, my part of the work being to put it in literary style, fill in the
> background, verify the dates and generally confuse the picture. It looks
> to me like a fifty-fifty proposition.[125]

Marjoribanks's book adopted the literary conceits of earlier unionist
histories by stereotyping the 'Ulsterman', in this case couched in the
language of his and his subject's profession. The 'North-East Ulsterman',
according to this assessment, was 'one of the most efficient jurymen in the
world, especially in dealing with guilt; he is acute, honest, and absolutely
fearless'.[126] The 'Northerner's' 'mind and manners' owed much to the 'dour
spirit of Scotland', which had 'been hardened and intensified far beyond its
native asperity'.[127] In contrast, the 'Southern Irish' were, according to
Marjoribanks, 'whimsical', 'talkative', 'impulsive' and 'mercurial' in
temperament. Henry Maxwell, in 1934, was harsher in his assessment; he
looked to the 1916 Rising for evidence of the true nature of the southern
Irish; referring to the murder of a policeman:

> The absolute lack of proportion in their hatred, the unmixed savagery of
> their vindictiveness, one might almost say the diseased egotism of their
> mentality, are all clearly revealed by the one incident as by the whole
> Civil War.[128]

And, he argued, if Ulstermen appeared hard and unbending, it was because
'the same tenacity and purpose in the service of what they hold to be right'

animated them, 'no less than when, in the service of the same probity, their rugged forefathers earned for themselves the reputation for steadfastness which gives to Covenantism its particular significance'.[129] Ian Colvin took over the biography shortly after Marjoribanks's death.[130] He wrote to Carson saying that his priority was to 'tell a story'; 'we must', he said, 'shape everything to that end':[130]

> I shall have to dive into Irish history in order to explain that fell and stark division of Ireland into two nations . . . In particular, I must explain historically the justice and the fears of the Protestant minority. A Statesman that ignores history is bound to come to shipwreck.[131]

Colvin's representation of Irish history was original in its metaphor but familiar, from past unionist histories, in its basic tenet; while Britain was 'one single mass of the same sedimentary rock, solid, united, uniform, coherent', Ireland was 'stratified and twisted in layers of apparently different and incongruous material, separate deposits, never united, at open or tacit enmity'.[132] He returned to a familiar theme of unionist writers, that of the native Irish unable to govern themselves, but 'held together by the adjacent sedimentary mass': 'Not even in Celtic times had the Irish been a united nation; since the conquest of Strongbow they had never lost an opportunity of insurrection'.[133] This line was already familiar from the work of unionist writers, such as Hamilton, Falls, Phillips and Chart. Ian Colvin quoted from a letter of Carson's to J.A.R. Marriot, MP, which reinforced, at the conclusion of the biography, the traditional unionist view of Irish 'natives': 'I quite agree that in the end it is a question of nationality, and the Celts have done nothing in Ireland but create trouble and disorder. Irishmen who have turned out successful are not in any case that I know of true Celtic origin'.[134] The picture Colvin painted of the protestant community was of an homogenous group. While the natives remained on the hills and the sandy coasts, or doing 'the menial and unskilled labour of the towns':

> The Protestants were a solid and integrated community, owning the land and the industries, with their own nobility – their Duke and their Marquess – their own gentry, business-men, farmers and workmen, knowing one another familiarly and keenly alive to their common interests and the menace of their common enemy.

This, then, was the community which, according to Colvin, provided Carson 'like another Oliver Cromwell, with the Ironsides of this civic struggle'.[135]

Ian Colvin did not, therefore, deviate from the pattern of unionist history already established by unionist authors in the 1920s. All of unionism's 'sacred dates' were covered in the biography: 1641 'was a rising of the dispossessed against the possessors' which developed into a 'general mania' of massacre, while the Battle of the Boyne was 'a war in which not merely men of one faith struggled against another, but men who had been dispossessed sought to exterminate their dispossessors'.[136] Dispossession was, for Colvin, a matter of evolution: 'Who shall find the clue to right and wrong in this time-tangled skein, or indict before a Court of Justice a process of evolution?'[137] The insurrections of the dispossessed culminated in 'the fifty-third rebellion of '98', whose design, 'the loyalists had reason to fear', was to 'exterminate the whole Protestant population'.[138] Grattan's parliament, a 'Protestant Parliament', was the parliament of that 'golden time'; and, in the 'hundred and ten years' which followed the Act of Union, Ireland, according to Colvin's narrative, was 'peaceful and prosperous'.[139] But, he noted, the fires of rebellion never died but 'subsided into a glow within their ashes'. This latent 'fire' was fanned into rebellion once more in 1916; the 'native Irish' grudge was against the 'loyal minority' 'whose faith they hated and whose possessions they coveted'.[140] There was, according to Colvin, 'no cause nor even pretext for rebellion': 'Ireland was lightly taxed, prosperous, under an easy Government, with no wrongs to redress, enjoying the freedom and the trade of the British Empire'.[141] His account of the 1916 rising bears a strong resemblance to that of W.A. Phillips's in whose narrative the rising was full of the 'brutal murders' of unarmed policemen, 'seething mobs' from the slums, mob violence and fire. In Colvin's account civilians were murdered in the streets, 'the scum of Dublin poured out of its slums to loot the shops; fires added to the general terror, and the fire brigade tried in vain to quench the conflagration under the rifles of the Sinn Feiners'.[142] In Colvin's final analysis, 'Irish Nationalism' was 'a class-war directed by the lower against the upper elements of society'.[143] This was similar to Ernest Hamilton's thesis, that harmony between 'settlers' and 'natives' was 'no more possible than it is between the dog with the bone and the dog without it'.[144] In common with unionist historians, such as Hamilton, Falls and Phillips, Colvin was not slow to criticise the British government, in particular their handling of the 1916 Rising:

> To modify policy as a result of violence, to pay the appearance of court to rebels, these, and not the execution of the ring leaders, were the psychological errors which brought to ruin the precarious edifice of Constitutional Government in Ireland.[145]

Discussing the Treaty negotiations Colvin noted that press attacks on the unionists were designed to screen the British government's policy, summed up by Carson as 'that pleasant way they have of trying to buy off their enemies at the expense of their friends'.[146] Henry Maxwell was harsher in his criticism: 'The British public have shut their eyes from weariness to the true state of affairs in Ireland, and politicians and the Press have pandered to their fatigue in forebearing to lift the veil'.[147] Although Colvin did not place the rising in terms of the Battle of the Somme, as past unionist writers had done, he did use the unity found in the war between the southern and northern recruits as the backdrop to the Irish Convention:

> About that time – on the 7th June, 1917 – the Irish Division and the Ulster Division stormed the Messines Ridge side by side. John Redmond's brother, Major Willy Redmond, who had appealed to the House of Commons 'as one about to die' three months before, was rushing forward

on the right of his battalion when he was struck by two bullets and was carried by stretcher-bearers of the Ulsters to the convent of Locre where a few hours later he died.[148]

But, these 'loyalties of war' made no difference to the 'age old animosities of the Irish race'. The southern Irish enemy, in Colvin's narrative, now had the single, identifiable face of Eamonn de Valera, who had 'organised the treacherous massacre of the Sherwood Foresters in Easter Week 1916 . . . [and] had incited the Irish to the boycott and murder of the police'.[149] Maxwell was melodramatic in his representation of de Valera's rejection of the Treaty, but it is an indication of the feelings which some unionists attached to the Fianna Fáil leader:

> His attitude, in which he was cordially supported by all those who, having intoxicated themselves with the dreadful exhilaration which comes with bloodshed and violence, could not forego their excitements, was to prolong the sufferings of Ireland indefinitely.[150]

Ian Colvin juxtaposed the death of William Redmond and political ascent of de Valera; 'the rebel', who won Redmond's East Clare seat 'boasting that he would make "English law" impossible and that "if Ulster stood in the way of Irish freedom Ulster would have to be coerced"'.[151] Reinforcing the point, Colvin quotes Carson's emotive Twelfth of July speech following the war:

> He spoke of the Irishmen who slept their last sleep on the plains of Flanders and France, in Mesopotamia, in Palestine, in the Balkans and elsewhere – men who had done their share not for the Irish Republic but for the British Empire. Was it to be their reward to give up all that they had won, to be false to all for which they had suffered?[152]

The second volume of the *Life of Lord Carson* was widely reviewed and well received; the *Sunday Times* felt it dealt with 'great events and great issues whose effects are by no means exhausted to-day', while the *Daily Mail* felt it gave 'new life to half-forgotten controversies'.[153] The latter was certainly one of the main achievements of the biography, although the use of words such as 'exhausted' and 'half-forgotten' indicate the growing British disengagement with unionism.[154]

Edward VIII abdicated in December 1936 and de Valera took the opportunity (presented by the subsequent difficulties of the royal family and the British government) to remove all references to the king and the governor general from the Free State's constitution. The following year he introduced a new constitution which ended the Free State's position as a dominion (the Dáil in future presiding over internal affairs) and retitled the state 'Éire'. More importantly, the 1937 constitution laid claim to the whole territory of Ireland, and accorded the catholic church a 'special position' therein. Éire was evolving into a state 'verging on the theocratic, with rigid censorship and a constitutional prohibition on divorce and family planning; a state compelling every child to learn Irish and turning its back, like Northern Ireland, on the cultural diversity of its people'.[155] But, as J.J. Lee has observed, protestant resentment of the 1937 constitution was more retro-spective than contemporary.[156] The constitution caused little surprise or heart-searching within Northern Ireland: the *Northern Whig* for instance quoted the prime minister James Craig as saying: 'It makes not a pin of difference what takes place in Southern Ireland as far as our position in the United Kingdom and the Empire is concerned'. The editorial in the paper argued that the new constitution would in fact only 'stiffen Ulster's resis-tance to any attempt to sever it from the British Crown or to diminish by one iota its full participation in the life of the British family of nations'.[157]

The accession of George VI that same year provided unionists with their final opportunity in this decade to proclaim their place in the empire. This was articulated in their message of congratulation to the king:

> The people of Northern Ireland look forward with complete confidence to the future, in the knowledge that Your Majesty's constant concern will be the happiness and prosperity of the United Kingdom and of the whole Empire, to which Ulster is proud to belong.[158]

It was also articulated in their message of sympathy to the royal family on the death of George V.[159] Unionists' response to the abdication was muted; they expressed their sympathy, through the government, to the royal family, and articulated their support for the king's successor, the Duke of York.[160] In his statement to the Northern Irish House of Commons James Craig spoke of Edward VIII with some affection: 'The late King, whom we here knew better and for longer as Prince of Wales, carries with him into retirement, our full appreciation of his services to the Empire and our best wishes for his happiness in the years that lie ahead'.[161] Craigavon was full of admiration for the British prime minister, Stanley Baldwin; in December 1936 he wrote to the primate of all Ireland: 'He is a wonderful statesman, and it only requires a *crisis* to reveal his unequalled powers.'[162] His speech on the abdi-cation emphasised above all the unity of protestants in the Northern Irish state in the face of the crisis:

> Although we may differ, and will continue to differ, from time to time on matters of local concern, there are four words in the Ulster language that everyone understands and appreciates, and with them I shall close my few remarks: God save the King.[163]

In a message to the BBC the Northern Irish prime minister suggested that it was not necessary to make reference to the circumstances leading up to the abdication, 'they are, in his present Majesty's own words, "unprecedented"'. In his own speech to the Northern Irish House of Commons he said: 'The burden has become a very heavy one, and it is our duty by extra loyalty – if that be possible – to lighten it in every way in our powers'.[164] The headline of the *Northern Whig*'s editorial indicated the emphasis unionists wished to place in the midst of the crisis: 'The Monarch Goes: The Monarchy Remains'.

> Even in this hour of grievous disappointment and deep humiliation, of frus-trated hopes and shattered illusions, those who have given King Edward

their loyalty and trust will not forget the great services he rendered to the British family of nations, both in peace and in war, throughout those years that seemed so rich in promise of future greatness.[165]

Memories were recalled of the visit of Edward VIII to the state (as the Prince of Wales to open the Stormont parliament), and the opportunity was taken to repeat his speech which linked the achievements of the state to the efforts of the Northern Irish in the First World War: there had been, according to the prince in 1932, no abatement of the 'patriotic devotion to the Empire' which the Northern Irish had 'proved so gallantly in the Great War'. Much had been achieved since then, said the prince, and the hope placed in the state by his father (when he came to open the Northern Irish parliament in 1921) had not been disappointed.[166] In this way unionists took the opportunity which this crisis within the monarchy offered to reaffirm the Northern Irish parliament and, by extension, the state.

George VI was crowned in May 1937 and this chance to proclaim their loyalty to the crown gave unionists a sense of security.[167] In a coronation statement Craigavon remarked that loyalty was no new characteristic of the people of Northern Ireland, and that the occasion of the coronations gave 'renewed assurance of its depth and sincerity':

> In these times of constant change and evolution in so many foreign countries it is a matter of profound satisfaction to every one of us that democratic institutions and representative government are still the foundation stones of the United Kingdom and the Great Dominions and Dependencies.[168]

The Northern Irish prime minister had his place in the coronation ceremony in London, bringing up the rear of the procession of prime ministers, and accompanied by four mounted RUC men.[169] King George and Queen Elizabeth paid a short one-day visit to Northern Ireland in July 1937. The ceremonies attending their visit took traditional form, and were full of pomp and pageantry:[170] 'The Royal Standard was broken on the quay, 21 guns sounded in salute and then a long sustained shout bore the Royal procession on their short journey to the City Hall'.[171]

> In the Garden of Remembrance outside 2,000 ex-servicemen were on parade; in the Council Chamber, the red uniforms of the county lieutenants, the black and gold of the Northern Ireland judges, and the red again of the City Councilors passed in quick pageantry to their allotted places. A flourish of trumpets heralded the arrival of the King and Queen, the King in the full-dress uniform of an Admiral of the fleet and wearing the ribbon of the Order of St. Patrick, the Queen in pale blue with a bouquet of carnations.[172]

A letter from Charles G. Wickham, the inspector general of the RUC, to Dawson Bates in February 1937 outlined the purpose of the visit: 'The object of the programme is to give all classes a show – the general public in the street and at the show ground. The "best people" at the lunch'.[173] 'The loyalists of

Ulster', according to the *Northern Whig*'s editorial, had 'dared much, endured much and sacrificed much, generation after generation, in attestation of their allegiance'.[174] The visit was seen by unionists as a high-profile opportunity to renew pledges of loyalty and allegiance to the crown. Around the route of the royal cavalcade twenty-four bands were stationed to play and entertain the crowds. In the Botanic Gardens special arrangements were made for the accommodation of 'approximately 400 cripples', while at the harbour, to greet the royal visitors, stands were erected for over 1,000 people, the majority of whom were children, who in addition were provided with flags.[175] It had been suggested to the cabinet secretary, Charles Blackmore, that representatives from a wide variety of groups and organisations be invited to help in the arrangements for the royal visit, so that 'as many persons as possible' would 'interest themselves in the arrangements in connection with [the] visit in order that it may be as popular as possible', and this is what was done.[176] At the rally for the royals in the Balmoral showgrounds, children took a prominent position, and were co-ordinated well in advance:

> All the uniformed Juvenile Organisations should be arranged round the Arena, as was done two years ago for the Duke of Gloucester's visit and their Majesties on arrival at the North Gate would drive very slowly round past the stands to the accompaniment of massed cheering by the children.[177]

And at the Royal Garden Party at Stormont (where another 'brilliant scene was staged', according to the *Northern Whig*) a variety of Northern Irish citizens, from dukes to members of the civil service, were presented to the king and queen.[178] At the time Craigavon was unwell and, although he greeted the royals on their arrival at Stormont Castle, he did not accompany them at the garden party. In his message of thanks to the governor of Northern Ireland the king spoke of the traditional manifestation of loyalism which they had witnessed on their visit 'in the vast cheering crowds and the beautifully decorated streets'. As the royal yacht sailed from Donegall Quay it did so to the air 'Come Back to Ireland' played by a band stationed on the quayside.[179] Unionists gained in self-esteem from this high-profile and public identification of the monarch with the state, and Northern Ireland, having experienced recent periods of violent disturbances, benefited from the order and ceremony imposed by the royal visit. W.S. Armour noted in his 1935 book, *Facing the Irish question*, 'Unless I have completely misread from a distance the Ulster Protestant Press, the only thing which a prudent editor actually can safely comment upon and remain "loyal" is the unhappy plight of the Irish Free State!'[180] Having made a point of the disorder in the Free State in comparison to the steadiness of their state, unionists were relieved to be given the opportunity to re-establish a more positive image of Northern Ireland and have this reflected in the press reports:

> In their minds they [the English] have a picture of an Ulster seething with dark and murderous plotters, of a Belfast trembling in danger of the knife and the pistol of the assassin and sternly ruled by a soldierly [*sic*] armed to the teeth.

Contrary to this image, the editor of the *Daily Dispatch* found 'a steady, industrious, contented people in a land of tranquil beauty, a friendly people ready to tell you their history and legend'.[181]

Given that the 1930s was a decade for unionist history and legend, this phrase was particularly apt. In the words of a *Northern Whig* editorial, in July 1935: 'The past cannot be and ought not be forgotten, for only in the light of history can the present be rightly interpreted'.[182] Three years after the pomp and ceremony of his state funeral, Carson was remembered again in Northern Ireland at a ceremony which was 'simple, moving and full of memories'.[183] In October 1938, a memorial plaque, commissioned by the Ulster Women's Association, was unveiled in his honour in St Anne's Cathedral. 'It was an historic occasion', wrote the *Northern Whig*'s reporter, 'Rich mingled with poor, Church with State to pay one more tribute to one whom Lord Craigavon described as 'the greatest man I have ever known – or any of you'.[184] Attended by Craigavon and Lady Carson, 'all around one caught glimpses of people prominent in Unionist circles'. As with the Carson statue, the Carson plaque was viewed as representing the essence of Edward Carson, and, by association, that of unionists: 'When they come here they will see embodied in bronze the courage, strength of character, and, perhaps, the most wonderful will power that can be depicted in such a way'.[185]

At the same time the unionist press was covering de Valera's statement that, with the threat of war, partition was a dangerous thing for the British government, 'because so long as it existed he would not co-operate with Britain in defence'.[186] Throughout the 1930s de Valera appeared, in unionist eyes, to be dismantling the settlement of 1921 – beginning in May 1933 by removing the oath of allegiance from the Free State's constitution, and progressing, by June 1937, to a new constitution. As the *Belfast Weekly Newsletter* reported on the occasion of the removal of the oath from the Free State's constitution:

> At all events, the work of getting rid of forms and symbols of the British connection, which Mr Cosgrave's Administration began, has progressed so well under Mr de Valera's direction that to-day the Free State is, indeed, a republic in all but name.[187]

This, coupled with the expression of self-confident catholicism in the Eucharistic Congress of 1932 and the internal disturbances within Northern Ireland, alarmed unionist observers. Henry Maxwell, in his 1934 publication, articulated this concern:

> As an outpost of Great Britain, the Imperial Province of Northern Ireland has her enemies both within and without her gates. Her footing in Ireland, beneath the hated flag of Britain, and under the odious banner of Protestantism, is not secure enough for her to bask in a fool's paradise . . . He that guardeth Israel must neither slumber nor sleep.[188]

Craigavon was quick to reassure the unionist faithful that the position of the Northern Irish state was unassailable.[189] Through the medium of the

Carson plaque and the occasion of the unveiling, unionists were given the opportunity to reaffirm their position. The unionist leadership could remind their audience, and themselves, that they had faced this type of threat before, and had overcome it. In an interview with the *Sunday Dispatch* and *Sunday Chronicle*, Craigavon reaffirmed the north's intention of remaining within the union in language familiar from unionist rhetoric through three home rule crises, and following the First World War.[190] Given unionists' past dealings with Westminster, there is some irony in his final remark: 'I firmly believe that public opinion in the United Kingdom would rise in indignation if any British Government showed the slightest signs of its intentions to betray the Loyalists of the North of Ireland'.[191] Three years later, during the Second World War, when the British government offered de Valera an end to partition in return for an end to Éire's neutrality, this professed unionist trust proved to be unfounded.

Notes and References

1   This chapter has been strongly influenced by David Chaney's essay 'A symbolic mirror of ourselves: civic ritual in mass society', in Richard Collins et al. (eds.), *Media, culture and society: a critical reader* (London, 1986). The three major festivals he considers are the Victory Parade of 1946, the Festival of Britain in 1951, and the coronation of Elizabeth II in 1953.

2   ibid., p. 250.

3   In addition to Lord Randolph Churchill's visit in 1886 and the activities of the UVF, there is a long history of theatrical unionist demonstrations which includes the Ulster Unionist Convention of 1892 and the signing of the Solemn League and Covenant in 1912.

4   David Chaney, 'A symbolic mirror of ourselves', p. 248. 'Such marking devices separated the political drama of this decade from contemporary reality, although not from the "real" politics of this time since they played an integral part in unionist identity building.'

5   'In a "garrison" colony', wrote W.S. Armour, 'if the garrison is to be maintained up to full strength, there is no place for independent opinion on any subject', *Facing the Irish question* (London, 1935), p. 58.

6   In the *Belfast Weekly News* editorial in July 1932 the editor made it clear what he thought that present and future were: 'Times are again not without cause for anxiety, and in the circumstances it is well that Ulster should make clear to all concerned that she stands where she has always stood, and that what she has is resolved to hold', *BWN*, 14 July 1932. For Alvin Jackson, Carson's unionism was of the romantic and nostalgic variety, *Sir Edward Carson* (Dundalk, 1993), p. 60.

7   Alvin Jackson, 'Irish Unionism and the empire, 1880–1920: classes and masses', in Keith Jeffery (ed.), *'An Irish empire?' Aspects of Ireland and the British Empire* (Manchester, 1996), p. 123, p. 143.

8   It was the protestant population within the state which worried the unionist hierarchy, more than the catholic community. As Oliver MacDonagh has noted: 'Proportional representation in parliamentary elections was abandoned by the Ulster Unionists at the first possible opportunity. But this, contrary to the general belief, was done to consolidate the Protestant vote rather than to under-represent the Catholic. Protestant splinter groups were seen as the prime

danger to security; Catholic alienation did not matter', *States of mind* (London, 1983), p. 138.

9   *NW*, 13 July 1935.

10   Nicholas Mansergh, *The unresolved question, the Anglo-Irish settlement and its undoing, 1912–72* (London, 1991), pp. 136–7.

11   The Earl of Crawford and Balcarres, the first commissioner of works, noted to the prime minister, Craigavon, that 'prominent people in Belfast' felt that Stormont was too far from the centre of Belfast for 'general public convenience', letter to Craigavon, 12 June 1922, CAB 9H/5/1.

12   John Vincent has edited David Lindsay's papers: *The Crawford papers, the journals of David Lindsay twenty-seventh earl of Crawford and tenth Earl of Balcarres, 1871–1940, during the years 1892–1940* (Manchester, 1984).

13   Craigavon to the Earl of Crawford and Balcarres, 9 Aug. 1921, CAB 9H/5/1.

14   A note attached reads: 'My dear James – This is a scold! – Forgive me – but I must be in a position to protect the British taxpayer'. Letter, Earl of Crawford and Balcarres to Craigavon, 12 Aug. 1921, CAB 9H/5/1.

15   St John Ervine, *Craigavon: Ulsterman* (London, 1949), p. 526.

16   Henry Maxwell, *Ulster was right* (London, 1934), p. 7. In the preface Maxwell acknowledges W.A. Phillips's *The revolution in Ireland, 1906–23*, Ronald McNeill's *Ulster's stand for union*, and Denis Gwynn's *Life of Redmond*. In his personal acknowledgements he thanks Gen. Sir Hubert Gough, who was commander of the Cavalry Brigade at the Curragh during the 'Curragh Mutiny', and H.M. de F. Montgomery. Special mention goes to Sir A.W. Hungerford, MP: 'the untiring Secretary of the Ulster Unionist Council, by whose generous encouragement and aid, given at all times and despite numberless calls made upon his time, the task of presenting these arguments had been rendered easy.'

17   Letter, Prince of Wales to the Duke of Abercorn, 17 Oct. 1932, FIN 18/12/60. The only reference to this wish was the decision of the opening committee not to have the districts surrounding Stormont light bonfires on the hills, CAB 4A/10/6.

18   'The long processional road, a veritable ribbon of white, lined by troops with their bayonets glinting in the fitful gleams of sunshine, made a striking approach', *BWT*, 26 Nov. 1932.

19   Minutes of the Stormont opening committee, 24 Oct. 1932. The committee members were: Sir Charles Blackmore, secretary to the cabinet, R.E. Thornley, Ministry of Finance, P.E. Shepherd (OBE), Ministry of Finance, C. Blake Whelan, Ministry of Finance, Major G.A. Harris (CBE), R.P. Pim, Ministry of Home Affairs, and the inspector general of the RUC.

20   FIN 18/1/399.

21   FIN 19/10/14.

22   Lt N.G. Scorgie, HMSO (London) to R.E. Thornley, Ministry of Finance, 25 Nov. 1932, FIN 19/10/14.

23   *Irish Times*, 16 Nov. 1932. The final estimate for the erection of Stormont was £1,125,000, which included Northern Ireland's 10 per cent contribution, FIN 19/4/4–5. Craig was aware that the building was a 'gift': '. . . we cannot repeat it often enough – that the British Government are making us a present of both our Parliament House and Administrative Buildings and the Royal Courts of Justice, and it is somewhat delicate and somewhat difficult to approach those who are making a present and tell them exactly what you want in that present . . . In all the circumstances we thought the generosity of the British Government was such that it would ill become any of us to criticise unduly what they intended to do for the benefit of our Province', *Northern Hansard*, vol. xiv, 11 Mar. 1932.

24   *Irish Times*, 16 Nov. 1932.

25   Draft of Craigavon's speech for the opening of Stormont, FIN 18/12/59.

26   'Ulster needs British protection and she is jealous of all that tends to weaken her connections with the Mother Country. She is dependent upon Great Britain for her very existence, and her dependence is manifest.' Maxwell added, somewhat limply, that: 'Ceaselessly day and night Ulster stands guard over the political and geographical Achilles heel of the Great British Commonwealth.' Henry Maxwell, *Ulster was right*, p. 9. Later it was the BBC and rituals such as the Festival of Britain which fulfilled this function.

27   *BWT*, 26 Nov. 1932.

28   Stand fast like our forefathers, who for freedom heard the call,
Did close the Gates and man the guns on historic Derry's Wall,
Remember our Boys at Thiepval – "No Surrender" was their cry,
When for that dear old Union Jack they volunteered to die.
Get out you Bolshie Sinn Fein band, we know of your vile hate,
Just strike your tents, get on the march before you are too late,
With our Navy Boys upon the sea and our soldiers hand to hand
Together we have always stood for freedom of our land
With England we will still unite and let our enemies see
Wherever the Union Jack doth fly, all men are equal free.
Together we'll shout with all our might and loud its echo ring,
Let Honour and Truth be our Guiding Star,
God Bless Our Gracious King.

Robert Waddell, 'A Welcome to the Prince', FIN 19/10/14. Craigavon received this poem from Thomas Morrison, 12 Nov. 1932, entitled 'Welcome!':
Hail Prince! Our Empire
Is looking on to-day.
Sincere in its desire –
It joins us as we say
Success to Ulster's Parliament
To open which our Prince is sent. FIN 18/12/61.

29   R.F. Foster makes this point in relation to the protestant ascendancy's drive to build magnificent public and private buildings in the eighteenth century, R.F. Foster, *Modern Ireland, 1600–1972* (London, 1988), p. 194.

30   Text of the speech of the Prince of Wales at the opening of Stormont, FIN 18/12/59.

31   R.F. Foster, *Modern Ireland*, p. 528.

32   *BWT*, 26 Nov. 1932. The city hall in Belfast, constructed in 1904, was perhaps more impressive structurally, but Stormont parliament had a more dramatic setting.

33   Edward Marjoribanks, *The life of Lord Carson*, 3 vols, i, (London, 1932), p. 2, p. 3.

34   Ian Colvin, *The life of Lord Carson*, vol. iii, (London, 1936), p. 401.

35   Although as Alvin Jackson has argued, 'it was Craig, and not Carson, who enthusiastically commended, and facilitated, the creation of a parliament for the six-county "Northern Ireland"', Alvin Jackson, *Sir Edward Carson*, p. 59.

36   *BWN*, 14 July 1932.

37   ibid., 2 July 1932.

38   Letters pertaining to attacks on catholics returning from the Eucharistic Congress, CAB 9B/200/1.

39   Letter, Salis to Lord Craigavon 26 July 1932. CAB 9B/200/1.

40   Letter, the Cabinet Secretariat to F. O'Reilly, 13 Mar. 1931, CAB 9B/200/1.

41   *BWT*, 25 June 1932.

42   ibid., 2 July 1932.

43   ibid.

44   Patrick McIntosh, the author's father, recalls how his mother brought him to listen to the service on the steps of the Mercy Hospital in Cork, where the nuns had set up a radio for people to hear the broadcast. He remembers the powerful singing of the tenor, John McCormack, but more pungently the smell of ether. This serves to illustrate that even those without radios in the 1930s were able to have access to important broadcasts, and also points to the communal nature of radio.

45   A statement he reiterated in the Northern Irish House of Commons: 'I have filled that office [in the Orange Order] many years, and I prize that far more than I do being Prime Minister', *Northern Hansard*, vol. xvi, 24 Apr. 1933.

46   *BNL*, 13 July 1933.

47   *IT*, 18 Mar. 1935. Denis Kennedy, *The widening gulf: northern attitudes to the independent Irish state, 1919–49* (Belfast, 1988), p. 167.

48   James Craig in an interview in the *BNL*, 22 Sept. 1911.

49   This dialectic between north and south appears often in unionist rhetoric; for instance, in a parliamentary debate Craig argued: 'It would be rather interesting for historians of the future to compare a Catholic State launched in the South with a Protestant State launched in the North and to see which gets on better and prospers more . . . I am doing my best to top the bill and be ahead of the South', *Northern Hansard*, vol. xvi, 24 Apr. 1934.

50   For a discussion and analyses of Carson's rise to power in Ulster see Andrew Gailey's 'King Carson: an essay on the invention of leadership', *IHS*, vol. xxx, no. 117 (May 1996) p. 73.

51   *BWN*, 11 July 1935.

52   Copy of letter from R.J. Lynn to Carson, 26 Oct. 1933, Carson papers, D1507/E/3/29.

53   *BWT*, 15 July 1933.

54   Sir Edward Archdale, *BWT*, 14 July 1933.

55   Ian Colvin, *Life of Lord Carson*, vol. iii, p. 439.

56   Alvin Jackson, *Sir Edward Carson*, pp. 29–41.

57   In 1919 at the commemoration of the Solemn League and Covenant unionist leaders focused on the Ulster Unionist Convention of 1892, recalling it as a moderate but effective example of protestant determination to resist government measures of which they did not approve. In 1933 at the unveiling of the Carson statue they recalled their resistance to the third home rule bill, and focused on the Solemn League and Covenant as resistance to British government policies through the threat of civil war. In the aftermath of the First World War it was inappropriate to use the threat of military force; in the 1930s when that war was a more distant memory it was less of a problem.

58   Edward Carson cited in the *BWT*, 15 July 1933.

59   Alvin Jackson, *Sir Edward Carson*, pp. 29–30.

60   St John Ervine, *Craigavon: Ulsterman*, p. 526.

61   In the *BNL* jubilee supplement the writer wrote of the Larne gun-running incident in terms of a 'Boys Own' adventure: 'Colonel Fred Crawford was the daring Ulsterman who carried out this dangerous undertaking', CAB 9B/225/3.

62   Lord Londonderry cited in the *BWT*, 15 July 1933.

63   Henry Maxwell, *Ulster was right*, p. 57. As Gailey argues: 'Above all, Carson was the embodiment of the "decent man" in politics, rejecting the lord chancellorship in 1916 and the wealth on offer at the bar to concentrate on the cause. He seemed thus that rare breed – a parliamentarian they could trust', Andrew Gailey 'King Carson: an essay on the invention of leadership', p. 73.

64   *The Observer*, 9 July 1933.

65 *The Times*, 1 July 1933.

66 *NW*, 10 July 1933.

67 Henry Maxwell, in his coverage of the prince's visit to open Stormont looked forward to the unveiling: 'the Prince drove away down the long processional avenue, at the head of which a yet unfilled pedestal stood in quiet expectation', *Ulster was right*, p. 10.

68 *NW*, 29 June 1933.

69 *BNL*, 10 July 1933.

70 *BT*, 29 June 1933.

71 *BNL*, 6 July 1933.

72 *BNL*, 30 June 1933. David Chaney, 'A symbolic mirror of ourselves', p. 249.

73 *The Observer*, 9 July 1933, and *BNL*, 10 July 1933.

74 *NW*, 10 July 1933.

75 The Craigavon demonstration was also noted for its diverse audience: 'masters and men of all grades were in the ranks', *BNL*, 25 Sept. 1911.

76 Bill Rolston, *An oral history of Belfast in the 1930s* (Belfast, 1987), p. 18.

77 Throughout the period of the late '20s and early '30s the unionist government kept a keen eye on the activities of both communists and fascists in the state. In the late 1920s there was an association in the minds of the government between fascists and protestants; one police report noted that their 'objects and principles' were 'excellent' and described various members as 'loyal'. For instance, a police report on Capt. Williamson, a former member of the Royal Irish Rifles, and the propaganda officer for the Belfast branch of the British Fascists, described him as a respectable man 'with a strong determination to support Loyalist ideas'. British fascists, Ulster fascists and the British Union of Fascists failed to gain much support in Northern Ireland because, as Loughlin argues, 'the unionist-nationalist conflict was too deeply entrenched to be easily displaced'. Communists in the north were treated somewhat differently to the fascists. From an early date they were associated with catholics and nationalists. This report on the Irish Unemployed Workers is typical of police reports on organisations felt to be communist:

> Most of them being of the low working class type, and many of them looked as if they had never done any honest work. From their appearance and standing it is thought that the organisation will be short lived. There is no doubt that it is in reality a Communist organisation, as those present at the meeting were of the extreme type of Socialist and Republican, who would glory in the downfall of constitutional government. However, they command no influence and have no standing, therefore they need not be taken seriously.

In most communist organisations the government saw the hand of the IRA; this was particularly the case during the Second World War when the government felt that monitoring communist meetings was a way of measuring subversive activity in the state, given that the IRA were proving more elusive in terms of surveillance, HA/34/1/386–557. For a more detailed consideration of fascists in Northern Ireland see James Loughlin's interesting 'Northern Ireland and British fascism in the inter-war years', *IHS*, vol. xxx, no. 116 (Nov. 1995), pp. 536–52. Ultimately, as J.J. Lee argues: 'Fascism was simply "crowded out" by the more familiar brands of resentment, which comfortably retained their market share of human frailty, J.J. Lee, *Ireland 1912–1985*, p. 254.

78 Ian Colvin, *Life of Lord Carson*, vol. iii, p. 368.

79 *BT*, 26 Jan. 1933.

80 The report continued: 'Recognising that fact the Ulster Unionist Council took charge of the arrangements for to-day's ceremony, which was attended by

thousands of Orangemen who marched to Stormont, by members of the Ulster Unionist Council, and by a very large representation of the general public', *The Observer*, 9 July 1933.

81   *BNL*, 10 July 1933.

82   ibid.

83   *Sunday Times*, 9 July 1933.

84   *BNL*, 10 July 1933.

85   ibid.

86   George V (1865–1936) acceded to the throne in 1910, and was crowned in June 1914.

87   *NW*, 13 July 1935.

88   'Indeed in a recent speech the Northern Prime Minister told distinguished visitors from London that the Northern Government was there for much the same reason as the original plantation of Ulster over three centuries before', W.S. Armour, *Facing the Irish question* (London, 1935), pp. 17, 18.

89   'The essence of a ritual is that a collectivity is postulated or affirmed which might otherwise only have an ambiguous social existence', David Chaney, 'A symbolic mirror of ourselves', p. 248.

90   Letter, Lord Craigavon to Sir John Gilmour, secretary of state, 16 May 1935, CAB 9B/225/3.

91   'The late Lord Londonderry let it be known that Mr Churchill was welcome to hold his meeting where he liked as long as he did not violate those historical traditions and memories connected with the Ulster Hall and Lord Randolph Churchill's visit in 1886', *BNL, JS*, CAB 9B/225/3, 4 May 1935.

92   *BNL*, JS, 4 May 1935, CAB 9B/225/3.

93   ibid.

94   'Then came the Great War, in which Ulster rallied wholeheartedly to the support of the Empire', ibid.

95   CAB 9B/225/1.

96   The sub-committee of the Northern Irish cabinet in charge of the celebrations were Mr Pollock, Sir Dawson Bates and Lord Charlemont.

97   Programme of 'Jubilee Gathering of Uniformed Youth Organisations' at Balmoral, 11 May 1935, CAB 9B/225/1.

98   ibid.

99   Charles Blackmore to Oscar Henderson, nd, CAB 9B/225/1.

100   *NW*, 19 July 1935.

101   *BWN*, 18 July 1935. This pattern was repeated in 1953 with the coronation celebrations when nationalists again responded with hostility to the royal visit.

102   *Evening News*, 19 July 1935.

103   Bill Rolston, *An oral history of Belfast in the thirties*, p. 47.

104   *BT*, 22 Oct. 1935.

105   *NW*, 23 Oct. 1935. In his speech to the Northern Irish House of Commons Craig said: 'I know I, myself, thought that while he was alive nothing possible untoward could happen to our beloved Ulster', *Northern Hansard*, vol. xvii, 22 Oct. 1935.

106   *NW*, 23 Oct. 1935.

107   Cabinet meeting, 4 June 1935, CAB 4/343/11.

108   CAB 4/343/1.

109   He was a man of 'indomitable courage, coupled with a charming simplicity, transparent honesty and a passionate love of country in its widest interpretation', according to Craigavon, *The Listener*, 30 Oct. 1935. Carson's biographer looked to his origins to understand the man: 'To understand him we must call to mind his origin – his mother, a Lambert, that is to say a "Cromwellian", his

father a professional man of Dublin, a city time out of mind owing much to the English, the capital of the Pale, the centre of English culture, commerce and law ... "People", he said, "do not easily tire who are fighting for their lives". He fought for the lives of his people', Ian Colvin, *Life of Lord Carson*, vol. iii, p. 441.

110 *Daily Mail*, 23 Oct. 1935.
111 *Morning Post*, 24 Oct. 1935.
112 According to John MacNeice, Edward Carson 'stressed the things which appealed inside and outside Ulster. He did not worry about the Pope. He reminded Ulstermen of their birthright', quoted in Jon Stallworthy, *Louis MacNeice* (London, 1995), p. 34.
113 *BT*, 25 Oct. 1935.
114 ibid.
115 *BNL*, 13 July 1935.
116 In a letter of condolence, The Revd Hewitt described to Carson's widow how his only three brothers had died in the First World War, two of them members of the 36th 'Ulster' Division: 'They both fell together on July 1st 1916, at the Somme. One of them had a large framed photograph of your distinguished husband, signed "Edward Carson". After my brother's death it passed into my possession, and I am proud, as he was, to have it', 25 Oct. 1935, D1507/E/4/398. Interestingly Gailey argues that many of Carson's achievements were negative, see Andrew Gailey, 'King Carson: an essay on the invention of leadership', *p. 85*.
117 This was supported by other nationalist members, for instance Patrick O'Neill (Mourne, Co. Down): '. . . it is surely not fair to ask others who did not believe in Lord Carson's policy, or in any of his works, to pay a portion of this sum', *Northern Hansard*, vol. xviii, 19 Feb. 1936.
118 ibid.
119 Ian Colvin to Lady Carson, 24 Oct. 1935, D1507/E/4/362. Gailey has argued that Carson lacked the overriding vision of the statesman. 'With change by 1914 plainly inevitable, he never displayed the imagination or inclination to shape a new Ireland, and this left his leadership strangely adrift,' Andrew Gailey, 'King Carson: an essay on the invention of leadership', p. 85.
120 E. Homberger and J. Charmley, *The troubled face of biography* (London, 1988), p. ix.
121 Text of the dust jacket of Ian Colvin, *The life of Lord Carson*, vol. ii (London, 1934).
122 His step-father, Lord Hailsham, wrote to inform Carson: 'My dear boy killed himself yesterday . . . He was in a state of acute nervous depression', D1507/E/2/28.
123 *Morning Post*, 11 July 1932, D1507/E/2/59.
124 Review from an unidentified newspaper, 11 Aug. 1932, D1507/E/2/31–61.
125 Edward Marjoribanks to Carson, nd, D1507/E/3/1–43. Marjoribanks's description of Carson: 'Behind the dogged and fearless politician, the ardent, tireless, relentless advocate, there has always been the sensitive soul of a simple Irish gentleman, which has sought and found expression in personal friendship', *The life of Lord Carson*, vol. i, p. 4.
126 Edward Marjoribanks, *The life of Lord Carson*, vol. i, p. 69.
127 ibid., p. 68. W.S. Armour argued that the trouble with the Irish was that they were 'a very quick-witted race', *Facing the Irish question*, p. 149.
128 Henry Maxwell, *Ulster was right*, p. 177.
129 ibid., p. 39. Maxwell cites W.A. Phillips's *Revolution in Ireland*, p. 45, regarding the nature of the southern Irish the 'unbusiness-like, happy-go-lucky temper of the southern Irish' to their 'Gaelic blood', to the 'soft and enervating climate' and to the 'disproportionate part' their religion had played in moulding their character.
130 'I should like nothing better than to do the book which would be much to my

own honour and profit as well as a pleasure to write, altogether from pleasing you', Ian Colvin to Edward Carson, 14 Apr. 1932, D1507/E/3/2.

131 Ian Colvin in this letter also outlined his secondary reading: 'I have been re-reading the story of the Ulster fight in the *Times* files, in Ronald McNeill's book, which is first rate, and in Denis Gwynn's life of Redmond', Ian Colvin to Carson, 28 Aug. 1932, D1507/E/3/9. He also referenced W.A. Phillips's, *The revolution in Ireland, 1906–23* (London, 1926). Colvin, *The life of Lord Carson*, vol. ii, p. 447. Interestingly, for the later chapters of this book which utilise novels as sources, Cynthia Ozick argues: 'A good biography is itself a kind of novel. Like the classic novel, a biography believes in the notion of "a life" – a life as a triumphal or tragic story with a shape, a story that begins at birth, moves on to a middle part, and ends with the death of the protagonist', Homberger and Charmley, *The troubled face of biography*, p. xii.

132 Ian Colvin, *The life of Lord Carson*, vol. ii, p. 10.

133 'Taken by themselves they had never been one nor could ever unite . . . that such a conglomerate would never be content under any rule of law devised by themselves, at least without a first ferocious settlement of old scores. Government by assent, forbearance in power let loose – for these, as Carson well knew, it was impossible to hope', ibid., pp. 10–11.

134 Ian Colvin, *The life of Lord Carson*, vol. iii, p. 441.

135 op. cit., vol. ii, pp. 75–6. The language is the same as that used in the *WNW* following the destruction of the 36th 'Ulster' Division at the Battle of the Somme in July 1916; placing the division in historical terms the newspaper reported: 'The same feelings which inspired Cromwell's Ironsiders animated all ranks and gave the Division an unconquerable spirit . . . they fear God and nothing else', *WNW*, 15 July 1916.

136 op. cit., vol. ii, p. 70. It is interesting to consider this focus on dispossession in the light of the Anglo-Irish War. At that time, in many of the unionist newspapers, it was portrayed as essentially anti-protestant, and an attempt to drive protestants out of southern Ireland.

137 ibid., p. 75.

138 ibid., pp. 13–14.

139 ibid., p. 15.

140 ibid., p. 57.

141 op. cit., vol. iii, p. 157.

142 ibid., p. 158. W.A. Phillips, *The revolution in Ireland*, pp. 98–9.

143 ibid., p. 441.

144 Lord Ernest Hamilton, *The soul of Ulster*, p. 192.

145 op. cit., vol. iii, p. 161.

146 op. cit., p. 406.

147 Henry Maxwell, *Ulster was right*, p. 15.

148 op. cit., *The life of Lord Carson*, vol. iii, p. 295.

149 op. cit., vol. iii, p. 403.

150 Henry Maxwell, *Ulster was right*, p. 271.

151 op. cit., *The life of Lord Carson*, vol. iii, p. 295.

152 ibid., p. 375.

153 *Daily Mail*, 15 Oct. 1934, *Sunday Times*, 21 Oct. 1934, D1507/E/3/32, D1507/E/3/34.

154 Ian Colvin's favourite review was that in the *Evening News*: 'Those who know the Dominion of Northern Ireland, at the present day, can witness to the righteousness of the battle which Carson and his friends fought just over twenty years ago, and be glad that the battle is not going unrecorded', *Evening News*, nd. Note from Ian Colvin to Edward Carson: 'All the reviews are kind but this is the biggest', D1507/E/3/30.

155 Jonathan Bardon, *A history of Ulster* (Belfast, 1992), p. 543.
156 J.J. Lee, *Ireland, 1912–85: politics and society* (Cambridge, 1989), p. 203.
157 *NW*, 6 May 1937.
158 Cabinet proceedings, nd, CAB 4/369/32.
159 'To assure His Majesty of our devotion to his Royal person, and of our sure conviction that his reign will, under the favour of Divine Providence, be distinguished by unswerving efforts to promote the virtue, prosperity, and contentment of the realm, and to guard the rights and liberties of His Majesty's faithful people', Cabinet meeting, 23 Jan. 1936, CAB 4/352/1-16.
160 CAB 4/368/1.
161 James Craig, *Northern Hansard*, vol. xix, 17 Dec. 1936.
162 Craigavon to the primate of all Ireland, 15 Dec. 1936, CAB 9R/5117.
163 James Craig, *Northern Hansard*, vol. xix, 17 Dec. 1936.
164 Prime minister's notes, CAB 9R/51/6.
165 *NW*, 11 Dec. 1936.
166 ibid.
167 This was reflected in Craig's article on the coronation for the *NW* coronation supplement: 'I am proud to accompany so many representatives from Ulster to participate in the Abbey solemnities. We shall take our place alongside other Prime Ministers, and thus emphasise the fact that Northern Ireland is wholeheartedly at one with them, and those for whom they have authority to act and speak in loyal devotion to their Gracious Majesties King George and Queen Elizabeth', *NW*, 11 May 1937.
168 Special coronation supplement of the *NW*, 11 May 1937, CAB 9R/51/12.
169 CAB 9R/51/11.
170 Coronation committee members: Sir Charles Blackmore, secretary to the cabinet, H.V.V. Thompson, minister of finance, W.A. Magil and Commander R.P. Pim, Ministry of Home Affairs, Lt. Col. Sir Charles G. Wickham, inspector general of the RUC.
171 *Morning Post*, 29 July 1937.
172 ibid.
173 Letter G. Wickham to Dawson Bates, 23 Jan. 1937, CAB 9R/51/15.
174 'Over and above all personal considerations, the visit of the King and Queen has meant for Ulster a renewal of its pledges of loyalty and allegiance', *NW*, 29 July 1937.
175 Coronation committee minutes, 28 Apr. 1937, CAB 4A/13/1/2 and 6 July 1937, CAB 4A/13/1/4.
176 Groups suggested: Lisburn urban council, Belfast chamber of commerce, Belfast chamber of trade, Royal Ulster Agricultural Society, Ulster Unionist Council, girl guides, boy scouts and boys' brigade, representatives from the trade unions. Letter, Oscar Henderson to Charles Blackmore, 26 Mar. 1937, CAB 9R/51/13.
177 HA 8/957/12. Tickets for Balmoral were issued through youth organisations, not the Northern Irish government.
178 List of those who attended the garden party: members of the senate and parliament, Belfast harbour commissioners, representatives from the Derry papers, Irish Society, Belfast water commissioners, Ulster Farmers' Union, the British Legion, Rural Development Council of Northern Ireland, Women's Institutes Northern Ireland, representatives of the chemists and druggists, Royal Ulster Agricultural Society, Queen's University Belfast, British Medical Association Northern Ireland, the Orange Order, Church of Ireland clergy, the Transport Board, Masonic Order, BBC, teachers' organisations, the Methodist Church in Ireland, Unionist Associations, RAF, RNVR (Royal Navy Volunteer Reserve), members of the post office, civil service, RUC, prison officers, dukes,

marquesses, earls, viscounts and barons of Northern Ireland, HA 8/957/2, *NW*, 28 July 1937.

179   *NW*, 28 July 1937.
180   W.S. Armour, *Facing the Irish question*, p. 10. Armour was the editor of the *Northern Whig* for twenty-one months.
181   Article by the editor of the *Daily Dispatch*, in the *Irish Times*, 30 July 1937.
182   *NW*, 13 July 1935.
183   *NW*, 24 Oct. 1938.
184   ibid.
185   ibid. Henry Maxwell saw Carson as: 'Tall, dark, and slender, with the uncompromising, almost menacing set of his countenance, the tremendous jaw and the whole indefinable strength and dignity of his bearing, he was in very truth the beau-ideal of a born leader of men', *Ulster was right*, p. 56. A.T.Q. Stewart continued the tradition of depicting Carson's physical appearance as a physical manifestation of his political ideology and that of his party: 'His height and powerful frame, and the determination of his features, gave an impression of immense strength and energy. His public face was set permanently in a scowl of righteous defiance', A.T.Q. Stewart, *Edward Carson* (Dublin, 1981), p. 39.
186   *BNL*, 24 Oct. 1938.
187   The *BWN*'s editorial drew parallels with the third home rule crisis: 'During the Home Rule agitation Irish Nationalists joined British Liberals in denouncing Ulster Loyalists for their obduracy in refusing to accept safeguards and guarantees under the rule of a Dublin Parliament. They are now being given a demonstration of the value of such safeguards as were inserted in the Free State constitution', *BWN*, 11 Apr. 1933.
188   Henry Maxwell, *Ulster was right*, p. 15.
189   Unionists were however concerned that the British 'in their desire for an overall settlement with the Irish Free State', would 'allow the future of Northern Ireland to be written into the agenda'. Nicholas Mansergh, *The unresolved question: the Anglo-Irish settlement and its undoing, 1912–72*, p. 305.
190   In 1919 Carson speaking to the unionist faithful at the Twelfth of July commemorations addressed the question of the British government versus the British people: 'I believe', he said, 'that when we appeal to the Great British Constituencies, which know the part we have taken in the war, whatever the Government may be, they will be with us to a man', *BNL*, 19 July 1919.
191   Cited in *BNL*, 24 Oct. 1938.

3. Broadcasting in Northern Ireland 1924–49

The BBC in Northern Ireland (BBC NI) played a significant role in creating an image of the state as a 'knowable community', as well as shaping an image of that society as a unified homogenous unit through the medium of broadcasting.[1] By providing listeners with access to music, drama, and other cultural resources, BBC NI helped to create the impression of a common, though not unproblematic, culture within the state and with the rest of the United Kingdom. Broadcasting contributed to the creation of the 'we-feeling' in the state but this was often not an inclusive 'we' but an exclusive one from which many felt alienated. This was reflective of the BBC's more general attempts 'to promote a sense of communal identity within its audience, whether at a regional, national or imperial level'.[2] The BBC's early ethos (until the late 1930s) was to promote social unity through 'the creation of a broader range of shared interests, tastes and social knowledge than had previously been the position of the vast majority of the population'.[3] In Britain, the BBC promoted the idea of a national culture, 'making the nation as one man' in Reith's words.[4] This was particularly the case during the Second World War, when the BBC made an increased effort to generate a sense of national unity through broadcasting;[5] however, the war was 'by itself generating a sense of social cohesion which made such exhortation seem not only redundant but even insulting'.[6] British 'national character' was contentious and had to be located by the BBC in the past to avoid exposing divisions within that society; in Northern Ireland where the past was as, if not more, contentious than the present, there was no common historical past to which BBC NI programme-makers could hark back in an effort to create the image of a common cultural heritage.[7]

BBC NI, then, made the state tangible through the range of images and symbols, events and ceremonies it broadcast; however, the image of the Northern Irish state as revealed by the station was not always one which unionists could support, and they were often critical of the programmes produced. Moreover, as the BBC developed, it evolved from simply serving the 'national culture' to gradually responding to the 'tastes of a popular audience'.[8] This meant that over a twenty-five-year period the BBC in Northern Ireland was faced with the difficulty that, in order to function, it had to deal with its audience as a unity, but was constantly reminded of the state's population as a diversity; it was almost impossible to presume a homogenous community whose interests it had to serve.[9] At the same time, and further complicating the picture, the BBC in Northern Ireland, as a British institution, became a focus of some of the anti-Englishness which was characteristic of much unionist literature and was a general feature of unionism's complex relationship with the British.

BBC NI sought to represent as homogenous a diverse and multi-layered society. And while regional stations such as BBC NI were expected to tap into local culture and talent for programme material, in Northern Ireland (where according to Ruby Hewitt it was difficult for unionists 'to think that an Ulsterman could have a great affection for "Ulster" without hating either Éire or England') this was to prove problematic.[10] Ultimately, the BBC in Northern Ireland was neither a crude promoter of unionism, nor was it a champion of any distinctive version of 'Irish' culture. It reacted to, and reflected, the state's social developments and political pressures and throughout this formative period it walked a political tightrope in terms of the image of the state it reflected to its domestic audience and to the wider British public. Despite this, the BBC became a primary definer of the identity of the Northern Irish. Few recordings from the BBC's early period in Northern Ireland are extant, nor are there many typescripts of the programmes or plays which were broadcast.[11] For this reason the early history of the BBC in the state is restricted somewhat to the strategies and intentions which lay behind programmes and schedules (and the reactions of senior BBC staff and the government to them), rather than to their actual realisation or effects.

Placed in close connection with the centres of political, economic and cultural power and authority in the state, the BBC in Northern Ireland became a channel that linked individuals to the wider community and to the process of government. (In particular, through its programmes, the BBC sought recognition of itself as a member of the establishment.)[12] Two men dominated the running of the BBC in Northern Ireland in this period, George Marshall (1932–48) and Andrew Stewart (1948–52); they were interchangeably known as the director or controller of the station. In its early history George Marshall has been frequently vilified by past authors as the oppressive face of unionism in the station.[13] This has largely been a case of mistaking a symptom for the cause. Marshall was a product of the BBC's early ethos, and followed in the path of previous directors to the Northern Irish station, such as Gerald Beadle, who had maintained the closest links with the Northern Irish government.

Gerald Beadle, BBC NI's second director, had endorsed the unionist government's early hopes of the BBC, that it would be biased in their favour, or at least responsive to their wishes. He came to the Northern Irish station two years after its establishment; 'mine was not a pioneering job', he wrote, 'rather it was a task of consolidation, which meant building the

BBC into the lives of the province and making it one of their public institutions':

> I was invited to become a member of the Ulster Club, where almost daily I met members of the Government; the Governor, the Duke of Abercorn, was immensely helpful and friendly, and Lord Craigavon, the Prime Minister, was a keen supporter of our work. In effect I was made a member of the Establishment of a province which had most of the paraphernalia of a sovereign state and a population no bigger than that of a moderate sized English county.[14]

This was in keeping with the overall role of BBC local station directors in the 1920s whose remit was to establish good relations with the civic authorities, other religious and civic bodies and, naturally, the public.[15] In a letter to Reith, the BBC's director general, in 1927, Beadle suggested that the position of the BBC in Northern Ireland would be 'strengthened immensely if we can persuade the Northern Government to look upon us as their mouthpiece'.[16] Although this was not allowed to happen, the BBC in Northern Ireland remained open to government pressure. Following a visit to Northern Ireland in 1943 R.W. Foot, the BBC's director general, reported that George Marshall's standing 'with all important contacts in that Region was high, and valuable to the Corporation'.[17] Marshall, a Scot, was a BBC man from the earliest days of the organisation, serving first in Glasgow, and later as director in Edinburgh and Newcastle-upon-Tyne. He came to Belfast as director in September 1932, at a time of heightened political and social tension in the state surrounding the Eucharistic Congress in Dublin, the opening of the new Stormont parliament and the social disturbances related to the Outdoor Relief Riots. Marshall was trained under John Reith's ethos that radio should bring into every home all that was best in human knowledge, endeavour and achievement, while avoiding that which was vulgar and hurtful.[18] This ethos was echoed by the governor of Northern Ireland who, in his speech to open the new station, spoke of the promise which broadcasting brought with it:

> Everything which tends to broaden one's mind and to enlarge one's outlook is to the good, and therefore I consider that a great boon has been conferred upon those who live in less populated districts of our Province, by the British Broadcasting Company.[19]

George Marshall remained as director of the Northern Irish station until 1948, throughout a period of insecurity in the state and he suffers in comparison to his successor Andrew Stewart. Stewart's period in Northern Ireland was the late 1940s and early 1950s when unionism's insecurities about the survival of the state had been, to an extent, allayed by the Ireland Act, and when the Belfast station was experimenting with and expanding into its own region, becoming less fearful of local resources. Stewart therefore comes across as a progressive controller. For a fair assessment, Marshall has to be viewed in the context of Northern Ireland in the period of the 1930s and 1940s (and the BBC at the same point of the corporation's development), and the tensions and pressures which were brought to bear on him as director have to be borne in mind. George Marshall was, however, responsible for encouraging an atmosphere of caution within the station and among staff about the type of programmes which could be produced, and for fostering a negative level of self-censorship.[20]

In *Television: a critical review*, Gerald Beadle argued that the BBC had been made responsible for the 'projection of Britain to the world through radio'.[21] For unionists the BBC had the power to project an image of the state (as a homogenous protestant community and an integral part of the United Kingdom) and its culture to a wide audience. It was a medium which unionists needed to control or at least maintain a strong influence over, and which they needed to constantly monitor. In addition, in the institution of the BBC the unionist government perceived a tangible expression of their union with the rest of the United Kingdom. George Marshall writing in the *Times* in August 1934 argued that Northern Ireland relied on broadcasting 'to strengthen and maintain the contacts with British opinion' which it desired.[22] In the late 1920s and early 1930s the Belfast station was 'radiating to its listeners most of the important London programmes', and occasionally programmes from Scotland, Wales and the North of England:

> Thus the broadcasting service reflects the sentiments of the people, who have always retained a lively sympathy with, and an unswerving loyalty to, British ideals and British culture. The chimes of Big Ben are heard as clearly in County Tyrone as they are in the County of Middlesex, and the news of the day emanating from the London Studio is received simultaneously in Balham and Ballymacarret.[23]

During his visit to Belfast in 1943, R.W. Foot was reported as saying that 'the BBC was the voice, not of London, but of Britain, and as an integral part of Britain and the Empire, Ulster's voice must be clearly heard'.[24] This attitude was to create its own problems in the late 1940s. To quote Edna Longley, 'the Unionist establishment was so terrified (for example in the BBC) of "local" culture turning out to be "Irish" culture that, forgetting Scotland and Wales, it affected an absurd Englishness – a mentality not dead yet'.[25] Ironically, it was the 'Ulster' accent which caused difficulty for the BBC in Northern Ireland. J.T. Sutthery, for the regional director in BBC NI, wrote to the BBC head office, in January 1935, commenting on one speaker's 'unusually attractive Irish voice', which he described approvingly in another letter as 'rich Irish'.[26] George Marshall himself noted that 'Ulster' speech 'should not be confused with Scots, as it is a curious hybrid of genuine Irish and lowland Scots which sounds well enough on the countryman's tongue, but is less pretty in the mouth of the man who wished to think he has no accent at all'.[27] Neither Sutthery or Marshall were, of course, from Northern Ireland.[28]

This question of accent excited sharp criticism of the station. In 1945, in a debate in the Northern Irish House of Commons over a BBC NI programme 'Women on the Land in Ulster' the MP with the original complaint (which was that the programme had been 'offensive and misrepresentative') expanded his argument and demanded that the state should have a separate broadcasting service of its own with exclusively 'Ulster staff': 'not "self-conceited and arrogant people from public schools in England" and "snobs with Oxford accents"'.[29] The debate broadened into an attack on the BBC generally, and centred to a large extent on the presence, and predominance, of English people on the staff of the station. John Nixon, MP, spoke of the 'empty-headed snobs' sent over from England to 'look down on' the Northern Irish; 'is it not time', he asked, 'we stood on our own dignity?'.[30] James Brown, MP for South Down, argued that the BBC constantly slurred and ridiculed the people of Northern Ireland: 'In Wales they have a Welshman in control, and in Scotland there is a Scotsman, but in Northern Ireland we have nobody who understands the position here – a person who is prepared to give fair play to Northern Ireland.'[31] The wrong people, according to Brown, were in charge of the BBC in Belfast, and they were 'self-conceited and arrogant'. Oscar Henderson, contributing to the debate, said that Radio Éireann told the world what Éire 'stood for, what their ideals are, and what their art and culture are'; why, he asked, could the BBC in Northern Ireland not do the same. Broadcasting House, he continued, was like a 'foreign country':

> We do not want the Oxford accent; we want the Ulster accent. If the Ulster people say to close the 'dure' we know they mean to close the door, and there is no need to be ashamed, or if they say to wipe the 'flure' we know it means to wipe the floor. As I say, we need not be ashamed. Our forefathers spoke that language.[32]

Following the war, more 'locals' (i.e. Northern Irish) were recruited to the BBC in Belfast, and the tension over the perceived bias in favour of English or Scottish staff was diluted somewhat. In the post-war period then, reflecting the wider BBC, BBC NI developed a more regional character. After 1945 more programmes were recorded outside of Belfast and, surveying the broadcasting year in Northern Ireland in 1947 the *BBC Yearbook* noted:

> To look back over the programmes of Northern Ireland broadcasting during 1947 is to get a lively and extraordinarily varied picture of life in the Province: a picture of past and present, showing the country, the towns, and the people as they were in past generations and as they seem today, reflecting the people at work in the fields and in the shipyards and factories, their creative efforts in the arts, their leisure interests and their tastes, their problems and their endeavours to solve them. In review, the programmes provide a vigorous and boldly coloured pattern in life in Ulster. [33]

During the Second World War some within unionist circles had felt that the BBC was not overly sympathetic towards them. 'There is', Sayers of the *Belfast Telegraph* told Andrews in December 1941, 'frequent disparagement of the North of Ireland [on the BBC], not so much by direct reference as by insinuation'.[34] In 1945, following the war, F.R. Adams wrote to Sir Ernest Cooper, director of information services for the Northern Irish government:

'On the face of it there seems to be some anti-Ulster influence at work among those who have the actual framing of the BBC programmes. If some anti-dote [*sic*] to this can be found it would be most useful.'[35]

The unionist government set many of the terms for the running of the BBC in the state, through direct and indirect pressure, particularly on the regional director. In April 1923, the private secretary to the minister of home affairs wrote to the cabinet secretary, Charles Blackmore, to say that the minister had no objection to proposals to erect a broadcasting station in Northern Ireland: 'Provided the right is conceded to the Government of Northern Ireland of stopping transmission at any time, if such a course should be considered necessary or desirable in the public interest'.[36] The Northern Irish government was never given that right, and they sought instead to influence what was broadcast from Northern Ireland, and where Irish topics were concerned on the BBC in general, through pressure on the Northern Irish controller and by personal representation to the director general of the BBC. This was in keeping with the policy of the British government, who, in the same way, reserved the right to appoint the BBC's governing body, the Board of Governors, and the ultimate right to veto any material to be broadcast by the corporation.[37] This was a strategy which the BBC, by the end of the 1930s, was predisposed to react to; the BBC was thus, according to Curran and Seaton, vulnerable to government bullying, 'as a result the most important constraint came to be the corporation's anxiety to pre-empt the threats'.[38] 'The assumption', Henry Fairlie wrote in an essay on the BBC in 1959, 'that underlies all the BBC's attitudes to authority [is that] it *ought* to be on the side of authority'.[39] This is not to say that the BBC was 'a crude agent of the *status quo*, rather it advocated acceptable change, in some areas, in certain circumstances, sometimes'.[40] Even though the BBC claimed independence, the British government did intervene in its conduct, and 'merely chose not to control it directly'.[41] And this was very much the pattern in Northern Ireland; for example, as they did in Britain, the media in Northern Ireland suppressed news of labour unrest during the war years, or simply chose to ignore it. In his monthly report for April 1944 George Marshall observed that a strike in the shipyards the previous month had looked 'likely to cause a complete stoppage of all transport and public utilities generally throughout the Province'.[42] Marshall and the BBC were asked to assist the unionist government 'by bringing a Group H transmitter into action and broadcasting announcements from time to time'.[43] The strike did not cause the expected disturbance, but the incident proved that BBC NI were willing to adopt a position of overt support for the government in a dispute between them and a section of the public; it could be argued that given their reliance on the government for their continued existence they had little option.

BBC NI did make small gestures of political independence in minor ways. In February 1949, when the director general of the BBC visited Belfast the guest list for dinner included not only Sir Basil Brooke, Maynard Sinclair, the minister of finance, and the speaker of the House of Commons, but also James McSparran a 'Nationalist. R.C. Member of the Northern Irish Advisory

Council'.[44] In a letter to the director of home broadcasting in London, Andrew Stewart argued that although the inclusion of McSparran was 'unusual' in such company it was important for the BBC to show that 'it was not tied to the Government's strings'.[45] On a basic level unionists hoped that the BBC in Belfast would counter broadcasts from Radio Éireann Athlone, Éire's broadcasting institution. Government pressure came more regularly in the form of meetings with BBC NI's controller to make him aware of their concerns. In the late 1940s, when Andrew Stewart became the director in Northern Ireland, he wrote to the director general of the BBC about the broadcasting, or not, of political appeals. Stewart wrote that the BBC's position had been explained to Sir Basil Brooke privately: 'since they are reasonable men they understand how the BBC is placed, although from their point of view it is not placed as their Party would wish'.[46] Nevertheless the station remained sensitive to unionist opinion; in July 1948, for instance, Andrew Stewart had a meeting with the prime minister and the minister of finance to discuss the 'possibility of the BBC being in a position to reply, through the Regional programmes in Great Britain, to any reports put out by the BBC of speeches made by Mr de Valera during his forthcoming campaign across the water'.[47] 'His object', wrote Stewart, 'will be to influence British public opinion against the continued political existence of Northern Ireland . . . Our policy has been for many years defined by my predecessor as follows: "The BBC does not permit attacks upon the Constitution of Northern Ireland"'. Stewart's concern was that other BBC regions might broadcast material to do with the de Valera visit, or indeed interview him. This, given that listeners in Northern Ireland could receive the national broadcast, would generate discussion, and such discussion according to Stewart 'would engender . . . not light but heat . . . Moderates on either side are few. Discussion is highly charged emotionally and in the past has led to bloodshed.'[48]

A recurring problem for BBC NI over several decades was that of elections and party political broadcasts.[49] In January 1938, Marshall wrote to the assistant controller about the upcoming Northern Irish elections and Lord Craigavon's views on political appeals via the wireless; 'he is strongly of the opinion', Marshall reported: 'that nothing of the sort should be attempted here, the reason being that the Opposition is so small and that there are so many conflicting interests, that a difficult situation would be bound to arise.'[50] Head Office agreed that such a 'difficult situation' was to be avoided, and suggested that should the opposition parties 'push for broadcasts' Marshall should inform them of the BBC's policy of impartiality:

> You should take the line that the BBC only broadcasts election speeches by agreement with all the main parties concerned, and that in this case the Government did not consent. In other words, the Opposition parties should be referred to the Government, with the information that you, the BBC will find time for speeches if a basis can be agreed by them and the Government.[51]

Marshall's successor, Andrew Stewart, faced the same problem, but a new prime minister, Sir Basil Brooke. In January 1949 Stewart reported his interview with Brooke about the party political broadcasts prior to the election to head office. Brooke, he noted, had no objection to the planned broadcast, however he was 'rather doubtful, that the argument would probably not be reasonable on either side. It might well be over-emotional, full of personalities, go too far, and become a slanging match'. Furthermore:

> The Prime Minister hoped that the Governors would be clear that this was not an Election where the issue is between the domestic policies of two major Parties, either of which would carry on within a set constitutional framework. The issue of this election was whether a part of the United Kingdom would remain within the United Kingdom or withdraw from its allegiance and join the Republic. The issue would be the constitutional position of Northern Ireland itself; in or out; King or Republic.[52]

A memo from the publicity officer of BBC Northern Ireland reported that the three parties had failed to come to an agreement over the allocation of broadcasts and, therefore, there would be no broadcasts.[53] Again, in 1952, the question of election broadcasts came up. There was an almost exasperated tone in Andrew Stewart's letter to the director of BBC South West:

> Frankly I don't see much point in making this offer for two reasons:
> 1. It is difficult to see how, under the Charter, we can utter propaganda for breaking up the United Kingdom.
> 2. Neither of the main Parties really wants to broadcast to propaganda: it is a two edged weapon and they will almost certainly do as they did the last time and get out of the problem by failing to agree in the allocations of dates.[54]

However, the BBC had to be seen to be independent; thus Harman Grisewood, director of the spoken word, wrote in a memo to the assistant director general: 'In brief, though I recognise the objections, I do not, on what is at present known to me, feel them to be stronger than the disadvantage to us of deciding not to make an offer'.[55] From the BBC's point of view, the major concern was that such broadcasts might lead the opposition parties (nationalists in particular) to 'say something so offensive about the Throne or Constitution as to bring odium on the BBC'. In such an event, given that they would see the text of the broadcasts prior to airing, the BBC would have to refuse to broadcast entirely.[56] Retrospectively, it seems almost inevitable that in September 1953 Belfast's regional director should be writing to the director of BBC South West that: 'One party has defeated the intention that lay behind the Governors' instruction. It is clear to me now that it is the unionists who do not want to broadcast and are quite happy to keep the others off the air . . . I am convinced that at all costs we should avoid a third repetition of this sterile process.'[57]

The 1930s was a period of world-wide slump, and the BBC in Northern Ireland reflected an image of the effects on the social and economic position of the state. A 1932 broadcast by the Northern Irish minister of commerce, J. Milne Barbour, entitled 'The Ulster Yet to Be' evoked the hope of improvement in the future.[58] And there certainly was a need for a better future. In Northern Ireland, between 1931 and 1939, 27 per cent of the insured workforce was unemployed. In 1938, 29.5 per cent of industrial workers were unemployed as compared to 23.8 per cent in Wales, the highest figure for any region in Britain.[59] Although unemployment gradually declined from 1935 on, 'there was here an industrial structure unduly geared to a declining range of traditional industries, coal, steel, textiles, shipbuilding'.[60] In 1932 the worst-hit trades in Northern Ireland were ship-building and the building industry; 'the two central planks of the Northern Ireland local economy were collapsing'.[61] The minister of home affairs, Dawson Bates, speaking in July 1932, indicated the extent to which the situation had deteriorated:

> I do not desire to take an unduly alarmist view, but there can be no doubt that unless some ameliorative measures are adopted there will be a large body of the population driven to desperation by poverty and hunger, and the only alternative to relief measures is to keep order by force, and for this purpose, in the face of widespread discontent, the existing force is not adequate . . . the situation is rapidly approaching a crisis.[62]

In Belfast alone, in 1932, there were 48,000 people unemployed, 48 per cent of whom were not receiving benefit.[63] The statistics for the shipyards speak for themselves; no ships were launched from Queen's Island between December 1931 and May 1934; the number of shipyard employees in 1930 was 10,428, in 1932 that figure was 1,554. By 1938 Belfast had the highest infant mortality rate compared to six other British cities, a high rate of death from infectious diseases, and chronically bad housing. This state of affairs was reflected in the Northern Irish regional programmes. In March 1937 the BBC in Belfast suggested a programme of four weekly talks during the month of July:

> Our present proposal is to get some intelligent unemployed person through the BBC place at Gateshead and have him over here for a month spending a working-man's holiday in various places in the province and giving a weekly talk from the studio of his experiences. This is a follow-up of an idea we put into practice a year or so ago when an Ulster unemployed man was sent off into the province with £3 in his pocket and told to make it last ten days and come back to tell us all about it.[64]

Again, proposing a talks series on nutrition for April/June 1939, J.T. Sutth-ery wrote to the director of talks in London:

> The particular problem of nutrition in Northern Ireland. This would deal with the food habits of the Ulsterman, his food tastes and prejudices, malnutrition in towns, suggestions for improvement . . . The subject is of peculiar interest in Ulster, as there is no doubt that the great majority of the working classes are definitely undernourished, or rather, badly nourished.[65]

In this period Northern Ireland was a state of great economic contrast.

Rolston notes that

> while tens of thousands suffered from malnutrition or had no clothes
> except those they stood up in, there were others who could afford to take
> up advertisements in local papers for world cruises and who continued to
> socialise on the scale to which they had previously been accustomed, the
> depression not withstanding.[66]

As for entertainment, it was above the means of the working class; inter-
viewed in Rolston's *An oral history of Belfast*, Frances Maguire recalls: 'Very
few people had a radio, and if you had a radio, by heaven, you were a step
above the buttermilk.'[67]

It is, of course, difficult to gauge the number or profile of radio listeners in
Northern Ireland with accuracy. In the early 1930s Northern Ireland's licences
made up only 1 per cent of the total number of licences in the United
Kingdom. The question of licence-holder records was highlighted in November
1947 in a letter from the BBC's director general to Harry Mulholland, the
chairman of the Northern Ireland Advisory Committee to the BBC. Mulholland had requested the extension of Listener Research to Northern Ireland;
'but', wrote the director general, 'it regrets that in view of the small proportion
of licences (the ratio of licences to population is half that of other Regions),
and in the light of Listener Research Department's past failure to establish a
sufficient number of interviewers and panel members in Northern Ireland it
does not consider the proposal practicable at the moment'.[68] For many years
the *BBC Yearbooks* gave a breakdown of radio licences per head of population;
in Northern Ireland licences increased four-fold between 1932 and 1939.[69] But
this of course does not include variables such as those who owned radios and
bought no licences, or those who did not possess a radio at all but had access
to someone else's. In addition, there was no breakdown of the geographical
distribution of licences, although because of poor reception elsewhere listeners were more likely to be concentrated in the north-east of the state. The *BBC
Yearbook 1934* noted that the 'more outlying parts of the Six Counties' were
not served at all by the BBC because of the weakness of the transmitter. This
situation improved somewhat with the installation of a new, and more powerful, transmitter but George Barnes in his 1948 report on the Belfast station
still noted that poor coverage was concentrated in the west of the state, 'the
Catholic fringe, which is both a fruitful source of programmes and the place
most cut off from British influence'.[70] The poor reception by radio owners due
to the quality of their wireless sets was also a factor in the make-up of BBC NI's
audience. This was a particular problem during the Second World War when
Craig noted that wirelesses in the state were not strong enough to receive
national broadcasts, and that subsequently 'sound advice given by the BBC
from time to time' did not 'penetrate to a large number of Ulster homes'.[71] One
may generalise therefore that the BBC's audience was not only predominantly
middle class, but also concentrated around the Belfast region.

In the 1930s the BBC organisation moved into a new phase when the
original local stations were replaced by the regional programme (produced
from the Midlands, North, South and West of England, Scotland, Wales and

Northern Ireland) and the national programme from London. The corporation now provided a two-channel service, dominated by and from London.
Regional stations produced their own material, which was sometimes taken
for the national programme, and also broadcast the national programme's
material. In the mid 1930s, for instance, the Northern Ireland station was
asked to take a regional programme called 'I was there – *Titanic* Survivor'.
This programme, according to Sutthery, was an 'awkward problem'; in a
letter to the programme director at head office he explained that:

> The 'Titanic', and everything to do with it, is an exceedingly sore point in
> Belfast history, as not only were some 40 Belfast people drowned –
> mostly rather important people – but also it was a very grave set-back to
> civic pride when this much-vaunted ship went out from Harland and
> Wolff's yard to sink on its maiden voyage.[72]

In 1947, Sir Basil Brooke intervened to have another BBC programme on
the *Titanic*, on the national service, postponed for a week when the date for
the original broadcast coincided with the date of the launch of a new
Cunard White Star liner from the Harland and Wolff shipyard.[73]

The role of the regional station was ostensibly to give expression to
everyday life and variety in the region. This was in contradiction to the
ethos of unionism in the period which was uncomfortable with the diversity
of the state, fearing that it would make it unstable. Lindsay Wellington, the
presentation director, suggested to the Belfast station that it would be better
to 'aim at quality rather than quantity where local pride' would allow:

> The great thing to bear in mind I think is that BBC programmes for
> Ulster listeners consist of two strands – the National Programme and the
> North of Ireland programme and not the North of Ireland programme
> with a National programme vaguely going on in the background.[74]

The tension between the Northern Irish station and London reflected
tensions across the board between the national and all the regional stations.
The Northern Ireland station's main contributions for national use were
documentaries, features, plays and Irish music.[75] In 1934 the Northern Irish
station was offering the national pool of programmes the Belfast Wireless
Orchestra, Cecil Chadwick at the organ of the Classic Cinema and Albert
Taylor's organ recitals from Rosemary Street Unitarian Church.[76] Replying to
a memo in January 1935 requesting 'a first class programme from each
Region for inclusion on National or Regional', J.T. Sutthery, of BBC Northern
Ireland, had a number of suggestions. The principal one was 'Bernard Shaw
speaking in London on absolutely anything he feels inclined', which Sutthery
felt would cost, 'at a guess, 50 guineas'. His list continued: 'Jimmy O'Dea and
Partner, the one and only first class Irish comedian. "Oul Belfast", a short,
light, Ulster sketch. An Irish singer. Big Male Voice Choir from the Wellington
Hall. The Orchestra'.[77] Again, in 1937, Henry McMullan, a producer in the
Belfast station, writing to the assistant director of variety, referred to a
Jimmy O'Dea revue: 'The music is all of the type that will appeal to the man

who has Irish blood in his veins about four generations back! In other words it will be "staged" Irish from beginning to end.'[78] Feature programmes developed a strong local flavour in this period; in the programme schedule for 1936, for instance, 'Six Men Went Forth' discussed famous 'Ulstermen'; Denis Johnson and Wilson Guy debated whether Belfast was Ulster; Sir Dawson Bates introduced a talk on town-planning in the state, and 'Home Again' featured 'distinguished Ulstermen' describing changes in their birthplaces since their childhood.[79] Anniversaries and opening ceremonies also provided limited opportunities for local broadcasting, particularly in the 1930s: the opening of the Royal Courts of Justice by the Duke of Abercorn in 1933, the tenth anniversary of the Royal Naval Volunteer Reserve in April 1934, and the opening of the King's Hall by the Duke of Gloucester the same year.[80] In June 1941 John Andrews, then prime minister, 'broadcast in celebration of the twentieth anniversary of the opening of the Northern Ireland Parliament, and spoke of Ulster's part in the war effort'.[81] Ursula Eason, a producer in Belfast, suggested to the BBC in London that they broadcast a special programme to mark the anniversary. Given the BBC's early war-time policy of conciliation towards southern Irish listeners, the response from London was telling. Rejecting the idea, the comments of some BBC executives included: 'I do not think that in these days we want to stress the tragic divisions in Ireland itself', and 'I'm inclined to leave the Ulster-Eire stew alone for the minute'.[82] Royal visits, too, provided material for broadcasting, and created a sense of a common experience with the rest of the United Kingdom: 'After the Coronation, commentaries were broadcast on Their Majesties' visits to Scotland, Wales and Northern Ireland; on His Majesty's review of Ex-Servicemen and women in Hyde Park; and on the Naval Review at Spithead'.[83] State occasions, for instance the funerals of Edward Carson and Lord Craigavon, also had their place in the station's broadcasts.

The issue of 'Irish culture' was a thorny one for the BBC in Northern Ireland and one which they failed to deal with effectively. Broadcasts were largely state-orientated and concerned with Britain and British culture, but given that up to 1949 the Irish Free State was a dominion, BBC NI was supposed to reflect Irish culture in general.[84] However, even a decade after the Second World War, there were few catholics employed in the Belfast station.[85] More overtly 'Irish' broadcasts were rare, although the BBC NI did broadcast occasionally from, for example, the Feis of St Colmcille in Derry.[86] As a reflection of the station's management of 'Irish' or catholic culture Sutthery pointed out the station's attitude to céilí bands in a memo to London in 1938: 'The ceilidh bands in existence in the Province are Catholic organisations made up of fiddles, piano, accordions, flute etc. and play for Catholic dances. We broadcast about 5 of these largely for policy reasons'.[87] Ten years later the whole issue of the céilí continued to irritate the unionist government who, without justification, saw in it a manifestation of catholic culture that was given too much attention by the BBC:

> The Prime Minister mentioned that he has impressed on Sir William
> Haley [the director general of the BBC] the fact that the great majority of

Northern Ireland people were not in sympathy with the ceilidhe type of programme, and that the undue prominence given to this kind of feature in local programmes was not justified.[88]

In fact, one reason why the 1940s witnessed an increase in 'Irish' music was the advent of the Second World War – as a result of the war, the Northern Ireland station's orchestra, which had supplied much of the station's classical and light musical output, was disbanded, and subsequently the station 'supplemented the national broadcasts of classical and light music by presenting traditional Irish music in the traditional manner with local combinations and solo artists': 'An Irish Rhythms Orchestra, flute bands, and ceilidhe bands have been featured in many programmes, and soft tones of the Uileann pipes – an instrument of great antiquity – reminded Irish music lovers of an art which is languishing.'[89] Unionists' objections to this type of broadcast were expressed by one correspondent to the prime minister, Basil Brooke, in February 1946: 'I think you will agree that, above all, we cannot allow any vestige of the Southern Ireland atmosphere having any suggestion of the Nationalists traditional music, to emanate from our Ulster Broadcasting Station'.[90] Unsurprisingly, in this atmosphere programmes in Gaelic were rarely broadcast by the BBC 'except for occasional Gaelic songs'; Marshall explained in one of his monthly reports that this was because Gaelic was not spoken in Northern Ireland.[91] The BBC NI series *Country Ceilidhe* is again illustrative of the problems 'Irish' culture caused. The series was broadcast from different locations throughout the state, and the programmes consisted of Irish dancing, singing and humour. The last programme in the series was broadcast in January 1947 from Derry. 'A very large crowd of dancers, singers, and Gaelic League enthusiasts took part', wrote Marshall:

> The programme went off satisfactorily despite information given to us by the police that the republican element were planning to make use of it to broadcast inflammatory party material. A number of police attended the performance and certain technical precautions were taken. The series of programmes has now come to an end, the BBC having carried out its plan as announced, despite the efforts of interested parties to control both the method and the material of the broadcasts.[92]

It is ironic that unionist critics at once objected to the predominance of 'Englishness' at the BBC in Belfast, and at the same time rejected programmes which dealt with local culture and which they perceived as representing southern Irish or catholic/nationalist culture. 'Local' culture was a sensitive area for the BBC in Northern Ireland because it was never clear when unionists might see 'local' as a cover for the 'Trojan horse for an Irish national culture'.[93] Local culture, when it did make it onto the airways, revealed the state as a diverse community containing elements of 'Irish' and catholic culture, among others, and exploded unionist attempts to present Northern Ireland as a homogenous protestant enclave.

In this context, Rex Cathcart has observed that for the catholic community in Northern Ireland, the BBC was the propagator of another culture, and appeared overly responsive to the wishes of unionism.[94] In terms of the broadcast of religious services, BBC NI, as early as 1930, was claiming that it tried to maintain a balance 'between the local and universal aspects of religion'.[95] St Patrick's day 1932 saw the first broadcast of a catholic service:

> The occasion was the Celebration of Pontifical High Mass at St Patrick's Roman Catholic Cathedral, Armagh, by His Eminence Cardinal MacRory in honour of the 1,500th anniversary of the Saint's arrival in the country, and the service was transmitted to America, via Dublin. The lifting of the ban on broadcasting in Northern Ireland on this occasion gave widespread satisfaction.[96]

This broadcast was followed in June by the broadcast of a service of commemoration in St Patrick's protestant cathedral in Armagh.[97] In 1945 the most notable religious events broadcast were the consecration of Dr W.S. Kerr as bishop of Down and Dromore and the funeral of Cardinal MacRory, the primate of all-Ireland.[98] The issue of the St Patrick's day broadcast was a recurring problem for the station, not because of religion *per se* but because of what the station represented as 'Irish' culture. This was the case in 1934 when the St Patrick's day programme 'Turf Smoke' 'gave rise to the largest volume of criticism during the year – both favourable and unfavourable'; 'Turf Smoke' 'consisted of music, poetry, songs and a spoken Epilogue and Prologue, and was designed to appeal to Irish men and women living away from their own country'.[99] Critics were either unhappy that the music used was too stage Irish, too representative of the Free State, too concentrated on Belfast industry, or devoid of genuine Belfast accents. Again referring to the lack of 'local' influence in the station, they argued that the staff of BBC NI was predominantly English or Scottish and could therefore not be 'expected to understand Irish feelings'.[100]

The issue of religion, in overt terms, died down as the station matured, or rather was manifested in terms of sport and drama. Sport was a regular broadcasting feature in Northern Ireland, in particular commentaries on the Ulster Grand Prix Motor-Cycle Race, and international rugby matches. During the war the presence of American troops in the state was marked by the broadcast of a baseball game: 'the first commentary in the Forces Programme on a baseball game between US army teams, and with broadcasts of American football'.[101] The Gaelic Athletic Association was, however, the cause of some controversy for the station. In May 1946, George Marshall wrote to the director general having received a request from the Ulster Council for the GAA asking for the same facilities granted to other sports bodies in Northern Ireland. Prior to the Second World War, GAA results had been broadcast by the BBC on Sundays, the major day for GAA fixtures, but Marshall pointed out that:

> As a result numerous complaints were received, to such an extent that the then Prime Minister, the late Lord Craigavon, intervened . . . it was decided to give up broadcasting such results on the grounds that they

were hurting the feelings of the large majority of people in Northern Ireland. Although there were certain protests when these were abandoned, they died down . . . You will appreciate that the Gaelic Athletic Association is entirely confined to the Nationalist party and obviously has a political flavour . . . On the other hand, things have moved on considerably during the last twenty years and I am inclined to think that, in fairness to the Nationalist sporting fraternity, we shall have to do something for them . . . there is almost certain to be a protest on the part of the Unionist party in Northern Ireland and that means practically the entire Protestant population who have always objected to Sunday sport.[102]

In a letter to the director general in May 1946 The Revd J.W. Welch (the BBC's religious advisor) advised head office about these sports bulletins: 'You ask about my opinion on the proposal of the Northern Irish director "leaving the political aspect entirely on one side" – but that is something which it is almost impossible to do in regard to Ulster'. As a solution to the problem Welch suggested broadcasting the results a day or two later, and continued:

> [results] which the BBC ought to give for the sake of its Nationalist and Roman Catholic listeners in the Northern Ireland Region. And, though I dare not rush in where angels fear to tread, I should have thought there was a certain value in showing our independence of the two contending parties in Northern Ireland, when we can do this without giving unnecessary offence to Christian feelings.[103]

This is eventually what was done. Equally, the BBC did not broadcast a commentary on the Twelfth of July parades. In May 1946 Marshall reported that he had been approached by the Orange Order; 'in past years', he wrote, 'I have always had the backing of the Prime Minister himself in this regard to our refusal to be associated with this political demonstration and I have no reason to alter my opinion as to its unsuitability. Quite apart from such considerations, the procession, as a programme feature, would be quite ineffective'.[104] While the station was not, therefore, a crude promoter of unionism and some attempts were made to represent the catholic community, equally it was not balanced in its representation of the communities in or the diversity of the state.

With the change-over to the regional scheme in the 1930s, and the subsequent expansion of local talks programmes, the problem for BBC NI became one of 'controversial' topics, which as we have already seen included sport, music, literature and the ever-present issue of religion. When the issue of politics was faced directly it was met with a predictable response. Henry McMullan suggested a series of talks, in October 1934, on 'the most famous man in each county of Ulster'; it was 'bound to be controversial', he felt, but 'of value to any listener interested in the history of Northern Ireland'. His letter concluded: 'These talks are still avoiding the questions of politics and religion. We have not yet found a satisfactory way of dealing with either of these matters owing, primarily, to the unwillingness of any speaker or body to co-operate in any scheme'.[105] The situation did not improve with time. George Marshall suggested a series of talks by 'prominent Ulstermen in London' in 1934. A rejection from the director of talks in London came at the end of December: 'I cannot see what prominent Ulstermen in London can have to say to Northern Ireland that could be of genuine interest to your listeners outside politics, which clearly would have to be avoided'.[106] Both the BBC in London and in Belfast were beginning to feel the boundaries of programme possibility in Northern Ireland. In a memo, in October 1936, the Northern Ireland programme director, J.T. Sutthery, outlined some projected programmes for the first quarter of 1937; under 'series talks' he proposed *How Ulster is Governed*. It was, he emphasised, 'entirely provisional' as the unionist government had not been consulted:

> Our idea is to present a series of eight talks showing what relation our Northern Ireland Parliament has to the Imperial Parliament, how we compare with a self-governing dominion or colony, and, in fact, to what extent we are autonomous. As you know, self-government in Northern Ireland is of a recent origin, and few people here know exactly to what extent we are independent, and there is, naturally, considerable pride in our dependence on and yet independence from London. (I hope you will understand this unintentional Irishism!)[107]

Within a fortnight Sutthery wrote again to London:

> This is to give you immediate notification that we have had to cancel our projected series 'How Northern Ireland Is Governed'. The reasons for this are of a political nature, and will be explained to you when next I am in Head Office. We have not yet thought of a series to take its place, but are still scratching our heads.[108]

A pattern had been initiated. In 1945, over a decade later, this same pattern was clearly visible in the controversy over the proposed series, *The Week in Stormont*, an issue which marked the pinnacle of the problem BBC NI faced in broadcasting political material. In September 1945 George Marshall proposed a series of talks to the prime minister entitled *The Week in Stormont*. The proposed speakers were backbenchers: 'invited to describe from their own point of view the work of the week in the House of Commons'.[109] The Northern Irish cabinet felt that the proposal 'did not commend itself' to them, for reasons which were explained to Marshall privately.[110] Marshall was clearly caught between two stools when he wrote to Brooke in November to say that the BBC's director general in London wished him to go ahead with the project.[111] In a memorandum responding to this new initiative Brooke invited his cabinet colleagues to suggest whether they should take 'further steps as may be practicable to press our objections on the BBC'. His memo continued:

> Not only do all the Opposition parties attack the Government on its legislative programme and its administrative acts, but the Nationalist members are aiming at the destruction of our constitution – a situation

for which there is no parallel in Great Britain. If the BBC proposal were adopted it would be a direct and powerful incentive to the development of a still more intensive 'anti-Partition' campaign inside the House – by means of motions and general debates – and this aspect of the proceedings of Parliament would be constantly exploited by the Nationalist members chosen to give the BBC talk.

In addition, Brooke feared that there might not be enough material for the series, and that 'in those weeks when comparatively minor matters were dealt with the radio talk would create the impression that our Parliament (as some of our opponents are constantly saying) is of little importance'.[112] Despite the prime minister's concerns, Marshall wrote to several Northern Irish MPs inviting them to take part in the series. Within days he received a reply, full of disapproval, from the cabinet secretary, Robert Gransden:

> Sir Basil expected to have the opportunity of discussing the introduction of this feature further with you . . . and while he recognises that no discourtesy was intended, he is surprised that steps were taken to approach individual backbenchers before any intimation was conveyed to him that the BBC had decided to proceed with the project.[113]

At the end of January Marshall notified Brooke that:

> Owing to the fact that very few members have expressed their willingness to co-operate in our proposed broadcast series of reports on the deliberations of the House of Commons in Northern Ireland, we are reluctantly compelled to abandon the scheme.[114]

It was a predictable end to the story, and confirms that the Northern Irish government presumed a power to influence what was broadcast in the state. In this case when the BBC did not comply with its wishes the government exerted pressure on the potential participants not to take part, and in this way sabotaged the programme.

Inevitably, the advent of the Second World War altered the circumstances of broadcasting in the state. The war years were not unproblematic for unionists, with the conscription crisis in particular complicating Northern Ireland's war-time experience. In September 1939 Craigavon notified the Northern Irish House of Commons that the Belfast station was being curtailed due to the war, but he assured his colleagues that Northern Ireland would still receive broadcasts from the regional stations in Scotland and the North of England and would through them get 'the fullest information that [was] handed to them by the various Government departments'.[115] The war made the public more seriously minded, and in terms of broadcasting the public's appetite for news broadcasts in Britain became 'insatiable'.[116] Reflecting this trend, in 1943, George Marshall pushed strongly for a weekly news bulletin from Northern Ireland: 'I feel', he wrote to the director general, 'that the claims of Northern Ireland, which has a separate Government and distinct problems of its own, should be considered quite apart from the other Regions'.[117] In a letter to the prime minister, Brian Maginess made the argument for a separate news service:

> Such a service . . . would in addition keep Northern Ireland before the public and would bring home to others in Great Britain what apparently the majority fail to understand, that is, that Northern Ireland is an integral part of the United Kingdom . . . that we are playing our part in the war and that we are not part of Éire.[118]

Belfast got its weekly service; and, as a means of monitoring their early newscasts, typescripts of bulletins were sent to London. On 27 May the main item of news was the docking in Belfast of the liner *Grisholm*, which was carrying British, Canadian and American repatriated prisoners of war. Another item concerned the Northern Irish exchequer:

> In the first ten years of the life of the Northern Ireland Parliament, the Province has contributed more to the British Empire's purse than the whole of Ireland from the day of the Union to the day the Ulster Parliament was established. Actually the whole of Ireland between 1817 and 1914 had contributed to the British Exchequer £25,000,000. In one year Ulster had contributed £35,000,000.

News for the 10 June 1944 covered the Normandy landings and the three-hundredth anniversary of the First Presbyterian Church in Rosemary Street in Belfast, while the news for 17 June was the announcement that the anniversary of the Battle of the Somme, 'in which the Ulster Division earned undying fame', would be observed on 1 July.[119] News broadcasts from Belfast continued to be carefully monitored by the station management itself; in 1949 the Belfast director Andrew Stewart warned staff that the news 'should report fairly upon happenings and affairs in or affecting Northern Ireland, giving due weight to matters of importance and real interest, avoiding the irresponsible and the merely sensational in presenting a balanced day-to-day summary.'[120]

Broadcasts were also made by the three Northern Irish prime ministers (Craigavon, Andrews and Brooke) throughout the war years. According to the *BBC Yearbook 1945* these were 'momentous contributions to broadcasting'. Craig in his broadcast pledged 'the resources of Ulster in the war effort' in February 1940; Andrews spoke on the occasion of the twentieth anniversary of the opening of the Northern Ireland parliament in June 1941; and Basil Brooke in January 1944, 'in a stirring Sunday evening postscript', gave a word picture of the part played by Ulstermen in the evolution of the two great democracies east and west of Northern Ireland'.[121] The changes brought about in the state by the war were also reflected by the station; for instance, the arrival of American troops in Northern Ireland in January 1943 was marked by the broadcast of special programmes involving American servicemen such as 'Billy Welcome's Day with the Doughboys' and 'Ack-Ack, Beer-Beer'. In addition the American troops broadcast military band concerts and camp concerts.[122] Other programmes dealt with that traditional unionist interest when dealing with America and Northern Ireland – 'American Presidents of Ulster descent'.[123] In 1946 the American connection was still being highlighted in BBC programmes such as that by historian W.F. Marshall 'on the great emigration from Northern Ireland to America in the eighteenth century, and the part that it played in the shaping of the United States of America'.[124] In 1945 the US services – army, navy and airforce – began to leave Northern Ireland and the BBC was there to mark their departure:

> The final link to be severed was the handing over of the last United States air station in the Province at Langford Lodge. The ceremony, attended by prominent American Generals and the Northern Ireland Prime Minister and members of the Cabinet, was broadcast from the American Red Cross Club in Belfast.[125]

In addition, state visits from the 'famous military war leaders General Eisenhower, Field-Marshal Sir Bernard Montgomery, Field-Marshal Lord Alanbrooke, and Field-Marshal Sir Harold Alexander' were broadcast by the station.[126]

In an interview with Rex Cathcart, Ursula Eason, the production director in Belfast, lamented the fact that during the war years Belfast had produced so few programmes for the home service: 'We just followed the news, read the monitoring reports and tried to keep in touch. I felt terribly sorry that people in Northern Ireland couldn't be reflected in any kind of way.'[127] Eason complained that 'people across the water in Britain simply did not know Northern Ireland, unlike Southern Ireland which they knew was neutral'.[128] 'We have concentrated mainly', wrote Eason to head office, 'on giving items representative of the music and culture of this Region only, and have not been able to contribute, except occasionally, to programmes of a non-local flavour.'[129] This was to remain the pattern throughout the war. War-time programmes dealt with the effects of the war on the people of Northern Ireland generally. It was the 'cult of the ordinary' according to Scannell and Cardiff; '"To-day in Ulster" reflected many war time activities such as the workshops for the blind, the blood transfusion services, nursery schools, welfare and evacuation centres. Speakers included the Duchess of Abercorn and W.B. Maginess, parliamentary secretary to the Northern Ireland Ministry of Agriculture'.[130] One of the most prominent war-time series was *Ulster's Half-Hour*, 'designed to reflect the cultural life and character of the people of Northern Ireland in wartime', which Basil Brooke inaugurated as follows in July 1943:

> The land of Ulster has known a rich history, and the people of Ulster enjoy a varied ancestry. Whether the producer looks at the battle-scarred walls of Derry, or the loveliness of Armagh, the ancient capital, or the old earthen boundary wall by the slopes of Slieve Gullion, known as the Black Pig's Dyke, he will find much to stir his imagination. And when he speaks to a farmer, an agricultural labourer, a factory girl, a shipyard worker, or a city businessman, he may find himself in touch with a descendant of the Presbyterian Scots who came as colonists in the seventeenth century, or the Huguenots who sought refuge from persecution and brought their knowledge of linen weaving to the Lagan Valley, or of

the sturdy, independent Northern clans who gave to the country many of her High Kings.[131]

War had altered the 'face of the country', but Brooke maintained that 'the spirit of resolution and friendliness' that characterised Northern Irish men and women remained unaltered.[132] Oscar Henderson was less complimentary about the programme: 'My heaven, if you only broadcast the speeches made in this House they would be a far greater asset to the Province than the *Ulster Half-Hour*, and the people would get a great deal more amusement.'[133] BBC NI's other war-time features included a twelve-year-old boy's experience of being an evacuee from Belfast, and a programme by Denis Ireland, *The Six Counties at War*, which highlighted war work in the state.[134] Further programmes focused on the celebration of Christmas in war time and eye-witness accounts of the Belfast blitz.[135]

Reflecting the increasing participation of women in war work and agriculture in this period, several programmes dealt on the one hand with the changing role of women in Northern Ireland, and on the other the transformation of their more traditional roles.[136] Programmes included *In and Out of Uniform: Talks about the wartime lives of Northern Ireland women*, *'My Wife's got a job': running a home in wartime*, *'Women Can't Do It': A talk by a worker in a Northern Ireland aircraft factory proving they can do it*, and *The Kitchen Front: A Northern Irish Housewife*.[137] Towards the end of the war one of the most controversial broadcasts was *Women's Page: Women on the Land in Ulster*, broadcast in January 1945. The title is self-explanatory, and the broadcast by Jeanne Cooper Foster dealt broadly with the position of women in rural Northern Ireland. The feature became the subject of questions in the Northern Irish House of Commons. It was 'a scurrilous broadcast' according to one MP, who then went on to demand that the government prevent the BBC from broadcasting such programmes, and 'secure for Northern Ireland the right to present to the peoples of Great Britain and the world the true conditions of the most loyal people on God's earth'.[138] The unionist press had, inaccurately according to Jeanne Cooper Foster, publicised her script as representing Northern Irish rural women as part of the farming stock. Hugh Minford said that the programme had portrayed farmers' wives and daughters as 'badly educated, badly clothed', and denied the freedom to choose their own husbands. 'Is the BBC', asked Minford, 'to open its doors to Fifth Columnists and Quislings to broadcast in such terms about the people of Ulster?'[139] George Marshall reporting on the controversy noted that the feature had been 'certainly of a challenging nature and resented by the Farmers' Union and Young Farmers' Clubs', the programme had urged women in Northern Ireland 'to be more independent and take a greater share in rural affairs and a fuller place in society'. Marshall was 'convinced that there was a great deal of truth' in the feature, and observed that what troubled the critics was 'the fact that the talk was broadcast across the water and thus might cause people in England to think that the Ulster farming community was somewhat primitive'.[140] It is ironic that while in this debate what the critics objected to was the dominance of

English culture at the BBC, it was ultimately British opinion of Northern Ireland which caused such concern.

The majority of war-time programmes produced by the Northern Irish station were for the domestic audience; few programmes made it onto the overseas or home services. At the bottom of Ursula Eason's report on the programmes produced in the early part of the war is a pencilled note which reads: 'I must say that, considering the limitations (cultural and mechanical) of the region, it has done pretty well.'[141] This did not mean that Eason did not try to get more Northern Irish-produced programmes onto the national airwaves. In a letter to the director of the features department, in September 1940, she proposed a feature on Edward Carson called *These Men Were Free*:

> 'Trouble' need not be anticipated. Any objections – so far as Ireland is concerned – would come from a small body of irresponsible people whose opinion is worthless and who are, in any case avowed enemies of England, so they don't matter in the least. The whole loyal population of the six counties would more than welcome a Carson feature, and paradoxically though it may seem, in Éire he is recognised and admired as a great man – he was of course a Southern Irishman – and in a queer way they are proud of him, although they may not agree with his ideals. Moreover he took up arms against Great Britain which in itself is always something . . . It would be hard to exaggerate the importance of such a feature in Northern Ireland.[142]

In further correspondence with Laurence Gilliam, the director of features, Eason proposed a second programme on Wolfe Tone:

> The fact that Carson lived more recently than Wolfe Tone makes little difference in this country where people's memories are long and where, in Northern Ireland at any rate, political feeling still hinges on the Battle of the Boyne in 1688 [*sic*]. We urge most strongly that Ireland, being in a peculiar position at the moment, should have two programmes, presenting both sides – i.e. one on Wolfe Tone and one on Carson . . . the fact that we are willing to present both sides would probably have a very forcible effect here at the moment.[143]

Eason's attitude reflected the British government's early war-time policy of maintaining good relations with Éire, a policy backed by the BBC in London. In the early years of the war the British government had no wish to alienate southern Ireland in the hope that the government there would rethink its position of neutrality. This policy was reinforced by the BBC's home service where programmes were specifically produced for southern Irish listeners and a conciliatory tone was adopted. On the question of partition, for instance, the BBC was directed by the Ministry of Information to ignore the topic entirely, or if forced to mention it, say that it was a problem for the Irish people to settle themselves.[144] However, the unionist government wanted no coverage of Éire that did not make clear that its position of neutrality was one to be criticised and disapproved of. In a letter from the Northern Irish prime minister, John Andrews, to George Marshall, this was made clear: 'I feel that the policy which the Ministry now seems to be adopting will be taken as weakness and to mean that Britain recognises that Éire is justified in maintaining her policy of independence and of opposition to the British Empire.'[145] In some programmes, the BBC attempted to target men and women from the south who were serving in the Allied forces. In a letter to the unionist government's publicity officer F.R. Adams, the Northern Irish information officer in London, explained this policy: 'The object of the broadcasts will be to interest "Ireland", North and South, and Irishmen everywhere, in the war effort by telling them, and the rest of the world, what Irishmen are doing for Britain in the fighting forces and other directions.'[146] This policy was received badly by the unionist government. Writing to the director general, Ogilvie, the prime minister complained that the policy 'would be an insidious form of propaganda which would entirely misrepresent the position of Northern Ireland in the United Kingdom and would slur over the neutral and most unhelpful attitude which Éire has taken up during the war'.[147] In a handwritten note at the end of this letter he suggested that Éire be left 'to plough her lonely furrow'. The policy remained, and Ogilvie wrote to Andrews in August 1941:

> You as; in your letter: 'Why not leave Éire to plough her lone furrow?'.
> We had long felt, however, that we ought to concern ourselves, not so
> much with Éire, as with those loyal men and women, tens of thousands
> of them apparently, who, leaving Éire, have joined His Majesty's forces
> here and elsewhere in the Empire and have thrown in their lot – plough-
> teams, lives and all – with our common cause.[148]

In general, George Marshall was concerned that nothing which offended the unionist government or community should be broadcast by the BBC in Northern Ireland, or on any of the corporation's services (home service, forces, or overseas). This applied equally to the drama department; in an effort to dictate the nature of the 'Irish' programmes produced, Broadcasting House in Belfast wanted Northern Ireland to be the sole region which produced them. In a letter from Eason to the director of the features department she complained about southern Irish plays being produced by the BBC in London and Manchester, feeling they should be done in Belfast and implying that BBC NI would do a better job:

> We do not want to suggest that we should do every Southern Irish
> production, as we are fully aware that our job here is principally to
> reflect Northern Ireland, but we very much hope that we may at least be
> given the opportunity of producing Southern Irish plays when they are
> suggested for the schedule.

She received a very terse reply from Val Gielgud, the director of features: 'You must not think that I am unreasonably arrogant if I retain what I conceive to be my right to prefer my own opinion as to what is or is not a good radio play, even though there may be different opinions.'[149] This again acts as a reminder of the ever-present spectre of 'local culture' for unionists. As early as 1930 the BBC was claiming that 'Ulster' had 'a drama of its own', but although the station presented some seventy plays a year, 'good quality' regional Northern Irish plays for radio were slow to develop.[150] BBC NI was more active in broadcasting other aspects of Northern Irish literature, particularly prose. Drawing on a range of authors, these broadcasts illustrated the diversity inherent within Northern Ireland culture. George Marshall wrote to the talks department in December 1935 of a proposed programme of talks to be called *Ulster Writers*. This programme of 'living authors connected with Ulster' was to include Robert Lynd, Helen Waddell (both of whom were anti-Unionist), as well as St John Ervine and C.K. Munro.[151] The programme was clearly a success; in February 1936 further correspondence drew attention to *Ulster Writers II*, the new series, which included Forrest Reid and Moira O'Neill, as well as Richard Rowley, Lynn Doyle, Canon Hannay (George A. Birmingham) and Denis Johnston.[152] As with the prose selection, George Marshall believed that the production of drama in the Northern Irish station should be limited to 'Ulster plays or plays with a definitely Irish significance'. 'For this reason', he wrote in 1935, 'we thought it proper to perform "She Stoops to Conquer"'.[153] The range of authors broadcast covered a selection from Northern Ireland, particularly George Shiels and St John Ervine;[154] but others who recurred who did not all possess Northern Irish credentials, and thus complicated the relationship between 'local' and 'Irish' culture, included Yeats, Lady Gregory, J.M. Synge, Frank O'Connor, Lennox Robinson and Oscar Wilde. The provisional arrangements for drama in Northern Ireland in the second quarter of 1937, for instance, included Yeats's *The Land of Hearts Desire*, Lady Gregory's *The Workhouse Ward* and *The Rising of the Moon*, George Shiels's *Insurance Money*, *The Pigeon* by Ian Priestly-Mitchell, *The Half-Door* by F.K. Fahy and *The Wedding* by Thomas Carnduff.[155] It was also the station's policy to present 'an occasional Shakespearean play'.[156] Throughout the war years, with the Belfast station largely limited to a domestic audience, the drive to broadcast plays of an identifiably 'Ulster' character on the home service intensified. Ursula Eason, writing to head office in October 1940, lamented that 'no play really representative of Northern Ireland has been included since the beginning of the war . . . We hope that it may be possible in the future to include plays by well known Northern Irish dramatists such as George Shiels.'[157] Her proposals often fell on deaf ears; in a letter in October 1941 she suggested St John Ervine's *John Ferguson*: 'it is a tragedy', she continued, 'and is very Ulster in atmosphere without being too dialect'. Handwritten notes on her letter from the director of the features department and the assistant director of drama read: 'Not wanted. Too gloomy', and 'I don't think this play makes "entertainment" in these times.'[158]

In the light of the British government's early war-time policy towards Éire, what the BBC in London wanted in terms of drama were southern Irish plays such as *Juno and the Paycock* – as a series of letters which streamed to Eason requesting it make clear; her letters in return suggested Lennox Robinson's *A Drama at Inish*, and works by George Shiels and James Stephens.[159] In May 1941 she suggested *Experiences of an Irish RM* as the

Irish serial play to head office:

> Living in Ireland, we are perfectly aware that a programme of this kind is
> not going to influence in any way the small party which might object to
> this book on the grounds of its being written by a Somerville, but it is a
> popular book amongst the Irish generally and a broadcast might achieve
> some purpose by pleasing the general body of Irish people and those who
> have not very strong political views. We do not, I imagine, hope to
> convert the fanatics by these programmes addressed to Éire listeners,
> but only to encourage waverers.

Eason's equation of fanaticism with holders of strong political views in Éire
is interesting, though not surprising in the context of the war. A pencilled
note at the end of this letter, author unknown, reads: 'We feel that the Irish
RM is too "county" and too Southern Loyalist to attract the Irish man-in-
the-street'. The *Irish RM* was dropped as the Irish serial play.[160] Denis
Johnston, the playwright and BBC producer, took up the campaign in June:

> Further to our previous correspondence on this subject, I wonder have
> you considered Frank O'Connor's novel 'The Saint and Mary Kate' or
> Peadar O'Donnell's 'Adrigoole'. It seems to me that to avoid the Anglo-
> Irish objection it would be necessary to consider some of the entirely
> modern authors, and these are probably the best known.[161]

Again, in 1941, Eason complained that the BBC had not broadcast 'a
genuine Ulster play' since the beginning of the war: 'from a policy as well as
any other point of view, I feel this is rather a serious omission'.[162] In an
interesting and revealing aside, Eason wrote to the assistant director of
drama with reference to St John Ervine's play *Boyd's Shop*:

> There is not any fear of offending Catholic opinion in Ireland, but last
> time it was broadcast a few Presbyterians were offended by the character
> of the young clergyman. I do not think, however, that we need worry
> about this and will do our best to soften anything that might be offensive
> in the adaptation.[163]

Once the war was over the BBC NI played a part in the retrospective
assessment of Northern Ireland's role in it with programmes such as George
Nash's series *Ulster at War* – 'a kind of stock-taking of the Province's valuable contributions to the Allied cause during the war' which focused on 'the
activities of the people in many other fields of production: the making of
munitions, ropes, textiles, the building of aircraft, the growing of food and
other efforts'.[164] Other war-time assessment programmes included *The
Fighting Men of Ulster* which dealt with 'four famous Irish regiments' and in
which 'many valiant episodes in war were dramatized in a rousing feature
programme', and the story of Northern Ireland's ports in wartime, *Atlantic
Bridgehead* by Denis Johnson, broadcast in 1945.[165]

Following the war unionist concerns centred on Éire and the anti-partition agitation which began to gain momentum. George Marshall's reports
reflect this growing political tension, referring, for example, to unionist

concerns about Éire propaganda concerning the 'abolition of the Border', particularly in America.[166] Nationalist politicians in Northern Ireland had decided to abandon their previous policy of abstention from parliament, their decision influenced by the election of the Attlee government, which they believed would be more sympathetic to their grievances.[167] The election of this government in July 1945 exacerbated unionist insecurity. Although labour had no definite policy to rescind partition, many within the party were anti-partition supporters. In the midst of this post-war anxiety Basil Brooke told a unionist meeting that 'he would like to have the Northern Ireland station of the BBC operating under the control of the Ulster Government'.[168] At an anti-partition rally in Glasgow one Northern Irish nationalist MP made 'a slashing attack on the BBC, which he claimed was entirely subservient to the Unionist Party and excluded all items of Gaelic or Irish interest from the news'.[169] Reporting in January 1947, Marshall painted a picture of the station as caught between these two political camps:

> *BBC and Political Bias*: The Belfast Unionist press gave considerable publicity to the report of the Conservative Central Office on the subject of broadcast talks and one newspaper printed a lengthy paragraph from their London correspondent, which was naturally weighted against the BBC and the Socialist Government. Our own reply was also published in full, together with the comment of the Conservative Central Office. 'The Irish News' (Nationalist Party Organ) had a leader on the subject, condemning the BBC in Northern Ireland for supporting the local Government in the programmes, news, etc.[170]

War-time broadcasting had 'had its own peculiar problems' he argued in the *BBC Yearbook 1945*:

> Geographically detached and separately governed, Northern Ireland has been subject to particular restrictions which tended to increase the inevitable limitations of broadcasting from the Regions in wartime. The position created widened the possibilities of programme building with local talent.[171]

With the war over, a period of assessment was appropriate. The BBC *Yearbook 1947* summarised the Northern Irish state:

> It is, in comparison with its opposite numbers on the other side of the Irish Sea, small in extent and in population. It contains only one large group of people living in an industrial city, the remainder being spread out over the six counties and mainly engaged in agriculture. It has its political problems, its own problems, its own Parliament, its own standards, and the Irish Sea, like every other main water barrier, tends to encourage a sturdy independence of thought and development.[172]

The BBC came back to life slowly in Belfast after the war. As already outlined, war-time isolation encouraged the Northern Irish to rely increasingly on their own resources for entertainment. Moreover, the presence of so many outsiders in the state during the war had forced them to place a greater emphasis on, and gain a greater awareness of, their own identity. This was reflected post-war in the increasingly regionalist ethos at the station.

Following the war, the BBC divided its channels into light, home and third, recognising that its audience was stratified and that it was no longer feasible to provide a unified national service.[173] There was also a drive by BBC NI to recruit more local people, a move which drew in creative writers such as Sam Hanna Bell and John Hewitt.[174] For some producers, the new atmosphere was limited to providing British listeners with an image of Northern Ireland which would improve tourist potential.[175] Nevertheless, the influx of locals did bring the station closer to the indigenous population. Local music and the arts were given a platform in series such as *In Ulster Now*, while *Writing in Ulster* provided a forum for the work of Northern Irish writers.[176] Andrew Stewart, who replaced George Marshall in 1948, backed this regionalist drive, encouraging producers to concentrate on Northern Ireland and to 'cultivate their own gardens'.[177] Stewart had a positive outlook in terms of what he thought the station could achieve; in a publication to mark the twenty-fifth anniversary of the BBC in Northern Ireland he wrote:

> If a community is in decay, its broadcasting will be moribund. In Northern Ireland we are far from that; with an energetic, industrious, cheerful, singing people and a hard working and devoted staff and the criticism and encouragement of the Advisory Council and committees, the BBC has idiosyncratic and splendid resources for the years to come.[178]

However, although Stewart was positively biased towards material from Northern Ireland he was cautioned ominously by the BBC's director general that Northern Ireland, was the only region of the BBC in which, out of exasperation from broadcasting, people might kill each other.[179] Not surprisingly this led to a cautious attitude within the station; in his 1948 report George Barnes wrote that while the BBC in Belfast was 'constitutionally more independent' than it was in London 'its fear of making a mistake, where the consequence is a fighting matter' prevented it from 'using the microphone as widely as in London or other regions'.[180] Stewart, therefore, was careful not to venture beyond the bounds of public, or governmental, acceptability; programmes such as one broadcast from Derry, which drew together a mixture of people (catholics and protestants) to discuss their economic and social problems, had all references to partition censored out.[181] The BBC in Northern Ireland continued to be concerned about its role in the state and in maintaining the niche in the establishment which it had negotiated for itself. Following the war the station developed a policy of conciliation within the community, 'the programme policy consequently accentuated what bound the communities together and neglected or ignored that which drove them apart'.[182]

During the 1950s and 1960s then successive controllers in Belfast 'pursued a consistent policy of reducing the constraints on broadcasting which they had inherited'.[183] More dramatic changes in the station took effect in the 1960s, changes largely associated with the introduction of television to the state in the late 1950s. As Rex Cathcart has argued, radio in the United Kingdom was gradually eclipsed by television in the period 1953–66.[184] With the influx of television programmes from England and the development of outside broadcasting in the state, Northern Ireland was being opened up to public scrutiny, both domestic and foreign. As a result, for instance, the first programme to discuss discrimination in the workplace was broadcast on 1962. Despite the increasing influence of television, however, the Northern Irish remained loyal to radio. This was for a number of reasons: television by comparison was expensive, and few could afford it, but in addition news and local broadcasts on television were scarce or at best brief. Television therefore lacked the local flavour which radio retained, and as a result BBC NI's home service and regional news remained prime listening for Northern Irish audiences. The BBC in Northern Ireland went through distinct phases; pre-war ignoring the nature of the state, post-war becoming more regionalist and adopting aspects of local culture which controllers felt would not offend unionist sensibilities, aspects which would highlight only the positive features of the state and underplay the negative or contentious. But the political developments of the 1960s in Northern Ireland (most prominently the civil rights disputes) over-ran BBC policy and forced broadcasters to reflect Northern Ireland as it was, warts and all.[185]

Notes and References

1   'These fellow-readers, to whom they were connected through print, formed in their secular, particular, visible invisibility, the embryo of the nationally-imagined community', Benedict Anderson, *Imagined Communities: reflections on the origin and spread of nationalism* (London, 1983), p. 47. In the context of this chapter, one could replace radio for print and fellow-listeners for fellow-readers.

2   David Cardiff and Paddy Scannell, 'Broadcasting and national unity', in James Curran, Anthony Smith and Pauline Wingate (eds.), *Impacts and influences: essays on media power in the twentieth century* (London, 1987), p. 157.

3   Paddy Scannell and David Cardiff, *A social history of British broadcasting: serving the nation, 1922–39*, vol. i (Oxford, 1991), p. 13.

4   Cited in ibid., p.10.

5   The Northern Irish entry for the *BBC Yearbook 1942* reflects this effort: 'From the results of their endeavour and of that of their staff, listeners to Regional broadcasts receive an impression of vigorous and many-sided activity, now very much enhanced in value to listeners here and in the Empire as an expression of the unity of the mother-country', *BBC Yearbook 1942*.

6   David Cardiff and Paddy Scannell, 'Broadcasting and national unity', p. 166.

7   Gerald Beadle, BBC NI's second director wrote that the 'fundamental unity of the English' was a 'great blessing and something they do not always appreciate as much as they should'. Gerald Beadle, *Television: a critical review* (London, 1963). But English unity was as much a construct as Northern Irish.

8   B. Waites, Tony Bennett, Graham Martin (eds.), *Popular culture: past and present* (London, 1982), p. 18.

9   Rex Cathcart says in the blurb for *The most contrary region: the BBC in Northern Ireland, 1924–84* (Belfast, 1984) that he wants to explore 'the way in which the BBC founded and developed in a society which enjoyed a large degree of political and social consensus, has coped with a profoundly divided society'.

Britain did not have that large degree of political and social consensus which Cathcart speaks of (in particular during this period ideas of the empire and the British nation were unstable), and while Northern Ireland was more diverse than the establishment wished to admit, it also had a degree of unity which has to be acknowledged.

10   Diary of Ruby Hewitt (hereafter RH), 16 May 1949.

11   The BBC Northern Ireland sound archive is housed in the Ulster Folk and Transport Museum, Cultra, Hollywood, Co. Down. Its holdings are more extensive for the 1960s and beyond. In a limited number of cases earlier recordings do survive, but they are predominantly of royal visits. The BBC's WAC also holds some extant Northern Irish scripts.

12   David Cardiff and Paddy Scannell, 'Broadcasting and national unity', p. 169.

13   Principally, George Marshall is portrayed in this way by Rex Cathcart's seminal work on the BBC in Northern Ireland, *The most contrary region: the BBC in Northern Ireland, 1924–84* (Belfast, 1984). Cathcart's work, which is largely a history of the corporation, contributes to the other literature on the BBC in Britain: Asa Briggs's five-volume institutional history of the BBC, *The history of broadcasting in the United Kingdom*, vols. i–v (Oxford, 1961–95), and Paddy Scannell and David Cardiff's first volume of *A social history of British broadcasting: serving the nation, 1922–1939*. Cathcart's assessment of Marshall's overt unionist bias is repeated, with no rethinking, in Scannell and Cardiff's *A social history of British broadcasting*.

14   Gerald Beadle, *Television: a critical review*, p. 23.

15   Paddy Scannell and David Cardiff, *A social history of British broadcasting*, p. 311.

16   George Beadle's report to John Reith, cited in Rex Cathcart, 'The BBC in Northern Ireland: 50 years old', *Listener*, vol. 92, no. 2372, 12 Sept. 1974.

17   Board of Governor's Meeting, 2 Dec. 1943, R1/1/16.

18   When he resigned in 1938 one newspaper described Reith as 'safe, responsible, reliable, the guarantor of the nation's cultural capital', Paddy Scannell and David Cardiff, *A social history of British broadcasting*, p. 17.

19   Typescript of the governor of Northern Ireland's opening speech, CAB 9F/165/1/1.

20   'The self-censorship', wrote George Barnes in his visit to the state in 1948, 'which a negative policy has engendered in the staff is increased by the absence of audience response'. He observed that the absence of listener research in Northern Ireland left the BBC in Belfast vulnerable to criticism from all quarters, G.R. Barnes 'My visit to Northern Ireland', 10/11 Nov. 1948, R34/731/4.

21   Gerald Beadle, *Television: a critical review*, p. 29.

22   George Marshall, *Times*, 14 Aug. 1934.

23   *BBC Yearbook 1930*.

24   *BT*, 24 Nov. 1943, P599.

25   Edna Longley, 'John Hewitt, 1907–87', *Fortnight*, Sept. 1987, p. 22.

26   J.T. Sutthery to BBC head office, Jan. 1935, R34/492/1.

27   George Marshall to BBC head office, 26 Nov. 1935, R34/492/1.

28   Interestingly, Andrew Gailey has argued in relation to Edward Carson that his accent was an asset: 'In a period when élite accents were increasingly anglicised, his brogue gave added appeal to his denunciations of English sophisticates and their velvet tongues', Andrew Gailey, 'King Carson: an essay on the invention of leadership', *IHS*, vol. xxx, no. 117 (May 1996), p. 72.

29   This report from Marshall concluded: 'One speaker compared the interior of Broadcasting House in Belfast to Palestine, but whether this was because of its sanctity or the fact that one member of staff is of the Jewish race, I have not been able to discover'. MR, Northern Ireland Region, Feb., 1945, R34/748/1.

30   *Northern Hansard*, vol. xxvii, 25 Jan. 1945.

31   ibid., 6 Feb. 1945.

32   ibid.

33   *BBC Yearbook 1948*.

34   John Sayers to John Andrews, 23 Dec. 1941, CAB 9F/165/2.

35   CAB 9F/165/1/1. In 1956, the Northern Ireland Tourist Board's general manager, R.J. Frizzell wrote to Robert Gransden about a BBC programme on the An Tostal festival in the Irish republic: 'What we have come to resent is what appears to be a special preference shown by BBC producers, directors, and feature programme directors for events occurring in the twenty-six counties. If they had the same interest and took the same trouble in equally attractive events up here there would be no reason for criticism, apart from the qualified opinion that they might show greater interest in events in the United Kingdom and in this part of Ireland', R.J. Frizzell to Robert Gransden, 18 May 1956, CAB 9F/165/2.

36   W.P. Henry to Charles Blackmore, 24 Apr. 1923, CAB 9F/165/1/1.

37   The BBC's charter, drawn up in 1926, forbade 'controversial broadcasting and editorial news'. Paddy Scannell and David Cardiff, 'Serving the nation: public service broadcasting before the war', in Waites, Bennett, and Martin (eds.), *Popular culture: past and present*, pp. 162–4.

38   James Curran and Jean Seaton (eds.), *Power without responsibility: the press and broadcasting in Britain* (St Ives, 1991), p. 145.

39   'Where the boundaries of accepted thought are crossed, there you will not find the BBC; where there is dissidence or protest, there you will not find the BBC; where there is irreverence or resistance to cant, there you will not find the BBC', Henry Fairlie, 'The BBC', in Hugh Thomas (ed.), *The establishment: a symposium* (London, 1959), p. 193, p. 205. Fairlie was a journalist with the *Daily Mail*.

40   Curran and Seaton, *Power without responsibility*, p. 149. 'Governments claim the right to define the national interest and expect the broadcasters, particularly in a crisis, to uphold their definition of it. To defend the public interest may mean challenging the government of the day – a risky enterprise for institutions that derive their authority to broadcast from the state', Scannell and Cardiff, *A social history of British broadcasting*, p. 10.

41   Curran and Seaton, *Power without responsibility*, p. 174.

42   MR, Northern Ireland Region, Apr. 1944, R34/748/1. George Marshall, and later Andrew Stewart, in common with other regional directors, submitted monthly reports to the board of governors on their own stations. Marshall's in particular are valuable reflections of the political developments in the state, although ironically he claimed that politics 'had no part' in his reports, MR, Northern Ireland Region, Jan. 1944, R34/748/1.

43   MR, Northern Ireland Region, Apr. 1944, R34/748/1.

44   The advisory council was established in 1946; its members were drawn from the professional middle classes. Initially of the twenty members of the council, only three were nationalists, which Marshall thought 'the right proportion'. Marshall's concern about the committee was that it was 'a bit on the young side'. In October 1946 it included a member of the Young Farmers' Club, an independent MP, a town clerk, a trade union secretary. a journalist, an architect, the daughter of the bishop of Down and Dromore, a unionist MP, the wife of a judge, the principal of a primary school, a barrister, a professor of Greek, the chairman of a company, a housewife and a church organist. The exception on the list was Samuel Megraw, shipyard plater, 'intelligent and representative man from the working classes. Candidate for local Parliament in Unionist interests'. Special meeting of regional directors, board meeting, 2 Oct. 1946, R1/1/14.

45   Andrew Stewart to the director of home broadcasting (Lindsay Wellington), 9 Feb. 1949, R6/64.
46   Andrew Stewart to the director general, nd, R34/556.
47   Report of the meeting of Andrew Stewart with Basil Brooke and the minister of finance, 19 Aug. 1948, CAB 9F/165/1/1.
48   Andrew Stewart to the director of home broadcasting, 14 July 1948. Stewart was merely voicing a concern, and he cited the director general's directive of 9 Oct. 1947: 'This raises special problems in Northern Ireland, in that the matter here is coloured by religious bitterness. The possibility of political and religious differences ending in violence is also an added responsibility . . . This does not mean that our policy must be static. Public opinion does change, and the BBC is doing today in Northern Ireland without protest things which it could not have done ten years ago. We must hope that the next ten years will see similar progress', R51/356/4.
49   This was also the case in Britain. See David Cardiff and Paddy Scannell, 'Broadcasting and national unity', p. 159.
50   George Marshall to the assistant controller (Lindsay Wellington), 14 Jan. 1938, R51/416.
51   Assistant controller to George Marshall, 19 Jan. 1938, R51/416.
52   Report of interview between Andrew Stewart and Sir Basil Brooke, 4 Jan. 1949, R34/556.
53   Publicity officer, BBC NI, 25 Jan. 1949, R34/556.
54   Andrew Stewart to the director of BBC South West, 24 Oct. 1952, R34/556.
55   Harman Grisewood to the assistant director general, 29 Oct. 1952, R34/556.
56   R.D. Marriott, controller BBC NI, to the director of BBC South West, 25 Aug. 1953, and 9 Sept. 1953, R34/556.
57   R.D. Marriott to the director of BBC South West, 25 Sept. 1953, R34/556.
58   BBC Yearbook 1932.
59   Jonathan Bardon, A history of Ulster, p. 529.
60   Kenneth.O. Morgan, The Oxford history of Britain (Oxford, 1993), p. 609.
61   Bill Rolston, An oral history of Belfast in the nineteen thirties (Belfast, 1987), p. 19.
62   Cabinet Minutes, CAB 4/304/21.
63   Bill Rolston, An oral history of Belfast in the nineteen thirties, p. 24.
64   Production director (BBC NI) to the director of talks, 19 Mar. 1937, R51/356/2. The BBC in Britain was also engaged in this type of talks programme, with 'eye-witness, first hand accounts by BBC staff "observers" of slum conditions in Glasgow, Tyneside and the East End' as well as unemployed people being brought to speak at the microphone. Paddy Scannell and David Cardiff, 'Serving the nation', p. 172.
65   J.T. Sutthery to the director of talks, 22 Nov. 1938, R51/356/2.
66   Bill Rolston, An oral history of Belfast in the nineteen thirties, p. 89. A.J.P. Taylor also highlights this contrast with living standards in England during the '30s: 'Yet at the same time, most English people were enjoying a richer life than any previously known in the history of the world: longer holidays, shorter hours, higher real wages. They had motor cars, cinemas, radio sets, electrical appliances. The two sides of life did not join up', A.J.P. Taylor, English history, 1914–45 (Oxford, 1965), p. 317.
67   Cited in Bill Rolston, An oral history of Belfast in the nineteen thirties, p. 88.
68   BBC director general to Harry Mulholland, BBC NI, 7 Nov. 1947, R6/64.
69   From 2.67 per cent in 1932 to 9.36 per cent in 1939, BBC Yearbooks, 1932–39.
70   G.R. Barnes, 'My visit to Northern Ireland', 10/11 Nov. 1948, R34/731/4. George Barnes was director of the spoken word for the BBC and was asked to make this report for the director general of the BBC, see note 20.

71 *Northern Hansard*, vol. xxiii, 4 June 1940.

72 J.T. Sutthery to the programme director, R51/356/1.

73 CAB 9F/165/1/1.

74 Lindsay Wellington to Mair, 14 Aug. 1934. There is an attached memo from Wellington (27 Aug. 1934) which says: 'Regions are allowed to cut out of the pool in favour of local programmes of importance', R34/492/1. Lindsay Wellington joined the BBC in 1924, he was presentation director in 1933, and director of programme planning in 1935.

75 'Programmes remain the final register and bearers of institutional intentions and assumptions about the scope and purposes of broadcasting and about the audiences to whom they speak', Paddy Scannell and David Cardiff, 'Serving the nation', p. 170.

76 Mair to Godfrey Adams, presentation assistant, London, 26 Apr. 1934, R34/492/1.

77 J.T. Sutthery (later Northern Irish regional programme director) to the presentation director, London, 9 Jan. 1935, R34/492/1.

78 Henry McMullan to the assistant director of variety, 30 Sept. 1937, R19/840/2. Henry McMullan joined the BBC in 1931, and took over as news editor, publicity man, and director of outside broadcasting in June of that year. He had previously been a journalist with the *Belfast Newsletter*.

79 *BBC Yearbook 1937*.

80 *BBC Yearbook 1934*, *BBC Yearbook 1935*.

81 *BBC Yearbook 1942*.

82 Rex Cathcart, *The most contrary region,* p. 117.

83 *BBC Yearbook 1938*.

84 David Cardiff and Paddy Scannell, 'Broadcasting and unity', p. 165.

85 See John Boyd, *The middle of my journey* (Belfast, 1990).

86 *BBC Yearbook 1933*.

87 J.T. Sutthery to Head Office, London, 16 Nov. 1938, R34/492/2.

88 Cabinet Publicity Meeting Minutes, 2 Mar. 1949, CAB 9F/165/1/1.

89 *BBC Yearbook 1945*.

90 R.J. Young to Sir Basil Brooke, 23 Feb. 1946, CAB 9F/165/1/1.

91 MR, Northern Ireland Region, 3 Feb. 1945, R34/748/2. In a letter to George Marshall the Northern Irish prime minister, John Andrews, wrote that 'Erse' (Gaelic) was objectionable because it was a 'language expressive of separation'. John Andrews to George Marshall, 18 Sept. 1941, CAB 9F/165/2.

92 MR, Northern Ireland Region, January 1947, R34/748/4. In the monthly report for February 1945 Marshall cited an *Irish Times* article dated 31 Jan. 1945 'with Bernard Shaw in which he was asked whether "the Irish revival would be accelerated by films in the native tongue shown in schools and picture houses to the rising generation or if the anglicising influences of the press, the BBC, Donham and Hollywood would be too strong, even for Mr de Valera's iron determination to restore the language?" He replied that Mr de Valera's unfortunate addiction to the hopelessly effete foreign language called Gaelic was almost as deplorable as Hitler's prejudice against the Jews. He added that all members of the Gaelic League (who are promoting the Irish language) should be shot as the worst enemies of their country, with, however, a recommendation for mercy to Mr de Valera'. MR, Northern Ireland Region, 3 Feb. 1945, R34/748/2.

93 Edna Longley, 'Progressive bookmen: politics and Northern Protestant writers since the 1930s', *Irish Review*, no. 1, 1986, p. 56.

94 Rex Cathcart, 'The BBC in Northern Ireland: 50 years old'.

95 'Some services are taken from St Martin-in-the-Fields, others from St Cuthbert's, Edinburgh. There are also frequent relays of services from various parts of the British Isles, and dovetailing into all is a scheme of local services most of

which originate either from St James's Parish Church or from Fisherwick Church Belfast', *BBC Yearbook 1930*.

96   *BBC Yearbook 1933*.

97   *BBC Yearbook 1933*. Mass was broadcast again in 1934 from Beechmont in Belfast; the celebrant was Dr MacNamee, bishop of Ardagh, and the service was presided over by Cardinal MacRory, *BBC Yearbook 1935*.

98   *BBC Yearbook 1946*.

99   *BBC Yearbook 1934*.

100   *BNL*, 21 Mar. 1933, cited in Rex Cathcart, *The most contrary region*, pp. 63–4.

101   *BBC Yearbook 1943*.

102   George Marshall to the director general, 14 May 1946, R28/189.

103   Rev. J.W. Welch to the director general, 28 May 1946, R34/492/4.

104   MR, Northern Ireland Region, May 1946, R34/748/3.

105   Henry McMullan (for the Northern Ireland regional director) to the director of talks, 26 Oct. 1934.

106   Director of talks to George Marshall, 28 Dec. 1934, R51/356/1.

107   J.T. Sutthery to the director of talks, 2 Oct. 1936, R51/356/1.

108   J.T. Sutthery to the director of talks, 14 Oct. 1936, R51/356/1.

109   Letter George Marshall to Basil Brooke, 17 Sept. 1945, CAB 9F/165/4.

110   Cabinet proceedings, 17 Sept. 1945, CAB 9F/165/4.

111   Letter George Marshall to Basil Brooke, 27 Nov. 1945, CAB 9F/165/4.

112   'It is obviously desirable that any talks of the character proposed should impress the public with the value and prestige of our Parliament . . . We should do all we can to prevent the BBC, a British radio service, from being made the medium of propaganda by Nationalist MPs for the further dismemberment of the United Kingdom', cabinet memo from Basil Brooke, 3 Dec. 1945, CAB 9F/165/4.

113   Letter, Robert Gransden to George Marshall, 12 Jan. 1946, CAB 9F/165/4.

114   Letter, George Marshall to Basil Brooke, 31 Jan. 1946, CAB 9F/165/4.

115   *Northern Hansard*, vol. xxii, 4 Sept. 1939.

116   Curran and Seaton, *Power without responsibility*, p. 161.

117   George Marshall to the director general, 10 Sept. 1943, R34/492/3. He was encouraged in his drive for a regional news service by Northern Irish MPs who raised the issue in Stormont, *Northern Hansard*, vol. xxv, 19 Oct. 1943.

118   Brian Maginess (junior minister in 1942, and minister for labour in 1945) to the prime minister, 22 Nov. 1943, CAB 9F/165/1/1.

119   Typescripts of Northern Irish news, R28/189.

120   Andrew Stewart, memo to staff, Mar. 1949, cited in Rex Cathcart, *The most contrary region*, p. 268.

121   *BBC Yearbook 1945*.

122   *BBC Yearbook 1943*.

123   ibid.

124   *BBC Yearbook 1947*.

125   *BBC Yearbook 1946*.

126   ibid.

127   Ursula Eason, cited in Rex Cathcart, *The most contrary region*, p. 106.

128   ibid.

129   Ursula Eason to Head Office, 24 Oct. 1940, R34/492/3.

130   *BBC Yearbook 1943*. David Cardiff and Paddy Scannell, 'Broadcasting and national unity', p. 166.

131   Copy of Basil Brooke's foreword to *Ulster's Half-Hour*, 29 July 1943, CAB 9F/165/5.

132   ibid.

133   James Brown's criticism was that *Ulster's Half-Hour* ridiculed Northern Ireland,

the programmes moreover contained 'accents never heard outside the BBC'. *Northern Hansard*, vol. xxvii, 6 Feb. 1945.

134 R34/492/3.
135 CAB 3A/96.
136 Unfortunately, there is a general lack of research into the response of government or society to the idea of working women during the war and after in Northern Ireland.
137 CAB 3A/96.
138 Hugh Minford, MP Antrim, *Northern Hansard*, vol. xxvii, 6 Feb. 1945.
139 ibid.
140 MR, Northern Ireland Region, 3 Feb. 1945, R34/748/2.
141 The signature is indecipherable, R34/492/3.
142 Ursula Eason to the director of features department, 17 Sept. 1940, R19/839/1.
143 Ursula Eason to Laurence Gilliam, 23 Sept. 1940, R19/839/1.
144 Rex Cathcart, *The most contrary region*, p. 323.
145 John Andrews to George Marshall, Sept. 1941, cited in Rex Cathcart, *The most contrary region*, p. 119.
146 Northern Irish London office to F.R. Adams, 8 July 1941, CAB 9F/165/2.
147 John Andrews to Ogilvie, nd, CAB 9F/165/2.
148 Ogilvie to John Andrews, 2 Aug. 1941, CAB 9F/165/2.
149 Ursula Eason to the director of features department, re: Irish plays, 20 July 1942, R19/840/3.
150 *BBC Yearbook 1933*.
151 Robert Lynd (1879–1949), born in Belfast, an essayist who 'retained his commitment to the idea of an Irish nation to the end'. Helen Waddell, (1889–1965), scholar and author, Robert Welch (ed.), *The Oxford companion to Irish literature* (Oxford, 1996), p. 321, p. 590.
152 Cannon Hannay, (1865–1950), born in Belfast, a cultural nationalist. Denis Johnston, (1901–1984), born in Dublin, playwright, joined the BBC in Belfast in 1938, moved to London in 1939 and became a war correspondent for the BBC in 1942, appointed director of programmes in 1948 but resigned and moved to New York. Leslie Alexander Montgomery (Lynn Doyle) (1873–1961), born in Downpatrick, *The spirit of Ireland* (1935), 'a guide book addressed to "the better class of English tourist", describes the "ordinary Irish" as "traveling steerage in every relation to life"'. *The Oxford companion to Irish literature*, p. 153. Richard Rowley (1877–1947), born in Belfast, founded the Mourne Press during the Second World War: his later collections such as *Ballads of Mourne* (1940) 'make use of rural settings and Ulster dialect', *The Oxford companion to Irish literature*, p. 502. Moira O'Neill, (1865–1955), born in Cushendun, her most popular series of poems, in Hiberno-English, were collected as *Songs of the Glens of Antrim* (1901), *The Oxford companion to Irish literature*, p. 450. Forrest Reid (1875–1947), born in Belfast, novelist, *The Oxford companion to Irish literature*, p. 494.
153 George Marshall to head office, 26 Nov. 1935, R34/492/1.
154 George Shiels, playwright (1886–1949) born in Ballymoney. St John Ervine, dramatist, novelist, biographer and critic (1883–1971) born in Belfast.
155 Drama assistant, BBC NI to head office, 30 Jan. 1937, R34/492/1.
156 *BBC Yearbook 1934*.
157 Ursula Eason to Head Office, 24 Oct. 1940, R34/492/3. This was in keeping with the attitude of Head Office to the regions from the early 1930s on, which meant that they kept a 'beady eye on the provinces to make sure they did not overstep the mark'. Paddy Scannell and David Cardiff, *A social history of British broadcasting*, p. 325.

158 Ursula Eason to the assistant director of drama, 23 Oct. 1941, R19/840/3. St John Ervine is the focus of later chapters.

159 R19/840/3. James Stephens, 1880–1950, born in Dublin, poet, novelist and short story writer.

160 Ursula Eason to head office, 13 May 1941, R34/492/3.

161 Denis Johnston to the director of features department, 19 June 1941, R19/840/3.

162 'A play by George Shiels or St John Ervine would be suitable, and St John Ervine's play "Boyd's Shop" at the Group Theatre had the rather extraordinary run, for a provincial repertory company, of 15 weeks . . . Other suggestions are, "His Last Day in Business" by George Shiels . . . and "The Jail Bird" by George Shiels, one of the best-known Ulster comedies and a very amusing play'. Ursula Eason to the director of features department, 19 May 1941, R19/840/3.

163 Ursula Eason to the assistant director of drama, Manchester, 20 June 1941, R19/840/3.

164 *BBC Yearbook 1948.*

165 *BBC Yearbook 1945* and *BBC Yearbook 1946.*

166 MR, Northern Ireland Region, Mar. 1946, R34/748/3.

167 'The fact also that the members of the Opposition have increased is a sign of the times and in recent public speeches both the Prime Minister and members of the Cabinet have been reiterating the need for solidarity and setting a strong face against the United Ireland propaganda'. MR, Mar. 1946, R34/748/3.

168 MR, Northern Ireland Region, Apr. 1946, R34/748/3.

169 MR, Northern Ireland Region, Oct. 1946, R34/748/3.

170 MR, Northern Ireland Region, Jan. 1947, R34/748/4.

171 *BBC Yearbook 1945.*

172 *BBC Yearbook 1947.*

173 David Cardiff and Paddy Scannell, 'Broadcasting and national unity', p. 168.

174 'New staff were appointed, staff returned from the services, and throughout the year the pattern of a Regional Service specially designed to meet the needs and views of the Northern Ireland listener was gradually evolved', *BBC Yearbook 1947.*

175 Rex Cathcart, *The most contrary region,* p. 8.

176 *BBC Yearbook 1947.*

177 Memo, Andrew Stewart to BBC staff, Mar. 1949 cited in Rex Cathcart, *The Most Contrary Region,* pp. 267–9.

178 Andrew Stewart in *The BBC in Northern Ireland, 1924–49* (Belfast, 1949).

179 'Try to extend the area of discussion. Try to get people talking to one another about their problems in Northern Ireland, but remember that you must only do so within the boundaries of public acceptability', Sir William Haley in discussion with Andrew Stewart, cited by Rex Cathcart, *The most contrary region,* p. 146.

180 G.R. Barnes, 'My visit to Northern Ireland', 10/11 Nov. 1948, R34/731/4.

181 Rex Cathcart, 'The BBC in Northern Ireland: 50 years old'.

182 Rex Cathcart, *The most contrary region,* p. 171.

183 ibid., p. 170.

184 ibid., p. 181.

185 ibid., p. 263.

4. The Festival of Britain and the coronation of Elizabeth II: performances of consensus in 1950s' Northern Ireland

The Festival of Britain in Northern Ireland in 1951 and the coronation of Queen Elizabeth II, in particular the coronation visit to the Northern Irish state, in 1953, were rituals which represented the unionist government's view of the Northern Irish state. To quote David Cannadine: 'Politics and ceremonial are not separate subjects, the one serious, the other superficial. Ritual is not the mask of force, but is itself a type of power.'[1] Through these ceremonies unionists made their view of society authoritative by invoking protestant loyalties 'towards a particular symbolic representation of the social order'.[2] Both events displayed unionist pageantry as propaganda, allowing the ruling élite to create a consensual surface image of Northern Ireland and its identity, and one which they hoped would cover any underlying tensions within the community. For unionists, the festival and coronation were not only a high-profile means of confirming Northern Ireland's place in the union, but acted moreover as a rallying point for the protestant rank and file, as had the rituals of the 1930s.[3] The impression given in the pages of the unionist press was of the community taking part in a significant way in the life of the state, and the wider United Kingdom, through the medium of these protestant events. The festival and the coronation reinforced the unionist community and government, while simultaneously expressing a particularly protestant, largely élitist interpretation of unionist culture. Politically, the late 1940s was a period in which the Northern Irish state was striving to create a more secure future for itself against the background of an uncertain past, and this appeared to have been achieved by the early 1950s. This seemed a positive period of economic growth for the Northern Irish state, with the Korean War providing the state's traditional industries of ship-building and linen manufacture with a new lease of life. The festival therefore promoted Northern Ireland as a modern industrial centre, and its cultural dimensions took second place to that concern. In contrast, the coronation was a celebratory affair, full of unionist self-confidence. Both events were part of the continuing process of the communalisation of the protestant state in Northern Ireland and both provide an insight into unionist priorities and political concerns in the early 1950s.

The Second World War, which ended in 1945, had allowed unionists to establish their separateness from the southern state and consolidate their strategic importance to the British government. Despite this, in the war's immediate aftermath, and at the beginning of a period of decolonisation within the British Empire, unionists believed themselves to be under threat from within their state, within the island and, more seriously, from Westminster where ultimately their constitutional survival lay. The election of a labour government at Westminster, and Clement Attlee as British prime minister, in July 1945, exacerbated unionist insecurity.[4] Although labour had no definite policy to rescind partition, many within the party were anti-partition supporters. In the immediate post-war election, unionists fought on an anti-socialist platform; but while they warned of the dangers to local industry of a labour government, they pledged to introduce whatever social reforms were passed in Westminster.[5] In addition, nationalist leaders in Northern Ireland decided to abandon their previous policy of abstention from both Westminster and Stormont parliaments. Their decision was influenced by the election of the Attlee government, which they believed would be more sympathetic to their grievances. In these circumstances the unionist government determined to preserve their state and set about consolidating their position. Since the establishment of the two states, unionists had feared that the Government of Ireland Act was being undermined by the Free State.[6] In 1948 when Éire's new taoiseach, John A. Costello, announced his government's intention to make the southern state a republic, it seemed that unionist fears were becoming a reality.[7] But Hugh Shearman interpreted this declaration of a republic positively, seeing it as a future measure which would deepen the divide between the two states and arguing that Northern Ireland was, in 1949, 'as strongly attached to Britain as it was at any time' during the previous seventy years. 'There seems little prospect', he wrote, 'of change in the system of political devolution by which Northern Ireland has remained a successful and useful unit within the United Kingdom during more than a quarter of a century'.[8] Indeed, of the three interested parties the unionists came out best in the negotiations over the Ireland Act in 1949: 'the weakest numerically of the three and self-evidently the most vulnerable, it had not only held, but had further consolidated its position'.[9] The southern Irish government announced that it was willing to give unionists any guarantees they required if they would accept reunification. 'They may bid as high as they please', Basil Brooke retorted, 'but our answer remains the same – Ulster is not for sale!'[10]

In direct response to the Éire government's declaration of the intention to become a republic, Brooke called for an election.[11] The theme unionists adopted reflected their anxiety that the southern state's moves towards a republic hinted at a renewed effort on the southern government's part to achieve a thirty-two county state: 'Our country is in danger', said Brooke, 'today we fight to defend our very existence and the heritage of our Ulster children.'[12] With this emotive electioneering, and traditional rhetoric, unionists won over 60 per cent of the poll.[13] The 1949 election illustrated clearly that, despite the war, little had changed in Northern Ireland, and, in fact, it served to underline the state's divisions.[14] But 1949 was also the year in which, it seemed, unionists' ultimate security was guaranteed by the Ireland Act which confirmed that Northern Ireland would only cease to be part of the United Kingdom with the consent of the unionist-controlled Stormont parliament. In this period of decolonisation then, unionists felt the need to affirm their own position in relation to Éire, and more importantly, within the United Kingdom.[15] This desire found expression in the royal visits to the state which followed the war and the two central ceremonies of the 1950s, the Festival of Britain in Northern Ireland in 1951, and the coronation visit of Elizabeth II in July 1953.[16] Through these ceremonies the official, that is government-approved, image of Northern Ireland was revealed as contradictory. On the one hand the government promoted the state and its people as distinctive and unique (which perhaps reflected the unionist government's concern at this time to maintain a level of autonomy in the face of labour legislation which they believed threatened them), on the other they supported Hugh Shearman's theory that 'in temperament and culture the people of Northern Ireland are British'.[17]

The Festival of Britain, organised by the labour government, was ostensibly convened to commemorate the centenary of the Great Exhibition of 1851.[18] With the intention of boosting the nation's morale it succeeded, according to one critic, in proving to the British population that they still possessed a 'vital and vigorous culture', were 'still at peace' with themselves and were 'secure in [their] heritage'.[19] In the words of the *Great Exhibition Centenary Official Committee* booklet:

> It is to provide a tonic and stimulus to the people of Britain after a decade of danger, fatigue and austerity and to provide inspiration and set standards on a scale beyond anything that can be achieved through speeches, posters and other regular media of the information services.[20]

In an essay on the festival, Michael Frayn uses the analogy of the organisation of the festival in Britain and the putting-on of a school play, a 'super-colossal school play, perhaps, to mark the end of a super-colossally long and trying term'.[21] The festival was not always a certainty either; when the Korean War broke out in 1950, 'the Press was full of gloomy speculations about the possibility of world war before the year was out' and the cancellation of the festival was mooted.[22] The feelings of pessimism are clear from this letter of Lord Ismay's to the chairman of the Festival of Britain Committee in Northern Ireland (hereafter FOBCNI), Sir Roland Nugent, in December 1950:

> For your private ear alone, the international situation looks to me so grim, that it may be necessary for the Council to consider the re-shaping of the programme for 1951 by modification, postponement, curtailment, and possibly cancellation of this feature or that.[23]

Sir Gerald Barry, the Festival of Britain's director, may have seen the festival as a tonic for the nation but, according to Adrian Forty, 'the Festival provided the illusion that Britain was recovering, which was very much what people wanted to believe but in reality the Festival concealed the fact that the patient was suffering a relapse'.[24]

In Northern Ireland, the festival primarily provided the state with the opportunity to publicise its industries, and, in the process, to display a distinctive culture and identity to itself and to the British public.[25] 'The Festival of Britain', read the official statement at the opening exhibition of the Northern Irish festival:

> Is a statement of strength – an account of enterprise in years that are past, an account of achievement to-day, an earnest of power for the future . . . We the women and men of Northern Ireland have played and are playing still our part in that endeavour . . . We have given much – and we have much to give.[26]

The festival in Northern Ireland also coincided with the thirtieth anniversary of the establishment of the Northern Irish state itself:

> Here in Northern Ireland it can be claimed, without boasting, that we stand at the end of a hundred years of remarkable progress, the speed and quality of which have been specially marked since we received a substantial measure of self-government 30 years ago.[27]

As David Harkness has argued, the 1950s held out the promise of a better life for all and 1951 was a positive year for the Northern Irish state;[28] although the elections in the south in May that year witnessed the return to power of de Valera and Fianna Fáil, the threat from the Irish republic seemed to have receded, symbolised by the disbanding of the Anti-Partition League.[29] Moreover, the north's traditional industries (ship-building and linen) which had begun to decline in the immediate aftermath of the Second World War were given a boost by the demands for shipping and textiles created by the Korean War.[30] The festival was an opportunity at the turn of the century, said A.A.K. Arnold, the secretary of the festival committee in Northern Ireland, 'to review our past and present'.[31] And in the circumstances, unionists could do so with some justifiable confidence. In the words of Britain's foreign secretary, Herbert Morrison, the festival was the people 'giving themselves a pat on the back'.[32] In his message to the festival opening the prime minister, Basil Brooke, spoke of 'Ulster's worthy share' in the celebrations: 'It is a day', he said, 'that signifies a decisive victory – not the winning of an armed conflict, but the triumph of the human will over pessimism and hostile circumstances.'[33] In addition to advertising its economic strength, the state's participation in the event stood as evidence to itself and others that it was a permanent feature within the United Kingdom.[34] Coming so soon after the declaration of the Irish republic this need to re-affirm a British connection is unsurprising. In an article called 'Festival will tell the Ulster story', Tyrone Guthrie wrote: 'the Ulster story is part of the larger story, part of its history and part of its present. Nevertheless we are a very individual part'.[35] This element of individuality within the United Kingdom reappears prominently throughout the official literature produced for the festival in Northern Ireland. James Loughlin has argued that references in the festival literature to Northern Ireland's unity with the United Kingdom 'acknowledged British national membership'.[36] However, these references can be seen as part of an established unionist tradition which clamoured for recognition as an integral and valuable part of United Kingdom, yet, paradoxically, by this very insistence appeared to be asserting something that was not self-evident. Other publications were quick to highlight Ulster's war efforts in 1914 and in the conflict just ended; one author spoke of: 'Northern Ireland's experience of a generation of sharing in war and in peace, in slump and prosperity . . . has severely tested that foundation of the Ulster constitution; and from the testing it has emerged powerfully strengthened'.[37] The rhetoric of the festival, in tune with traditional unionist rhetoric, was also full of references to the inheritance the British owed to the sacrifices of their forefathers; 'If we are to be worthy of our heritage', said the Archbishop of Canterbury, 'to preserve it and to add to it, we must keep to the same sure foundations on which our fathers built.'[38]

The Festival of Britain in Northern Ireland was organised in three parts: the Festival of the Arts, which ran between May and September 1951, and was organised by CEMA (the Council for the Encouragement of Music and the Arts, which later became the Arts Council),[39] and the rest of the festival projects, organised by the Festival of Britain Committee in Northern Ireland (FOBCNI).[40] The third part of the festival was its major exhibition, the Farm and Factory Exhibition at Castlereagh, which was organised exclusively by the ministry of commerce. Initially, there was a question of what Northern Ireland's festival title should be. Some favoured 'Ulster', but, as William Leitch of the Parliamentary Counsel Office at Stormont explained to the ministry of commerce, this was not a viable suggestion: 'The objections to the use of the word 'Ulster' are to my mind geographical and possibly political rather than legal. As this Festival emphasises our connection with the rest of the United Kingdom I would say that 'Northern Ireland' is to be preferred'.[41] However, from the outset the overriding concern of the Northern Irish government in relation to the festival was economy.[42] The financial difficulty facing the FOBCNI was elucidated in a letter to the committee from Col. Haughton, its first chairman:[43]

> If too much is spent all sorts of questions will be raised in Parliament no matter how brilliant Northern Ireland's participation may prove to be – and – if too little is spent and a shabby picture of Northern Ireland's life and industry is shown the Public will say – quite rightly – 'It would have been better not to participate than to stage such a miserable reflection of our own character and aspirations'.[44]

The emphasis on economy increased when the department in charge of festival organisation switched to the Ministry of Commerce.[45] The original FOBCNI had been organised by the Ministry of Education; members were appointed by S.H. Hall-Thompson, minister of education, and many of them remained on the committee for the duration of the festival's organisation.[46] 'The remarkable thing about [the festival] is that it has not been dictated from above or imposed by a Government department', said A.A.K. Arnold. However, the Northern Irish government held the purse for the festival's funding, and it was unlikely that events which did not have their approval would be supported. This was made clear in a FOBCNI internal memo in November 1949: 'in Northern Ireland the financial responsibility, and therefore the main executive responsibility, is that of the Northern Ireland Government, who will meet the expense of most official projects in Northern Ireland'.[47] In addition, while the FOBCNI had executive responsibility for festival projects, projects also had to have the approval of the festival council in Britain.[48] From the beginning, therefore, all were made aware of the need for prudence, and groups were invited to take part in the festival on a voluntary basis, that is with no financial support from the government.[49] A.A.K. Arnold explained the position to CEMA's standing committee in January 1950:

> The local Festival Committee had no financial resources of its own; the implementation of schemes and policy involving Government expenditure recommended by the Committee subject to approval of the Ministry of Finance, was the responsibility of the appropriate Ministry or Local Authority concerned and would be borne on the vote of the respective Ministries.[50]

Sobering notes such as this from the ministry of finance to Arnold kept the festival committee in economic line: 'It is necessary to emphasise that where possible savings should be effected in respect of Festival projects and it is presumed that the various Committees will keep this in mind and will not aim at expenditure of the maximum approved in each instance.'[51] 'We Ulster people are citizens of no mean country', said Sir Roland Nugent, 'and our industrial and agricultural reputation stands high in the Empire . . . This very fact has tended to overshadow the less material qualities of the Ulsterman and his ability in the creative and cultural sphere.'[52] CEMA was given a very limited budget for its projects, the greater part of the funds being allocated to the government's Farm and Factory exhibition at Castlereagh.[53] This emphasis is unsurprising given the government's concern to promote new manufacturing industry in the state in order to compensate for the rise in rural unemployment caused by the increase of technology, particularly the use of tractors, in farming.[54]

The composition of the festival committee in Northern Ireland, and its sub-committees, reveals much about the government's perception of the role of the festival which, contrary to all contemporary speeches, was as a glorified trade show. Interestingly, Asa Briggs notes that what annoyed British conservatives about the Festival of Britain was its 'anti-commercial' tone.[55] In an internal FOBCNI memo it was noted that the committee members were 'not all necessarily intended to represent specific organisations or sections of the population', but in fact they did largely represent the business and industrial concerns of Belfast.[56] The festival's organisers were keen that the festival should not be considered Belfast-centric:

> Although Belfast, as the capital city, is the official centre of our Festival of the Arts and the place where the Ulster Farm and Factory Exhibition and the Traveling Exhibition aboard the Festival ship 'Campania' will be seen, I would like to make it clear that all parts of Northern Ireland have an opportunity of taking part in the Festival.[57]

There were, therefore, local celebrations which included, for example, an industrial exhibition at Armagh, 'Augher through the Ages', a Ballymena through-the-ages event, and a shopping exhibition in the local temperance hall at Banbridge.[58] Ultimately, however, the festival centred on, and was reflective of, the state's capital and its élites. The festival committee was headed by Sir Roland Nugent, speaker of the Northern Irish senate, who was appointed at the suggestion of the prime minister, Basil Brooke. Other members included representatives from government bodies, ministries and trade unions, as well as figures from municipal corporations and private enterprise.[59] Given its composition, it is little surprise that initially the committee wanted the festival's main exhibition to centre on ship-building; they decided on the Farm and Factory exhibition only when it was discovered that the Scottish committee had thought of the ship-building theme first. Local committees were staffed by members of the local authorities, and by local religious and civic dignitaries. The claim by the local authorities sub-committee's final report was, therefore, exaggerated:

> The Festival did much to strengthen and unite the people and bring home to them the value of their great British heritage . . . The bringing together of the people, in all walks of life, on Festival committees will, no doubt, have a most beneficial and lasting effect on the community.[60]

It is interesting to consider who the 'people' were. Henry Diamond, nationalist MP for the Falls, argued that the festival was for one section of the Northern Irish population alone:

> I am all in favour of industrial exhibitions that tend to increase the trade and industry of the Province but at the same time it is regrettable that the auspices under which this exhibition is to be held should be the local Festival of Britain Committee . . . The people for whom I speak are anxious for the prosperity of this area, but they resent, and bitterly resent, any attempt at co-operation with either the Festival of Britain Committee in Britain or anything of that nature so long as part of the country is occupied . . . The Festival of Britain Committee may be all right in Britain, but we are in another country and there is nothing particular that the people here feel they should celebrate . . . I am opposed to it particularly since it divides the people. The exhibition will be one of those functions that are held from time to time to which the followers of the Government will give their support with a great deal of ballyhoo, and which another substantial section of the population will certainly boycott.[61]

In the early phase of festival organisation, Northern Ireland's festival committee was anxious to define its role and its power; both, they discovered, were minor and limited:

> The fact that its [the festival council in Britain] advice is in practice accepted as an authoritative direction is a phenomenon of administrative expediency from which the members of the Council appear to derive little encouragement. The Committee for Northern Ireland passed through a similar state of enlightenment, if not disillusionment, last year, and the part which the Government is playing in the Festival in Northern Ireland is now fairly well defined.[62]

In a letter from Sir Roland Nugent to Andrew Stewart, controller of the BBC in Northern Ireland, Nugent explained that the role of the FOBCNI was 'mainly advisory and supervisory', with the executive work carried out by the government of Northern Ireland, the local authorities and CEMA.[63] And CEMA itself had no real authority.[64] In a memo to CEMA's standing committee in January 1950, A.A.K. Arnold reminded them that: 'Projects approved by the Northern Ireland Committee were reviewed by the Official Committee and authority to incur expenditure then sought – in the case of CEMA – from the ministry of education'.[65] In January 1950, the CEMA minutes noted that they were 'responsible to the Festival Committee for policy and to the Ministry of Education for financial approval'.[66] CEMA was responsible for the organisation of all events for the Festival of the Arts in Northern Ireland.[67] The question of who controlled the festival was clarified when the issue of the playing of the national anthem at festival events organised by CEMA arose and some members queried whether it was necessary; CEMA's standing committee were informed that 'the present practice was arrived at as a result of a Cabinet ruling and that as the Festival in Northern Ireland was being run under the Government auspices, Sir Roland Nugent was quite definitely of the opinion that the present policy should not be modified for Festival activities.'[68]

'An occasion such as this', said the president of CEMA, Dame Dehra Parker, 'presents us for the first time with an opportunity to prove what our regional contribution to the arts can be, and to demonstrate regionally the artistic qualities of the Ulster spirit – as distinct from the industrial.'[69] Although the unionist government's overriding concern was to advertise the state's industrial potential, civic and drama weeks were held throughout the state, bringing 'the true Festival spirit to almost every area', according to Sir Roland Nugent, 'or perhaps it would be more accurate to say that the spirit is already there and the Festival will provide an apt occasion for its manifestation'.[70] CEMA organised art, drama, architecture, and musical events, including plans for the first Irish ballet. 'Irish folk songs and dances find their place in a programme', wrote the *Belfast Newsletter*, 'which will include a new Irish ballet based on a poem "The Dancer" by the Belfast poet, Joseph Campbell'.[71] In addition, there were two nights of open-air dancing at the Botanic gardens and Belfast castle, free of charge.[72] Tyrone Guthrie took charge of the drama projects, and established a theatre group, the Northern Irish Theatre Company, to perform several plays during the course of the festival.[73] Also, as part of the festival, John Luke was commissioned to paint a mural in Belfast city hall which would represent the history of Belfast and its industries. John Hewitt headed the CEMA sub-committee on art which arranged for, among others, a photographic exhibition entitled 'Georgian Architecture in Northern Ireland', sponsored by the Arts Council of Great Britain, an exhibition of contemporary Ulster art and a special CEMA collection of works by Ulster artists.[74] One of the festival's most successful events, organised by Lady Antrim's sub-committee on culture, was an exhibition called 'Our Ulster Heritage in Town and Country'. With the intention of helping to create a better understanding of 'Ulster heritage', it attracted over 8,000 visitors in little over a week.[75] Another exhibition of interest was the Exhibition of Northern Ireland Books and Manuscripts. The exhibition was organised by John Babbington, the city librarian in Belfast, under the direction of Lady Antrim's sub-committee on culture.[76] In a broadcast on the festival for BBC Northern Ireland's Home Service, John Babbington outlined the exhibition:

> What has been attempted is to show how almost every aspect of life and letters in Northern Ireland is reflected in the written and printed word. So there are sections dealing with the land itself, with the people and their way of life, their history and government, their arts and their crafts, with their agriculture and industry, their prowess in scholarship.[77]

Predominantly, the material exhibited concerned the plantations, the Siege of Derry, William III, the linen and flax industry, the growth of Belfast as a city of industry and commerce, including the growth of the harbour, and the growth of the university. Represented in a much smaller way were items more identifiably 'Irish' (such as a late seventeenth-century Gaelic manuscript, a manuscript book of Irish songs and a collection of Ulster folk songs). It was an exhibition which the chairman of CEMA, John Lindsay, thought reflected 'almost every aspect of life and letters in Northern Ireland'. It was certainly representative of the official version of Northern Ireland's past, and very revealing about its vision of the present, particularly in its promotion of the state as having an established history as a centre of commerce and learning.[78]

The difficulty over the involvement of the catholic church in the festival in Northern Ireland revealed the state to be less homogenous than the unionist government claimed. In Britain, liaison between the festival council and the churches was maintained through the Festival of Britain advisory committee of christian churches.[79] In Northern Ireland, this was not the case. Sir Roland Nugent outlined where he saw the difficulty with the involvement of the catholic church in Northern Ireland's festival; in a memorandum to the Northern Irish cabinet he wrote:

> There is no working liaison between the Roman Catholic Church and the Protestant Churches represented on the United Council of Christian Churches and Religious Communions in Northern Ireland, and

approaches to the different denominations would be likely to meet with unequal response for political reasons.[80]

And his memo continued:

> Although the easiest line would doubtless be to take no action, such a course might at a later stage expose my committee and possibly the Government to criticism from a section of the Churches, while to approach only that element from which a willing response could confidently be expected would be to invite criticism of another kind.[81]

All the main churches in the state, including the catholic, were invited by the festival committee to co-operate in the festival on their own responsibility.[82] Personally, Nugent felt that the churches should not be asked to participate at all; however, 'if the Cabinet thinks otherwise then he [Nugent] would suggest a United Service in St Anne's and an invitation to the head of the Roman Catholic Church to hold a service'.[83] The matter, however, did not solely rely on the decision of the Northern Irish cabinet.[84] Nugent noted in a letter to the Dean of St Anne's, the Revd R. Elliott, in January 1951 that the festival committee, in fact, had had no response from the catholic church to invitations to take part in the festival.[85] While the festival committee received 'favourable and sympathetic replies from most of the Churches approached', they received no response at all from the catholic authorities.[86] CEMA's standing committee noted in June 1950 that 'there would be a religious pageant in St Anne's Cathedral . . . and that the Jewish community and the Christian Scientists each proposed to arrange a programme of religious music'.[87] When the united service did take place in St Anne's it was given official endorsement by the presence of government officials; Sir Roland Nugent read the lesson, and the congregation was made up of 'men and women distinguished in public life in Northern Ireland'.[88] Separate united services in protestant churches took place throughout the state to launch festival weeks in the various locations. As the final report of the civic authorities sub-committee concluded, 'One of the most striking features of the Festival in Northern Ireland was the holding of United Church Services by the Protestant congregations. Ministers of religion joined forces, and the services, usually in the open, were most impressive and uplifting'.[89] They were, according to the voluntary organisations' programme, an indication of 'the way of life' in Northern Ireland in 1951.[90] Ultimately, in keeping with its attitude towards the state, the catholic church took no part in the festival.[91]

Offering a different version of life in Northern Ireland was *The arts in Ulster*.[92] Edited by the author and BBC producer Sam Hanna Bell, the poet John Hewitt and Nesca Robb, it was an official festival publication which included essays by various writers on areas of the arts in the state.[93] A sub-committee headed by John Hewitt was established to oversee the project.[94] Andrew Stewart felt that the sub-committee had not made it 'quite clear to Mr Sam Hanna Bell that his introduction should portray the background of Northern Ireland out of which developments in the various arts had arisen'.[95]

And in his editorial piece Bell took the opportunity to address the less idealised aspects of Northern Irish society out of which the various arts had evolved. 'There is a problem', he wrote, 'for the Ulster writer; our history, for historical reasons, is still warm from the hands of zealots . . . here in the work of these scholars, so far as the writer is concerned, is our history cooled and tempered for us.'[96] Initially, it was proposed to publish a book on the history of the theatre in Northern Ireland, but this idea was shelved in favour of a book on the arts.[97] Nearly all the contributors to the book were on one or other of the festival's sub-committees.[98] Hewitt and Robb were already members of CEMA's art committee, and Hewitt was also on its standing committee; while David Kennedy and Nelson Browne were members of the sub-committee on culture.[99] But not all who were invited wished to take part in the publication; in a letter to Bell the author Michael McLaverty explained why he would not take up the offer to contribute to *The arts in Ulster*: 'Surely you don't expect an Irish Nationalist like myself to subscribe, implicitly or explicitly, to Festival of Britain activities. I couldn't do so until our broken country is healed.'[100] The festival was clearly seen by some as solely a political celebration of British culture and the union.[101]

The compilation of the book was not without its tensions among the editors. In particular, Nesca Robb wrote to John Hewitt, in June 1950, complaining about John Boyd's article on prose:

> We've got to keep politics out of this as far as is humanly possible . . . This is a book on the Arts in Ulster – not a disquisition on the Irish question . . . Therefore all unavoidable references to politics should be as brief and as neutral as they can possibly be made . . . I should think it equally improper to use a work of this kind for covert propaganda of a different colour. This is after all, a semi-official publication financed out of public funds . . . If some of the contributors could be persuaded to adopt a more cheerful less scolding tone it would be as well – no one wants them to be fulsome – but this is by way of being a Festival book, and we'd better try to make the best of our wares, such as they are![102]

In his piece, John Boyd had argued that literature was 'closely wedded' to history, particularly social history. 'There have been many complex problems of politics and economics', wrote Boyd, 'problems which have affected every one of us.'[103] His assessment of 'Ulster' prose was not in accordance with those who wished to highlight the Britishness of the Northern Irish state and its culture: 'Ulster is part of Ireland, which is part of the British Isles, which is part of Europe. Our literature should belong to our own country, to the British Isles, to Europe.'[104] Boyd also questioned the quality of Northern Irish literature directly:

> We have not produced a dramatist of the stature of Shaw, a poet of the stature of Yeats, a novelist of the stature of Joyce – to mention three Irishmen whose importance is recognised in Europe; and in the nineteenth-century we did not produce a novelist who is now regarded as of permanent worth.[105]

This was a repetition of Sean O'Casey's article in the journal *Time and Tide* in 1944 which criticised the quality of Northern Irish literature. At the time the article was viewed as a blatant attack on 'Ulster's' cultural integrity and drew a bitter response from St John Ervine in a series of articles in the *Belfast Telegraph* between September and October 1944, entitled 'Ulster: the real centre of culture in Ireland'.[106] In his conclusion John Boyd quoted Æ, defining a writing genius as one who was 'just as likely to kick his own country as to bless it'; according to Boyd that was what Northern Ireland's best living authors were trying to do. Bell left no doubt as to his position on the matter, and indicated his priority for the tone of the book in this letter to Hewitt: 'I don't give a damn if Nesca Robb likes this contribution or not – I do and I know as much and probably more of this aspect than she does. After all it has taken quite a lot of courage on J.B.'s part to say what he has said. I back him in his "waspishness".'[107] Nesca Robb's concern reflects the tension which surrounded the work of writers in Northern Ireland and their relation to the state in this period. This was in keeping with the work of writers such as Bell, John Hewitt, W.R. Rodgers and Louis MacNeice who provided an alternative vision of the state throughout the 1940s and 1950s and who were often seen as challenging the *status quo*.[108] The reviewer for the *Belfast Newsletter* paid little attention however to Boyd's article, highlighting instead Nelson Browne's article 'Poetry in Ulster', and stressing the fact that 'at least one of the contributors to *The arts in Ulster* thinks that the growth of the arts in our midst has been stimulated by the separation of Northern Ireland from the rest of the country.'[109] This accorded with Bell's point that 'it would be a matter for concern if observers, watching the coming and going in a vivid, voluble, and involved community, were agreed that what they saw was simple, static, and incapable of more than one interpretation'.[110] But this in itself was contrary to the unionist government's priority for the festival, which was intended to provide an image of Northern Ireland as a homogenous, industrious and exclusively protestant society. Although Boyd's article appears uncontentious, given the image the government were trying to promote, suggestions that 'Ulster' was part of Ireland and not of Britain (but the British Isles) were bound to offend unionist sensibilities.

Roy Strong argues, in *A tonic for the nation*, that the Festival of Britain was 'fiercely nationalistic, and anti-imperialist'.[111] In this it was contrary to the ethos of unionism, which throughout the festival in Northern Ireland loudly claimed its place in the empire and its homogeneity with Britain. Hugh Shearman visited the South Bank Exhibition in London for the *Belfast Telegraph* in June 1951, and noted the lack of 'Empire' in the proceedings: 'A curious omission from the exhibition is the Empire. Here and there its existence could be discovered, but it is not stressed as a major item in British life'.[112] Shearman felt, however, that it was a mark of 'our assurance and perhaps our courtesy to visitors from other empires, that the Exhibition refrains from rubbing it in' – the might of the British Empire, that is.[113] Typical of this attitude was the experience of Willy de Majo, the co-ordinator and chief designer of the Farm and Factory Exhibition at Castlereagh: 'Once

I got appointed there were questions raised in the Ulster Parliament. Somebody said "If we have to get a designer from across the water, why not an English Englishman instead of a Yugoslav Englishman?".[114] Ultimately what did cause excitement among the festival organisers was the planned visit of the king and queen to open the Farm and Factory Exhibition at Castlereagh. The civic authorities sub-committee, which had noted a lack of enthusiasm for the festival in March 1950, suggested that 'if the possibility of Royal Patronage and a royal visit could be made known, it would be a great stimulus to Local Authorities in promoting plans for the Festival'.[115] The FOBCNI felt that 'the royal visit in June would set the seal on the Northern Ireland Festival Programme'.[116]

In June 1951 George VI was too ill to travel to Northern Ireland, and so Queen Elizabeth and Princess Margaret opened the Farm and Factory Exhibition.[117] This royal visit gave unionists their first chance since the declaration of the Irish republic, and the Ireland Act, to proclaim their loyalty to the crown and claim their place in the empire.[118] The *Northern Whig* detailed the routes and times of the royal visit a week before the actual visit – in fact the press had made the royal visit known as early as February 1951.[119] In June the *Belfast Telegraph* reported:

> Happily the occasion was blessed with perfect weather, so that the crowds had a splendid view of the royal visitors as they drove in an open car from Dufferin Quay through the centre of the city to Castlereagh, where they saw the Festival Farm and Factory exhibition.[120]

Costumes being all-important in a ritual, details of both royal outfits were provided; Princess Margaret wore a silver grey taffeta coat and a dress of dusty pink, while the queen 'looked fresh and charming in a lightweight ensemble of powder blue, with off-the-face hat of the same colour surmounted by a feather sweeping downwards. She carried a grey handbag and wore slingback court shoes to match'.[121] The queen opened the exhibition and was introduced to Lord Ismay and Sir Gerald Barry by Sir Roland Nugent. Also present were the members of the festival committee and the various sub-committees. Princess Margaret toured the exhibition with Willy de Majo, the minister of commerce and Mr Rebbeck. According to de Majo: 'The Minister knew very little about the exhibition and as you know the procedure is that you don't address royalty unless they speak to you, so I was walking behind and kept feeding the Minister and telling him what was what.'[122]

Reporting to the festival council in London, Mrs J. Mackie, chairman of the voluntary organisations sub-committee, outlined the exhibition: 'There has never been an Exhibition like this before in Ulster, or indeed in Ireland, and we hope that visitors will find there a new understanding of the character and achievement of our people'. 'We see the Festival', she continued, 'not only as a holiday tonic but as having a lasting practical value.'[123] According to Sir Roland Nugent, the Castlereagh exhibition set out 'to tell a story, the story of the craftsmanship and productive skill of our people as seen in those activities that make up our chief contribution to the material resources of the United Kingdom. It shows how Ulster earns its living.'[124] The exhibition was almost entirely industrial; exhibits included the shirt and collar industry, the ropemaking industry, the pottery industry, the woollen industry, the tobacco and cigarette industry, the poplin industry, the whiskey industry, the aerated and mineral waters industry, textile machinery and the cotton industry, as well as a farm of the future and one of the past.[125] J.D. Stewart, who had broadcast on the festival for the BBC programme *Ulster Commentary*, was the author of the Farm and Factory Exhibition guidebook.[126] In it he saw the trade and industry show as a manifestation of the character of the Northern Irish:

> It shows that through peace and war, slump and boom, we have kept on trying. with faith and skill and patience, to improve ourselves and our environment. We have preserved old skills and applied them to new problems. We have worked and we have won.[127]

The minister of education, who closed the Farm and Factory Exhibition, hailed it as a triumph 'for designers, architects, artists and gardeners'.[128] But it was Nugent's words which were the most accurate, the exhibition showed how Northern Ireland 'earned a living', and when the exhibition was over the site returned to work as a factory.[129]

The importance of the exhibition to the organisers was made clear in October 1950. In a broadcast publicising the festival for the BBC in October 1950, Sir Gerald Barry, the director general of the Festival of Britain, neglected to mention the Farm and Factory Exhibition.[130] There was an immediate, and very angry, reaction from Sir Roland Nugent:

> I don't want to overstate the case, but I would like to say how glad we should be if, for their future guidance, the attention of the BBC could be drawn to the fact that we are not just a far-flung outpost of curiosity value, but an exhibition centre – and Arts Festival centre – on the United Kingdom programme.[131]

A.A.K. Arnold also wrote a letter of complaint to the Festival of Britain's director of public relations, Paul Wright:

> I have been receiving so many black looks and sarcastic telephone calls that I thought it best to let you know, for the record, without going over the ancient wrongs of Ireland. The reference to Northern Ireland, they say, was pretty obviously dragged in as an afterthought, and although it said that we were busy preparing, totally neglected to say what for. The Ministry of Finance, who are spending over £175,000 on us, and with whom our troubles are by no means over, now shoot us glances of incredulity and mistrust 'What price your Farm and Factory Exhibition?', they seem to say. As for the Ministries of Commerce and Agriculture they have practically disappeared into the Slough of Despond. No one is more conscious than I am of our shortcomings and our insignificance; but Ulstermen are so sensitive beneath those hard exteriors. Please remember us next time.[132]

Wright responded to this very emotional letter, admonishing Arnold for his criticism:

> We always remember you, and a great deal of thought is given to preserving the national balance in publicity, and giving Northern Ireland, in company with the other important regional centres, its fair share of the limelight.

'But', Wright concluded, 'an hour's radio show about the Festival, which has to entertain, as well as inform, cannot fail to be sketchy, and leave a great many gaps'.[133] The reaction of the Northern Irish organisers to the perceived slight by Barry illustrated not only the importance they placed on the Farm and Factory Exhibition, but their general feelings of inferiority in relation to the rest of the United Kingdom.[134] In contrast, Nugent made no complaints about BBC Northern Ireland's home service's coverage of the festival; broadcasts were made by many of the organisers, including Nugent in November 1950:

> Now when people are bored and depressed – 'feeling frustrated' is I believe the modern catch word – it's not a bad thing for them to pull themselves together and, in the old phrase 'count their mercies'. The Festival will give us all a chance to do this, to realise the great things the country has done.[135]

J.D. Stewart, the dramatist, gave over several *Ulster Commentary* programmes to advertising the festival.[136] Of course, Stewart was already a part of the festival and his play, *Danger, Men Working*, was included in the drama programme. In September 1950 he spoke of the festival as something which everyone could enjoy: 'Everyone is to see it and enjoy it and – more than that – everyone may take part in it'.[137] Arnold felt that this broadcast 'should certainly encourage efforts by local authorities, who are at last beginning to wake up a bit'.[138] Stewart was in tune with the festival organiser's ethos; 'one of the objects of the Festival too – to show the community to the community, and make us admire each other and each other's handiwork.' 'It will make us all a little more aware. Aware of the community, of all our partners in it, and hence, of ourselves.'[139]

The closest connection the Northern Irish state had to the rest of the United Kingdom in the festival came in the shape of the 'Festival ship' – the *Campania* – which travelled around the coast of Britain carrying the dominant festival message of unity.[140] The *Campania* had been built by Harland and Wolff in 1943, and it returned to Belfast's Pollock dock in August for a week, giving the Northern Irish the opportunity to see a miniature version of the exhibition on the South Bank. That exhibition told the story of Britain in three parts: 'The Land of Britain', 'Discovery' and 'The People at Home'.[141]

> Its view of history was patriotic, evolutionary and non-expansionist. All references past or present to divisions of rich and poor, of class, of state as against private education, of state as opposed to private medicine were of course, glossed over as officially it was non-political.[142]

This question of a united nation was as problematic in Britain as the question of a united community was in Northern Ireland. As Barbara Dorf has noted, whole areas of Britain were ignored by the organisers of the festival, particularly the midlands and the north. And although organised by a labour government, the festival lacked input from those of a working-class background.[143] In a famous description, Michael Frayn identifies those who organised the festival in Britain as 'herbivores':

> In short, the Herbivores, or gentle ruminants, who look out from the lush pasture which are their natural station in life with eyes full of sorrow for less fortunate creatures, guiltily conscious of their advantages, though not usually ceasing to eat the grass.[144]

Those who organised the festival in Northern Ireland were not quite gentle 'ruminants', but members of the government, senior civil servants, industrialists and established members of the intelligentsia. The struggle seemed to be between the bureaucrats, ever aware of the financial drain that the festival was making, eager to promote Northern Ireland as a progressive industrial centre, and those concerned with the state's cultural representation, who wanted to do something lasting and significant in terms of the arts through the festival. In the end, the only strong statement, in cultural terms, was made by Bell's *The arts in Ulster*, whose introduction at least questioned the *status quo*.

Above all, the Festival of Britain in Northern Ireland was a chance for the unionist government to extol, with little opposition except from a select number of writers, the achievements of their state. It was a festival for Northern Ireland's business interests. In Britain the tories feared that the festival would be used to advertise the achievements of the labour government.[145] When labour lost the general election in the autumn of 1951 Churchill lost no time in destroying most of the buildings constructed for the festival, including the spectacular 'Skylon'.[146] The new minister of works, David Eccles, explained that the South Bank site was cleared with such haste because it was to be transformed into a garden to be used for the celebrations of the coronation in 1953, 'an appropriate Tory version of the spectacular to succeed the socialists of Britain'.[147] As Michael Frayn has noted, the festival did not evoke popular public enthusiasm in the same way that royal pageantry had in the past, and was to again in the coronation celebrations of 1953: 'the Festival was a rainbow – a brilliant sign riding the tail of the storm and promising fairer weather'.[148] In 1956 the Northern Irish journalist Martin Wallace argued that 'undue sensitivity to outside opinion' was the dominating characteristic of the Northern Irish state and 'another illustration of the mirror-image concept'.[149] In Northern Ireland the festival was not a mirror in which unionists could see their image and identity reflected, nor a window on the empire but, to use Roy Strong's phrase, an enchanted glass in which they attempted to conjure up a specific image of the state as progressive, industrial and united, an image in keeping with the stereotype of the 'Ulsterman' already established by past unionist writers.[150] The Festival of Britain in

Northern Ireland expressed one dimension of a complex unionist identity, displaying something which earlier unionist writers had articulated, a pride in the state's industry, and a belief in its progressive and modern nature. Unionism's response to the coronation evidenced another (albeit more familiar) side of unionism, one which was deeply loyal and sentimentally attached to the crown and empire as embodied in the monarchy. Unionism's reaction to these two events reveals a complexity within itself, but also an inherent pragmatism. Unionists were willing to accept the labour government, and the festival as a labour project, because of their desire to promote their state's industries and progressive image, and as John Hewitt had argued in 1949, because they wished 'to cling to those standards of life' which the labour government had raised or maintained.[151] Finally, unionism's reaction to the Festival of Britain in comparison to the coronation was in keeping with the general reaction felt throughout the United Kingdom, where the royal occasion caused far more public excitement and enthusiasm.[152]

All this stood in contrast to the coronation of Elizabeth II in June 1953, and the coronation visit to Northern Ireland in July of the same year, which were embraced with all the spectacle, symbolism and importance that the Northern Irish government could muster.[153] Their significance was highlighted by the editor of the *Northern Whig*, who argued that such ceremonies were 'alive and vital, an imperishable part of the life and the way of life of Britain and the British people, for the golden thread that runs through them and gives them true significance is of the spirit'.[154] The importance of the royal visits to the state was in direct proportion to its contemporary political circumstances; thus, in 1942 the royal visit provided a morale boost in the midst of the war; following the war, in 1945, it acted as a rallying point of unity for the Northern Irish; in 1949 a 'cheerful visit' by Princess Elizabeth and Prince Philip as the Ireland Act made its way through parliament and 'resentment rumbled on in Dublin, seemed to symbolise in the popular mind the removal for ever of a dangerous revanchist threat'.[155] In 1953, it was an occasion for unity with the theme of family and an expression of a new age of modernity centred around the symbol of the new young monarch.[156] In a changing world, royal ritual was familiar to the Northern Irish, and through its almost timeless pageantry (apart from the players themselves, little changed in the pattern of royal visits over the decades), and their role in it, unionists were reassured of the continuity of their place in the empire and the union. Moreover, unionists gained a sense of security from the high-profile and constant identification of royalty with their state. Nationalists in general however did not share in the unionists' pleasure in the royal visit; Henry Diamond, MP for the Falls, for instance, claimed that he was speaking to 'prevent misrepresentation' by unionists about the universal welcome for the royals in Northern Ireland: the visit was, he claimed, an endorsement of partition. The government, he continued, used royal occasions to 'make life very difficult for those who disagree with them in principle':

> At the same time, on occasions like this, in connection with the Empire and Imperial festivities feelings of persecution are aroused against the

nationally-minded minority in this area . . . so long as that attitude . . . persists there can be no question either of loyalty or even of enthusiastic acceptance of other people's celebrations on occasions like this.[157]

Thomas Henderson, MP for the Shankill, rebutted Diamond's claims, arguing that 'all creeds and classes not only in Northern Ireland but throughout the great British Commonwealth of Nations' were looking forward to the coronation 'with pleasure and joy', 'even His Holiness the Pope has asked Roman Catholic people of all countries over which he rules to pray for our young Queen.'[158] Nevertheless, nationalist objections to the visit persisted and, as will be shown later, expressed themselves in civil disorder.

The coronation visit came a year after the death of King George VI, who was, in the words of the editorial of the *Belfast Telegraph*, 'The Good Man as King': 'during the years of the blitz "the King is still in London" was a saying that was an inspiration to the people of the capital in hard circumstances'.[159] In 1942, the king and queen had paid a morale-boosting visit to the Northern Irish state. Because of the war, it was a low-key affair in comparison to previous – and indeed later – royal occasions.[160] The three-day visit included visits to the Harland and Wolff shipyards and the Short and Harland aircraft factory, as well as inspections of WRNS (Women's Royal Naval Service), the Home Guard, Civil Defence personnel, American army units, British Army and RAF units and British and American navies.[161] Given the recent entry of the USA into the war the prominence accorded them on this visit was not surprising.[162] It combined with the king as 'man of the people' theme: 'During the visit the King and Queen sat down to lunch with one hundred doughboys – enlisted men of the American Army – in a barrack mess, and drank coffee from big china pint mugs.'[163] This was a visit for the benefit of the troops and the war workers: 'Their path to the quay of a small Northern Irish town was lined by the men who are fighting and winning the Battle of the Atlantic – British and American sailors.'[164]

Elizabeth II's coronation visit to the state in 1953 inherited much, in form and organisation, from its most recent precursor in 1945, when the king and queen and the then Princess Elizabeth had visited Northern Ireland:

> The final visit of His Majesty to Ulster was probably the most exciting of all. It was on July 18, 1945. Victory had been won. The long night of the war was over and Ulster put on her best finery to give the King, who was accompanied by the Queen and Princess Elizabeth, an unforgettable reception.[165]

The royal visit of 1945 had been an opportunity for unionists to proclaim their loyalty against the backdrop of the Second World War; the northern state's 'pride and its boast', wrote the editor of the *Northern Whig*:

> Is that it is part and parcel of the United Kingdom, one with England, Scotland, and Wales, part of the Mother Country. Close on 25 years of self-government have not turned the eyes or the mind of its people outward; rather have they served to strengthen the feeling of oneness

with the sister countries of the United Kingdom and deepen the loyalty to the Crown.[166]

As guests of the Northern Irish governor, the royal family were greeted at Government House by two Lambeg drummers. On the first night of their visit they appeared in the courtyard of the house 'in response to the cheering of several hundred people gathered round the entrance'. They were cast 'as the heads of a happy household' returning home 'after a long absence'.[167] From the beginning of the war the Northern Irish government had placed much emphasis on the contribution made by the state to the Allied war effort, particularly in terms of the state's production of munitions, shipping, rope and fabric. War workers were, therefore, given prominence in the events organised for the king and queen's 1945 visit.[168] This included a workers' garden party in the Botanic gardens, to which 5,000 war workers from throughout the state were invited.[169] There was also a royal visit to the shipyards, where 'grimy, hoary-headed workmen craned their necks to the utmost to see her Royal Highness, and when the car had passed, they turned to those apprentices, not blessed with high status and asked, "Did you see her?"'.[170] The more formal side to the visit was the reception at Stormont; there the international character of the Allied war effort was highlighted:

> Members of the Senate were accommodated on both the Government and opposition benches and immediately behind them on the right were a number of officers representative of the British, USA and Belgian Armies, with all His Majesty's Lieutenants for the six Ulster counties and county boroughs.[171]

Given its importance as a military base during the war, Londonderry was also honoured with the royal presence: '"We'll guard old Derry's Walls", played by a 'B' Specials band, greeted the King and Queen and Princess Elizabeth when they arrived by royal yacht at Princess Quay Derry, yesterday'.[172] And at the Guildhall the royals took the salute of servicemen and women.[173] The more overt royal pomp was left to the visit to Queen's University 'where the splendour of the academic gowns – the gold, the purple, the red, the black and the green – lent a touch of pageantry to a scene of immense dignity.'[174]

On his death, the *Belfast Telegraph* noted that George VI had based his personal life and his official career on his family happiness.[175] The 'family' theme was carried through when Princess Elizabeth was crowned Queen Elizabeth II in June 1953.[176] 'Perhaps the omens are propitious', wrote the editor of the *Northern Whig*, 'for never was the Monarchy so close to the people, never has the Sovereign so fully represented the whole nation'.[177] The visit to Northern Ireland of Queen Elizabeth II, in her role as 'the symbolic custodian of national unity and communal values', was important to the unionist government in that it helped to lessen any antagonism which protestants in the state held towards them.[178] In this context, the queen acted as a symbol of family solidarity, and solidarity was a key unionist concern in this period. The coronation visit to Northern Ireland was cast then in traditional terms, and there was an added emphasis, as the Korean War drew to a close, on militarism.[179] This included a priority accorded to women. In Londonderry, for example, 'it was appropriate that the women's services should be given places of honour in the vicinity of the Guildhall. Detachments of the WRNS, WRAC and WRAF were on parade in Whittaker Street and Shipquay place'.[180] Within the ranks of the troops there was an international air which reflected the broad effort of nations (under the auspices of the United Nations) involved in the war. In the reports of the unionist press, there was a tension between depicting this royal occasion as a traditional ritual, and as a democratic celebration. Military personnel and elements of pageantry were given priority, but in view of the fact that the Northern Irish government was keen to emphasise its continuing worth as a military base this is not surprising.

The unionist press gave copious coverage to the coronation ceremony, publishing among other things a detailed map of who would attend the coronation and where they would sit in Westminster Abbey, in this way allowing the Northern Irish reading public to feel they were part of the royal pageant. Given their large audience, the unionist press were strategically well placed 'to promote a national consensus around a potent symbol like the Crown'.[181] The coronation's level of public access was an innovation; to quote David Chaney:

> It was because previously mysterious parts of traditional ritual became literally visible that this coronation, more than any other royal ceremonial, marked a turning point between symbolism articulating constitutional relationships and ritual as dramatic spectacle.[182]

The coronation year was also the year in which television in Britain came of age. This meant that the priority in media terms was accorded to the new medium and radio was left to follow its traditional routines. In this respect Northern Ireland was relatively unaffected; although there were television sets in the state which received the coronation programme, the medium was scarce.[183] As the *Whig* reported:

> Until the middle of the afternoon most of the people were inside their homes or in with friends or neighbours to hear the BBC broadcasts of the ceremony and the processions in London. If they possessed a television set or were fortunate to watch one they saw what must have been a perfect projection of the scenes in the Abbey and in the streets of London. Both the sound and television went without a hitch.[184]

The television transmission did go without a hitch; the RUC kept a guard on the television transmitter at Glencairn to ensure that no attempt was 'made to interfere with the station and so prevent the local TV relay of the coronation ceremony and parade in London'.[185]

Though scarce, television caused subtle changes in the way in which the coronation was represented to the listening and reading audience in Northern Ireland. In the press coverage there was an added sense of the immediacy of the coronation ritual. The *Whig* assured its readers, for instance, that its correspondent had a seat in the Abbey from which he would be able to describe 'in detail the great service there'.[186] The radio coverage was improved by the television coverage; the head of outside broadcasts (sound) for the BBC noted that because of the television monitor he was able to 'advise commentators about things that were taking place which they were missing'.[187] The reports of the coronation were full of theatrical detail:

> Only the Queen was still. Motionless, she sat in King Edward's Chair, holding in her hands the Sceptre and Rod. From above brilliant lights beat on the gold carpet of the theatre – the Crossing of the Church – in which the great drama of the coronation was played.[188]

The readers of the main Northern Irish newspapers had been prepared for the spectacle days in advance: 'On Tuesday the Abbey will be peopled by peers in their red and ermine; by knights in their silken mantles of colour according to their Order; by heralds in their tabards; by archbishops in their copes'.[189] Northern Ireland's capital was given its role in the great drama through scene and atmosphere:

> The greater part of Belfast lay amazingly still and quiet yesterday morning – no smoke from the factories; hardly any traffic in the streets; few pedestrians; the shopping centres deserted. The bunting and flags looked like the backdrop and scenery trappings of an empty stage, just before the show.[190]

Belfast corporation ensured that the city would be suitably prepared, placing ads in the press 'requesting that owners of business premises, shop-keepers and householders' would 'arrange to have their premises suitably decorated for the coronation'.[191] The *Northern Whig* detailed the colour and exotic nature of the coronation procession through London:

> Here were courageous saronged men of the Federation of Malaya Police – all with gallantry decorations – Fiji Islanders in their sulu skirts proud of their war-time reputation of being the world's best jungle fighters, West and East African troops, men from the Windward Islands, Sarawak and Aden.[192]

Lord Brookeborough, representing Northern Ireland at the ceremony, broadcast a special radio 'programme of homage' from London; he spoke in, by now traditional, terms of the Belfast shipyards and the number of American presidents of 'Ulster' ancestry. Northern Ireland was, he said:

> A small but fertile country. A land of sun and showers, of farms and industry. A rugged coast – with rugged people. We have more than played our part in feeding these islands in war and peace – and our linen spans the earth. But first and last we are loyal – and here and now from loyal Ulster men and women I bring our loving greetings to Her Majesty the Queen.[193]

To mark the coronation, bonfires were lit throughout Britain and Northern Ireland; bonfires throughout the state 'flared up to become part of a gigantic chain of light stretching all over the United Kingdom'.[194] Northern Ireland's celebration of the coronation was in keeping with the rest of the United Kingdom with parades, fancy dress parties, sports events, performances by bands and religious services. The majority of events, such as those held in Whitehead, were youth orientated:

> In Whitehead the main features were a fancy dress parade and a sports meeting. About 500 children paraded to the sports field, where a programme of 26 events was run off. The children were afterwards provided with free ice-cream, chocolate and minerals.[195]

The state was traditionally bedecked with bunting and flags, and the citizens were portrayed as a united community celebrating to the full on the eve of the coronation around the figure of the monarch:

> On Shankill Road, where every side street looked like Coney Island, with illuminated windows and royal emblems and gay coloured lanterns hanging outside almost every house, and bonfires big enough to blister the paint on the homes of those who danced around them, thousands of people celebrated until after midnight.[196]

These festivities aside, the editor of the *Northern Whig* summed up what he believed the coronation symbolised: 'Amid the rejoicing, then, Coronation Day calls upon us, as it does upon the Queen, to renew our faith and to re-dedicate ourselves to the service of God and our fellowman'.[197] The 'fellowman' referred to was, of course, a member of the British Commonwealth; 'men do not live by bread and power alone and the Commonwealth still sets an example that is the wonder of nations who see us as too often we fail to see ourselves'.[198] The festivities for the coronation were seen as a means of uniting the diverse commonwealth in a common celebration. In London a lunch was held for representatives from the commonwealth countries; those guests included, naturally, Basil Brooke but also Frank Boland, the ambassador of the Irish republic to Britain. The response of the Irish republic to the coronation had been measured, although Cardinal D'Alton, the catholic primate of Ireland, issued a press release expressing the wish that during the new queen's reign 'all of us who love the old historic Ireland' would hope to see the country 'restored to its natural unity'.[199]

The 1953 coronation visit was on a far grander scale than the one-day visit of the king in 1937.[200] It was a celebratory affair for unionists, reflecting their self-confidence in this period.[201] However, contrary to the image portrayed by the unionist government and press it was not a cause of celebration for the whole of the Northern Irish community. Nationalist MPs in Northern Ireland 'publicly repudiated the [queen's] right to reign over Northern Ireland'; speaking retrospectively against the visit, one nationalist MP claimed that the occasion of this royal visit was taken by unionists as an opportunity to suppress any views which were contrary to theirs:

Surely the hon. and learned Member need express no surprise if on an occasion, a very public occasion, such as the recent Royal visit, the representatives of the majority of people in this country, and at least of the minority in the Six Northern counties, attempt to put forth their point of view . . . should we have hidden ourselves away for the sake of the facade that the Unionist Party presents on occasions.[202]

In more direct protest, the IRA planted bombs in Belfast and in Kilkeel, Co. Down; and in Newry, where nationalists controlled the council, the flying of patriotic bunting on council property was forbidden.[203] Elsewhere in the state, in areas which were divided between nationalists and unionists, the flying of bunting also became a cause of contention.[204] This was not a celebration for Northern Ireland's catholic population then, a fact ignored by the unionist government, as they had ignored their non-participation in the festival.[205] The extent to which nationalist opinion gained a response from unionists was epitomised in Derry where 1,300 police (a third of the RUC's force) were drafted in to ensure that there would be no nationalist disturbances during the coronation visit to the city. But, as so often with unionist shows of unity, this coronation visit was a chance to reaffirm protestant solidarity, and paper over tensions within the protestant community. One incident clearly exposed this underlying tension; in June 1952 the minister for home affairs, Brian Maginess, had banned an Orange march on the Longstone Road, a nationalist area near Annalong, Co. Down. In the face of Orange protests his decision was rescinded the following month but the incident, in conjunction with the nationalist hostility towards the coronation and the subsequent mediation by the RUC between catholics and protestants, was seen as a sign by some unionists that the government was following a policy of appeasing the nationalist population. In direct response, in the elections at the end of the coronation year, seven independent unionists challenged the government, standing on a platform of 'ultra-Loyalism, anti-Catholicism, and social and economic populism'. Brian Maginess was challenged in his own constituency and attacked specifically over the government's purported appeasement of catholics during the coronation. Willie John McCracken, who opposed him, and his supporters accused the RUC (and thus by extension the government) of having stood 'idly by', allowing the IRA to take over the town of Dungiven, and stopping the Boveva band from playing. Brookeborough intervened, speaking at one of Maginess's election meetings, and promising his audience that the Union Jack would not be prevented from flying in any part of the state in future. Although Maginess retained his seat, his vote dropped by over 3,000. As with Brookeborough, the unionist government responded quickly to this criticism from within its ranks, and the new minister for home affairs, G.B. Hanna, ordered an enquiry into the incident at Dungiven. As a result, 1954 saw the introduction of the Flags and Emblems Act which made it an offence to interfere with the Union Jack, and gave the police the right to remove other flags which might provoke a breach of the peace; this was clearly aimed at the tricolour, and Hanna 'apologised that he couldn't ban the Tricolour outright as this was a matter of foreign policy reserved to Westminster'.[206]

Against this background then, the emphasis of the 1953 royal visit was on traditional royal procession, high-profile spectacle, and overt protestant unity. The visit of 1953 was predicted as one of the 'most colourful of royal visits for many years': 'For the Queen has sent before her a detachment of the celebrated Yeomen of the Guard, who will precede the royal Party at formal indoor processions, and a group of State Trumpeters, who will greet the Queen and the Duke with fanfares at several engagements'.[207] From the outset, public accessibility was a key feature of the organisation. For instance, at a meeting of the coronation committee, 'Lord Glentoran referred to the desirability of providing an open car in order that the public might have a good view of the royal visitors'.[208] In January 1953 the General Purposes and Finance Sub-Committee of Belfast corporation proposed 'a fireworks display on the banks of the Lagan and in connection therewith suggested that arrangements be made for a barge to be provided for the conveyance of the Belfast City Orchestra who would perform Handel's Water Music and music for the royal fireworks during the display'.[209] The visit of the new queen echoed, often directly, that of the royal family in 1945. Again, as guests of the governor of Northern Ireland at Government house, Hillsborough, the royals were welcomed by two Lambeg drummers (as the previous king and queen had been in 1945).[210] In a special feature on Hillsborough castle the *Belfast Telegraph*'s reporter wrote:

> All roads lead to Hillsborough, that ancient town in the heart of the country were [*sic*] once stood the stronghold of the Magennises. On this site the first-born of Sir Moyses Hill, that gallant soldier who served the first Elizabeth, built a castle. Now, here is the home of the Governor of Northern Ireland, representative in Ulster of Queen Elizabeth the Second. How strangely interwoven are the strands which bind us to our past.[211]

Again, as in 1945, the royal couple made an impromptu appearance on the balcony of Government house 'responding to the fervent calls of "We want the Queen! We want the Queen!" from thousands of adults and children who had assembled outside Government house, Hillsborough, to acclaim them on the first evening of their coronation visit'.[212] There was an insistence in the unionist press that the Northern Irish public's response to the queen was an immense and a 'spontaneous' outpouring of emotion: 'The size of the crowds, the fervour of their loyal greetings in Ulster's towns and countryside, looking its loveliest in these hot July days – these cannot be "bespoke" or made to order'.[213] What could be assured was the presence of civilian bands at various point along the processional route.[214] The lining of the streets with troops as the royals made their way through the city proved difficult, as the RUC's inspector general illustrated, 'by reason of the long distances involved'.[215] The children waiting to see the royals in Ormeau Park, and the people of Ballymoney, were portrayed as having anxiously awaited their arrival.[216] This royal occasion was one of interaction with the general public, indeed the public played a starring role in the performance; at a garden party in Brooke park 'wave after wave of cheering' reverberated as the royals arrived, while 'in the enclosures more than 2,000 citizens representing every walk of life were waiting' to greet them.[217] But the celebration of the visit was not restricted to those who could attend the parks visited by the royals; 'while the main routes through Belfast and other towns are gay with colour', wrote the *Northern Whig*'s reporter, 'the real beauty and originality is to be found in the back streets which will never see royalty, but whose loyalty is none the less for that'.[218] While they may not have had the presence of royals 'two of Belfast's little streets will be honoured to-day when the prime minister, on his way to Aldergrove to greet the Queen, will stop off to admire their decorations'.[219] That evening the governor hosted the state dinner, which again the papers gave minute details about. The thirty-two guests were entertained in the 'splendid surroundings' of Government house:

> The simple elegance of the room was otherwise unadorned, the long windows looking out on the lawns at one side, and on the other the walls filled with portraits of men and women famous in Ulster history, that of the Duke of Abercorn the first Governor, being nearest the centre, and that of Lord Carson at the further end.[220]

As with the royal visits of the 1930s and 1940s, this visit allowed the Northern Irish state to confirm both the harmony and homogeneity of the state, and its secure place in the empire.

Having stayed at Government house on the first night of their arrival, the royals spent the following day visiting the traditional sites: Queen's University, the City Hall, the Balmoral show and Stormont parliament. The most militaristic of all the events was the Balmoral show. Balmoral had an established place in unionist tradition as a display ground for the unionist faithful, most notably when Bonar Law visited Belfast in 1912. In 1953, a similar military aspect was notable: 'The massed standards, the gleaming sheen of the medals and the regimental bearing of the veterans, many of whom had seen service in the Boer War, all contributed to probably the most impressive scenes ever staged at Ulster's historic parade ground'.[221] At the Whitla Hall, attention switched to the outfits of the principal ladies:

> She [the queen] was wearing a coat frock of blue shanting with a close fitting straw hat of the same shade. A touch of navy on the hat matched her gloves and bag, and on the lapel of her frock was a diamond brooch ... Lady Wakehurst ... was wearing a gown of nut brown taffeta with sailor hat to match and coat of dusky lemon. Lady Brookeborough was in a silk frock of hyacinth blue, with small hat of black straw with veil, black gloves and bag.[222]

The visit to the Whitla Hall was a spectacular affair, and not only because of the queen's outfit: 'The colour came from the gilt adornments of the Trumpeters, the bright uniforms of the Yeomen of the Guard, the robes of the mayors of various boroughs, and the sunlight which cast bright gleams'.[223] In the presence of mayors, members of the cabinet and leaders of the various protestant denominations, Brookeborough reminded his audience of the great occasion of the coronation ceremony in London, 'which had acted on the emotions of a people who had gone through trials of war and peace'.[224] Again, the prime minister was recalling for the audience the bonds which united Northern Ireland with Britain, and the emphasis was on their continued unity under the new monarch. On her final day the queen paid a visit to Stormont, and her speech to the Northern Irish House of Commons was traditional:

> As your Queen I am now even more closely concerned with the affairs of Northern Ireland, and I assure you that I shall always strive to repay your loyalty and devotion with my steadfast service to you, and may God give you wisdom and faith in your labours.[225]

The banner headline of the *Northern Whig* on 3 July echoed this message:

> 'I shall always strive to repay your loyalty and devotion'
> Queen's Pledge to Province.[226]

The visit of the queen to the Northern Irish parliament was, then, full of significance for unionists, and was marked by all the trappings of royal ritual: 'As her Majesty descended the Central Staircase to the Great Hall a flourish of trumpets was sounded by the State Trumpeters'.[227] The Yeomen of the Guard lined the staircase of Stormont as the queen listened to the traditional response from the speaker of the Northern Irish House of Commons: 'It is our heartfelt prayer that Your Majesty may be blessed with health and strength long to reign over us, and to safeguard and enrich the ancient constitution to which we in Northern Ireland are proud to be heirs'.[228] The queen's three-day visit was represented by the media in great detail: 'But thereafter, until Friday evening, the Queen will spend almost all her waking hours among her people, the ordinary people of Ulster who are renowned the world over for their loyalty and the boisterousness of their welcomes'.[229] The last day of the visit epitomised the processionary nature of this royal occasion; Queen Elizabeth travelled through Northern Ireland's hinterland by train, the *HMS Rocket*, and by sea to Derry. The train itself became a manifestation of the traditional tone the organisers were striving for. Built in 1911, it was appropriate for use as a royal transport; according to the *Northern Whig*'s reporter: 'No modern plastics could possibly compete with the magnificent aged mahogany panelling. No ultra-modern could better the simple dignity of its form'.[230] The train's original purpose had been as a transport for systems inspections in the state; now in 1953 it was being used as a vehicle for royal inspection. The Northern Irish public were informed in some detail of the minute decor of the train: 'The Royal suite is furnished in easy chairs, covered with pale grey Ulster linen; the floor has a gold carpet, and heavy glass ash trays in the form of four-leaf clover stand on the occasional tables'.[231] This 'magnificent' ten-coach train of blue and cream stood under guard at the GNR terminus at Belfast awaiting the arrival of its royal passengers.[232] The procession through the Northern Irish countryside was also well reported, again with the emphasis on the accessibility of the queen for the public:

From Ballymena the journey continued through Cullybackey, Glarryford, Dunloy to Ballymoney. This part of the journey was through Ulster's agricultural heart with its rolling fields and well-kept farms; then on to Coleraine, the broad River Bann, and the sea. To Coleraine, where at the request of the Governor, Lord Wakehurst, the site of the royal dais was changed so that more people could see their Queen.[233]

Derry was the peak of this royal visit:

Londonderry, second city of the Province, to-day put the seal on the triumph of the Queen's coronation visit to Northern Ireland. The ancient city famous for its loyalty to the Crown gave Her Majesty and the Duke of Edinburgh one of the most spontaneous and moving welcomes of their lives.[234]

There was no mention in the press of the added numbers of police drafted in for the day, or the fears of nationalist disturbances. Rather it was noted that the majority of people had the day off so that 'the opportunity of seeing the Queen and the Duke of Edinburgh was made easy for all'.[235] The attention which came with the royal visit also provided the opportunity to highlight the port's military importance: 'As the frigate, dressed overall and with the royal Standard at the masthead, steamed slowly through the historic waters of the Foyle, she signified Londonderry's new-found place as one of the principal naval bases in the United Kingdom'.[236] On the 1 July the story of the royal visit was juxtaposed in the *Belfast Telegraph* with reminiscences of the Battle of the Somme, in an article entitled 'When Orange sashes were worn by the British Army'. 'From a testing immediate past', the editor of the *Belfast Telegraph* concluded, 'we have emerged into a harassing present and a difficult future'.[237] Above all, this was the value of the coronation visit in that it manifested in a traditional, high-profile way the permanent position of the Northern Irish state within the United Kingdom, and the unity of the protestant community behind the symbol of the monarch.

As Hammerton and Cannadine have concluded: 'The planning, staging and celebration of a ritual is not just a means by which people explain society to themselves: it is also, of itself, an expression, a product, of tensions and conflicts, links and shared assumptions of that society'.[238] In common with the rituals of the 1930s, the coronation visit and the festival made the Northern Irish state's identity, as perceived by unionists, tangible to a domestic and foreign audience. The image projected was of a protestant, industrial, homogenous community free of disharmony, although this was clearly not the case. In reality both the festival and coronation were dominated by Northern Irish protestant élites; priority in both was accorded to the unionist government, industrialists, civic authorities, and protestant religious leaders. They were expressions of protestant consensus, even on a superficial basis, and a reinforcement of the protestant hierarchy. Moreover, the coronation testified to the enduring place of the monarchy in the fabric of Northern Irish protestant culture and identity. Each occasion was aided by the unionist press which conjured up interest and excitement about the events in the public sphere, and gave the protestant population at large a sense of involvement. These performances were examples of ritualised consensus, full of references to a protestant past which appealed directly and exclusively to unionists.[239] In a similar way to the rituals of the 1930s, these rituals in the 1950s united Northern Ireland's unionists in a display of strength, and at the same time betrayed their continuing defensiveness in the face of criticism from within their own ranks.

Notes and References

1   David Cannadine, 'Introduction: divine rites of kings', in David Cannadine and Simon Price (eds.), *Rituals of royalty: power and ceremony in traditional societies* (Cambridge, 1987), p. 3.

2   Elizabeth Hammerton and David Cannadine 'Conflict and consensus on a ceremonial occasion: the Diamond Jubilee in Cambridge in 1897', *The Historical Journal*, vol. 24, no. I (1981), p. 112. Although this is more traditionally associated with the discussion of royal pageantry, such as the coronation, it also applies to the Festival of Britain in Northern Ireland since both were government-dictated ceremonials which took traditional form. Moreover, the festival included a royal visit.

3   Catholics played no significant part in either event. But then the attitude of the catholic community towards both was a matter of indifference to the unionist authorities: their initial impulse was to ignore the problem except when they had to face the matter directly as when they had to decide what to do about church participation in the festival, or when they had to draft in extra police to prevent nationalist disturbances during the queen's coronation visit to Derry.

4   Although this petered out by 1946 by which time, according to Bew, Gibbon and Patterson, the unionist government became convinced of Attlee's goodwill towards them. 'The Home Secretary, Chuter Ede, rebuffed the attempts of both the Northern Irish Labour Party and the "friends of Ireland" group of backbench labour MPs to raise issues such as electoral law and practices, discrimination and the Special Powers Act in Ulster'. See P. Bew, P. Gibbon and Henry Patterson, *The state in Northern Ireland, 1921–72: political forces and social classes* (Manchester, 1979), p. 121.

5   ibid., p. 116.

6   De Valera's request, in 1947, that the British government should make a declaration that they wished to see an end to partition alarmed the unionist government.

7   According to Basil Brooke, Éire's decision to become a republic was ' "the last stage of that deplorable journey" that had taken the south of Ireland from the Free State to total separation'. Dennis Kennedy, *The widening gulf: northern attitudes to the independent Irish state, 1919–49* (Belfast, 1988), p. 239. Brooke saw the declaration of a republic as the end of a journey, drawing the thread back to the establishment of the two states, underlining the unionist belief that the settlement of 1920/21 had always been under threat from the southern state, that they had been correct in their defensiveness about their own position, within the island and within the union.

8   Hugh Shearman, 'Recent developments in Anglo-Irish relations', *World Affairs*, Apr. 1949, p. 163.

9   Nicholas Mansergh, *The unresolved question: the Anglo-Irish settlement and its undoing, 1912–72* (Avon, 1991), p. 336. The Ireland Act was the British Government's response to Ireland's departure from the Commonwealth. In it they guaranteed Northern Ireland's status.

10 John Bowman, *De Valera and the Ulster question* (Oxford, 1982), pp. 267–9.

11 'This legislative affirmation of Ulster's right to remain part of the United Kingdom is the necessary counterpart of the acknowledgement of Southern Ireland's secession from the British Commonwealth', *Ulster Commentary*, editorial, Jan. 1950.

12 David Harkness, *Northern Ireland since 1920* (Dublin, 1983), p. 120.

13 The election victory for unionists was also a sign of the government's acceptance of the labour government's measures of welfare reform.

14 The Northern Irish Labour Party was entirely squeezed out in the election, leaving the Stormont parliament polarised, with nationalists as the only opposition.

15 The Attlee government granted self-government to India, Pakistan, Ceylon (Sri Lanka) and Burma between 1947 and 1949. Unionist fears were recognised by the British government in October 1948: 'The people of Northern Ireland would undoubtedly regard Éire's secession from the Commonwealth as a serious threat to them; and, whatever mitigation of the practical consequences of secession might be acceptable to the United Kingdom government, it was likely that the government of Northern Ireland would feel bound to adopt rigorous measures in protection of their interests', Ronan Fanning, 'The response of the London and Belfast governments to the declaration of the Republic of Ireland, 1948–49', *International Affairs*, vol. 58, no. I (1981–2), p. 100.

16 In the same way texts such as John Blake's *Northern Ireland in the Second World War* reinforced and reminded readers of Northern Ireland's war-time contribution, while St John Ervine's *Craigavon: Ulsterman* affirmed unionism and the state through a celebration of Lord Craigavon, while at the same time boosting unionist self-esteem through criticism of the southern state and its citizens.

17 Hugh Shearman, *Northern Ireland: its government, resources and people* (HMSO, 1949). This complexity is also revealed in this statement from Dinah McNabb in the House of Commons: 'This Festival will be an act of national reassessment and an affirmation of faith in the future, and Northern Ireland, with its wealth of native poetry and drama, its outstanding craftsmanship, its many advances in the arts and sciences, will be able to make a worthy contribution to this great Festival, a Festival which will demonstrate to the world the undaunted courage and patriotism of the British people', *Northern Hansard*, vol. xxxiv, 28 Feb. 1950.

18 Roy Strong points to the festival's precursor, the British Empire Exhibition at Wembley in 1924: 'The exhibition set before the survivors [of the First World War], and a new generation, the myth of Empire as a way of life and the future'. In fact, 'at a late stage of designing the Festival . . . it was suddenly realised that no provision had been made for an exhibit to recall 1851', in Mary Banham and Bevis Hillier (eds.), *A tonic for the nation: the Festival of Britain* (London, 1976), pp. 7–12.

19 To quote the king at St Paul's Cathedral: 'This Festival of Britain has been planned, like its great predecessor, as a visible sign of national achievement and confidence', *BNL*, 4 May 1951. Kenneth O. Morgan (ed.), *Oxford history of Britain* (Oxford, 1993), p. 637.

20 Extract from the *Great Exhibition Centenary Official Committee*, 17 Feb. 1949, CAB 9F/176/1.

21 Michael Frayn, 'Festival', in Michael Sissons and Phillip French (eds.), *Age of austerity, 1945–51* (Oxford, 1986), p. 307.

22 ibid., p. 329.

23   Lord Ismay, chairman of the Festival of Britain Council, to Sir Roland Nugent, 3 Dec. 1950, COM 4A/8.

24   Adrian Forty, 'Festival Politics', in *A tonic for the nation*, p. 26.

25   A state-controlled festival, it manifested the close links between the government and industrialists, something which Bew, Gibbon and Patterson dismiss in *The state in Northern Ireland*, pp. 102–28.

26   *NW*, 30 Apr. 1951.

27   Sir Roland Nugent, *NW*, 30 Apr. 1951.

28   David Harkness, *Northern Ireland since 1920*, p. 124. There were some significant social and economic improvements in Northern Ireland in the post-war period, in education, social welfare, housing. See D.S. Johnson 'The Northern Ireland economy, 1914–39', in L. Kennedy and P. Ollerenshaw (eds.), *An economic history of Ulster 1820–1939* (Manchester, 1985). Ironically, although the '50s was one of the most successful periods in the history of the state, it was still one of the least developed of all UK regions.

29   De Valera was closely associated with the Anti-Partition League, paying great attention to it and its activities on his tours of the USA, Australia and Britain in the later '40s.

30   'At one point in 1951 sixty-eight vessels were either being built or on order, and twenty-one thousand men were fully employed on Queen's Island'. Linen manufacturers also experienced a boom both due to the Korean War and to the fact that linen's main rival rayon was in short supply. In 1951 76,000 were employed in the textile industry. Jonathon Bardon, *A history of Ulster* (Belfast, 1992), p. 613.

31   *NW*, 1 May 1951. The Northern Ireland festival was one of twenty-three festivals to be held throughout the United Kingdom. A.A.K. Arnold was deputy principal in the ministry of commerce and he was recommended by the ministry of finance as chairman of the Northern Ireland council for the festival. Letter from ministry of finance to Sir Robert Gransden, cabinet secretary, 13 Aug. 1949, CAB 9F/176/2.

32   Michael Frayn, 'Festival', p. 310.

33   *NW*, 31 May 1951.

34   The king's speech encapsulated the ethos of the festival: 'We have not proved unworthy of our past, and we can do better in the years ahead . . . In this Festival, then, we look back with pride, and forward with resolution', *BNL*, 4 May 1951.

35   Tyrone Guthrie, in *Ulster Commentary*, 1950. For more details of Guthrie's festival involvement see note 73.

36   James Loughlin, *Ulster unionism and British identity* (London, 1995), pp. 52, 157–8.

37   Estyn Evans, *Northern Ireland: a new guide book with an introduction by E. Estyn Evans* (London, 1951).

38   *BNL*, 4 May 1951.

39   In addition to CEMA a smaller sub-committee on culture was organised by R.C. Grubb in June 1949; its role was to cover any areas not already being dealt with by CEMA and in April 1950 the agenda included a discussion on erecting plaques to famous citizens from the state, a book exhibition, an exhibition of public records, a poetry competition and a documentary competition. This sub-committee became known as Lady Antrim's committee on culture, its members were J.A.S. Stendall, director of the Belfast Museum and Art Gallery, J. Nelson Browne, College of Technology Belfast, David Kennedy, St Malachy's College Belfast, Dr Estyn Evans, QUB, J. Babbington, city librarian, Belfast, H.W. McMullan, BBC, and Miss P. O'Connor, secretary to the committee, COM 4A/6.

40   Lindsay Keir, president and vice-chancellor of Queen's University, Belfast, was nominated by the Northern Irish government as the state's representative on the central council of the main Festival of Britain Committee.

41   William A. Leitch to J.C. McLaughlin, 29 Nov. 1949, COM 4B/9. The issue of calling Northern Ireland 'Ulster' had arisen with the declaration of the Irish republic; in 1948/49 when the British government was drawing up a new bill to define its relationship to the new republic and Northern Ireland, what eventually became the Ireland Act, the Northern Irish government wanted the state's official name to be 'Ulster'. Ronan Fanning, 'London and Belfast's response to the declaration of the Republic of Ireland, 1948–49', p. 106. Article 4 of the 1937 constitution in the Free State changed its name to Éire; in Northern Ireland this prompted discussions about whether the state's name should be changed to 'Ulster', but some unionists feared that it would reduce 'the status of government loans by suggesting they were only of local standing', and that 'the amendment in name might suggest other changes in the Government of Ireland Act of 1920', Nicholas Mansergh, *The unresolved question*, p. 306.

42   At one of the earliest meetings of the Festival council in London, Sir Roland Nugent was keen to establish that 'the scale of the Festival activities and expenditure in Northern Ireland should be in conformity with that in Great Britain in so far as it reflected the policy of economy being followed by the festival organisation', minutes of the Festival of Britain council, 9 Dec. 1949, COM 4A/7.

43   Col. Haughton was replaced by Sir Roland Nugent as chairman of the FOBCNI.

44   Col. Haughton to FOBCNI, 3 Mar. 1949, COM 4A/2. The CEMA standing committee were also anxious to insure that the 'scale upon which anything is undertaken will compare not unfavourably with the scale of similar activities in Great Britain', Minutes, 4 Jan. 1949, AC1/2/1.

45   This happened in September 1949, and A.A.K. Arnold replaced R.C.W. Grubb as secretary.

46   The members appointed in Nov. 1948 were D.H. Alexander, A.G. Algeo, J.P, the Countess of Antrim, L. Arndell, R.W. Berkley, S. Clarke, Col. S.G. Haughton (chairman), E.T.R. Herdman, A.J. Howard, J. Keating, Dehra Parker, MP, Denis Rebbeck (vice-chairman) and R.C.W. Grubb (secretary), COM 4A/2.

47   The memo continued: 'If any approved Festival projects, in their carrying out by the executive bodies concerned, appear to diverge from or to be taking on a character not in accord with the policy or standards of the festival, the Committee is empowered through the Minister-in-Charge that they should cease to be recognised as Festival projects', FOBCNI memo Nov. 1949, COM 4A/2.

48   Letter Leonard Crainford, secretary of the Festival of Britain, to L. Arndell, the representative from the Ministry of Education, 27 Apr. 1949, COM 4A/25.

49   The civic authorities had their own festival sub-committee which noted in its final report that: 'The Festivities in most of the large towns were organised by Festival Committees set up by local councils but in the smaller towns and villages voluntary Festival Committees spared neither time nor money to make their Festival events memorable occasions', Nov. 1951, COM 4D/8.

50   CEMA standing committee, 11 Jan. 1950, AC1/2/1.

51   Letter, J. Cook, at the Ministry of Finance, to A.A.K. Arnold, 25 Apr. 1951, COM 4A/4.

52   *NW,* 4 May 1951.

53   'The Ministry of Finance had agreed to an overall gross figure of £59,000 and a net figure of £27,500 for CEMA Festival projects', memo A.A.K. Arnold to CEMA standing committee, 11 Jan. 1950, AC1/2/1. The file on the cost of the Farm and Factory Exhibition held by PRONI is closed at present.

54   The promotion of new industry was always going to be difficult in Northern Ireland given that it had no fuel source, the high cost of importing fuel and the cost of cross-channel transport. Despite the boom in shipping and textiles in the early 1950s, Northern Ireland remained the most disadvantaged region of the United Kingdom at that time. Jonathon Bardon, *A history of Ulster*, p. 618.

55   Asa Briggs, *History of British broadcasting* (5 vols, London, 1961–95), vol. iv, p. 19.

56   COM 4A/2.

57   FOBCNI (nd) Sir Roland Nugent, COM 4A/2.

58   COM 4/E/1/13.

59   The other members were Dr D. Rebbeck (director of the Belfast shipyards), James Alexander (secretary of the Belfast harbour commissioners), the Countess of Antrim, L. Arndell (the representative from the ministry of education), R.W. Berkley (director of the Belfast Steamship Company), W.H.N. Downer (general and financial secretary of CEMA), E.T.R. Herdman (linen and country interests, Co. Tyrone), A.J. Howard (director of scientific developments at the ministry of commerce), J. Keating (trade unions representative), Nelson McMillan (chairman of the Northern Irish Tourist Board), Mrs J.A. Mackie (chairman, voluntary organisations sub-committee), Councillor J.H. Norritt (Belfast Corporation) and Andrew Stewart (controller, BBC Northern Ireland), COM 4A/2.

60   Festival of Britain in Northern Ireland local authorities sub-committee, final report, Nov. 1951, COM 4D/8.

61   *Northern Hansard*, vol. xxxiv, 17 Oct. 1950.

62   Letter, A.A.K. Arnold to William Scott, permanent secretary to the ministry of finance, 20 May 1950, COM 4A/25.

63   Sir Roland Nugent to Andrew Stewart, 22 Nov. 1949, COM 4A/2. The members of the official committee (i.e. government) c. 1951 were W.H. Smyth, minister of education, H.E. Jones, minister of commerce, W. McCauley, minister of health and local government, and A.A.K. Arnold, secretary, COM 4A/4.

64   W.H.N. Downer sought to gain assurances from Grubb that 'approvals and assurances conveyed on behalf of the Festival Committee' would have 'official support and authority'. W.H.N. Downer, general and financial secretary of CEMA, to R.C.W. Grubb, secretary of the FOBCNI, nd, but probably August 1949, AC1/2/1.

65   A.A.K. Arnold to the CEMA's standing committee, 11 Jan. 1950, AC1/2/1.

66   CEMA minutes, 11 Jan. 1950, AC1/2/1.

67   The make-up of CEMA's standing committee in July 1949 was: Dame Dehra Parker, MP (chairman), A.C. Williams (vice-chairman), W.J. Hardie, John Hewitt (chairman, art committee), A.S.G. Loxton (chairman, drama committee), C.J. McKisack (vice-chairman, music committee), W.H.N. Downer (general and financial secretary), J. Loudan (organiser) and Andrew Stewart, controller, BBC NI, who attended for festival items. The committee remained substantially the same; however, by 1950 Dehra Parker was no longer chairman, she was replaced by A.C. Williams. Over the course of time additional members were added; these were Lt/Col John F. Hunter, R.H. Semple, W.J. Sloan, J.A.S. Stendall and A.A.K. Arnold (secretary controller, Festival of Britain Committee in Northern Ireland), AC1/2/1.

68   Minutes of CEMA's standing committee, 13 Oct. 1949, AC1/2/1.

69   Dame Dehra Parker was minister for health and local government, as well as president of CEMA. *BNL,* 4 May 1951.

70   Sir Roland Nugent, cited in the *NW*, 30 Apr. 1950.

71   *BNL*, 30 Apr. 1951.

72 Jack Loudan article, *NW*, 3 May 1951. There was a separate sub-committee set up to deal with folk songs and dances, but their recommendations centred around such issues as whether people should dance on the grass or on a platform at Botanic gardens, and not on the type of music to be played, COM 4A/21.

73 The programme for the festival was comprehensive, with items from agricultural and horticultural shows to drama. Plays directed by Tyrone Guthrie for the festival were: George Shiel's *The Passing Day*, J.D. Stewart's *Danger, Men Working*, St John Ervine's *Uncle Tom*, and Lynn Doyle's *Fiddler's Folly*. The festival clearly did not catch the imagination of John or Ruby Hewitt: 'A John Boyd programme on BBC tonight to tell what was coming off in Festival poor enough – Tyrone Guthrie spoke on Dramma [*sic*] John Luke on his mural (badly) George McCann in his Derry panels, was good. Johnny about the Lavery show – in which he has no interest'. Ruby Hewitt's diary, 2 Mar. 1951, D3838/4/6. The Hewitts visited the Farm and Factory exhibition in Castlereagh in August 1951: 'The lay out is very attractive but it isn't a great show really', RH, 3 Aug. 1951, D3838/4/6.

74 Arts festival posters and catalogues, COM 4/E/1/12.

75 In a book published in 1951, called *The town in Ulster*, the author Gilbert Camblin considered that it was important for people to know the background to the creation of 'Ulster'; 'this background', he argued, 'must prove invaluable to all who are concerned with the future development of the Province', Gilbert Camblin, *The town in Ulster* (Belfast, 1951), p. 5.

76 The original idea came from the former deputy keeper of PRONI, D.A. Chart, on behalf of PEN 'A project which the Northern Centre of the International P.E.N club is laying before that body [CEMA] officially . . . is the organisation of an exhibition of books printed in Ulster or by Ulster authors since 1921', D.A. Chart to Dehra Parker, 14 Jan. 1949, COM 4A/34. 'The City Librarian was being authorised to proceed with the planning, in conjunction with Queen's University and Linenhall Library, of a Northern Ireland Book Exhibition, which will be recognised as an official Festival feature', Civil authorities sub-committee minutes, 14 Mar. 1950. The members of this sub-committee were Councillor J.H. Norritt, G.C. Gamblin (Town and Planning Institute), E. Doran and T. McVea (Association of Municipal Authorities of Northern Ireland), J. Keating (main committee), J. Knipe (Ministry of Health and Local Government) and S.M. Morgan (deputy controller), COM 4A/35.

77 John Babbington, BBC, NI HS, 9 May 1951, COM 4A/69.

78 'No nation can be great if its citizens are mean of spirit. Where there is no vision the people perish. One thing above all else the Festival has already done – it has given us vision', Sir Roland Nugent, *NW*, 30 Apr. 1951.

79 'The Cardinal Archbishop of Westminster . . . appointed one of his clergy to keep in touch with the Dean of Westminster on matters relating to the Festival . . . the Dean will, on the Festival Council, be in a position to speak for all the Churches, including the RC Church', memo from Sir Gerald Barry, director general of the Festival of Britain, to the FOBCNI, 24 Sept. 1949, COM 4A/56.

80 Memo from Sir Roland Nugent, 27 Feb. 1950, COM 4A/56.

81 Cabinet memorandum by Sir Roland Nugent, re. churches' participation in the Festival of Britain, nd, CAB 9F/176/1.

82 FOBCNI, memo 14 June 1950, COM 4A/2.

83 Memo from Sir Roland Nugent to the Northern Irish cabinet, 2 Feb. 1950, COM 4A/56.

84 The Northern Irish government agreed to Nugent's suggestion that 'a formal invitation to all Churches to co-operate in Festival arrangements, leaving the

responsibility for subsequent action to the Churches themselves', memo from Sir Roland Nugent, 27 Feb. 1950. Noted that cabinet agreed, 8 Mar. 1950, COM 4A/56.

85   Sir Roland Nugent to Dean R. Elliott, 11 Jan. 1951, COM 4A/56.

86   FOBCNI, 14 June 1950, COM 4A/2. The following churches and religious groups were invited by the festival committee to take part in the festival: non-subscribing presbyterians, church of Ireland, salvation army, baptists, christian science committee, presbyterian church, anglicans, catholic church, methodists, jews, congregational church, reformed presbyterian church, quakers, COM 4A/56.

87   AC1/2/2, 19 June 1950.

88   Report in FOB voluntary organisations' programme, nd, COM 4D/8.

89   FOBNI civic authorities sub-committee, final report, Nov. 1951, COM 4D/8.

90   COM 4D/8.

91   While there is no note in the archdiocesan archives in Armagh of the cardinal's response to the festival, there is some evidence of the hierarchy's general attitude to state occasions in Northern Ireland. For the coronation visit in 1953 Cardinal MacRory was invited to nominate somebody to act as a representative when the queen visited the Whitla Hall. MacRory responded that while he appreciated the invitation, he regretted that 'in the present circumstances' he was 'unable to avail of it'. Cardinal MacRory's secretary to the minister of home affairs, 14 May 1953. This can be taken as typical of the official attitude of the catholic hierarchy towards the Northern Irish government, although the presence of the monarch undoubtedly gave it a particular edge.

92   Both Sam Hanna Bell (hereafter SHB) and John Hewitt wanted the image on the book's cover to 'show only Ulster'. SHB to Hewitt, 1 Sept. 1950. Bell also wanted 'Ulster' in the title, not 'Northern Ireland', SHB to Nesca Robb, 28 Aug. 1950, SHBP. This issue of what to call the state had already arisen with the very title of the festival in the state; then as with Bell, the government wanted 'Ulster' in the title, but they were unable to use that name.

93   Apart from the editorial committee of Sam Hanna Bell, John Hewitt and Nesca Robb, there were the CEMA committee representatives: Dame Dehra Parker (president), W.J. Hardie (vice-chairman of CEMA's standing committee), W.H.N. Downer (general and financial secretary) and D. McDonald (secretary), SHBP. Dame Parker suggested that Cyril Falls should be invited to contribute, editorial board meeting 2 Nov. 1950, SHBP. Nesca Robb was suggested as an editor because, to quote Andrew Stewart, controller BBC NI, 'it was important that a woman should be represented on it'. CEMA minutes 11 Jan. 1950, AC1/2/1. Nesca Robb published several books including that for which she is best known *William of Orange*, vol. i (London, 1962), *An Ulsterwoman in England, 1924–41* (Cambridge, 1942), and a book of poetry, *Aras ecologues and other poems* in 1970. *The arts in Ulster* was in addition to the official Festival of Britain in Northern Ireland publication which covered all aspects of festival activities in the state.

94   The sub-committee included John Hewitt, Professor G.O. Sayles, Andrew Stewart, W.H.N. Downer, Jack Loudan and Dehra Parker. Minutes of CEMA's standing committee, 10 Nov. 1949, AC1/2/1. The decision to appoint Bell was taken at the sub-committee's meeting, 2 Dec. 1949, COM 4A/51. An early title is scribbled in the corner of these minutes which reads 'Northern Lights, the Arts in Ulster'.

95   Minutes of CEMA's standing committee, 8 Dec. 1949, AC1/2/1.

96   SHB, *The arts in Ulster* (London, 1951) p. 18. Although Robb and Hewitt were joint editors, Bell clearly saw himself as the main editor. In a letter to W.H.N. Downer, he wrote: 'Finally, one name can be put on the spine – that is mine –

but I should still wish to have Dr Robb and John Hewitt associated with me on the title page', SHB to Downer, 13 Oct. 1950, SHBP. Bell was born in 1909 of emigrant Ulster parents. He returned to live in Northern Ireland with his mother's family in 1918 when his father died. Having held a variety of jobs, and backed by Louis MacNeice, Bell joined the BBC in Belfast following the Second World War. Already writing short stories by the 1940s, and a founder editor of the northern periodical, *Lagan*, with John Hewitt and Robert Davidson, *December bride* was the first of four novels he was to write between 1951 and 1987 (these were *The hollow ball*, 1961, *A man flourishing*, 1973, *Across the narrow sea*, 1987) and this in addition to a broadcasting career, which spanned nearly twenty-five years. As both broadcaster and writer, Bell contributed to the creation of an 'Ulster' identity which often found itself at odds with unionist or the BBC's version of reality in the state. For a further discussion of Sam Hanna Bell, see chapter 6.

97   Perhaps the history of the theatre idea was dropped because the festival committee could not get funds to build a permanent theatre in the state for festival year. W.H.N Downer informed R.C.W. Grubb of CEMA's decision on the book, 27 July 1949, AC1/2/1.

98   List of the contributors to *The arts in Ulster* and their articles: SHB, 'A Banderol: an introduction', Denis O'D. Hanna, 'Architecture in Ulster', David Kennedy 'The Drama in Ulster', John Hewitt 'Painting and sculpture in Ulster', John Boyd 'Ulster Prose', J.N. Browne, 'Poetry in Ulster', Nevin Foster, 'Music in Ulster'.

99   John Hewitt and Nesca Robb were members of CEMA's art committee, along with L. Beaumont, J. Christie, D.O'D. Hanna, Lt. Col J.F. Hunter, J.D. McCord and the Countess of Antrim, COM 4A/8.

100   Michael McLaverty to SHB, 29 Sept. 1950, SHBP.

101   There were some suggestions by nationalists in the House of Commons that since it was only the government which supported the festival, that funds for it should come from the unionist party, see *Northern Hansard*, vol. xxxiv, 28 Nov. 1950.

102   Nesca Robb to John Hewitt, 16 June 1950, SHBP. Reviewing *The arts in Ulster* for the BBC NI HS series *The Printed Page*, Rayner Heppenstall was critical of the 'celtonia' of Bell's introduction and the 'disgruntled regionalism' of Hewitt's piece on art. BBC NI HS, 30 Mar. 1951, COM 4A/69.

103   John Boyd, 'Ulster Prose', in *The arts in Ulster*, p. 100.

104   ibid.

105   ibid.

106   *BT*, 13 Oct. 1944.

107   SHB to John Hewitt, 12 July 1950, SHBP.

108   For a further discussion of these writers, see chapter 6.

109   This reviewer also made an interesting point: 'One result of the separation was the establishment of a BBC station in Northern Ireland, and that station has had a cultural effect in this region which ought to be recognised and is perhaps not sufficiently acknowledged by the contributors', *BNL*, 22 Mar. 1951.

110   SHB, 'A Banderol', p. 14.

111   Roy Strong, *A tonic for the nation*, p. 8. Exhibitions were 'designed to show the ingenuity of the British people in using the resources available to them, and to this extent, though not in any overt political way, it was a highly nationalistic affair', Adrian Forty, 'Festival politics', p. 35.

112   Hugh Shearman, *BT*, 5 June 1951.

113   ibid.

114   Interview with Willy de Majo in *A tonic for the nation*, p. 155. H. Lynch-Robinson was the architect for the exhibition, and Willy de Majo was based in London.

115 Minutes of the civic authorities sub-committee, 14 Mar. 1950, COM 4A/35.

116 FOBCNI, 19 Mar. 1951, COM 4A/2.

117 The king only cancelled his visit on 30 May, two days before the opening of the Farm and Factory Exhibition. In Britain the tory establishment was, initially, critical of the festival, given that it was organised by the labour government. As well as giving appointments on festival committees to titled citizens, the establishment was brought around to the festival, or in any case was not so openly critical of it, after March 1950 when the king and queen became patrons.

118 This is reflected in the speeches made by unionists in the Northern Irish House of Commons. Nationalists in the house predictably objected to the visit of the royals, for instance Henry Diamond, MP for the Falls, *Northern Hansard*, vol. xxxv, 20 Feb. 1951.

119 *NW*, 26 May 1951. 'Ulster royal visit not expected to be confined to Belfast', *BT*, 8 Feb. 1951. The royals also visited Campbell college, the city hall, Stormont and Government house.

120 The *Belfast Telegraph* also noted that in order to control the crowds expected to line the royal's route 4,800 yards of street barriers had to be erected, *BT*, 31 May 1951, and *BNL*, 2 June 1951.

121 *BNL*, 2 June 1951.

122 Interview with Willy de Majo in *A tonic for the nation*, p. 158.

123 Report given at the festival council, 21 Feb. 1951, COM 4A/8.

124 Sir Roland Nugent's foreword to the Farm and Factory Exhibition guidebook, COM 4E/1/6.

125 'Although this is organised for us by the Northern Ireland Government, and not by Festival Headquarters, it ranks nevertheless as one of the six or seven official Festival Exhibitions throughout the United Kingdom'. Report given to the festival council, 21 Feb. 1951, COM 4A/8. List of exhibits, COM 4/B/15–24.

126 A.A.K. Arnold described the exhibition in an article for the *NW*, 1 May 1951: 'models; intricate and colourful animated displays; a cinema; an 1851 farmstead; a modern working farm fully stocked; a "farmhouse of the future" – all attractively set out with cafes and bars, a restaurant, gardens, bandstand, lagoons, fountains and a play centre for children'.

127 Farm and Factory Exhibition guidebook, COM 4E/1/6.

128 COM 4A/44.

129 A.A.K. Arnold in a letter to Sir Roland Nugent in February 1951 wrote: 'it is the only spot in the building where one can explain to visitors why they can't sell lawn mowers at the Exhibition or present one to the King and Queen', 23 Feb. 1951, COM 4A/4. It was hard to get away from the idea of the Festival in Northern Ireland as a great trade show with some arts thrown in for distraction. Even the winning poem in the poetry competition organised by Lady Antrim's subcommittee on culture had as its topic the linen industry: 'A black flax dam, a field of linen snow,/Linked opposites: the scar on the soul/ of every Ulsterman'. From May Morton's 'Spindle and Shuttle', COM 4A/69.

130 The FOBCNI had its own sub-committee in charge of publicity: F.R. Adams (chairman and publicity officer for the Northern Irish government), W.H.N. Downer, D. Haldane, F. Barry, J.C. McLaughlin, J.R.D. Oliver, G.L. McKelvey, V. Bradley, J. Bishop, J. McCausland, H. Lynch-Robinson, R.J. Frizzell, A.A.K. Arnold, S.M. Morgan, P. Riddell.

131 Sir Roland Nugent to Sir Gerald Barry 16 Oct. 1950. Nugent in this letter exonerated the BBC in Northern Ireland from any criticism, they were he said 'most co-operative', COM 4A/69.

132 A.A.K. Arnold to Paul Wright, 18 Oct. 1950, COM 4A/69.

133 Paul Wright to A.A.K. Arnold, 23 Oct. 1950, COM 4A/69.

134 This may not have been without foundation; while Wales and Scotland were full committees, Northern Ireland was a sub-committee of the festival council, COM 4A/2.

135 Nugent developed the most extraordinary metaphor: 'I am tired of hearing well-meaning foreigners talk as if the British Lion had become a mangy Tom Cat. He may have a few bits of sticking plaster on him. Small blame to him after the last ten years. But he's a pretty good Lion still, and next year he will smarten himself up, throw a party, and just show 'em', Sir Roland Nugent, BBC NI HS, 8 Nov. 1950, COM 4A/69.

136 In all, the festival featured in some sixty-two programmes on BBC NI HS, COM 4A/69.

137 J.D. Stewart, *Ulster Commentary*, BBC NI HS, 26 Sept. 1950, COM 4A/69.

138 A.A.K. Arnold to Harry McMullan, BBC producer, 29 Sept. 1950, COM 4A/69.

139 J.D. Stewart, *Ulster Commentary*, BBC NI HS, 7 June 1951, COM 4A/69.

140 Roy Strong, *A tonic for the nation*, p. 14. In Northern Ireland a whole section of the population (the catholic community) was ignored by and ignored the festival.

141 From the FOB guidebook to the *Campania*, COM 4/E/1/4.

142 Roy Strong, *A tonic for the nation*, p. 8.

143 'There was almost no one of working-class background concerned in planning the Festival, and nothing to suggest that the working-classes were anything more than lovably human but essentially inert, objects of benevolent adminis-tration', Michael Frayn, 'Festival', p. 307.

144 ibid.

145 For the conservatives, 'spending the taxpayers money on doing the taxpayers good was suspect', according to Michael Frayn, 'Festival', p. 319.

146 The 'Skylon' was a metal structure, erected on the South Bank, the emblem of the festival, representing 'belief in modernity, and optimism for the future'. Over six million visited it in 1951; within five months, and as soon as the conserva-tives were back in government, it was dismantled, *One foot in the past*, BBC 2. 'It was said that "like Britain it has no visible means of support"', Adrian Forty, 'Festival Politics', p. 72.

147 Adrian Forty, 'Festival Politics', p. 38.

148 Michael Frayn, 'Festival', p. 325.

149 Martin Wallace, 'Government of Northern Ireland', D2833/D/12/1/19.

150 'A generation later, in the aftermath of the Second World War, the Festival of Britain offered neither a mirror nor a window but rather an enchanted glass in which somehow the organisers, shorn of the magic of Empire, attempted to reconstitute a future based in a new secular mythology', Roy Strong, *A tonic for the nation*, p. 8.

151 John Hewitt, *The New Statesman and Nation*, 19 Feb. 1949.

152 Michael Frayn, 'Festival', p. 319.

153 The organisation of the coronation visit rested solely with the Northern Irish government, and Belfast corporation. A sub-committee was appointed by the general purposes and finance committee of Belfast corporation to consider arrangements in relation to the coronation visit. CEMA had three members on this committee: W.H.N. Downer, W.H. Smyth (MBE), J.A.S. Stendall (OBE). Minutes of CEMA's standing committee, 13 Jan. 1953, AC1/2/2.

154 *NW*, 3 June 1953.

155 David Harkness, *Northern Ireland since 1920*, p. 121.

156 The prime minister Basil Brooke in his statement on the coronation said: ' . . . our earnest hope that the new Elizabethan era may be rich in opportunity and achievement throughout Her Majesty's wide realms', *Northern Hansard*, vol. xxxvii, 20 May 1953.

157   ibid.

158   ibid.

159   The paper also listed all the visits George VI had made to the state in 1924, 1937, 1942 and 1948, *BT*, 6 Feb. 1952.

160   John Andrews, the Northern Irish prime minister, noted to Dawson Bates: 'Although the recent royal visit was shorn of a great deal of the pageantry and ceremonial with which it would have been surrounded in peacetime, nevertheless, the arrangements involved much arduous work', 30 June 1942, CAB 9R/66/1.

161   CAB 9R/66/1.

162   American troops lined the processional avenue into Stormont when the king and queen visited the House of Commons.

163   *Irish News,* 27 June 1942, CAB 9R/66/1.

164   Statement issued by the Ministry of Information, Northern Ireland Region, 1 July 1942, CAB 9R/66/1.

165   *BT,* 6 Feb. 1952.

166   The editor also spoke of the deep affection of the people of Northern Ireland for the sovereign, and continued: 'Although Northern Ireland is separated from Great Britain by the narrow waters of the North Channel, the Province does not regard itself as an overseas possession', *NW,* 18 July 1945.

167   *NW,* 18 July 1945.

168   Admission cards to this event were distributed to war-workers through the firms in which they were employed, CAB 4/629/12.

169   *NW,* 18 July 1945.

170   *NW,* 19 July 1945.

171   *NW,* 18 July 1945.

172   *NW,* 20 July 1945.

173   There was a real sense of theatre about this visit. In a letter to F.R. Adams, the Stormont publicity officer, the lord mayor of Derry wrote: 'I understand it is usual for the Press to supply a small sort of Album of photographs for an event such as we staged in Derry in connection with the royal visit on Thursday', 21 July 1945, CAB 9R/69/2.

174   *NW,* 19 July 1945.

175   *BT,* 6 Feb. 1952.

176   J.G. Blumler, J.R. Brown, A.J. Ewbank, and T.J. Nossiter note that chief among the moral values the coronation endorsed was family values. 'Attitudes to the monarchy: their structure and development during a ceremonial occasion', *Political Studies,* vol. 19, no. 2, 1971, p. 152.

177   *NW,* 1 June 1953.

178   J.G. Blumler et al., 'Attitudes to the monarchy', p. 152.

179   The armistice in the Korean War was signed on 27 July 1953.

180   *BT,* 3 Aug. 1953.

181   J.G. Blumler et al., 'Attitudes to the monarchy', p. 152.

182   David Chaney, 'A symbolic mirror of ourselves: civic ritual in mass society', p. 258.

183   Elaborate sound and vision coverage of the coronation visit to Northern Ireland was arranged by the BBC with 'a team of top flight commentators (one of whom was Richard Dimbleby) and three complete TV camera units' to cover 'every aspect of the royal tour', *NW,* 1 July 1953.

184   'Eight hundred ex-servicemen from Ulster and Éire, 200 of them disabled, watched the ceremony on nine television sets in the Ulster Hall. Reception was perfect', *NW,* 3 June 1953.

185   *NW,* 1 June 1953.

186 *NW*, 2 June 1953.

187 David Chaney, 'A symbolic mirror of ourselves', p. 258.

188 *NW*, 3 June 1953.

189 *NW*, 1 June 1953.

190 'Within a few hours, however, the stage was crowded with an animated and colourful crowd of actors as the city in the afternoon went en fete for the coronation', *NW*, 3 June 1953. Northern Ireland was also given its part in the celebrations with the inclusion of some of its citizens in the queen's coronation honours list. Included were the lord mayor of Belfast, J.H. Norritt, who received a knighthood, and Sir Frederick Rebbeck, chairman and managing director of Harland and Wolff, who received a KBE.

191 GPFSC, 15 May 1953, LA7/2EB/186.

192 'The Sultan of Zanzibar, in brilliant blue, sent the crowd wild with approval as he waved and smiled in the rain', *NW*, 3 June 1953.

193 ibid.

194 The primary torch was lit by the deputy lord mayor H. Holmes, and then carried in relays by 135 boy scout runners to light the 'Coronation bonfire' on the top of Cave Hill.

195 *NW*, 3 June 1953.

196 *NW*, 2 June 1953.

197 ibid.

198 *NW*, 4 June 1953.

199 *NW*, 2 June 1953.

200 Initially the Northern Irish cabinet believed that the coronation visit to the state would be for one day only, CAB 4A/39/1. The 1953 coronation visit inherited much from the 1937 coronation visit, as this note from the coronation committee illustrates: 'Mr Blake Whelan outlined the arrangements for floodlighting and decorating Government buildings on the occasion of Coronation Day in 1937, and the Committee decided that similar action should be taken on this occasion', Coronation committee, 9 Dec. 1952, CAB 4A/39/2.

201 By comparison, the jubilee celebrations of 1935 were held against the backdrop of unrest within the state and perceived threats to the state from the Free State. That royal occasion therefore marked the fact that the Northern Irish state had survived. In addition, the coronation celebrations for George VI were muted by the circumstances in which he gained the throne. Despite this, the 1937 coronation, and indeed the abdication crisis, gave unionists a chance to reaffirm their loyalty to the crown and claim their place in the empire.

202 Henry Diamond, MP for Falls, *Northern Hansard*, vol. xxxvii, 7 July 1953.

203 Ed Moloney and Andy Pollak, *Paisley* (Dublin, 1986), p. 63. There were other incidents in which bunting and decoration caused altercations, see *Northern Hansard*, vol. xxxvii, March/May 1953.

204 In Cookstown catholics removed flags and streamers, while in Derrymacash, outside Lurgan, catholics put up the tricolour in response to the erection of the Union Jack. The most notorious incident was in Dungiven, Co. Derry, where the plans for a coronation children's parade were interrupted by catholics with hurley sticks who objected to the inclusion in the parade of the Boveva flute band, a notoriously bigoted Orange band. The matter was settled when a large Union Jack was removed from one of the floats, Ed Moloney and Andy Pollak, *Paisley*, p. 63.

205 Nationalist objections were commented on in the Northern Irish House of Commons, see *Northern Hansard*, vol. xxxvi, Jan. 1953 for example.

206 Ed Moloney and Andy Pollak, *Paisley*, pp. 64–6.

207 *NW*, 1 July 1953.

208 Coronation committee, 7 Oct. 1952, CAB 4A/39/1. Members of the committee
     were the prime minister, Sir Basil Brooke, the ministers of finance and home
     affairs, Lord Glentoran, the lord mayor of Belfast, Senator Sir George Clark,
     D.S. Rodgers, Sir Robert Gransden, Adrian Robinson, Capt. T.D. Morrison, W.N.
     McWilliam. In addition to this committee a sub-committee of the general
     purposes and finance committee of Belfast corporation was established to
     orchestrate details of the visit, such as decoration of the city. Members of this
     committee were Councillor Norritt, lord mayor, Councillor Harpur, deputy lord
     mayor, Alderman McKee, councillors Bell, Geddis, Jefferson, McCallum,
     McGrath and Tougher. On 18 Nov. 1952 they co-opted the president and secre-
     tary of the Belfast chamber of commerce and the junior chamber of commerce,
     a representative of the cinema and theatre associations, the chairman and
     secretary of the Belfast harbour commissioners, and a representative of the
     Royal Ulster Constabulary, LA7/2EB/185.
209 GPFSC, 21 Jan. 1953, LA7/2EB/185.
210 'Hillsborough was in carnival mood for the first evening of the Queen's visit. The
     Lambeg drummers were out, and the streets and nearby roads were crowded
     with spectators and thousands of cars', BT, 2 July 1953.
211 BT, 1 July 1953.
212 NW, 1 July 1953.
213 BT, 3 July 1953.
214 It was decided that between fifteen and twenty civilian bands would be neces-
     sary for the routes and the royal garden party later, Coronation committee, 12
     Feb. 1953, CAB 4A/39/4.
215 Coronation committee, 10 Apr. 1953, CAB 4A/39/5.
216 'For almost four hours prior to the arrival of the train, spectators were taking up
     position close to the station, and in the railway yard, also bedecked with flags,
     hundreds of school-children had been allotted places', BT, 3 July 1953. Children
     were also incorporated into the coronation celebrations by means of souvenirs
     provided by the government, GPFSC, 14 Apr. 1953, LA7/2EB/186.
217 BT, 3 July 1953.
218 NW, 1 July 1953.
219 ibid.
220 ibid.
221 NW, 3 July 1953.
222 BT, 2 July 1953.
223 ibid.
224 The protestant denominations were represented by the archbishop of Armagh,
     Most Revd J.A.F. Gregg, the moderator of the General Assembly of the Presby-
     terian Church in Ireland, Rt Revd J.E. Davey and the president of the Methodist
     Church in Ireland, The Revd R.M.L. Waugh, BT, 2 July 1953.
225 BT, 3 July 1953.
226 NW, 3 July 1953.
227 BT, 3 July 1953.
228 ibid.
229 NW, 1 July 1953.
230 ibid.
231 'The locomotive which will pull the royal train on Friday, will carry on its front
     a large shield bearing the "Ulster banner" – the centre piece of the Govern-
     ment coat of arms, and will be flanked with two royal cyphers in blue and
     gold', ibid.
232 ibid.
233 BT, 3 July 1953.

234 ibid.
235 ibid.
236 ibid.
237 *BT,* 1 July 1953.
238 Hammerton and Cannadine, 'Conflict and consensus on a ceremonial occasion',
     p. 146.
239 ibid., p. 145.

5. Official reflections of Northern Ireland in the 1940s and 1950s

In Northern Ireland the period of the Festival of Britain and the coronation of Elizabeth II was framed by the publication of two semi-official texts, St John Ervine's *Craigavon: Ulsterman* and John Blake's *Northern Ireland in the Second World War*.[1] Neither text sold in any great number, but both acted as textual affirmations for the unionist government and the state; both were part of the process of assimilation into the canon of protestant and unionist myth and history of the state's founding father, James Craig, and the Second World War, the most recent sacred date for protestants.[2] Ervine and Blake's texts also contributed to what Norman Vance calls the warrior myth; they continued a tradition which unionist politicians and writers had established in the aftermath of the First World War, which linked unionist claims to British identity to their sacrifices in Britain's wars.[3] The Second World War allowed unionists to consolidate their position within the United Kingdom; it also allowed them to establish, in terms of identity, their separateness from the southern state and their oneness with the British Empire.[4] With Éire remaining neutral, Northern Ireland and its ports became strategically important to the Allied war effort; this was in addition to supplying war material, such as shipping and textiles.[5] The state acted as an air base and a base from which the Allies could monitor the German U-boats, which patrolled the waters off Donegal and Malin head attacking shipping. Northern Ireland's strategic importance in the Battle of the Atlantic was something which writers, such as Hugh Shearman, were later to emphasise constantly. The state's important strategic role induced confidence amongst unionists that following the war their state would be maintained in the union. Participation in the war created a bond between Britain and Northern Ireland, which the bombing of Belfast in the spring and early summer of 1941 underlined.[6] As Roy Foster has noted: 'Just as in 1918, Ulster emerged from the war with its position strengthened and its vociferous claims to special treatment ensured a hearing.'[7]

The period between 1939 and 1949 was, however, one of uncertainty for unionists.[8] In the years before the outbreak of the Second World War the unionist government's political insecurity and obsession with maintaining the union with the United Kingdom had grown in response to the evolution of de Valera's overtly catholic southern state. The Free State's abolition of the office of governor general and the removal of the king from its constitution in 1936 exacerbated growing unionist fears that the settlement of 1920–21 was being undermined. Those fears were confirmed with the publication of de Valera's 1937 constitution which laid claim to the whole territory of Ireland.[9] The intervention of the Second World War was providential for the unionist state, although initially this did not appear to be the case. Within the first two years of the war the British government had decided not to enforce conscription in Northern Ireland at the risk of offending the nationalist population. Moreover, in 1940, against the background of the evacuation from Dunkirk and the fall of France, they offered de Valera Irish unity in return for his government's support of the Allied war effort. From a unionist perspective this was an unwelcome return to the political situation which they had faced during the First World War; then, as now, they felt they had done their duty to the crown and their loyalty had not been repaid.

In 1939 Éire had declared herself neutral, vindicating past unionist allegations of its inherent disloyalty and unreliability, and leaving the way open for unionists to play the role of loyal patriotic subjects without competition.[10] To quote Basil Brooke:

> Éire is neutral. Ulster is at war. There are many results of this, but I shall mention only one. The bases in the South, which might have saved lives and shortened the struggle in the long and terrible Battle of the Atlantic, have been denied the fighting forces . . . Throughout the history of Ulster our people have been consistent in their attitude of loyalty to Great Britain and of identification with the interests of Great Britain.[11]

Yet despite this unionist advantage, the British administration was still willing to undermine the Northern Irish state in order to gain the use of Éire's ports. Again, rebellion appeared to gain the reward while loyalty was penalised. The unionist administration's practical fears about this British offer to end partition were defused when de Valera rejected the plan. It was patently obvious to unionist ministers, however, that the Westminster administration would not maintain the Northern Irish state out of a sense of benevolence. It was in this way that the Second World War was providential for unionists, for through their service on behalf of the crown and the empire they could bring the moral pressure of a debt owed to bear on the British government in order to preserve their state.[12]

As stated earlier in the discussion on the role of broadcasting during the war, to emphasise their loyalty to the crown unionists had to be seen to be enthusiastically supporting the war effort, and it was in this context that the conscription issue came to dominate in the Northern Irish state as a 'potent affirmation of Northern Ireland's constitutional status'.[13] Craigavon particularly drew great attention to the large number of recruits from Northern Ireland, and focused on conscription as the ultimate sign of loyalty.

However, contrary to official and popular unionist belief, and subsequent propaganda, recruiting during the Second World War was disappointing in Northern Ireland, and catholics did join the British forces. While Craigavon was anxious to have conscription, John M. Andrews (then minister for finance and later his successor) feared that those loyalists who joined up would lose their jobs to those who did not, 'namely disloyal Catholics and southerners seeking war time work in the north'.[14] St John Ervine argued the same point as Andrews in his biography of Craigavon, using the example of recruiting in the First World War: 'During the last war, Ulstermen who volunteered for service were replaced in offices and factories and workshops by Southern Irishmen who came North to higher wages'.[15] He continued: 'Men who, returning from the war, found their civil occupations filled by men who had never been near the war, who were, in many cases, pro-German in feeling, and were prompt with jeers at them for having gone to the war.'[16] Ervine drew his example up to the present day: 'Everything that Craigavon had done and believed in his life culminated now in this position: that Éire, after her fashion, was standing aside, that Ulster, after her fashion, was standing with the Empire people.'[17] Following the bombing of Belfast in May 1941, the issue of conscription emerged once more. In a cabinet meeting, the Northern Irish government noted:

> It further considers, particularly in the light of recent heavy enemy attacks, that the principle of equality of sacrifice and service underlying conscription is essential to promote the degree of corporate discipline which is necessary if our people are to withstand the tide of total war and play their full part in the national effort.[18]

Nationalist opposition to the suggestion of conscription for Northern Ireland was automatic.[19] In May 1941, Cardinal MacRory issued a statement against the possibility of conscription:

> That the people of all creeds and classes in Belfast have recently suffered heavily at the hands of the Germans, though regrettable as it may be, does not touch the essence of the question, which is that an ancient land made one by God, was partitioned by a foreign power against the vehement protest of its people, and that conscription would now seek to compel those who still writhe under this grievous wrong to fight on the side of its perpetrators.[20]

Nationalist objections to conscription centred around a belief that were it enforced it would affect them more than others.[21] In Northern Ireland 30,000 were already in the forces and 30,000 were medically unfit. According to Fisk, 'Nationalists reasoned that the outstanding forty eight thousand represented Catholics since the shipyard, engineering and aircraft works – industries with "reserved" occupations – employed mostly Protestants'.[22] The RUC's inspector general, Sir Charles Wickham, told Churchill that conscription would fall heaviest on the catholic population in Northern Ireland; as a result 'many will cross the border but from those who remain wide resistance to the enforcement of the Act may be expected'.[23] It is likely that some protestants, fearing that their jobs would be taken by those not conscripted, welcomed the fact that the Northern Irish state would not have conscription:

> Loyalists did not have to oppose conscription because of the ferocity and obstreperity [sic] of Nationalist resistance. For this reason, popular perceptions at the time may have held that the disloyal section of society prohibited Northern Ireland from contributing fully to the war effort. This popular perception, to some degree lives on today.[24]

Again, the British government decided against conscription for Northern Ireland.[25] 'The British decision', prime minister John Andrews said, 'would be loyally accepted in the North as having been taken by those in the best position to decide what was most likely to further the British Empire's struggle for justice and freedom'.[26] The poor recruiting levels were thrown into relief by the failure of the Northern Irish government to effectively mobilise the state's workforce; compared to Britain where unemployment 'plummeted' according to Peter Clarke,[27] unemployment figures remained high in Northern Ireland throughout the war.[28] But unionists were anxious to focus on statements such as that made by Winston Churchill in a letter to John Andrews in 1943:

> Only one great channel of entry remained open. That channel remained open because loyal Ulster gave us the full use of the Northern Irish ports and waters and thus ensured the free working of the Clyde and the Mersey. But for the loyalty of Northern Ireland and its devotion to what has now become the cause of thirty governments or nations we should have been confronted with slavery and death, and the light which shines so strongly throughout the world would have been quenched.[29]

The picture was not, therefore, one of simple oppositions as promoted by the unionist government; recruits from Northern Ireland and Éire, catholics and protestants, joined the Allied war effort 'for various reasons and for different purposes despite and with little regard for the political relations between the three states of Northern Ireland, the Irish Free State and Great Britain'.[30] The Northern Irish state's participation in the war was not therefore a simple display of loyalty.[31]

Throughout the war years, unionists continued to be highly sensitive to any criticism of their state, even when it came from the most predictable of places. In 1944 the playwright Sean O'Casey wrote an article in the magazine *Time and Tide* which questioned whether Northern Ireland had ever produced anyone of the calibre of Yeats. It was viewed by unionists as an attack on Northern Ireland's cultural integrity. The Northern Irish author and playwright St John Ervine responded with a series of articles in the *Belfast Telegraph* entitled 'Ulster: the real centre of culture in Ireland', which catalogued the great men of science, the military and the arts which Northern Ireland had produced. Ervine concluded his final article: 'As Éire recedes more and more into the background, becoming of less and less interest to the world, the six counties will be seen, I prophesy, to shine with many coloured lights that may yet scatter Éirean darkness.'[32] At a difficult time of war and rationing these articles flattered unionist self-esteem; however, they were articles which were broad in their praise of Northern Ireland, including in that term, geographically, the whole of the Ulster province, and, politically, nationalists as well as unionists.[33] It was the variety and richness of Ulster culture which Ervine implied that the rest of Ireland lacked. Stormont's cabinet publicity committee noted O'Casey's article, which it referred to as 'scurrilous', and Ervine's rejoinder, which it thought 'excellent'.[34] The Northern Irish government's London press officer even wondered whether the unionist government had commissioned the articles.

The official reaction to these articles goes some way to explaining why the Northern Irish government at first supported Ervine as Craig's biographer, but also why they eventually had to withdraw that support. Initially, the unionist government were keen to have this successful author, and declared unionist, as the official biographer, and as a promoter of a positive image of the Northern Irish state and unionism following the Second World War. Even when the Northern Irish government had decided not to officially support the biography, prime minister Brooke wrote to Ervine expressing the hope that he would 'not interpret it as detracting in any way from the Government's high admiration for your genius as an author to which indeed universal recognition has justly been accorded'.[35] Ervine's unionism was independently held and individualistic in nature. Thus, while his biography was overtly critical of Éire and many of its leading citizens, he was not dictated to by official unionism. When the government had made it clear to him that they were not supporting the biography, Ervine responded by saying that in fact he had 'not solicited the sanction or approval of the Government', and that as far as he was concerned he was the official biographer because he had been appointed by Lady Craigavon; the government in his opinion had no responsibility for the biography and could therefore not dictate to him.[36]

St John Ervine came to prominence as a polemicist for unionism against a background of insecurity and a developing unionist defensiveness during the early years of the war.[37] He was invited to become Craig's biographer in the tense atmosphere generated by British negotiations with Éire over neutrality and partition, a year after the death of the only premier the state had known. By 1941 Ervine had been a successful dramatist, critic, and novelist for over a quarter of a century. His political writing began in 1915 with a short and highly critical book on Sir Edward Carson; but this monograph was to prove to be an aberration.[38] According to John Boyd, the playwright and critic, Ervine would have become

> One of the most widely recognised Irish prose writers if he had not imaginatively and emotionally renounced his birthright as Irishman and Irish writer: a renunciation which neither Shaw nor Joyce nor O'Casey – all fellow exiles and all extremely critical of Ireland – ever made.[39]

His early work had explored the tensions and sectarianism of Northern Ireland, and Ireland in general, but as the ethos and identity of the Free State developed into a conservative catholicism Ervine chose to identify himself with Ulster and the British Empire, although not Britain itself.[40] As Vance points out, 'Ervine could never think of himself as English either and was very proud of his Ulster accent'.[41] His aggressive unionism was then largely a reaction to, as well as a means of rejecting, the Free State and its ethos, and the embodiment of both in the person of Eamonn de Valera. In a letter to George Bernard Shaw in 1923 he wrote that the very thought of Ireland made him feel like vomiting.[42] By the 1920s unionism was the only means by which Ervine felt he could retain within his identity an Irishness, which he believed was not accommodated by the Free State, and a Britishness that would encompass his Ulster regionalism. As he wrote in the preface to the biography of Craig:

> Our province xists [sic] because Great Britain exists, because the United States of America exist, because the British Commonwealth of Nations exists; and its history cannot be separated from theirs, nor can it be told in disregard of their existence.[43]

And he explained to Dame Dehra Parker: 'Don't imagine that I am anti-Irish. I'm not. I'm anti-Eirean, anti-Republic. But I want Ireland in the Commonwealth. If I were anti-Irish, I'd want it put out.'[44] In 1949, when *Craigavon* was published, unionists feared that the move towards a republic would mean a renewed effort on the part of the southern government for a thirty-two county state. This anxiety finds articulation in Ervine's text: 'its [Northern Ireland's] life is so closely knit with the commonwealth's that to wrench them apart would be to ruin Ulster irreparably and Ireland in the end'.[45] This was also a period of decolonisation throughout the British Empire, with self-government being granted to India, Pakistan, Burma and Ceylon between 1947 and 1949. It is in this context that Ervine's *Craigavon: Ulsterman* should be read.[46] Ironically, the government's primary concern about the biography was the concluding section in which Ervine suggested that a united Ireland would be possible if the Irish republic returned to the commonwealth. Robert Gransden noted: 'This quite clearly could not be included in the "official" Life on the basis of his conclusions that a unified Ireland can be contemplated on the return of Éire to the Commonwealth. If anything is certain, it is that this was not Lord Craigavon's view.'[47]

It was Lady Craigavon who invited Ervine to write the biography of the late Lord Craigavon, the architect of the Northern Irish state, the man who 'had built up a Parliament from the bare ground, building it when the hands were few and materials scanty and troubles thick'.[48] 'It was mainly Lord Carson who laid the foundations of the Ulster state', said John Andrews, 'it was Lord Craigavon who erected the structure and made it impregnable'.[49] Lady Craigavon was 'prompted' to have a biography because of her 'keen desire for the world to know, and especially the English people, how much they owed to him for his great successful fight to keep Ulster in the

Empire'.[50] Ervine was approved of as Craig's biographer by the unionist government, contact with senior Stormont civil servants was established, and arrangements were made for him to have access to official files.[51] Although Ervine should not have had access to all government files, a process was engineered by the government through which he could.[52] Robert Gransden explained this to Lady Craigavon in a letter in April 1941, when he suggested Ervine as biographer:

> Keeping in contact as the work proceeds with such members of official circles as he thinks may be able, from their knowledge of the events, to help with the text. Those circles would, the Prime Minister is sure, be able to offer material assistance, and it could also be arranged that the author could be allowed to see any document or letter bearing on the part of the text concerned which would enable him to judge whether he had done the subject justice.[53]

Lady Craigavon supported Ervine's access to government papers and assured John Andrews that he was trustworthy: 'he would not be indiscreet in anyway, and would submit any points to you that he was doubtful as to the wisdom of publishing'.[54] St John Ervine himself undertook 'not to publish anything of which the government disapproved'.[55] Once the government decided to withdraw its support from the biography, it became concerned about the level of access which Ervine had had to official papers and official help, as this letter from Brooke to Lady Craigavon indicates: 'The question also arises as to the use of material derived from official letters and other documents of a confidential nature'. In an effort to disassociate his government from the work Basil Brooke reminded Ervine that: 'In view of the Government's decision it will, of course, be necessary to delete all reference to help received from officials in the compilation of the work'.[56] Ervine replied that he accepted that:

> The thanks I return to officials in the preface might be regarded by some people as implying that the Northern Ireland Government is in some way responsible for the book; and I am, therefore, as you demand expunging these thanks, though I do so with deep regret.[57]

As for access to official papers, he denied that he had ever seen such documents or material; 'so far as I know there is nothing in the book which is not available to the general public in Government and other publications'.[58] But this point continued to concern the government; Gransden drafted a letter to Ervine in August 1946 noting that they were glad to have his assurances that he had made use only of 'such material as is already a matter of public knowledge'.[59] Throughout the war years, while the biography was in progress, he remained popular with the unionist government; his advice, for instance, was sought by the publicity committee on the composition of a panel of Ulster writers they hoped to organise to submit articles to journals and so on.[60] Although approved of, Ervine was never one of those panellists, and while he had government sanction he was not an official apologist for unionism and held his views independently of Stormont patronage. And because the administration could not control or at least be sure of influencing what he produced he was too much of a risk to be an establishment figure.

Ervine's professed intention in *Craigavon* was to give the facts of Craig's life and to expand and interpret the 'beliefs and political faith of Ulster Unionists' in terms of the late prime minister's life: 'For he, more than any single individual, embodied these beliefs and maintained this faith, both in what he said and did and in what he was'.[61] Craigavon had been overshadowed by Carson in political life, and in death he was overshadowed by the Second World War. His commemorative text was Ervine's *Craigavon: Ulsterman*, published in 1949.[62] Lord Craigavon had become so closely associated with the Northern Irish state by 1940, in fact, that this biography can be profitably read in terms of Craig as Ulster, or Craig as the Northern Irish state, in much the same way as Carson in the 1930s became the embodiment of unionism's glorious past. In death Edward Carson came to embody ideal unionism and the ideal unionist; James Craig came to embody Northern Ireland itself, a political reality rather than a political philosophy. Describing the partnership between Carson and Craig, Ervine noted:

> These seemingly incompatibles, the saturnine and moody Southern Irish egoist, and the severe Ulster humourists [*sic*], rocklike in their rigid attachments and extraordinarily unmoved by swift emotions, though quick in response to moods according with their principles, caught fire from each other.[63]

While Edward Carson had stood for a more restrained constitutional form of unionist resistance in the face of the third home rule bill, James Craig had represented 'a more narrowly focused and localised Ulster Unionist resistance'; 'this unaffected man, the symbol of his people' was to remain a parochial politician throughout his career.[64] According to J.J. Lee: 'He could at times show physical and even moral courage well above the ordinary'.[65] Patrick Buckland sums him up thus: 'Big, bluff, stolid and kindly-looking with a large, red, craggy face, his appearance reflected much of his character – humane, unimaginative, a man who could be relied upon to do a competent job'.[66] Foster is more direct, and whilst acknowledging Craig's organisational skills, describes him trenchantly as 'unimaginative but devout'.[67] Craig's successor John Andrews thought him 'a great Ulsterman, a great Irishman, a great Imperialist. His love of country was innate, sincere and strong'.[68] For Ervine, 'In accent and mind and manner, in body and belief, James Craig, born and bred in the County of Down, was unmistakably marked by his people and his country. He was an *Ulster*man [*sic*].'[69]

Craig encapsulated then, even for later historians, all the particularly 'Ulster' characteristics which unionists claimed to represent, and which they claimed were synonymous with 'Ulstermen'.[70] Even Craig's voice, as he made his war broadcast in February 1940, is portrayed by Ervine as possessing stereotypically Ulster characteristics: 'As the cool tones of his clear and manly voice, full of firm Ulster notes, came across the air, many who listened felt themselves encouraged by his strength and sincerity'.[71] Indeed, Ervine claimed, contrary to the accepted unionist stereotype, that 'Ulstermen' were extroverts, while 'Southerners' were 'neo-introverts, suffering severely from ingrowing minds and ingrowing souls'.[72] More traditionally, he echoed the pattern of 'Ulster' characteristics established by earlier unionist historians, and repeated by Carson's biographers Marjoribanks and Colvin. Although he accepted that the southern Irish were 'valiant', for him they were also 'servile' and lacked moral courage.[73] On their own, he argued, the Celts would perish, 'or if they survive, exist only in a low condition of culture, if not in a state of servitude'.[74] In the same way he commented on the progressive, and industrial, nature of Northern Ireland, which he dated from the union, in comparison to the Republic of Ireland:

> We emphasise the fact that the history of Ireland since the Union has been of two distinct tendencies, one of which we believe to be right and in accordance with the general progress of mankind, the other of which we believe to be wrong and in accordance with the general retrogression of mankind.[75]

The Gaels failed to succeed as industrialists, he argued, because 'extreme volatility, coupled with impatience and lack of perseverance, do not result in great business'.[76] For Ervine, Ireland's greatest age was that of the union 'when the policy of admixture of peoples was attaining its perfection'.[77] This argument is familiar from D.A. Chart's 1927 history of Northern Ireland which argued that following the union, 'the province as a whole continued contentedly on that career of economic progress'.[78] And Ervine maintained that the union lived on 'up there in the iron North' in 'Ulster men of spirit'.[79]

While the biography of Edward Carson had played a part in the collectivisation of unionism in the 1930s, Ervine's biography of Craig had an alternative agenda. His purpose in writing the book, he claimed, was 'to try to translate my countrymen, the Ulster people into such terms that those who misunderstand and misinterpret them, shall at least perceive that we have reasons for our attitude towards our fellow-countrymen'.[80] It was a more personalised account, reflecting Ervine's own political feelings strongly, and was overtly unionist and aggressive towards southern Ireland in general and de Valera in particular: 'The prime purpose in my book is to prove that Craigavon was right in doing what he did. An essential factor in that purpose is proof that his opponents were in the wrong.'[81] His agenda is immediately apparent in the photo of Craig published on the inside of the front cover of the book. The photo depicts Craig making his broadcast on BBC Northern Ireland in February 1940: 'de Valera had proclaimed the neutrality of Éire on the outbreak of the War, but Craigavon told his listeners that the Ulster people were "King's men, and we shall be with you to the end"'.[82] The biography was then largely an attack on Éire and its position of neutrality during the Second World War.[83] In this way it can also be read as a legitimising narrative of contemporary unionist history and the Northern Irish state.[84] Ervine did not spare the British from criticism either; according to Ervine their war-time offer to Éire to end partition was a resurrection of the 'old fight', and an offer 'to sacrifice his [Craig's] people in a fruitless effort to propitiate the unprofitable'.[85] In 1949 unionists learned that Britain would not consider the Irish republic a foreign country and that it 'would continue to enjoy the rights of commonwealth membership'. This they believed was 'surrender to Éire' on the part of the British and they were highly critical of the arrangement.[86] Ervine's biography thus gave vent to unionist hostility to British negotiations with Éire during the war, and following it; he described the negotiations, in which Northern Ireland was the 'bait', as ridiculous and offensive.[87]

Craigavon: Ulsterman was a self-confident piece of chauvinistic unionist writing. In a period of change, it acted to reinforce the unionist population; as one review noted it 'struck many shrewd blows' for the honour of the Northern Irish state.[88] But the biography could not ultimately be supported by the unionist government. Robert Gransden, who was Ervine's main government contact, thought that Ervine had given 'a true and moving picture of the man', but he believed 'that many of the references to Southern Ireland would stir up bad feeling and would probably create a reaction against the Biography, notwithstanding its many outstanding merits.'[89] Gransden suggested that two books be created out of this one; the first volume on the life of Lord Craigavon would have government sanction, while the second, a history of the period, could be published under Ervine's own auspices. And he concluded his letter: 'I have been prompted solely by my desire to see a life of Lord Craigavon that will rank as the standard Biography without becoming the centre of a bitter political controversy that might tend to obscure a fine picture of a truly great man.'[90] The tone of Ervine's *Belfast Telegraph* articles, one of unambivalent hostility towards Éire (which Ervine surmised was full of 'bleating Celtic twilighters, sex-starved Daughters of the Gael, gangsters and gombeen-men'[91]), was still evident in 1946. A Stormont press office memorandum of April 1943 cautioned staff that in dealing with the subject of Éire a 'moderate attitude' was to be adopted; such an attitude would, the memo continued, 'redound to Ulster's credit', and preferably in Britain.[92] Ervine's biography of Craig was neither moderate in its attitudes, nor did the unionist administration feel that it was likely to redound to their credit. F.R. Adams, Stormont's publicity officer, reviewed the biography in draft for Brooke:

> Instead of being primarily a biography, with the history introduced to throw into higher relief the portrait of the man, the book is predominantly a political history, with the figure of Lord Craigavon appearing and disappearing – sometimes disappearing for so long that the reader has almost forgotten him.[93]

The biography was, he felt, full of a 'bitterness of spirit' and often 'gratuitously offensive', and was likely to irritate and infuriate readers. The attacks on de Valera, Adams believed, were used 'as a foil to bring out Lord Craigavon's qualities – a proceeding which in itself is hardly flattering to the subject of the biography, whose personal merits needed no heightening by this method'.[94] Lady Craigavon herself accepted that 'a certain amount of criticism of Éire was bound to be necessary', but she suggested that Ervine might do this 'in a less controversial manner'.[95] Dame Dehra Parker in a letter to Ervine said she was:

> Quite certain, that, whatever his fundamental views or his personal feelings, James was an Irishman, as well as an Ulsterman, and that he would not have cared to have his Biography intermingled with such scathing criticism of Ireland and the Irish, past and present – no matter how true the strictures were.[96]

Robert Gransden concluded that the historical material 'together with his [Ervine's] conclusions as to the character of the Southern Irish as a whole should be detached from the official biography' and published independently by the author if he wished.[97]

Ervine's introduction had set the tone for his attitude towards southern Ireland and its citizens:

> [Ulstermen] deny that the Southern Irish, however witty they may be, have any sense of humour. And they decline to be deceived by charm, the most over-rated characteristic that mankind possesses: a characteristic which every crook and confidence trickster must possess, for how, otherwise, could he hope to earn a living by his frauds and deceits . . . [they] are inept and incompetent controversialists, not only because they are romantically indifferent to, and averse from, fact, but because they bring to every discussion irresponsible and frivolous minds. They are not serious men. They have no gravity.[98]

De Valera was the focus for much of Ervine's ire (as much an embodiment of Éire as Craig was of Northern Ireland), and was described as introverted, solitary, reclusive and forbidding of people; 'like all men of unconvivial and monastic character, [he] is indifferent to morality'.[99] He also criticised the English in racial terms as speaking in thin-lisped and disemvowelled voices; they were, he argued, people who imagined 'toleration and indifference to be identical, and are convinced that a man is free from bigotry when he is only free from principle'.[100]

Lady Craigavon was 'greatly distressed at the large amount of scurrilous material directed against Southern Irish personalities': 'there were various personal remarks about people in it that I felt "my PM" would not have liked'.[101] Her principal objection was that the book's historical content 'dwarfed' the biography, which she considered 'charming': 'I should not like my PM's name mixed up with so much of the Southern Irish matter, as it had really nothing to do with him, except at certain moments of political history'.[102] Reporting to the publicity committee, Robert Gransden did not feel that Ervine would accept his advice to 'eliminate the offending passages'; nor did he.[103] Ervine had already, in the light of advice from Dehra Parker and Robert Gransden, removed large sections of text from the biography.[104] But reviewing a redraft of the biography in March 1946, Sir William Scott noted that little had changed. In his opinion, 'the book was of exceptional interest', but given the 'vigorous attacks on prominent Roman

Catholic prelates and Southern Irish public men' that 'the Government should not be associated with the publication'.[105] However, along with Dehra Parker, Scott believed that 'a great deal of what is said in the biography needed to be said'.[106] The government felt ultimately, however, that the biography would be 'likely to inflame political and sectarian passion and provoke trouble between the adherents of rival parties', in addition to which the final chapter was 'out of harmony with the views of Lord Craigavon and the present Government of Northern Ireland'.[107] Brooke notified Lady Craigavon of the government's decision, but she asked that she be allowed to make a final attempt to persuade Ervine to amend his text, so that it would have official approval.[108] 'I would be so distressed', she wrote to Ervine, 'if the book appeared, disowned by the Northern Government, and was the cause of any discord, as I know J. himself would abhor anything of the kind'; Ervine was asked to 'fall in with their views, so that they can give it their full blessing'.[109] Brooke informed Ervine that the government decision had been reached with the deepest regret, and was based 'solely on grounds of public policy'.[110] Ervine responded with a lengthy letter refusing to bend to the government's will:

> If I choose to mingle biographical and historical facts for reasons that seem to be good and substantial, even if it be unorthodox to do so, that is my business and none of the Government's . . . Our people are continually maligned and disparaged in the British Press, even in the Conservative papers . . . For attempting a rebuttal of these and other charges, I am accused of attempting to foment 'party bitterness and rancour'![111]

Ervine, nevertheless, agreed to include in his introduction a passage which left no doubt in the public mind that the opinions expressed in the biography were entirely his own: 'To avoid all possibility of misunderstanding, I think it well to add that the Government of Northern Ireland has no responsibility whatever for the book, and that all opinions expressed in it, and not attributed to other people, are mine'.[112]

Craigavon: Ulsterman was published in 1949 without the official approval it had begun with.[113] The unionist press responded enthusiastically to the biography; while Hugh Shearman in the *Northern Whig* thought it 'racy, readable and sometimes pleasantly preposterous'.[114] Chief amongst newspapers which praised Ervine was the *Belfast Telegraph*. 'In some quarters', it noted in its weekend supplement,

> it will inevitably be rated as over provocative, but its sturdy author will remain undismayed. He has struck many shrewd blows for the honour not only of the Down in which James Craig was born and bred and buried but of his own native Ulster whose gratitude will be his reward.[115]

The *Irish Times* was, however, highly critical:

> James Craig has not been well served by his biographer; and the tragedy is that St John Ervine might have written a splendid book. He has the

talent; he has the style; he had the material. Where he has failed is in
his inability to subordinate his personal prejudices to the objective
demands of his subject . . . A brilliant pen has been steeped in venom
and dipped in gall. One leaves this book with a feeling of almost personal
shame.[116]

Ervine's work was at times full of bitterness and invective towards the
Irish republic, but while this made it a political liability, it also had its benefits for unionism. It reminded readers of recent unionist sacred dates
interwoven with the political life of James Craig (the third home rule
controversy, the Solemn League and Covenant, the First World War, the
setting-up of the Northern Irish state, the opening of Stormont, the state's
role in the Second World War), and recalled how trials had been overcome
through unionist unity and the steady leadership of James Craig. Lord
Craigavon was buried next to the Stormont parliament, whose creation and
construction he had 'enthusiastically commended and facilitated'.[117] One
reassuring symbol for unionists of the permanence of the Northern Irish
state was joined with the other: 'They could say to him as Adam said to Eve
in Milton's epic: Our state cannot be sever'd, we are one'.[118] Merely to be in
Craig's company, wrote Ervine, was to feel reassured and for many unionists
Ervine's outspoken and impolitic biography was equally reassuring.[119] It
acted to reinforce unionist self-confidence and sense of community: 'Within
their own terms of reference', J.J. Lee has argued, 'no generation in modern
Irish history has been more successfully led in their own time than were the
Protestant people of the North by James Craig, Ulsterman.'[120] Sir William
Scott advised his government against endorsing Ervine's biography, warning
that the 'outspoken comments' in *Craigavon* would 'give rise to a considerable amount of discussion'.[121] This is not to say that it did not articulate
some unionists' feelings of hostility towards Éire and the British administration. Ervine's biography can be seen as having provided a necessary
pressure valve, providing unionists with a high-profile outlet for their feelings towards contemporary events, and an articulation of some of their
genuinely held but, at the time, politically sensitive beliefs.

John Blake's *Northern Ireland in the Second World War*, begun in 1941
and published in 1956, marked a development in unionist writing from that
of St John Ervine. Although Ervine received Stormont support in the 1940s
he could not, with any consistency, be led by the will of the unionist administration. In the final analysis, this meant that for official purposes he was a
liability. Blake's work, on the other hand, was based not only on the research
of Stormont's civil servants and regimental historians, but its foundations lay
in draft mini-histories of the various government departments which were
written by the government's own officials. Apart from the opening chapter,
Blake's voice is almost entirely stifled. The history carries his name but ultimately it was a government 'product' in a way that the work of Ervine never
was. However, in the same way as *Craigavon*, *Northern Ireland in the
Second World War* acted to affirm unionism, capitalising on Northern
Ireland's involvement in the Second World War, continuing the warrior myth
and textualising this latest protestant sacred date.

Northern Ireland in the Second World War was intended to represent the Northern Irish state's part in the war in the way in which the unionist government wished it to be remembered. In addition, it echoed and templated many of the stereotypes created by earlier unionist historians, such as Ernest Hamilton, W.A. Phillips, James Logan and D.A. Chart, of Northern Ireland and 'Ulstermen'. 'Though the province was small', wrote Blake, 'nevertheless it contained hidden strength; and its greatest strength derived from the character of the Ulster people.' That 'character' was identifiably protestant, although Blake does concede that 'the whole background of the Ulsterman, whether Presbyterian, Episcopalian, Methodist or Roman Catholic, runs counter to emotional display'. But this is a token reference. 'Geography, history, tradition and religion all in some sense differentiated Northern Ireland from Éire' according to John Blake. The 'Presbyterian-Scot' settlers were 'dour, fervent, conscious of high destiny, taught self-reliance' and brought these elements to the 'Ulster' character, while the 'Anglo-Scottish' added 'vigour, enterprise, dogged determination and much individuality'. The contribution from the 'Irish' was 'the romance that is peculiarly Irish'.[122] These were the individuals James Logan described as contented to delight in diligence and duty,[123] while Chart had identified men from the north of Ireland as being the most individualistic on the whole island.[124] For Cyril Falls, Northern Irishmen were marked by constancy and tenacity.[125] Blake follows this traditional rhetoric:

> More than that, he was capable of translating into other spheres the deep unquestioning loyalty which religious conviction breeds. His vision might be limited, but to what he could see he unswervingly adhered . . . The Ulsterman, indeed, is wholehearted in the causes he adopts.[126]

Similarly Hamilton had identified 'unquestioning loyalty' as a characteristic of the planter: 'their word, once given, was binding even to death'.[127] Blake saw in the First World War the proof of the quality of the 'Ulsterman': 'His worth on the battlefield, indeed, had been frequently demonstrated and not least in the First World War . . . when he supported Great Britain in 1939, as previously in 1914 he did not count the cost'.[128] Clearly, however, the cost could be counted:

> But all this was willingly accepted as part of the price of loyalty to King and country and readiness to serve in a cause which she counted just. Here, indeed, is the true measure of her war service, one that, because it is hidden in the recesses of the half-conscious mind, defies external analysis.[129]

Blake argued that a combination of all these factors, including the leadership of Craig, had brought Northern Ireland into the war: 'Because of all this – background, tradition, religion and character – the devotion of a majority of her people was one of Northern Ireland's principal contributions to victory in the Second World War'.[130]

Northern Ireland in the Second World War rehearsed the by-now traditional unionist interpretation of Northern Ireland's history, and the process, historical as well as legislative, by which the state had come into existence. Blake also drew comparisons between the unionists' position in the face of the third home rule bill and Americans in the American War of Independence:

> As with many Americans in the age of their revolution, so now with the Ulster Unionists the question was not so much home rule but who should rule at home; and, representing a minority as they did, they could not see how, in a united Ireland separated from Great Britain, they could hope to rule at home.[131]

This association with the Americans is not surprising following the stationing of Americans in Northern Ireland from 1942. John Blake's narrative also linked unionist opposition to home rule to their support of the war effort:

> That philosophy, which formerly had sustained Ulstermen in their dour opposition to home rule, now underlined their conviction that political destiny and material advantage lay in the preservation of the British connection. Northern Ireland, composed of six of the old nine counties of Ulster, conceiving that the war against Germany was a righteous cause, was, as in the old days, again prepared to fight and to believe herself right.[132]

Tracing developments from the home rule controversies of the 1880s up to the Government of Ireland Act, Blake used language appropriate to the aftermath of a war ostensibly fought to protect the rights of small nations: 'In so far as the protection of minorities must figure among the aims of the modern democratic state, the point could not be evaded that special provision ought to be made to meet the demands of the spokesmen of the North.'[133] Interestingly, Blake in this instance discussed the rights of minorities in terms of the position of unionists on the eve of the settlement of 1920. In addition, he considered northern nationalist and southern unionist objections to the Government of Ireland Bill, but while explaining that the latter's objections rested on the fact that they would be subject to a 'parliament in Dublin which would be wholly controlled by Sinn Fein', he did not draw the obvious conclusion of his argument that northern nationalists would similarly object to a Northern Irish parliament dominated by unionists.[134]

The message throughout Northern Ireland's official war history was that the British government had a debt to repay to the unionist government and people for their strategic war-time contribution. In the foreword Lindsay-Keir and Professor G.O. Sayles (professor of modern history at Queen's University Belfast), members of the war history advisory committee, summed up the book's purpose; it would, they believed, 'correct any impression that the part of Northern Ireland in the winning victory has been unduly emphasised'.[135] And they continued:

> Her [Northern Ireland's] most valuable opportunity to ensure the Allied victory came, as is generally agreed, with the battle of the Atlantic, to which one chapter has accordingly been almost exclusively devoted . . . In that vital struggle Northern Ireland was indispensable.[136]

Of course, comparison was also made with the First World War and the part played by unionists; many 'still recalled how the Ulster Division had been mutilated, almost annihilated, on the Somme in July 1916', but, 'as in 1914, so now, duty prescribed that the people of Ulster must mobilize all their resources in the common cause, that of the unity and freedom of the British Commonwealth and Empire'.[137] This is a telling paragraph, indicating that the unionist government saw itself as having fought the war to prevent the break-up of the United Kingdom, presumably by the altering of the Government of Ireland Act of 1920, something which they had feared in the years immediately before the outbreak of the conflict in Europe. Blake voiced some of that concern: 'The Government of Ireland Act (1920) might prove no more than a pious aspiration, an outline on paper of a possible scheme of government. Would it suffer the fate of Cromwell's paper constitutions?'[138] He made no claims that unionist loyalty was to the British administration; he is quite clear that Northern Ireland's war efforts were motivated by their desire to remain within the United Kingdom and not for the freedom of smaller countries.[139] During the Second World War unionists had seen British willingness to 'sacrifice' Northern Ireland for their own ends in an offer of unity with the Éire government over the Treaty ports. Blake, therefore, referred to unionist loyalty to the British crown and to the country but never, significantly, to the British government:

> Northern Ireland, like other parts of the United Kingdom, suffered for her faith. All the evils of total war were her lot, and not least damage, bombing and death . . . But all this was willingly accepted as part of the price of loyalty to King and country and readiness to serve in a cause which she counted just.[140]

While emphasising the debt owed to Northern Ireland for its war-time effort, Blake's text indicated a continuing unionist fear that the British administration would, or at least could, abandon the state. And, moreover, that without the moral pressure of a debt owed this was likely to happen.

In the first chapter of the official war history Blake refers to Randolph Churchill's famous quotation in the late nineteenth century that 'Ulster will fight and Ulster will be right':

> Thus articulating the instinct of Ulstermen to render unswerving loyalty to a cause conceived in justice, in his own way he helped to strengthen those bonds of intimacy which allowed men and women from Northern Ireland to fight and strive side by side with the people of Great Britain in the world wars of the twentieth century.[141]

He depicts Northern Ireland's relationship with Britain as one of equals fighting and striding 'side by side', as unionist politicians and commentators had done during the First World War. Unionists' rhetoric, following the Second World War, focused on their position within the empire and on maintaining the *status quo*. Blake outlines the continuity in the make-up of the Northern Irish government from 1921 to the eve of the Second World War: 'The architects of government in Northern Ireland, by a combination of skill, determination, hard work and imagination, had by 1939 produced a working system of administration capable of adaptation without undue loss of efficiency in the event of an emergency.'[142] Although he later contradicts this contention: 'When hostilities with Germany began in September 1939, Northern Ireland, judged by the exacting standards of modern war, was in some respects ill-prepared.'[143] This rhetoric echoed the unionists' position following the First World War with regard to the Free State. The nationalist south in that period was depicted as treacherous and disloyal while the unionists in Ulster had proven their loyalty by their willingness to sacrifice themselves for the empire. Following the Second World War unionist rhetoric was more muted but the message was similar. To quote Blake:

> In the struggle against Germany the Government of Éire preferred to observe a policy of neutrality, a position which was maintained through-out the Second World War. In Ulster, however, the old loyalties prevailed. If to most of those living in the South neutrality was a rational policy, to their neighbours in the North it was an evasion of duty.[144]

Thus in 1939, as in 1914, unionists represented the southern Ireland as having shirked its war duty while they had given the ultimate proof of loyalty in their efforts on behalf of the Allied forces.

The Northern Irish government had begun to plan their official war history as early as 1941. D.A. Chart, the deputy keeper of the Public Records Office of Northern Ireland, was approached by the unionist govern-ment in 1941 to collect and write the history.[145] He began to write drafts as early as March 1943.[146] From the start he was considered and considered himself the official author: this is clear from his correspondence. In a letter to the commissioner of valuation looking for newspaper sources he wrote: 'If so, I should be greatly obliged if they could be sent to this office, which is at present engaged in gathering material for a history of the War Effort of Northern Ireland, which I have been officially deputed to compose'.[147] In the end, an impressively large, comprehensive and valuable scrapbook of news-paper cuttings relating to the war was compiled. Chart requested that government officials keep the project in mind when recording and collating their department's records.[148] Several meetings were held with the principal civil servants in each department to discuss the way in which they could aid Chart's project.[149] At times these civil servants were cautious about co-oper-ating, as this note of Chart's reveals:

> Some of the members of the committee were uneasy about premature disclosure, so I told them that there would be no publication until the end of the war and that even then the matter in the history would be submitted to and approved by the department concerned. This seemed to settle that particular doubt.[150]

Despite the sobering influence of Stormont's civil servants, Chart was keen that there should be some lighter moments in the history: 'Any illuminating detail or matter of what might be called human interest helps to brighten a history and this particular one (though the matter will mostly come from officials) is not intended to be too official in tone'.[151] He also had the support of a small committee, created in 1942 and headed by Professor Lindsay-Keir.[152] The committee's task was simply to advise the government on the collection of material for the project, and to make suggestions as to the format it might eventually take. There is a peculiar irony in these arrangements given that the war was raging in 1941. Moreover, it was not going well for the Allied forces; it was not until 1943 that the balance of power shifted in favour of the Allies. The Stormont government's plans for their war history, in common with the official United Kingdom war history which was also being organised at this time, displays admirable optimism that theirs would be the winning side.

In 1943 the Home Office in London suggested the publication of a more popular pamphlet publicising Northern Ireland's war effort, complementing the official war history. Sir Alexander Maxwell of the Home Office wrote to Robert Gransden:

> The Home Secretary suggests that at an appropriate time the story of Northern Ireland's part in the war ought to be published . . . The Home Secretary has in mind some suitably illustrated pamphlet under some such title as 'Northern Ireland's Part in the War for Freedom'.[153]

This pamphlet, Sir Wilfrid Spender felt, could be taken home as a momento by the American and British troops stationed in Northern Ireland.[154] Spender, however, outlined one of the publication's major problems: 'It might not be very judicious for the Government to boast of Ulster's part at a time when, in official circles, there is a good deal of criticism of what our workers are doing and also criticism of the lack of response of our young men in joining the fighting forces'.[155] The question of conscription reared its head once more. Robert Gransden was in favour of the idea; 'what is now proposed is a more readable and racy account of what we are doing':

> The publication would be more attractive if written up by an outsider of the calibre of Mr St John Ervine than if it were left to an editor in official circles, and I do not think there should be any difficulty in Departments giving such an individual the necessary particulars to enable a connected story to be told.[156]

Chart believed that the proposed pamphlet would damage the market for the official history 'as it would probably disclose many of the otherwise exclusive features of the official history'.[157] In addition, he argued that: 'No satisfactory publication could be made at present, nor, indeed, so far as I can see until the war is finished, because not until then will it be possible to speak freely of the extent of Ulster production of munitions etc'.[158] He ultimately recommended against the publication. Professor Lindsay-Keir suggested that if the pamphlet were to go ahead it should be organised under the auspices of some group other than the war history committee:

> It is, however, felt that the responsibility already resting on the Committee, and particularly on Dr Chart, who has to deal single-handed with

both the collection of material and also with the actual writing of the Official War History of Northern Ireland, would make it advisable for some other body than the Committee itself to undertake the work.[159]

Basil Brooke, however, supported this project and recommended to Maynard Sinclair that St John Ervine be approached to act as author.[160] Sir Wilfrid Spender saw a difficulty with Ervine:

> Mr St John Ervine, in his publication of Lord Craigavon's life, is making it clear that he is writing an appreciation of Lord Craigavon at Lady Craigavon's request, but that it does not in any way represent a historical biography. He therefore told me that he felt justified in bringing into the picture those factors which were most favourable to his subject without having the necessity of introducing anything of a critical character. He emphasised the fact that his publication would be entirely unofficial. There is, of course, no question of any Government subsidy to this biography. I am a little doubtful, however, whether in a Government-subsidised publication one is justified in picking and choosing one's contributions in the same way.[161]

Despite this objection, and with the prime minister's backing, Ervine was invited and accepted the authorship, with Chart's help.[162] Ervine, acknowledging Chart's contribution, requested that his name appear as joint author of the pamphlet.[163] However, Chart was anxious to separate this pamphlet from the official war history:

> The Committee, has, however, been rather inclined to keep the official history and Mr Ervine's work completely separate as there might be some tinge of propaganda about the latter, which would diminish the historical authority of the former. I do not know how they would view my being at the same time collaborator in the popular brochure and official historian and I would like to consult them about it.[164]

By November 1944, in an effort to overcome the difficulty of selecting an appropriate author, John Blake was suggested as a suitable choice.[165] Interest in the pamphlet was fuelled by the publication of a white paper by the British government which detailed the United Kingdom's war record. The Northern Irish government felt that the publication of a similar white paper on Northern Ireland's record would be unwise, since Northern Ireland would 'suffer by comparison with the United Kingdom figures'. The publicity committee 'recognised that a record of Northern Ireland's war effort should be available, but agreed that the necessary material could be included in the popular history and not published as a White Paper'.[166] In June 1945 Robert Gransden noted that St John Ervine was now unable to undertake the authorship and Jack Loudan was recommended as his replacement.[167] However, Sir Wilfrid Spender observed in a memo, in September 1945, that Loudan 'would not be disappointed if ultimately he did not undertake the editing of the projected History'.[168] Ultimately the idea of the pamphlet was dropped altogether.[169]

John Blake, a lecturer in the history department at QUB, was appointed as the author of the official war history by the unionist government in 1945.[170] In his acceptance letter to the prime minister, Sir Basil Brooke, he wrote: 'The invitation which you have so kindly extended to me both confers a privilege and imposes a responsibility. I shall be honoured to accept the privilege and privileged to fulfil the responsibility'.[171] He considered his appointment as official war historian an honour, as did the university's administration.[172] And it was a responsibility, but not for Blake alone. D.A. Chart had done much of the groundwork for this history; it was he who had made all the initial contacts with the government departments and others in the shipbuilding industry, the railways and so on. Moreover, he had drafted several pieces on areas of the war, and sketched the outline of the project as a whole by the time Blake took over.[173] Maynard Sinclair, in a letter to Lindsay-Keir, felt that the appointment of Blake over Chart was a sensitive issue which had to be handled carefully:

> I am quite agreeable to the appointment of Mr Blake to assist in the preparation of this publication and to pay him an honorarium of £250 for his services in this connection. While it has, of course, nothing to do with me, I would suggest that in conveying this decision to Dr Chart it might be better that this should be done by you personally rather than at a meeting of the Committee.[174]

In 1945 Chart was made editor of the war history, but he was no longer its author.[175]

The unionist government's wish to have an official version of their state's war record written involved many others, although it was a very minor operation in comparison to the organisation involved in the *History of the Second World War: United Kingdom* series. Although Blake was the author, a combination of civil servants and historians contributed significantly to the work.[176] He had at least seven civil servants individually researching and writing up the war histories of their own departments.[177] From a memorandum recording an interview between Sir William Scott and Blake in May 1946 it is clear that this was a government priority:

> Scott affirmed that, in his view, the existing system was to be preferred, that is, the system by which specified individuals (preferably one in each department) were detailed to write up the history of their own respective departments in war time.[178]

Clearly, the unionist government was taking no risks in the representation of their departments' and the state's war record. This team of civil servants was organised by Blake following the end of the war, although Chart had already established this arrangement prior to the armistice.[179] Blake did make some of his own contacts, particularly within Queen's University. This letter to Professor T.T. Flynn of the zoology department is typical of the sort of approach that was made:

> I have heard it rumoured, indeed, that you were toying with the idea of preparing an account of the casualty services and their achievement under your direction. I don't know whether this is true, but I hope it is so, because, if so, then I would like you if you can and if you will to furnish me with whatever information you think may help me in the writing of the Official War History.[180]

This was the nature of Blake's requests, by and large; individuals were invited to contribute by writing up short narratives on their area of experience, which Blake would then incorporate into the wider narrative of the history.[181] In addition, appeals were made in the English press for information on anyone from Northern Ireland who had been involved in the war.[182]

Despite the fact that the official war history took ten years to produce, Blake's commitment to the work does not appear to have faltered.[183] There are occasions, however, when his correspondence with Black, the war history advisory committee's secretary, indicated impatience with the subject matter:

> I am immersed in the Ministry of Commerce Registry (Linenhall Street) ploughing a deadly furrow through the indexes, and occasionally, looking at the contents of a file. In this vast desert there are only a few oases, and yet one has to cross miles and miles of sand! It is I fear, pretty monotonous. Every day, I become more convinced that the *writing* of the History is the least of my jobs.[184]

The following year produced similar complaints: 'I am now in the throes of drafting another chapter on Ocean Convoys, and it would be impolite for me to put down on paper exactly what I think about it'.[185] But such complaints were to be expected given the drawn-out nature of the research project, and by and large Blake found his task a relatively painless one. 'In any case', he wrote to Lindsay-Keir in 1947, 'so far as routine difficulties are concerned I invariably encounter such ready co-operation from the government that up to the present time all such incidental difficulties have been adjusted smoothly and happily'.[186] Ironically, despite this official co-operation, the long delay in completion was primarily due to the involvement of so many civil servants. The subject matter itself was also a contributory factor; as Chart wrote in 1942: 'I pointed out that the book would be at least partly intended as a guide to future administrators, if such an emergency occurred again, and would try to relate substantially what had been done by the departments.'[187] Delays were unavoidable given the large amount of paperwork needed to supply the various civil servants with drafts of chapters which related to their departments, as well as copies for ministers and members of the war history advisory committee.[188] Blake himself pointed to the interference of individual Stormont government departments as the major delaying factor in the progress of the war history:

> The re-drafting of this chapter has taken a very great amount of time, much more than I can really afford to devote to it. This partly arises from what I regard as special pleading . . . This indeed is where the trouble

arises. Time and again, a department, viewing the script from its own angle, fails to see the whole point that is being made, and unless I keep my eyes skinned the general pattern suffers.[189]

This letter from the Ministry of Commerce is illustrative of the sort of objections departments had:

> I suggest that, in giving an historical account, it is particularly necessary to remember that the reactions of people at the time were governed by the limited extent of their knowledge from day to day and that consequently, unless those limits can be made perfectly clear, a false impression can easily be given when writing after all the cards have been played on the table.[190]

Slow progress was inevitable given the process which the various draft chapters had to go through.

In addition to Stormont officials, London officials also reviewed drafts and on occasion objected to the bias of Blake's text.[191] For example, a draft of chapter nine was sent to the Home Office, the Ministry of Supply, the Ministry of Labour, the board of trade, the treasury, the Ministry of Agriculture and Fisheries, the admiralty and the security authorities in London.[192] In May 1952, Acheson wrote to Black, informing him that the Home Office had objected to references to 'Ulster' as a province, 'because the area of the Northern Ireland Government is not the same as the old province of Ulster'.[193] The Ministry of Materials objected to the over-praising of a Belfast ropeworks:

> The firm no doubt did quite good work but they were only one of many in the UK engaged in the production of ropes and cordage for the war effort. It is misleading to select a comparatively small user of cordage to make the implication that a large proportion of requirements was met from Belfast.[194]

More damningly, Brigadier H.B. Latham, of the cabinet office historical section in London, felt that it was 'quite the most absurd Official Military History' he had read:

> To follow every ship across the oceans, because it was built in Belfast and to boost at all times the actions of the Army units based in Northern Ireland may lead to a 'complete nonsense' and indeed may make the latter look ridiculous in the eyes of the rest of the Army.[195]

Although Lindsay-Keir felt that the 'pride of place should be given to the part played by Northern Ireland in relation to trans-Atlantic convoys', he argued that Blake was over-emphasising the work of Belfast-built ships.[196] Progress was, in this way, also hampered by the existence of the war history advisory committee led by Lindsay-Keir. Established in 1946, with Blake's approval, the committee consisted of Professor David Lindsay-Keir, D.A. Chart, Professor Sayles, Sir William Chart, J.F. Caldwell and F.R. Adams.[197] It gathered at regular intervals to discuss the history's progress, comment on work already completed and address any problems which might have arisen. It is clear from the minutes that all areas of the history were carefully reviewed by the committee, and that towards the end drafts of chapters were sent to the various departments for final approval. This process no doubt contributed to the length of time the project took to be completed.[198]

John Blake then, to all intents and purposes, was a research director.[199] The influence of these civil servants is apparent in the finished product.[200] For example, in an early plan of the book Blake used the names of government departments as chapter headings, indicating the broad topics which he would cover: 'Ministry of Education – evacuation of children, their return, education, etc. Ministry of Food – food production and rationing'.[201] He also made extensive use of the regimental histories available, particularly those of regiments with a high quota of Northern Irishmen.[202] Combined with the influence of civil servants, this created a turgid and largely dull history. To quote the harsh but astute *Times Literary Supplement* review in 1957:

> It is not, however, a book for the ordinary reader. It is a mass of facts and statistics, it covers the performance of every industry in Ulster, as well as following every service unit connected with Ulster to battlefields all over the world. The result is a collection of information, much of which is part of the general history of the Second World War, which has been assembled to proclaim Ulster's contribution to the Allied cause. There is no doubt that both collectively and individually the Northern Irish did much to help the destruction of the Nazis and their allies, but it is questionable whether this provincial history of the war is either necessary or dignified.[203]

Unlike the *TLS*, the unionist government believed the history necessary precisely because it proclaimed Northern Ireland's contribution to the war. Responding angrily to the *TLS* review Blake wrote to Black: 'What an insult to the people of Northern Ireland and indeed, if I may say so, to all Irishmen everywhere.'[204] Reminding British political and public opinion of the strategic importance of Northern Ireland in times of crisis was one of the central aims of Blake's work. To quote Cyril Falls's review: 'The subject is inspiring, that of a community which accepted all that war entailed as "part of the price of loyalty to King and Country" in a war held to be just'.[205] In November 1956, the month of the book's launch, the information service at Stormont noted that: 'The Official War History provided an excellent foundation for several feature articles emphasising the importance of Northern Ireland to the United Kingdom in peace and war'.[206] The Northern Irish government's desire for such a history went deeper than the need for positive publicity, and reveals the continuing concerns of unionists for the state's survival twenty years after its establishment. Given the anxiety caused by the declaration of an Irish republic in 1949, this is not altogether surprising. Above all, however, Blake's work was aimed at reinforcing in the minds of the British public and politicians the common bond which war had created between Northern Ireland and Britain, a bond which unionists believed would ultimately prevent future Westminster administrations from abandoning them.[207]

Within the island and within the United Kingdom, unionist security was copper-fastened by the Ireland Act of 1949, which confirmed that in no event would 'Northern Ireland or any part thereof cease to be part of His Majesty's Dominions and of the United Kingdom without the consent of the Parliament of Northern Ireland'.[208] It appeared that loyalty had gained its reward.[209] But, as with the Government of Ireland Act of 1920, the Ireland Act of 1949 seemed to promise what it in fact did not.[210] Stormont ministers believed that they were now in control of their state's destiny, at the whim no longer of the policies and aspirations of others.[211] This gave them a self-confidence which can be seen in the Festival of Britain in Northern Ireland and in the triumphal celebrations for the coronation visit of Elizabeth II. They failed to appreciate that ultimate legislative supremacy lay with administrations at Westminster which in the past had shown themselves willing to interfere with Northern Ireland's political existence.[212] The Northern Irish administration had looked to the 1920 Government of Ireland Act to ensure their security.[213] The next twenty years had presented them with a different reality. After a decade of watching the southern government undermine the arrangements made for them under the 1920 Act, unionists were then faced with the British government's willingness to embrace a united Ireland in 1940. In the years following the armistice in 1945, unionist politicians realised that they would have to create further barriers to maintain the state which they controlled. This determination to resist the British government had emerged in the years following the First World War. Speaking to his cabinet in May 1922 Craig had set the tone for government of the Northern Irish state; 'What we have', he said, 'we will hold.'[214] This continued to be the policy of the unionist government, and in this respect their role in the Second World War was of vital importance, for it allowed them the moral high ground. Westminster could not disown, or even threaten to disown, them given this wartime association. 'Without the help of the North', said Ernest Bevin, the British foreign secretary, 'Hitler would unquestionably have won the submarine war and the United Kingdom would have been defeated':

> That would have brought Hitler at once to Dublin and they would have made the Irish become as slaves. Until the majority of Northerners were persuaded, therefore, that it was in their interests to join the South, the British people would oblige us to give them guarantees that they would not be coerced.[215]

After 1945, in a period of rapid decolonisation, there was an increased need for unionists to secure their political moorings to the British state, and it is in this context that the official war history should be read. While an important part of the development of unionism's literary tradition, Blake's *Northern Ireland in the Second World War* and Ervine's *Craigavon: Ulsterman* contribute significantly to an understanding of official unionism's self-perception and reflect unionists' political aspirations in the post-war period.

Notes and References

1   Ervine's *Craigavon: Ulsterman* had official approval removed when the first drafts were seen by Stormont civil servants and ministers, but it did have official support while being written and, privately, prominent unionists approved of it, as this letter from Dehra Parker to Ervine illustrates: 'As a study of Irish events, politics and character, I find it enthralling. I love the parts about James and your obvious understanding of his most loveable, able and upright character, AND his strength and single-mindedness. But, if you want my true opinion, at this stage – I wish there were more of him and a little less about Southern Ireland. I do hope this comment won't hurt or offend you? I feel that you have the material there for two separate books?', Dehra Parker to St John Ervine, 10 Nov. 1945, CAB 9H/16/1.

2   While there are no sales figures available for either book, Judge James Brown, who helped St John Ervine in part of the research for the book on Craigavon, recalled that Ervine was disappointed that the book had not sold better. Interview with Judge James Brown, 29 Feb. 1996.

3   Although, as Norman Vance points out, the tradition of Irish soldiering for Britain during the First and Second World Wars was a long one and existed before the development of Ulster militarism, and had little to do with the politics of nationalism or unionism. Norman Vance, *Irish literature: a social history. Tradition, identity and difference* (Oxford, 1990), pp. 190–1.

4   In addition the welfare state was extended to Northern Ireland following the war, enhancing this gap between north and south.

5   Ervine argued that it was Northern Ireland which had allowed Éire to maintain its position of neutrality; ironically it was Éire's position of neutrality which gave Northern Ireland the opportunity to fulfil a vital strategic role for the Allies.

6   The Belfast Blitz involved four German attacks; as a result 1,100 people died and 56,000 houses were damaged.

7   Following the war the central funding authorities in Britain were more sympathetic to Northern Ireland's need for subventions; the idea of a 'balanced' budget was dropped; the state shared fully in the new welfarism; between 1946 and 1951 parity was established between Britain and Northern Ireland's services and taxation levels; unemployment funds in both areas were amalgamated, R.F. Foster, *Modern Ireland, 1600–1972* (London, 1988), p. 559.

8   In addition, as Brian Barton has argued, these early war years were ones of tension within the Northern Irish cabinet itself, tension which led to the resignation of Andrews and the election of Brooke as prime minister in 1943. Brian Barton, 'The impact of World War II on Northern Ireland and on Belfast–London relations', in Peter Catterall and Seán McDougall (eds), *The Northern Ireland question in British politics* (London, 1996), pp. 50–3.

9   Article 2 of the 1937 Constitution claimed that the national territory consisted of the whole island of Ireland, see note 28.

10   The Northern Irish government objected when the British government refused to enforce conscription; however, such complaints from the Stormont government were largely to cover up poor recruiting figures in Northern Ireland, see note 28.

11   Copy of the speech of prime minister Basil Brooke to the members of the Thirty Club in London, 14 July 1943, CAB 3A/116.

12   Cyril Falls's review of Blake's *Northern Ireland in the Second World War* highlighted this point: 'The loss of Queenstown or Cobh, of Berehaven and of Lough Swilly, through Southern Irish neutrality, was a deadly handicap in the Battle of the Atlantic. Ulster filled the void. Sir Winston Churchill believed that it made the difference between defeat and victory. "But for the loyalty of Northern

Ireland", he said, "we should have been confronted with slavery and death"',
      BBC NI Home Service, 21 Nov. 1956, CAB 3F/1/10.

13   Brian Barton, 'The impact of World War II on Northern Ireland and on
      Belfast–London relations' in Peter Catterall and Seán McDougall (eds.), *The
      Northern Ireland question in British politics*, p. 58.

14   Liam Canny, 'Recruiting in the Irish Free State and Northern Ireland for the
      British armed forces during the 1939–1945 war', unpublished MA dissertation,
      QUB, Sept. 1995, p. 49.

15   Ervine, *Craigavon: Ulsterman,* p. 547.

16   ibid., p. 548.

17   ibid., p. 551.

18   CAB 4/475/15.

19   This included a large protest meeting of nationalists in Corrigan Park. A petition
      was signed: 'We pledge ourselves solemnly to one another to resist conscription
      by the most effective means at our disposal, consonant with the law of God', *Irish
      Press,* 24 May 1941, cited in Canny, 'Recruiting in the Irish Free State', p. 59.

20   Cardinal Joseph MacRory, 23 May 1941. Department of Foreign Affairs files, P70,
      National Archives, Dublin. ibid., p. 58.

21   Northern Ireland had approximately 212,000 men between the ages of eighteen
      and forty-one, eligible for conscription. The state also had 104,000 reserved jobs,
      most held by protestants. Liam Canny, 'Recruiting in the Irish Free State', p. 59.
      In Britain by 1945 two out of every five men of military age were enlisted. Peter
      Clarke, *Hope and glory, Britain 1900–1990* (London, 1996), p. 200.

22   Robert Fisk, *In time of war: Ireland, Ulster and the price of neutrality* (London,
      1983), p. 443.

23   ibid., p. 446.

24   Liam Canny, 'Recruiting in the Irish Free State', p. 64.

25   The issue of conscription was raised for the last time in 1943. But Sir Charles
      Wickham, inspector general of the RUC, noted that 'there is behind the scenes a
      large amount of co-operation between the South and the services and conscrip-
      tion would kill this'. This seems to have settled the conscription matter once and
      for all. Memo, Sir Charles Wickham to the Northern Irish cabinet, 28 Apr. 1943,
      CAB 4/540/6A.

26   *Irish Independent,* 28 May 1941.

27   Peter Clarke, *Hope and glory,* p. 209.

28   Liam Canny provides an interesting argument for unionist discomfort with the
      conscription problem; in October 1941 Churchill proposed the setting-up of an
      Irish Brigade to show appreciation for the numbers of recruits from Éire who
      joined the British forces. Troops would be drawn from two units based in North-
      ern Ireland, one in England, the Royal Irish Fusiliers, the Royal Inniskillen
      Fusiliers and the London Irish Rifles. 'Many government officials in Northern
      Ireland objected because the unit might expose poor performance in their
      recruiting efforts. L.G.P. Freer, liaison officer to the Northern Ireland cabinet,
      wrote a letter to Robert Gransden, Northern Ireland cabinet secretary. "There is
      also the difficulty that our recruiting effort has not been as good as it might have
      been, the proportion of men from Éire in the battalions affected may be high".'
      Liam Canny, 'Recruiting in the Irish Free State', p. 62.

29   Letter, Winston Churchill to J.M. Andrews, on 'the occasion of his relinquishing
      the office of Prime Minister of Northern Ireland', 6 May 1943, CAB 3A/116.

30   'Most of these young people gave little thought to the politics of the time. A policy
      of neutrality did not influence recruits from the Irish Free State. Likewise,
      recruits from Northern Ireland gave little thought to Irish neutrality'. Liam
      Canny, 'Recruiting in the Irish Free State', p. 66.

31   'The Stormont Government had been embarrassed at the comparatively low rate of voluntary enlistment with only 38,000 volunteers out of an eligible male population of 212,000 and they probably hoped that conscription would cover up this lack of enthusiasm among loyalists to fight for the embattled Empire', Joseph Carroll, *Ireland in the war years* (Newton Abbot, 1975), p. 108. Moreover, the state suffered from recurring labour disputes, 'an inferior output' from its munitions factories compared to British firms, and 'pervasive apathy towards civil defence'. Brian Barton, 'The impact of World War II on Northern Ireland and on Belfast-London relations', p. 48. See Peter Clarke's description of the social effects of the war in Britain: 'Saving for victory, digging for victory, sewing for victory – this was a war in which everyone could "go to" and do their bit on "the home front"', *Hope and glory*, pp. 207–15.

32   Ervine, *BT*, 13 Oct. 1944.

33   Norman Vance, *Irish Literature; a social history*, p. 192.

34   CAB 9F/123/14. I am grateful to Seán McDougall for initially drawing my attention to this reference.

35   Letter, Basil Brooke to Ervine, 19 July 1946, CAB 9H/16/1.

36   'I regarded it solely as something that I could do for my own place and people. You will, I am sure, understand that I feel aggrieved by the implication, made several times in your letter and the Memorandum, that the Northern Ireland Government has some responsibility for the book. It hasn't any, and I am willing, if it be desired, to make this plain in my preface', letter Ervine to Basil Brooke, 30 July 1946, CAB 9H/16/1.

37   Born in Belfast 1883, died 1971. Broadly his career was spent from 1911–15 in the Abbey Theatre, West End comedies in the 1920s, and a return to 'Ulster' themes in the 1930s and 1940s.

38   In it Ervine argued that Carson had 'never said or done anything in the whole of his political career to denote that he possesses any constructive faculty whatever', *Sir Edward Carson and the Ulster Movement* (Dublin, 1915), p. 52. According to Vance, the book also 'tried to side step the problem of identity: "There are not two Irelands and two kinds of Irish man: there are four millions of Irish"', Norman Vance, *Irish Literature: a social history*, p. 185.

39   John Boyd, *Threshold*, Summer 1974.

40   Early plays included *Mixed Marriage* (1911), *The Magnanimous Lover* (1912), *The Orangeman* (1914) and *John Fergusson* (1915).

41   Ervine wanted to join an Irish, not an English, regiment in the First World War, and was commissioned in the Royal Dublin Fusiliers. Norman Vance, *Irish Literature: a social history*, p. 184.

42   Ervine to George Bernard Shaw, 1923, cited in Norman Vance, ibid., p. 189.

43   Ervine, *Craigavon: Ulsterman*, p. vii.

44   'Moreover, I cannot condone in my friend what I condemn in my foe. If a German behaves badly, well, he's a German and I don't expect anything better from him. But I expect something a lot better from my friend, and if he fails, I condemn him more severely than I condemn my enemy'. Letter, Ervine to Dehra Parker, 22 Dec. 1945. CAB 9H/16/1.

45   Ervine, *Craigavon: Ulsterman*, p. vii.

46   Ervine was also offered the authorship of a more popular history of Northern Ireland in the Second World War, but although he accepted the project he never completed it and the project was dropped eventually.

47   Letter, Robert Gransden to Lady Craigavon, 24 Dec. 1945, CAB 9H/16/1. Similarly in this letter from Basil Brooke to Lady Craigavon, 5 June 1946: 'Further, as you can well understand, we cannot subscribe to the conclusions contained in the last paragraph', CAB 9H/16/1. And in these notes on the biography prepared

by the publicity officer, F.R. Adams: 'Many will feel, indeed, that it is contrary to what Lord Craigavon knew to be practicable and believed to be desirable in view of the Government of Ireland Act, 1920, which he accepted as a final settlement', CAB 9H/16/1.

48   CAB 9F/123/67, Ervine, *Craigavon: Ulsterman*, pp. 551–2. Cyril Falls was also considered by Lady Craigavon as a possible author, CAB 9H/16/1.

49   Draft of John Andrew's radio broadcast on the death of Lord Craigavon, 25 Nov. 1940, CAB 9H/16/1.

50   Letter Lady Craigavon to Ervine, 22 June 1946, CAB 9H/16/1.

51   Once he had been appointed as biographer several government ministers let it be known that they would be willing to meet and talk with him. Robert Gransden, the Northern Irish cabinet secretary, was the principal reader of the book in draft form. A special lunch was convened to introduce Ervine to the cabinet and Ervine was also given a room in Stormont Castle to work in. In addition, Ervine was a frequent house guest at Lady Craigavon's.

52   'The strict official rule was that normally cabinet and other similar secret papers should not be open to writers of biographies, but the then prime minister told Lady Craigavon that, keeping within this strict official rule, every facility would be afforded the author'. Cabinet publicity committee meeting, 28 May 1946, CAB 9H/16/1.

53   Letter, Robert Gransden to Lady Craigavon, 21 Apr. 1941, CAB 9H/16/1.

54   Letter, Lady Craigavon to John Andrews, 14 Feb. 1941, CAB 9IF/16/1.

55   Ervine to Lady Craigavon, 30 Mar. 1941, CAB 9H/16/1.

56   Letter Basil Brooke to Lady Craigavon enclosed, draft of letter, Basil Brooke to Ervine, June 1946, CAB 911/16/1.

57   Letter, Ervine to Brooke, 30 July 1946, CAB 9H/16/1.

58   ibid.

59   Letter, Robert Gransden to Ervine, 8 Aug. 1946, CAB 9H/16/1.

60   CAB 9F/123/14.

61   Ervine, *Craigavon: Ulsterman*, p. vii.

62   Ostensibly a biography, it acted as a criticism of Éire and its policy of neutrality and a vindication of James Craig's leadership which had brought Northern Ireland to its position as the Atlantic bridgehead.

63   Ervine, *Craigavon: Ulsterman*, p. 190.

64   D.G. Boyce, *Nineteenth century Ireland, the search for stability* (Dublin, 1990), p. 234. Ervine, *Craigavon: Ulsterman*, p. 612. '"Distributing bones" was the phrase favoured by the ageing Craig (now Lord Craigavon), as he trundled around his province happily agreeing to classify a road to the Portstewart golf-links as first class, or advocating huge expenditure on Musgrave Street police barracks after an ex-public-school cadet complained about conditions there'. R.F. Foster, *Modern Ireland, 1600–1972*, pp. 556–7. Craig's parochialism is evident from the vast number of letters, housed in PRONI, sent by citizens of the Northern Irish state to the prime minister about a variety of concerns, PM 2.

65   J.J. Lee, *Ireland, 1912–85* (Cambridge, 1989), p. 138.

66   Patrick Buckland, *James Craig* (Dublin, 1980), p. 1.

67   R.F. Foster, *Modern Ireland, 1600–1972*, p. 465.

68   *Northern Hansard*, vol. xxiii, 26 Nov. 1940.

69   Ervine, *Craigavon: Ulsterman*, p. xx.

70   Ervine cites a contributor to the *Westminster Gazette*, 7 Nov. 1922: 'No man in the United Kingdom is so typical of the people he leads. He is the concentrated essence of Ulster in a sense that Lord Carson never was'. ibid., pp. 569–70.

71   ibid., p. 551.

72   ibid.

73 ibid.
74 This is Ervine's version of the native not being able to govern themselves, again familiar from earlier unionist histories, ibid., p. 607.
75 ibid., p. viii.
76 ibid., p. 608.
77 ibid., p. 607.
78 D.A. Chart, *A history of Northern Ireland* (Belfast, 1927), p. 24.
79 Ervine, *Craigavon: Ulsterman*, p. 612.
80 ibid., p. xviii.
81 Letter, Ervine to Brooke, 30 July 1946, CAB 9H/16/1.
82 Ervine, *Craigavon: Ulsterman*, inside front cover.
83 In this way, although Craig dies and is buried by p. 561, Ervine's narrative continues for another sixty pages of vitriol against the Irish republic and its ministers. The 'young in Éire' also came in for Ervine's criticism; they were 'educated very strictly on a syllabus which inculcates a loathing of the British, are no better than the dotards: they join an adolescent ignorance of ordinary facts to an incoherent passion which disturb the minds of the judicious and render hope of better feeling in the future delusive'. ibid., p. 556.
84 'The justification of his life's work', according to Robert Gransden, 'is the Ulster bridgehead of 1939–1945', letter, Robert Gransden to Ervine, nd, but probably October 1945, CAB 9H/16/1.
85 Ervine, *Craigavon: Ulsterman*, p. 555.
86 David Harkness, *Northern Ireland since 1920* (Dublin, 1983), p. 119.
87 Ervine, *Craigavon: Ulsterman*, p. 556.
88 *BWT*, 26 Aug. 1949.
89 Letter, Robert Gransden to Ervine, nd, but probably October 1945, CAB 9H/16/1.
90 ibid.
91 Ervine to Shaw, nd, cited in Norman Vance, *Irish literature: a social history*, p. 189.
92 CAB 9F/123/14.
93 Notes on the text by F.R. Adams, 4 July 1946, CAB 9H/16/1. Adams was a Yorkshire man, and a former editor of the *Northern Whig*.
94 ibid.
95 Letter, Lady Craigavon to Brooke, 23 June 1946, CAB 9H/16/1.
96 Dame Dehra Parker felt that Ervine's overt bias against Éire detracted from the 'value of all you say of our first P.M. and the North', although she did also say that she felt he had said many things that needed to be said: 'you make a damning indictment of "National" [*sic*] character and policy'. She suggested that this sort of commentary would be better in a separate book. Dame Dehra Parker to Ervine, nd, CAB 9H/16/1.
97 CAB 9F/123/67.
98 Ervine, *Craigavon: Ulsterman*, p. x.
99 'Ulstermen know that De Valera, in almost everything he says and does, is wilful and wrong. His mind is commonplace and narrow. He has no sense of humour or accommodation . . . he likes hard facts. The harder they are, the better he likes them', Ervine, ibid., pp. 571–572.
100 ibid., pp. ix–x.
101 CAB 9F/123/67. Letter, Lady Craigavon to Robert Gransden, 20 Feb. 1946, CAB 9H/16/1.
102 Letter, Lady Craigavon to Robert Gransden, nd, CAB 9H/16/1.
103 'He [Gransden] had written a private letter to the author giving his personal view that the background of Irish political history against which the portrait was drawn was not what Lord Craigavon would have wished', 28 May 1946, CAB 9F/123/67.

104 'I am influenced by your very reasonable statement that *my* opinion ought not to be part of a book expounding Craigavon's but of an entirely separate book', letter, Ervine to Robert Gransden, 19 Dec. 1945, CAB 9H/16/1.

105 CAB 9F/123/67. Robert Gransden wrote to Sir William Scott, permanent secretary to the Ministry of Finance, saying that in any case 'minor amendments will not meet the position. The whole conception is wrong, and the biography would have to be re-written to a large extent', 4 July 1946, CAB 9H/16/1.

106 Letter, Sir William Scott to Brooke, 21 May 1946.

107 Draft statement of why the Northern Irish government could not approve of the biography, nd, CAB 9H/16/1.

108 Letter, Lady Craigavon to Basil Brooke, 9 June 1946, CAB 9H/16/1.

109 Letter, Lady Craigavon to Ervine, 9 June 1946.

110 Letter, Brooke to Ervine, 19 July 1946, CAB 9H/16/1. Sir William Scott suggested that the biography be allowed to be published: 'It is almost certain to raise something of a storm, but so long as the Government is not associated with it there should be no ground for the generation of inter-State ill-feeling', letter, Sir William Scott to Robert Gransden, 2 July 1946, CAB 9H/16/1.

111 Letter, Ervine to Brooke, 30 July 1946, CAB 9H/16/1.

112 Ervine, *Craigavon: Ulsterman,* p. xx.

113 'It was thought, however, that if bitter feeling is aroused the Government would be asked whether they approved or otherwise of the publication of the Biography and it was felt that the only course open was to indicate definitely to the author that the Government did not agree that certain parts of the work should be linked in any way with an authentic life of Lord Craigavon', 28 May 1946, CAB 9F/123/67.

114 *NW*, 18 Aug. 1949. The *BNL* review was written by D.L. Savory and was also favourable. The *Irish News* on the other hand felt that Ulster had been 'singularly unfortunate in her apologists, and Lord Craigavon in his biographer', *IN*, 19 Aug. 1949. Both the *Observer* and the *Sunday Times* (21 Aug. 1949) felt that Ervine was overly concerned with 'the cause as distinct from the man', CAB 9H/16/ 1.

115 *BWT*, 26 Aug. 1949.

116 *Irish Times,* 20 Aug. 1949, CAB 9H/16/1.

117 Alvin Jackson, *Sir Edward Carson* (Dundalk 1993), p. 59.

118 Ervine cites this poem 'A conservator, call me, if you please/not a creator nor destroyer: one/Who keeps the world safe', Ervine, *Craigavon: Ulsterman,* pp. 567–8.

119 *ibid.,* p. 561.

120 J.J. Lee, *Ireland, 1912–85*, p. 257.

121 CAB 9F/123/67.

122 John Blake, *Northern Ireland in the Second World War*, (Belfast, 1956), pp. 34–5.

123 James Logan, *Ulster in the x-rays* (London, 1923), p. 53.

124 D.A. Chart, *A history of Northern Ireland,* p. 15.

125 Cyril Falls, *The birth of Ulster,* p. 254.

126 John Blake, *Northern Ireland in the Second World War,* p. 35.

127 Lord Ernest Hamilton, *The soul of Ulster* (Belfast, 1917), p. 31.

128 John Blake, *Northern Ireland in the Second World War,* pp. 34–5. Similarly, when writing about the First World War, James Logan wrote: 'Under no compulsion, but willingly, with the courage of their forefathers and with lion-hearted bravery, they heard the call of duty and obeyed', Logan, *Ulster in the x-rays,* p. 170.

129 John Blake, *Northern Ireland in the Second World War,* p. 535.

130 ibid., p. 35.

131 ibid., p. 4.

132 ibid., p. 2.

133 ibid., p. 4.

134 ibid., p. 5.

135 ibid., p. xv.

136 Germany's defeat, in particular its attempt to 'throttle' the Atlantic route, 'in the end was a measure of the strategic advantages arising from, among other factors, the rocklike devotion of Northern Ireland', ibid., pp. xv, 46.

137 ibid., p. 3.

138 ibid., p. 7.

139 'Resolutely determined to preserve at all costs the political connection with the British Commonwealth and Empire, their wartime alignment was the logical outcome of a position consistently maintained since the controversy over Irish home rule had first flared up in 1886', ibid., p. 1.

140 ibid., pp. 534–5.

141 ibid., p. 1.

142 Blake's narrative highlights the *status quo*; the government had won a 'striking victory' in the elections following the establishment of the Northern Irish state: 'It was this Government, later in office, still directed by Craig (Lord Craigavon, as he had become), and substantially unchanged, which was to be confronted some eighteen years afterwards by the problems arising from war between the United Kingdom and Germany', ibid.,pp. 7, 15.

143 ibid., p. 47.

144 ibid., p. 2.

145 'This Office has been entrusted with the task of compiling a record of the war effort of Northern Ireland', note of D.A. Chart's, 18 Dec. 1941, CAB 3B/18.

146 'To avoid a great rush of work after the war is over I am intending to write the history so far as it can be ascertained under the various sections when they have gone sufficiently in to the past for survey, making a beginning with the events of 1939–41', letter, D.A. Chart to L. Allen, Ministry of Labour, 4 Mar. 1943, CAB 3B/20. J.B. Meehan of the Ministry of Finance was appointed as his assistant, letter, J.B. Meehan to F.W. Haslett, ARP officer, civil defence, 14 July 1943, MPS 2/3/505.

147 Letter, D.A. Chart to the commissioner of valuation, 24 Dec. 1941, CAB 3B/18. 'As you will probably have heard I have been appointed to write an official History of the War Effort of Northern Ireland', D. A. Chart to Clarke, chairman of Northern Ireland Road Transport Board, 8 Mar. 1944, CAB 3A/16.

148 CAB 3A/16 & CAB 3B/18. 'As the meeting was arranged for the Official Historian to indicate what sort of information he would wish to receive and for the heads of branches to consider what they could supply and in what way, the proceedings tended to take the form of an enquiry from each person as to the nature of his work and the particulars he could supply', note of a discussion as to the furnishing of details for the war history by various heads of branches on the works side, Ministry of Finance, 17 Aug. 1944, CAB 3B/1 8.

149 'The meeting was to discuss the lines on which a general account of the war work of the Ministry of Commerce might be drawn up for my use as Official Historian of the War Effort', note of an interview with James Stewart and R.H. Wrights, Ministry of Commerce, 19 Jan. 1944, CAB 3A/16.

150 Note of an interview with the Northern Irish production executive committee, 21 Feb. 1944. Attended by W.D. Scott, the permanent secretary of the Ministry of Commerce, and representatives of the admiralty, the Ministry of Supply, the Ministry of Aircraft Production, Factory and Storage Control, Ministry of Labour, machine tool control, CAB 3A/16.

151 Letter, D.A. Chart to W.D. Scott, permanent secretary of the Ministry of Commerce, 26 Mar. 1943, CAB 3A/16.

152 Other members of this committee were Sir Arthur Quekett, Robert Gransden and F.R. Adams, CAB 3B/20.

153 Extract letter from Sir Alexander Maxwell of the Home Office to Robert Gransden, 10 Feb. 1943, FIN 18/23/319.

154 Providing this sort of propaganda was not new to the Northern Irish government; in 1943 'Ulster: The British Bridgehead' was published. 'Its main purpose', according to Robert Gransden, 'was to inform our American visitors and others about our constitutional position and war-time achievements', letter, Robert Gransden to Sir William Scott, 11 June 1945, FIN 18/23/255.

155 Memo of Sir Wilfrid Spender's, 18 Feb. 1943, FIN 18/23/319.

156 Letter, Robert Gransden to Sir Wilfrid Spender, minister of finance, 17 Feb. 1943, FIN 18/23/319.

157 Letter, D.A. Chart to Sir Wilfrid Spender, 24 Feb. 1943, FIN 18/23/319.

158 ibid.

159 Letter, D. Lindsay-Keir, vice-chancellor QUB, to prime minister Basil Brooke, 29 June 1943, FIN 18/23/319.

160 This letter would indicate that he took little notice of Keir's letter of 29 June 1943. 'I think that this is a project which would best be left to a writer of the eminence of Mr St John Ervine. Of course, I do not know whether he would be prepared to undertake the work as it would necessarily involve the closest contact with Dr Chart's organisation, but I believe he is coming over here later in the month and perhaps he might be sounded on the matter', letter, Basil Brooke to Maynard Sinclair, 2 July 1943, FIN 18/23/319.

161 Memo of Sir Wilfrid Spender's, 18 Feb. 1943, FIN 18/23/319.

162 'I am glad to be able to inform you that Mr Ervine is agreeable to undertake this task. I understand that he has been in direct communication with Dr Chart, who has supplied him with certain information', letter, Sinclair to Basil Brooke, 8 Sept. 1943, FIN 18/23/319.

163 Letter, St John Ervine to Sinclair, 29 Dec. 1943: 'Dr Chart's name ought to appear as part author of the pamphlet. His work is really the substantial part of the pamphlet and it would be best justice to acknowledge this by including him in the authorship', FIN 18/23/319.

164 Letter, D.A. Chart to the private secretary, Ministry of Finance, 11 Feb. 1944, FIN 18/23/319.

165 'It may be that the appointment of Mr Blake may solve the problem in as much as Mr Blake's qualifications may be such as to fit him for the preparation of a popular version of the History of the War Effort', letter, W.D. Scott to Robert Gransden, 1 Nov. 1944, FIN 18/23/319.

166 Extract from minutes of the publicity committee, 19 Dec. 1944. Members were the minister without portfolio, minister of labour, minister of education, parliamentary secretary to Ministry of Finance, secretary to cabinet government press officer, FIN 18/23/319.

167 Letter, Robert Gransden to W.D. Scott, 9 June 1945. Cabinet publicity committee, 5 Aug. 1945, FIN 18/23/319.

168 Memo of Wilfrid Spender's, 11 Sept. 1945, FIN 18/23/319.

169 5 Oct. 1945, FIN 18/23/319. The Ulster Unionist Council published a pamphlet by Prof. D.L. Savory, 'The War Effort of Northern Ireland', in 1947.

170 'Mr John W Blake, M.A, Queen's University, Belfast, has been appointed as author of the Official History of Northern Ireland's War Record, in which capacity he will work in collaboration with Dr Chart', letter, W.D. Scott to W.A. Carson, registrar general, 20 Aug. 1945, CAB 3B/18. Blake was considered for the post as early as March of 1945, but an unspecified query arose about his suitability. It was not mentioned again, so presumably it came to nothing. At the cabinet meeting of 22

Mar. 1945: 'It was decided that the appointment of an author should be left in the Prime Minister's hands', CAB 4/619/12. There is a gap in the minutes of the war history committee covering the period Oct. 1944 to Jan. 1947, the period in which Chart was made editor and Blake appointed as author.

171   CAB 9B/3.

172   Letter of Lindsay-Keir's, then vice-chancellor of the university, expressing his pleasure at Blake's appointment. Keir continued to support the history and acted on the war history advisory committee, CAB 3B/3.

173   Interim note, 6 Mar. 1944 of topics to be treated in the official history of Northern Ireland's war effort: '1)Historical Outline, 2)Fighting Services, 3)Civil Defence, 4)Agriculture and Food, 5)Industry, 6)Finance, 7)Transport and Communications, 8)Social Services and Education, 9)Welfare', FIN 18/23/319.

174   Letter, Maynard Sinclair to the vice-chancellor Lindsay-Keir, 30 Oct. 1944, FIN 18/23/319.

175   'I have been appointed by the Government of Northern Ireland editor of the war record of the Province and anything bearing on war production here would be greatly appreciated', letter, D.A. Chart to Hynes, Ministry of Supply, 7 Sept. 1945, CAB 3A/16.

176   In particular Black, the secretary to the war history advisory committee, who responded efficiently to Blake's copious requests for articles, government publications, books, and statistics, CAB 3B/4. Interestingly, during the writing of the Northern Irish Official War History Blake was contacted by Professor J.R.M. Butler of the cabinet office in London. Butler was involved in the official war history of the United Kingdom under the direction of Professor Keith Hancock. He wrote to ask Blake to recommend candidates 'in connection with the official [U.K] war history'. Of the four Blake recommended, one was Hugh Shearman; Blake wrote: 'Here is a young man of about thirty, who certainly has the ability to do the sort of thing that you have in mind . . . He comes from a distinguished Northern Protestant family, and his sympathies are Northern . . . He is not very malleable, but he does possess quite unusual gifts'. Blake also suggested a female Ph.D student for the post but suggested that, being a Roman Catholic, she was probably not the sort of candidate Butler would want, CAB 3E/17.

177   Civil servants who wrote up the war histories of their various departments: Ministry of Finance, Mr Darling; home affairs, Ms Jessie Campbell; public security, Mr J.B. Meehan; commerce, Mr R.H. Wright; labour, Mr Thomas Elwood; agriculture (this ministry issued annual reports which were used instead); education, Mr W.R.J. Downer.

178   CAB 3B/6.

179   'It is my intention to arrange to have the help of selected individuals in some of the Ministries, when I come to consider the War Record and achievement of each and all of the Ministerial Departments'. This arrangement was initiated by W.D. Scott, letter, Blake to E. Rea, Ministry of Education, 7 Dec. 1945, CAB 3B/6.

180   Blake to Professor T.T. Flynn, department of zoology, QUB, 11 Mar. 1946, CAB 3B/6.

181   'I do not want you to attempt anything in the nature of a finished narrative. I would be more than pleased if you could supply me with the essential factual material, and, allow me, in the event of my wishing to go behind your material access to the administrative records upon which your story will be, presumably, based', letter from Blake to A.J. Alloway, director of extra-mural studies, QUB, 11 Mar. 1946. Blake wanted Alloway to supply information on the activities of the committee responsible for education among the armed forces, CAB 3B/6.

182   The appeal was very broad, any information was welcome. There are no details

as to the precise nature of the appeal, letter, D.A. Chart to Blake, 20 Dec. 1945, CAB 313/6.

183 D.A. Chart remarked in a letter to L.J. Mason, 26 Oct. 1944: 'It is a continual surprise to me how the scope of the history steadily increases', CAB 3B/18.

184 Blake to Black, 8 Apr. 1948, CAB 3B/4.

185 Blake to Black, 9 Nov. 1949, CAB 3B/4.

186 Blake to Lindsay-Keir, 13 Oct. 1947, CAB 3B/6.

187 Note of conversation with Crone at the Ministry of Commerce, 15 Jan. 1942, CAB 3A/16.

188 'I am afraid that the examination of this chapter, one of the longest, has taken some time, and in the end neither the War Office nor the security authorities had any observations to make', letter, Acheson to Black, 25 Nov. 1953, CAB 3F/1/19.

189 'I shall continue to do the best I can to meet all the suggestions which Departments – whether in Belfast or in London – put forward, but the experience of this chapter is a clear warning to me that disastrous results may follow if I go too far', letter, Blake to Black, 30 Nov. 1951, CAB 3F/1/19.

190 Letter, A. Farrell, Ministry of Commerce, transport division, 2 Aug. 1950, CAB 3F/1/18.

191 'The closest links were maintained between the Northern Ireland Committee and similar committees working in Great Britain under the authority of the War Cabinet and by this means it has been found possible to construct the framework of the Northern Ireland History in close conformity with the United Kingdom design', memo of the prime minister, Basil Brooke, 20 Mar. 1945, CAB 4/619/4.

192 In December 1953 A. Acheson, of the cabinet office in London, wrote to Black asking for '18 copies of the completed book for the Official circulation, I had not contemplated that any copies would be required for distribution to individuals. Professor Blake, however, is anxious that those members of our Historical Staff who have seen the various chapters in draft and have given him personal comments should also see the revised chapters in their context. This means that I must increase my request from 18 copies to 33 copies. In addition, it would assist us if you could send me three copies of each chapter separately as it is rolled off', 7 Dec. 1953, CAB 3F/1/19.

193 Letter, A. Acheson, cabinet offices, London, to Black, 22 Mar. 1952, CAB 3F/1/19.

194 Letter, A. Acheson to Black, 22 Mar. 1952, CAB 3F/1/19.

195 Brig. H.B. Latham to A. Acheson (cabinet office), 8 Dec. 1952, CAB 106/331 PRO London. I am grateful to Dr Keith Jeffery for drawing my attention to these references.

196 He also felt that, if material were cast in different terms it would read more impressively: 'I am not quite happy about the last sentence of the top para [sic]. "Statistics show . . . from Belfast"). It might be that 6% is so low a proportion as to throw some doubt as to the real value of the Northern route, and I would favour expressing the proportion either in terms of ships or tonnage', letter, David Lindsay-Keir to Black, 7 Aug. 1950, CAB 3F/1/18.

197 Letter, Robert Gransden to John Blake, 16 Dec. 1946, agreeing to the setting-up of the committee. David Lindsay-Keir was the vice-chancellor of QUB, D.A. Chart was the deputy keeper of the PRONI, F.R. Adams was head of Stormont's publicity committee, J.F. Caldwell was a senior civil servant, Robert Gransden had been Craig's private secretary and was the cabinet secretary.

198 Concerns were raised intermittently by the war records committee about the length of time the project was taking, on one occasion, in March 1949, Blake responded by saying 'he felt he must carry out his task as well as he was able but

it would not be possible, with his other commitments, to do this to his full satisfaction if the time factor was to be regarded as of paramount importance', CAB 3E/14 is the file of the papers of the Northern Ireland war records committee and, after 1946, the minutes of the advisory committee, CAB 9CD/177 contains the minutes of the war records committee up to 16 Oct. 1944.

199 D.A. Chart had done so much of the groundwork for the book that his help was invaluable. There was a steady and cordial correspondence between him and Blake.

200 A friend (identified in the file by his initials as 'J.E.T.') of Blake's, who had read a draft of the book, wrote to him November 1948 complimenting him on the work: 'For the most part the author effaces himself like the civil servants who furnish him with so much of his material', CAB 3B/3.

201 CAB 3E/16.

202 These included, among others, the North Irish Horse, the Royal Irish Fusiliers, and the Royal Ulster Rifles.

203 *Times Literary Supplement,* 25 Jan. 1957, cited in CAB 3F/1/9.

204 Blake to Black, 28 Jan. 1957, CAB 3F/1/9.

205 Cyril Falls's review on BBC NI HS, 21 Nov. 1956, CAB 3F/1/10.

206 'These, "angled", to interest the United States Press, were circulated through British Information Services . . . In addition, the history provided a "scoop" in the shape of a story on the identity of the first U.S. soldier to set foot in Europe during the Second World War; this was accepted by Reuter and the Press Association for world-wide distribution', CAB 9F/123/53.

207 'It will be a great pleasure to me once again to recall memories of the inestimable value of Northern Ireland to our common cause, and of the illustrious part you yourself played', letter from Winston Churchill to Basil Brooke thanking him for the complimentary copy of the Official History, 22 Jan. 1956, CAB 3F/1/10.

208 Ireland Act 1949, section one.

209 While the moral debt owed did influence the British government's support for the Northern Irish state, there were other factors. The Imperial government's official working party concluded in January 1949 that: 'So far as can be forseen it will never be to Great Britain's advantage that Northern Ireland should form part of a territory outside His Majesty's jurisdiction. Indeed it seems unlikely that Great Britain would ever be able to agree to this even if the people of Northern Ireland desired it'. Brian Barton, 'The impact of World War II on Northern Ireland and on Belfast-London relations', p. 65.

210 Interestingly, the original constitutional declaration desired by the unionist government was that '"any alteration in the law touching the status of Northern Ireland as a part of the United Kingdom or the relation of the Crown to the parliament of Northern Ireland shall require the assent of that parliament as well as of the parliament of the United Kingdom" – a more impregnable guarantee than the formulation ultimately achieved in the wording of the Ireland Act of 1949', Ronan Fanning, 'London and Belfast's response to the declaration of the Republic of Ireland, 1948–49', *International Affairs,* vol. 58, no. 1 (1981–2), p. 106.

211 At a cabinet meeting in December 1948 to arrange a meeting between Northern Irish and British ministers to discuss the finer details of the Ireland Act, Brooke argued that they should give priority to 'strengthening Northern Ireland's position so as to eliminate the possibility of interference by a government in Whitehall now or in the future and on anticipating any pressure which might be exercised by the government of Éire to force Northern Ireland to make concessions on the partition issue', Ronan Fanning, 'London and Belfast's response to the declaration of the Republic of Ireland, 1948–49', p. 107.

212 Moreover, Clement Attlee noted to colleagues that the Ireland Act could be altered by a subsequent parliament, Ronan Fanning, 'London and Belfast's response to the declaration of the Republic of Ireland, 1948–49', p. 110.

213 Although, as Nicholas Mansergh has pointed out, the Government of Ireland Act 1920 was not the guarantor of security that the Northern government would have hoped. See Nicholas Mansergh, *The unresolved question: the Anglo-Irish settlement and its undoing 1912–72* (Avon, 1991), p. 249.

214 Cited in Ervine, *Craigavon: Ulsterman*, p. 478.

215 Ernest Bevin, cited in Ronan Fanning, 'London and Belfast's response to the declaration of the Republic of Ireland, 1948–49', p. 113.

6. Alternative visions of Northern Ireland in the 1940s and 1950s

In 1965, the poet W.R. Rodgers argued in a memorandum to the Arts Council on literature and writers in Northern Ireland:

> Language is fundamental to society: words, spoken or written, are a unique means of communication. Because they can express concepts and ideas, and can precisely give us past, present, and future tenses (as music, painting, sculpture, cannot) they are the basis of social activity, the vehicle of our history.[1]

Before the Second World War, creative writers in the state had made 'no serious attempt . . . to encapsulate the character of the province or its people', reducing the 'Ulster' elements to little more than local colour.[2] The character, identity and image of Northern Ireland and the Northern Irish was dominated largely by unionist historians, biographers, journalists and government officials.[3] During the war, however, many Northern Irish writers adopted a regionalist ethos, and began looking to their own area to a much greater extent for cultural inspiration, and as a means of defining themselves and their writing. The war accelerated this development, forcing the Northern Irish to rely on themselves and their own resources.[4] Ironically, the war also exposed Northern Ireland in a greater way to the outside world, having been a 'neglected backwater', 'so the presence of so many outsiders must have forced upon people an awareness of their identity'.[5] Following the Second World War protestant writers such as John Hewitt, W.R. Rodgers, Sam Hanna Bell and Louis MacNeice[6] provided an alternative version of Northern Irish culture against the backdrop of, and often in contrast to, official commemorations and official literature.[7] Alternative in this context does not necessarily imply opposition, but rather a variation on the image being projected of the Northern Irish state, the place and its people. Through their writing, they brought to the state an alternative social self-examination, and more critical reflections on the identity of Northern Ireland and the Northern Irish. It is important to remember that these writers were still part of an élite, articulating a largely protestant version of

180

Northern Irish culture. Indeed, many of them had active roles in the state's institutions, such as the BBC. This however did not mean that they were uncritical of the unionist government or the state. In fact, against a backdrop of royal visits, festivals celebrating the unity of the United Kingdom and official unionist literature, these writers appeared as the dissenting protestant voices of the 1940s and 1950s in Northern Ireland.[8]

The 1940s brought a chance for a reassessment of Northern Irish identity, and the poet John Hewitt forged a place as the representative voice of the period; he 'set about spreading the gospel of regionalism in articles, reviews, broadcasts, lectures and letters to the press'.[9] A number of prominent writers in Northern Ireland adopted this regionalist ethos to various degrees, although one of its problems was the lack of an agreed definition amongst them of what precisely it was or meant.[10] Hewitt outlined what he believed regionalism was in a talk given on BBC Northern Ireland in November 1945:

> Ulster is not a nation, yet she has ceased to be just a colony, for those of us who are of English or Scots extraction, have been here long enough to form a distinct people together with descendants of earlier immigrations . . . But now, although there are many surface differences and some fairly deep ones among our people, we have lived long enough together to be more like each other than unlike . . . We are not big enough to form a nation, but we have our own attitude of mind, our own place on the map . . . we are compelled to preserve our emotional and, dare I say, spiritual integrity, to turn our hearts and our intimate affections to some unit smaller than the nation – but larger than the townland – to what is called the Region. In our own case to Ulster.[11]

Hewitt believed that Northern Ireland had a distinct identity of its own which needed to be developed, so that it would be 'no mere echo of the thought and imagination of another people or another land'.[12] Although, again, Hewitt's concept of 'Ulster', according to Roy McFadden, 'omitted that part of it on the west of the Bann'.[13] Hewitt argued that the Northern Irish had an identity which, while part of Britain, was also separate from the United Kingdom:

> we would be strangers in the capital;
> this is our country also, no-where else;
> and we shall not be outcast on the world.[14]

For Hewitt, it was regionalism which offered the chance to 'transcend sectarian division in Northern Ireland', and he feared that without this new ethos the 'old severing prejudices' would 'trouble again', leaving Northern Ireland 'precariously perched' upon a 'melting iceberg'.[15] Politically, and more specifically, Hewitt supported the idea of a federated British Isles, which would incorporate Ireland, although he would also have accepted a federal Ireland politically separate from Britain. Art and culture according to him would supply the emotional legitimacy for the region; 'to enable this, art and high culture were to grow from rootedness, out of traditional identity'.[16] Through regionalism, he hoped that protestants, in particular, would come to perceive themselves as 'a group living long enough in Ireland to have the air in their blood, the landscape in their bones, and the history in their hearts'.[17] He articulated this hope in 'Conacre':

> This is my home and country. Later on
> perhaps I'll find this nation is my own
> but here and now it is enough to love
> this faulted ledge, this map of cloud above,
> and the great sea that beats against the west
> to swamp the sun.[18]

In 'The Colony', Hewitt further reinforced his belief that, despite feelings of alienation, Ireland was still his country, 'since birthplace and habitation define allegiance as much as dubious ancestry, he is at the same time Irish'.[19]

John Hewitt was the linchpin of the Northern Irish literary scene, which, although it had no central arena, manifested itself within many forums (such as the BBC and PEN)[20] in the late 1940s and early 1950s. A small group of writers, of which he was a member, made up the 'New Literary Dinner club' in 1950. Started by the BBC producer and novelist Sam Hanna Bell, this club included John Boyd (a producer in the BBC), Joe Tomelty (the dramatist and also involved in the BBC), J.D. Stewart (again a dramatist who was involved in the BBC), David Kennedy, Seamus Campbell and Roy McFadden.[21] Most Northern Irish writers in this period found a forum in the BBC.[22] Through his position at the BBC, Sam Hanna Bell, for instance, acted as a promoter of other writers, as he recorded in *The arts in Ulster*: 'Since 1945 practically every Ulster writer has contributed, at one time or another, to the Northern Ireland Region of the BBC'.[23] Hewitt was himself on the BBC's advisory council, as well as being a regular broadcaster, as were J.D. Stewart and Joe Tomelty. Many writers were also involved with PEN, an organisation which provided an opportunity for writers to meet with other writers, as well as politicians, civil servants and members of the BBC. It was very much an élite group.[24] PEN's annual dinner in 1954, for example, was attended by John Hewitt, who was chairman of PEN that year, R. Marriott, the controller of the BBC in Northern Ireland, Sir Robert Gransden, secretary to the Northern Irish cabinet, and Dame Dehra Parker, minister of health and local government.[25] As well as being a social forum, PEN members also attended lectures, such as John Boyd's on 'Why Lagan Failed', D.A. Chart's on 'Two kinds of storytelling', and Douglas Young, the leading Scottish socialist, who spoke about Lallans.[26] According to Roy McFadden, there was no great commitment among the members of PEN 'to writing as a troublesome art and the meetings were usually tepid'.[27] The visit of Douglas Young in 1949, however, was not without incident. Following his lecture on Lallans the Hewitts' friends gathered in their house:

> That night we had Joan and John Stewart, George Davy and Elizabeth, Mercy and George McCann plus some Pat Maguire he phoned to ask if he could bring. Edith and Roy McFadden. Barbara Hunter, Denis Ireland and

Joe Tomelty and when J and DY came from the dinner they brought Andrew Stewart and his wife.[28]

George McCann rang Ruby Hewitt the following day to say that Pat Maguire was a detective. Some days after that the Hewitt's Cushendun cottage was broken into: 'I could see', wrote Ruby Hewitt:

> How the authorities were worried about Dennis Ireland being invited to meet Douglas Young who was Chairman of the Scottish Nationalist Party and J. phoned Dennis [sic] to invite him and no doubt his phone calls would be tapped. Again they may not understand J's approach to his regionalism and suspect him as trying to pull wool over their eyes and it might appear to them our cottage could be used in some way for unloyal purposes. It must be difficult for our authorities to think that an Ulster-man could have a great affection for 'Ulster' without hating either Éire or England.[29]

As Edna Longley has argued, 'Unionists themselves have always paranoically perceived Ulster local culture, Scots or Irish or both, as the Trojan horse for an Irish national culture.'[30]

In the 1930s John Hewitt was involved in the Workers' Educational Association, and in 'various fringe gatherings, political and cultural'.[31] He associated with 'socialists, reformers, people of strong views, "the assertors, the protestors", as he put it himself'.[32] As well as working with his wife Roberta (Ruby) for the Peace League, and in anti-fascism agitation, he also assisted with an investigation into the Special Powers Act by the National Council for Civil Liberties, where he became 'acquainted with the nature of state authority and its techniques of the opened letter and the tapped telephone'.[33] Equally, Hewitt had little time for nationalism, describing Northern nationalists in 1942 as 'sectarians, a Redmondite rump stupefying in snugs and clubs'.[34] This background, in combination with his policy of regionalism, was to cause Hewitt trouble in the 1950s.[35] In her diary entry for 31 December 1951, Ruby Hewitt noted that her husband felt he had to stop broadcasting on the BBC Northern Ireland series *Ulster Commentary*.[36] Hewitt was applying for the directorship of the Ulster Museum, where he was already assistant director: 'He cannot say what he really feels he should and keep his job', Ruby Hewitt wrote,

> [he] must be careful what he says on air as people think he is a commu-nist. It worries me that one should be lacking in courage for things that are right and yet as Director he would be free to do many things that would give him pleasure and I don't think it would do him any harm as a man or poet.[37]

As a minor example of what could happen when one was not careful, Ruby Hewitt recorded an evening in 1949 which John Hewitt spent in Bangor as the chairman of a discussion for the BBC called 'An Ulster Char-acter'. Hewitt's role was to be deliberately provocative, and he 'said a lot of hard things about the Ulster people'. A member of the audience later went to

Bangor Council 'and had a resolution passed by one or two votes condemning the BBC for allowing Johnny to say uncomplimentary things about the Ulster people. It was in the papers. The BBC were not worried'.[38] This was, of course, in a period of heightened unionist sensitivities, coming shortly after the declaration of the Irish republic, and prior to the reassurance of the 1949 Ireland Act. The Hewitts, in an effort to secure the museum's directorship, attended 'very dull' events, with 'all the best people'; 'we are there to be seen', wrote Ruby, 'Such going's [sic] on'.[39] Famously, John Hewitt did not get the job.[40] According to Edna Longley, he paid the price for consorting with catholics and communists.[41] In March 1957, Hewitt was appointed to the Herbert Gallery in Conventry, and exiled himself from Northern Ireland for fifteen years.

Through the 1940s and '50s John Hewitt was constant in his promotion of local culture, in whatever form that took, and was anxious that 'Ulster' writers and writing would get their fair share of attention. In November 1943, for instance, he wrote to W.R. Rodgers about a recent Seán O'Faoláin publication, *The story of Ireland*, complaining that 'there's scarcely a reference to Ulster and not a single illustration of this province'. He suggested that Rodgers write a similar book on 'Ulster', 'this would stop St J-Ervine doing it'.[42] Hewitt, although 'always ready to praise any author who had made an impact in one way or another', was equally willing to criticise.[43] Reviewing *Now in Ulster*, a slim anthology of writing from Northern Ireland published in 1944, he complained that none of the writers included had shown

> any awareness of contemporary needs; no one even appears to appreciate the sharp conflicts of our time. We do not suggest that there must be 'propaganda', in art, but we do say that art must draw its vitality from contact with everyday life.[44]

Hewitt's concern was that there was a sharpness in Northern Irish life and literature which its authors were failing to acknowledge and reflect. It was a concern echoed by the reviewer of *Northern harvest: anthology of Ulster writing*. This volume, edited by Robert Greacen, and published in 1944, included pieces by Denis Ireland, W.R. Rodgers, Michael McLaverty, John Hewitt, and Colin Middleton. The reviewer, Keidryan Rhys, believed that the 'Hampstead big names' – Robert Lynd, Helen Waddell, St John Ervine, and Forrest Reid – were included as 'reader's bait' because Greacen was unsure of the talent of the others. And, he continued,

> One dominant impression, however, that stays in the mind is that they do not feel free in themselves to write as they wish: this accounts for a certain tameness in their work, especially when treating the political aspect, which is inseparable from any discussion of Ulster.[45]

Here again are references to the 'tameness' and the lack of freedom evident in the writers' work. Rhys did commend the Greacen anthology on the basis that it did not include any pieces on Belfast's traditional industries: 'How nice to come across a Belfast publication which isn't an organ of the ship-building or linen industry.'[46]

The genre of writing Rhys referred to, what amounted to basic propaganda, was one which the writer Hugh Shearman was to make his own in this period. He represented the sort of writing, and writer, which Hewitt most objected to.[47] Following the elections called by Basil Brooke in response to the declaration of the Irish republic, Shearman and Hewitt engaged in a brief correspondence in the pages of the *New Statesman and Nation*.[48] The elections, the most violent since those held in 1921, led to a polarisation of Northern Ireland's politics, with Northern Irish labour being eliminated, and the nationalists left as the only opposition in the Stormont parliament to the unionist party.[49] In his letter, Shearman argued that Ulster unionists were on the left of the British conservative movement: 'For several years now the government of Northern Ireland has not only co-operated on terms of real cordiality with a Socialist government in Britain, but has paralleled a very large part of that Government's legislation'.[50] He agreed with W.R. Rodgers's summary in 1943 that this was merely a pragmatic policy on the part of the unionist government to ensure the continuation of Northern Ireland's economic benefits.[51] 'The Ulster worker votes Unionist', wrote Shearman:

> Because he has no wish to vote away his old age pension, his unemployment benefit, his State medical services, the educational opportunities that are being made available for his children, the better conditions and pay he gets or the exporting industry in which he works.[52]

John Hewitt responded to this letter the following week, agreeing that the 1949 election had been a 'clear declaration' of Northern Ireland's 'desire to cling to those standards of life which have been maintained or raised by the Labour government at Westminster'. However, he maintained that unionist MPs at Westminster were 'indistinguishable from the Right Wing of British Conservatism': 'Hence we have the anomaly of British Governmental legislation being attacked furiously at Westminster, only to be enacted after a short interval by members of exactly the same party at Stormont'.[53] In his essay for *The character of Ireland*, Martin Wallace summed up this state of affairs wryly: 'Although Unionist MPs at Westminster often disapproved of Socialist legislation in the years after 1945, the Stormont government swallowed most of it without a cough'.[54] Hewitt's central argument was that there had been 'a failure of essential democratic machinery' in Northern Ireland. This was not only due to unionists, but also to Northern Ireland labour which, he felt, had lacked unity, and to nationalists who had lacked coherent policies. As a result, he maintained, there was now no coherent opposition to the unionists in the Northern Irish parliament. In 1949, Northern Ireland was, Hewitt concluded, a congested state, threatened with apoplexy.[55]

This was not the image of the state promoted by Hugh Shearman who acted as a moderate apologist for the Northern Irish government in the 1940s and early 1950s.[56] Between 1942 and 1971 he published some half-dozen books relating to Northern Ireland, commissioned sometimes by the unionist government, or with their patronage.[57] Certainly, in his writing, Shearman could be relied upon to follow the government's requirements faithfully, and not to alarm a British audience. In 1946, he cautioned the unionist government that in dealing with the British public it should be remembered that

> there is a strong and in many ways admirable tendency, particularly among English people, to assume something can always be said on the other side; and that tendency comes quickly into action at any suspicion of a disproportionate presentation or a brief dismissal of certain themes or too highly selective account.[58]

Shearman's career had begun with a small biography of Craigavon, *Not an inch*, in 1942.[59] In this study he adopted a moderate tone; in comparing the characteristics of Craig and de Valera, for instance, he wrote:

> The two traditions stand out proud and tough; and those who can sympathise with one find it very hard to sympathise with the other . . . What could Mr de Valera know of life in an Ulster Presbyterian family? How can a member of the Ulster Unionist Council learn to appreciate the ways of thought of a Gaelic-speaking Sinn Fein schoolmaster?[60]

Shearman's attitude to Éire's war-time neutrality was almost benevolent: it was, he wrote, a decision 'reached and followed with sincerity'.[61] In the light of British negotiations with Éire over neutrality and partition, Shearman's book reflected unionist hostility towards the British government. Thus, wrote Shearman, Craig, concerned in the Northern Irish state's early years with its survival, 'learnt that British sympathy was not to be truly relied on in this respect'.[62] Shearman reminded his readers that the British government's underestimation of 'Ulster' had 'already gone near on one occasion to causing a civil war in the British Isles', this an oblique reference to the third home rule crisis of 1912–14.[63] Shearman's next political work was *Anglo-Irish relations*, published in 1948. The intervening six years, since *Not an inch*, had brought a change in Shearman's attitude – reflecting a change of attitude among unionists generally. Shearman has himself accounted for this development:

> With regard to the war there was a big change in people's attitudes towards Germany towards the significance of the war and so on. Once the information came out about the extent of genocide and so far as de Valera's attitude . . . it wasn't their war, it was someone else's war. But after the war, people couldn't see it that way really. It was seen as a crusade against horrible things, a lot that we know now was not known during the war, we didn't know about the extermination camps. There was a change of tone between *Not an Inch* and the 1948 publication.[64]

Thus, in *Anglo-Irish relations*, the tone was one of general hostility towards Éire; in it Shearman embraced all things identifiably 'Ulster' and British as a means of rejecting the rest of Ireland:

> The Ulster Unionist preference for the name Ulster as a synonym for Northern Ireland has probably owed much to the dislike of many Ulster

people to being called Irish, feeling that the word Irish has come to have a restrictive meaning which excludes them.[65]

The emphasis on a separate Northern Irish identity was combined in this book with a stress on Northern Ireland's contribution to the war effort.[66] Éire's neutrality came in for harsh treatment in *Anglo-Irish relations*:

> As it was, with Northern Ireland serving alike as a lightening conductor and a reserve of defensive strength, Éire managed to retain its neutrality to the end and was the best fed and most comfortable country in Europe.[67]

De Valera was no longer the 'Gaelic-speaking Sinn Fein schoolmaster', but 'rigid', and filled with 'insensitive self-righteousness'.[68] According to Northern Ireland's prime minister, Basil Brooke, Éire's decision to become a republic was 'the last stage of that deplorable journey' that had taken the southern state from the Free State to total separation.[69] Brooke saw the declaration of a republic as the end of a journey, in this way drawing the thread back to the establishment of the two Irish states and underlining the unionist belief that the settlement of 1920/21 had always been under threat from the Free State, that unionists had been justifiably anxious about their own position, within the island and within the union. Writing in *World Affairs* in April 1949, Shearman expressed the disdain unionists now had for the Irish republic; with reference to Éire's wish to leave the commonwealth, he wrote:

> One explanation which has been suggested is that consciously or unconsciously there has been a tendency for Éire ministers to stress the Nationalistic aspect of public life in order to draw attention away from the grave condition of social backwardness and economic stagnation in which Éire has sunk.[70]

In this piece Shearman rejected Irish nationalism:

> The symbols, heroes and traditions of Irish Nationalism which deeply move the emotional and rhetorical temperament of the people of Éire only bore and repel the practical and executive temperament of the people of Northern Ireland.[71]

Shearman's change in attitude between 1942 and 1948 reflected the changing political scene in Ireland and Britain. It also preceded the passing of the Ireland Act in June 1949, which confirmed that the Stormont parliament, dominated by unionists, would decide the future of the Northern Irish state.[72] In his conclusion, therefore, Shearman expressed the hope that the British government would

> show a protective recognition of the Ulster community's special needs and interests and an awareness of its very honourable record of contributing through war and peace to the common safety and welfare of the British Isles and the Commonwealth as a whole.[73]

Shearman's next book was *Ulster*, a tourist publication written in 1949 in which he catalogued the prominent men from Northern Ireland, writers such as Forrest Reid, St John Ervine, Louis MacNeice and W.R. Rodgers, and artists such as Sir John Lavery, Paul Henry and William Conor. 'The Northern Ireland government', he wrote, 'and the municipal authorities have steadily tried to help and foster art, music, historical research, field studies, archaeological work and other cultural activities.'[74] Predictably, the book also contained references to the importance of 'Ulster' in 'defence of Britain's lifeline during the darkest period of the war of 1939–45'.[75] Shearman produced two other propaganda booklets for the Northern Irish government: *Northern Ireland: its history, resources and people* (HMSO, 1946), and *How Northern Ireland is governed* (HMSO, 1951). He was not, however, the government's first choice for *Northern Ireland: its history, resources and people*. In a letter to Louis MacNeice, in March 1944, the Northern Irish cabinet publicity office offered him the commission and outlined the purpose of the pamphlet: 'It should give a clear picture to English and Scottish teachers (and pupils) of the history and position of Northern Ireland in the United Kingdom'.[76] The pamphlet, they wrote, would be free of propaganda. During this period MacNeice was writing propaganda pieces aimed at an American audience, scripts for the BBC in London about 'bombed buildings representative of the Anglo-American heritage'. In addition to this, the cabinet publicity committee in Northern Ireland was prompted in its choice by MacNeice's booklet 'Meet the U.S. Army', which it had considered 'admirable'. There was, of course, a difference for MacNeice between propaganda work for the BBC, or British Council, during war time (work which he considered vulgar but which had its value) and propaganda work commissioned by the Northern Irish government promoting his native place, about which he had never been that positive:

> A city built upon mud;
> A culture built upon profit;
> Free speech nipped in the bud,
> The minority always guilty.[77]

It is ironic that when MacNeice did submit a typescript for the British Council booklet on Northern Ireland later in 1944, its blatant treatment of violence and religious discrimination in the state meant that it was considered 'most unsatisfactory' by the Northern Irish government. MacNeice, however, was 'unable to undertake' the commission and Shearman was subsequently offered it.[78]

Hugh Shearman's initial draft of *Northern Ireland*, following in MacNeice's footsteps, was also rejected by the Northern Irish cabinet publicity committee, although for different reasons. The cabinet publicity committee's objections to Shearman's text centred on the pamphlet's use of terminology and the inaccuracy of its information. His redraft was also heavily criticised, as these notes from the Northern Irish Ministry of Education illustrate:

Pg 12. Sub-title - 'The Experience of the Ulster Colony, 1641–1885'. I do not think it should be implied that Ulstermen were 'colonists' at so late a date as 1885.

Pg 13, line 17. The description of the Battle of Boyne as a 'slight . . . defeat' would scarcely meet with general approval in N. Ire.

Pg 16 and 17, lines 26 and 1. The reference to 'docile Roman Catholic workers' might give offence to English Roman Catholics.[79]

The point about offending English catholics is reminiscent of W.R. Rodgers's anecdote in his article for the *New Statesman and Nation* in 1943, in which he recounted how American troops were stationed in 'an Ulster village, a stronghold of Protestant propriety':

> Being Catholics these troops went to worship at the local Catholic church. They refused to go again, and the master of the local Orange lodge offered them the Orange Hall for worship. A friendly gesture to an ally in wartime, yes. But a distinction drawn between the Catholic and the Catholic Irishman.[80]

In July 1944, Robert Gransden, the cabinet secretary, noted that the cabinet were dissatisfied with Shearman's final draft. They concluded that he would have to rewrite the entire pamphlet or that another author would have to be appointed.[81] Ultimately, Shearman made the required changes.[82] The copious and minute criticisms irritated him at times, however; in a letter to R.S. Brownell, he complained:

> If we go whittling it down . . . we pass imperceptibly into a bald state-ment of the historical Ulster Unionist case, and we have a booklet which might more fittingly be issued from Glengall Street than from your department . . . We create prejudice not by the sins of our ancestors, but by skating over the sins of our ancestors.[83]

The last straw for Shearman was the suggestion that he make the pamphlet more 'popular':

> Then about this business of being 'popular'. The subjects I have been asked to set down information about aren't very popular. Ulster Union-ism and Protestantism haven't produced any Bonny Prince Charlie and the people here don't wear kilts and blue paint.[84]

Interestingly, when the English Ministry of Education eventually reviewed the pamphlet, they requested that the section headed 'The Volunteers, the Covenant and the Gunrunning' should be deleted, believing perhaps that in the aftermath of the Second World War stories of loyal British citizens importing German arms to defy the British government would be inappro-priate.[85] The pamphlet was eventually produced and, indeed, went into several editions up to the 1960s. In July 1946 Hewitt criticised *Northern Ireland: its history, people and resources,* with W.R. Rodgers's approval: 'the Shearman brochure . . . was sadly pedestrian. I'm glad you took him up on it, for it's only dogged watch-doggery that will waken the Van Winkles'.[86]

Despite the criticism, and on the strength of this first pamphlet, Shearman was offered the commission of another pamphlet, *How Northern Ireland is governed*, published in the Festival year, 1951. In 1953 he was offered the commission of *Modern Ireland*, a successor to D.A. Chart's 1927 school text *A history of Northern Ireland*.[87] Shearman explained how the Ministry of Education, through R.S. Brownell, presented the proposed text to him:

> There again Brownell was in touch with me – he said these schools are trying to get across that Sir Basil Brooke had caused the potato famine! He said nuns particularly had a nice way of doing it . . . Brownell was worried about history being written in a highly political way, in a mythological way.[88]

The Northern Irish press officer in London thought Shearman's book a 'carefully written history' which 'adequately' explained the development of Northern Ireland and would leave 'no doubt in the minds of readers as to the present position of Northern Ireland'.[89] Given their stated concerns about the politicisation of history, it is interesting that the Northern Irish government should have chosen a government apologist as the author of this text.

Despite his role as propagandist, Hugh Shearman is not without his surprises. Having published *Not an inch*, in 1942, Faber published his two novels, *The bishop's confession,* in 1943, and *A bomb and a girl*, in 1944.[90] Both novels centre on men who are alienated from their contemporaries, and within their communities. *The bishop's confession* is the fictional memoir of Percival MacPeake, a church of Ireland bishop, in which the reader is invited to learn 'without reservation his exact feelings about nearly everything that has vitally impinged on his life's career, everything from bed-knobs to eschatology or from sex to assassination'.[91] Interestingly, given that the novel was published during the uncertain days of the Second World War, MacPeake, the central character, argues that the struggle for self-security was the driving motive of 'the great institutions, the churches, the government, the political parties, the army, business'.[92] The novel charts the course of MacPeake's life from his birth in 1875 to his appointment as bishop following the First World War. The son of a Belfast linen magnate, he leads a privileged life, entering Trinity College in Dublin to study for the church of Ireland ministry. This first novel is set in Belfast at the turn of the century, although MacPeake's university career in Dublin allows for comparisons between the two cities:

> It feels like a more ancient city than Dublin. It feels more like the capital of a country . . . It <Dublin> is a worldly, everyday Anglo-Saxon sort of city . . . Belfast always seemed to me to be more in touch with ancient tradition.[93]

The novel's consideration of social propriety centres on Elizabeth, the bishop's sister, who is divorced by her husband for adultery and is subsequently disowned by her entire family, apart from the bishop. Many years later, she contacts the bishop to tell him she is destitute and dying from creeping paralysis; he rescues her, and makes her final months comfortable.

While his sister has led a decadent and promiscuous life, MacPeake has only experienced repressed and abstract love; his greatest love, for instance, is an actress whom he meets only briefly and has no real relationship with. In general, his attitude to women is unreal; he longs for a 'fairy princess', of the sort he heard in his mother's readings of Grimm's fairy tales. Despite the fact that her life ends in poverty and paralysis, Elizabeth's life is understood to have been more far more fulfilling than Percival's which, although a success in society's terms, has been a frustrating and ultimately lonely one.[94]

The central theme of *The bishop's confession* is class, the exploration of which reveals the lack of social or religious integration within Northern Ireland, and in particular between the various protestant churches. All MacPeake's reflections on other religions are related to the class they represent, rather than their theological differences: 'The Roman Catholic Church was not strong outside the so-called working classes, the small tenant farmers, the freeholders created by the operation of the land acts, and the labourers'.[95] He maintains, for instance, that the church of Ireland was 'the only church in the country that was supported by people from all classes'.[96] He grows up regarding catholics as poor and ignorant, 'often individually very good people, but led astray by the stupid rather than malignant activities of their priests', and presbyterians as 'sometimes very good people' also but 'it was not as gentlemanly a thing to be a Presbyterian' as to be a member of the church of Ireland.[97] It is interesting that MacPeake considers presbyterians as only 'sometimes' very good people, while catholics are 'often' very good. Conversely, according to MacPeake, there were few presbyterians amongst the prison population in Ireland, which he argued was made up of catholics and members of the church of Ireland. Catholicism and presbyterianism aside, two incidents reveal MacPeake's complete disdain for evangelicalism. The first is when the workers at MacPeake's father's mill experience a religious revival, and the foreman writes to Mr MacPeake encouraging him to be saved. Mr MacPeake fires him: '"He ought to know quite well", said my father, "that he ought to attempt no interference in the religious affairs of his betters".'[98] In the second incident MacPeake meets an evangelist on the train on his way to study in Trinity College, Dublin: 'I felt hot all over with embarrassment, and at the same time his filthy fingernails nearly drove me to cry out loud to him to let my hand go.' He surmises that 'a man who started talking about religion in a train was a person to be treated with suspicion and kept strictly at a distance'.[99] At Trinity class boundaries are reinforced in the divinity school which is divided between high and low church views; MacPeake socialises with the high churchmen: 'all the better intellects in the divinity school tended to do the same', 'the low churchmen sometimes tended to be of a lower social class'.[100] MacPeake's first congregation is in east Belfast, but he soon moves to a seaside village which is in the process of developing as a tourist village:

I felt that the more intelligent middle-class city visitors who came in the summer created an opportunity which ought to be well used. They ought

to be given somewhat different material from what I was accustomed to
give to my more primitive native audience at other seasons.[101]

When MacPeake finally loses his faith he sees that too as a sign of 'culture
and intelligence': 'I knew better than to mean it, and I was only preaching it
because it was good enough for the lower classes.'[102]

Shearman's second, and last, novel, published in 1944, was *A bomb and
a girl*, 'the story of a criminal and a study in the psychology of crime',
according to Shearman's preface. The antagonism which Shearman
displayed towards the British government in *Not an inch* manifested itself
in this novel in the uncomplimentary portrayal of the two Englishmen, one
of whom is eventually murdered by a protestant student. In the novel's
preface Shearman was keen to stress that, although the story was set in
Queen's University in the late 1930s, when Shearman himself had
attended Queen's, there was no connection between the staff in his novel
and the staff he had known during his college career.[103] The characters in
this novel are painted in broad strokes; the aptly named Officer is an overt
fascist, the catholic students are harmless and ignorant, the Englishmen,
although ineffectual, have superiority complexes, while the sole unionist
in the novel, Professor Oliver, is not only intellectually, but also physically,
superior to everyone else. The novel's principal character, Stanislas,
comes from a middle-class protestant family and is alienated from his
contemporaries, far more than MacPeake was, seeing them as intrinsically
flawed: 'as he was an alien among them and unskilled in the ordinary
schoolboy activities, the other children often made fun of him'.[104] He is an
egoist, an arrogant character whom it is hard to like:[105] 'He collected
historic names and titles and dreamed long and constantly of himself as
the centre of great events and the arbiter of the destinies of Europe'.[106]
Topically, given the date of publication, his first contact with another
student at Queen's is with Officer, who has been to Germany, is full of anti-
semitism, and extols the virtues of fascism; 'do you know', he asks
Stanislas, 'that there's a Jewish world conspiracy to overthrow civilization,
to degrade our race and reduce us to slavery and impotence?'[107] At his first
Latin lecture Stanislas sits with 'two small, serious boys with intensely
black hair and bewildered faces': 'They were a little untidy and rather
unshaven, and their finger-nails were not very clean. Stanislas at once
decided that they were Roman Catholic divinity students.'[108] (Similarly,
when MacPeake, in *The bishop's confession*, meets the evangelist on the
train to Trinity one of the signs of his unsuitability are his dirty finger-
nails.) Shearman depicts these catholic divinity students as ignorant, and
lacking in ambition; asked by Stanislas if they are doing honours, one of
them, Michael Jeremiah O'Herlihy, remarks:

> No. Oh a pass is enough for us. You see, the learned chaps goes into the
> orders like the Jesuits. But for the ordinary secular mission it's not learn-
> ing you want. It's the fire and zeal and the enthusiasm.[109]

Shearman's single unionist character, the English lecturer, Professor Oliver, is depicted in positive terms as being full of 'justice, friendliness and moderation':

> Professor Oliver was very evidently a great man . . . he was regarded as the most polished and commanding speaker of the Ulster Unionist Party . . . in spite of himself, he was profoundly impressed by Professor Oliver.[110]

While Stanislas identifies himself as British, both the novel's Englishmen are described in overtly negative terms. Standing in stark contrast to Professor Oliver is Professor Steinbrenner, the Latin lecturer, who victimises Stanislas. Professor Steinbrenner is English, has a coarse complexion, talks in 'wheedling' tones and makes unwanted sexual advances to the female undergraduates: 'He had a pale, greasy-looking face and thin, sandy hair. His eyes were very close together'.[111] Moreover, Professor Steinbrenner 'after his first discovery that all the people in the north of Ireland were not gunmen or even Orangemen, had decided that it was a very comical, backward place where he could show people a thing or two'.[112] Stanislas decides to murder Steinbrenner, and does so by blowing him up during a lecture. Although the police are convinced of his guilt they do not have enough evidence to arrest him; they turn to the professors of the university to help to trap him by provoking him to attack another lecturer. However, the professors are unwilling to place themselves in danger. The provost of Queen's asks the police sergeant whether Stanislas cannot just be arrested; 'no indeed', answers the sergeant, 'you can do no such thing. This is a free country. You can only do that sort of thing with Sinn Fein rebels and communists'.[113] The provost, the other Englishman in the novel, is not only a weak character but, in common with Professor Steinbrenner, also hates Ulster:

> He felt that he hated Ulster people. They were rude, violent, dishonest, cynical, with no cultural polish, no reverence for beautiful things, and a frank, cheerful disrespect towards that unwritten code of honour and precedent which ought to govern the intercourse and behaviour of gentlemen and scholars. He was among a little nation of criminals, iconoclasts and boors.[114]

Stanislas is never prosecuted for Professor Steinbrenner's murder. The knowledge that he has murdered intimidates not only his university professors, who subsequently allow him to pass through his college career with honours, but also his superiors in the civil service, where equally he is given promotion through passive intimidation.

These are interesting novels which, in the context of the war period, provide a unionist writer's perspective on Northern Irish society. They confirm Hugh Shearman's negative attitude towards the British in this period; more generally they explore the complex relationships which existed not only between unionists and the British, but within the protestant community itself. (This anti-Englishness also emerged in W.R. Rodgers's article, 'Conversation piece: an Ulster Protestant', in *The Bell* in 1942.)

Moreover, Shearman's novels reflect the diversity within a largely élite, protestant community. In *The bishop's confession* Shearman highlights the diversity which results from the association of religion with social class, and the novel reflects the class tensions of the 1930s, when it was written. Interestingly, neither novel devotes much attention to the position of the catholic community in Northern Ireland, or indeed to the Free State. This accords with the major concerns of the unionist government in this period, which was to maintain unity, or the appearance of unity, within the protestant community. However, neither do Shearman's novels portray Northern Ireland as a homogenous protestant enclave, and his acknowledgement of diversity and disharmony within the Northern Irish state stands in contrast to his work as an official writer for the unionist government.

While they share an acknowledgement of diversity, and a place on Éire's censor's list, Shearman's attitude and tone in his work overall stands in contrast to the attitude of other Northern Irish writers like, for instance, Sam Hanna Bell.[115] Although both writers take account of the sectarian nature of the state in their novels, Shearman was concerned largely with the experience of élite protestantism. Bell's concern was to represent 'different sections' of Northern Ireland, presenting a balanced image and celebrating its population's diveristy. Of course, Sam Hanna Bell's profile was quite different from Shearman's. Bell had already begun to write short stories and articles before Louis MacNeice encouraged him to join the BBC following the Second World War. In 1943, with John Boyd and Bob Davidson, he founded the periodical *Lagan* as a northern counterpart to *The Bell*.[116] *Lagan* shared John Hewitt's regional ethos as its first preface written by John Boyd illustrated:

> A writer must be conscious of the changing attitudes of the common people, that is, of the governed to their governors; he must be conscious of the inherent contradictions in our society, and of the intricate relationship between a maladjusted society and a maladjusted individual; he must be conscious of the social use of literature as a drug or antiseptic: in short, he must be conscious that the struggle for a way of writing is part of the struggle for a way of life.[117]

Against the unionist ethos of the period, Sam Hanna Bell blurred the edges and allowed diversity within the picture he painted of the state. As a BBC producer from 1945, he spent much of his time providing a voice for different sections of the community in Northern Ireland. In addition he played an important role in the Festival of Britain in Northern Ireland, as one of the editors of the festival's principal arts publication *The arts in Ulster*. He strove to present a balanced picture of the state, and one which ran counter to the image which unionism promoted. In an article for BBC Northern Ireland's twenty-fifth anniversary in 1949, he wrote:

> This balance is essential, not only from the point of view of policy, but because different sections contribute different aspects to the complete programme – from one comes, say, music, old ballads, and tales; from the other the ready answer, the quick practical mind, the humour rather than the wit of the Ulster countryside. It would be misleading to press the comparison; for the characteristics I have mentioned aren't limited

to either side; but it is the wise producer who on entering a farmhouse understands the significance of the picture over the fireboard.[118]

In 1942 W.R. Rodgers had used this image of the farmhouse as a signifier of identity and a way of exploring the differences between the stereotyped characters of catholics and protestants in the state, and with positive bias accorded to the latter:[119]

> In the first you will have been received charmingly and emotionally and with all the grace of the Gael. In the second case, by contrast, you will have been received churlishly and thoughtfully, and with all the dourness of the Scot. But let me say that in the first house it is 'easy come, easy go'. For no sooner will you depart than your character and conduct, looks and likes, may well be torn to pieces. In the second house, once you have been accepted you have made friends for life. Your character will have been established and your reputation secured. There will be loyalty to you in your absence, and one which will speak for you in the presence of your enemies.[120]

These traits, described by Rodgers, particularly loyalty and reticence, had been established as characteristically protestant by unionist writers in the 1920s and 1930s.[121] As John Wilson Foster argues, 'a religious upbringing establishes habits of mind which clothe the secular and, openly or secretively, the creative life'.[122] The stereotyped portrait of catholics was echoed in Hewitt's poem 'The Colony':

> They worship Heaven strangely, having rites
> we snigger at, are known as superstitious,
> cunning by nature, never to be trusted,
> given to dancing and a kind of song
> seductive to the ear, a whining sorrow.
> Also they breed like flies.[123]

Through his novels, it is clear that Bell embraced Hewitt's regionalism, supporting the concept of a Northern Irish people with a unique culture and identity. As a producer he travelled throughout Northern Ireland with the folklorist Michael J. Murphy collecting stories and lore for the BBC series *Fairy Faith*; it was a collection which Professor Delargy of the folklore commission described as 'the most important work in Irish folklore in modern times'.[124] In 1956 Bell published a collection of stories on Ulster folklore and customs. In its preface he wrote: 'All that I bring to these pages is a lively curiosity in what my fellow-citizens do and how they do it, and the good fortune that in my daily work as a BBC features producer this curiosity is encouraged'.[125] Bell chose to make this collection representative of the 'historic province of Ulster', and not the Northern Irish state. And he reminded his readers that he was not afraid of blurring the edges of identity: 'here and there the story runs beyond the confines of the Northern Province, for a custom is no more susceptible to borders than is the social activity from which it arises'.[126]

His first novel, *December bride*, was published in 1951, the festival year.[127] It is interesting, though perhaps not surprising, that this first novel should have highlighted the unique, often violent, nature of life within a religiously dominated society. It concerns the lives of the Echlin brothers, Frank and Hamilton, and their relationship with Sarah Gomartin, against the background of community disapproval. Sarah becomes involved in a sexual relationship with both brothers, sharing herself 'between them both in body and in mind' after her mother and she go to keep house at the Echlin's farm. She bears a son, and later a daughter, by one or both men. In an interview in 1987 Bell spoke of his childhood in relation to *December bride*: 'I was brought up for the next, terribly impressionable, three or four years in Raffrey . . . *December bride* is set about that period and it came quite naturally to me to put it there'.[128] Written following the Second World War and set in the aftermath of the First World War, *December bride* reflects the sombre mood felt in Northern Ireland in 1918. A *Belfast Telegraph* editorial in July 1919 summed up the atmosphere in the province succinctly: 'We claim one thing and one thing only but we never get it, and that is to be left alone'.[129] It is significant that Bell set his novel in this period of Northern Ireland's history, a period in which unionists were, as in the late 1940s, searching to secure the state's, and their own, political position and future within the United Kingdom.

Themes common to many rural novels of the period are present in *December bride*: the hunger for land, the tensions between siblings, defying the will of the community and the prevailing morality.[130] John Hewitt, in a letter to W.R. Rodgers, noted that it was the best 'regional' novel of the period. 'A bit loamy and dour-peasantry', he remarked, 'but with moments of fine evocation'.[131] But it was more than a pastoral portrait of rural Ulster.[132] Viewed in the context of Northern Ireland in the late 1940s and early 1950s, the tension within the novel offers an insight into the atmosphere of the period. The fatalistic structure of the novel mirrors this feeling. Beginning with the marriage of Sarah to Hamilton when they are both in their fifties, the novel employs a flashback technique to sketch the path which has led to this muted ceremony. The introductory scene in which the couple are married sets the oppressive tone:

> Echlin took his bride's hand, and with her assistance managed to press the ring over the first gnarled joint of her finger. But the lower knuckle, hard and dented as a chestnut, was too large for the ring and Sarah timorously drew her hand back. Sorleyson caught it abruptly. 'I think we should manage to do it properly', he said, and tried to press the ring down to the root of her finger. As she winced, he lowered her hand with a look of annoyance, leaving the ring turning loosely in the middle of the fleshless concave finger.[133]

There is then a backdrop of fatalism from the start, the reader knowing that Sarah will inevitably conform to society's demands. *December bride*, in common with much of Bell's work, actively sabotages the notion of a homogenous protestant enclave. In addition to the tensions within the presbyterian community the novel touches on the mutual bigotry between the Echlins and the Dineens, their catholic tenants. 'We have with us', wrote Bell in 1951, 'still in Northern Ireland an antique conflict, resolved long ago in Western Europe – the conflict of religious dogmas, encrusted with loyalties, prejudices, and racial aspirations.'[134] This was not quite the representation of the state the Northern Irish government aspired to, particularly in festival year. But for Bell, the unionist ethos was 'so cloying that almost anything came as a relief', and his work clashed with the image the unionist publicity machine was striving to project of Northern Ireland as a progressive, modern and united society.[135] Hugh Shearman had concluded his 1951 pamphlet, *How Northern Ireland is governed*, on a positive note: 'the central framework of the Northern Ireland constitution remains the same, and it has shown its capacity to meet with considerable success many new and often highly unexpected situations and to adapt itself to the demands of a changing community and a changing world.'[136] This idealised vision of the Northern Irish state naturally found firm patronage in Stormont, and in such circumstances, with political dissent coming more and more to include creative endeavour, Bell's work made him a creative subversive.[137]

There are no heroes in *December bride*; even Sarah, whose independence we could admire, compromises ultimately to give her daughter the opportunity to start married life with respectability. At the very least, *December bride* makes the claim that such diversity is acceptable, and answers John Hewitt's call for more sharpness in Northern Irish literature. Mr Sorleyson, the representative of authority in Bell's novel, consistently pressurises Sarah to marry one of the brothers. Yet, even he, faced with the harmony of the lives of Sarah and the Echlin brothers, finds his arguments for Sarah to marry hollow and contrived, ultimately admitting that 'his insistence that she should marry one of the men was only a nod to the world'.[138] It is tempting to see Sarah's beration of the minister as an articulation of Bell's own philosophy: 'And what was it ye said?', she demands. 'To marry one of the men. To bend and contrive things so that all would be smooth from the outside, like the way a lazy workman finishes a creel.'[139] Through his work Bell was quick to emphasise Sarah's point that that which appeared smooth and harmonious to the eye could be contrived to cover diversity and disharmony within. For him, this was not problematic, his image of Northern Ireland was a complex tableau, one which prevented it from conforming to unionism's rigid vision. 'I think', he wrote in 1951, 'it would be a matter for concern if observers, watching the coming and going in a vivid, voluble, and involved community, were agreed that what they saw was simple, static, and incapable of more than one interpretation.'[140] It was a mark of his career that there was always more than one possible interpretation.

In 1955 Sam Hanna Bell produced the *Return Room*, the poet W.R. Rodgers's portrait of his childhood in Belfast, and 'probably one of the finest feature programmes devised in Northern Ireland after the war'.[141] In it, Rodgers described his puritan upbringing: 'Gay goes up and grim comes down. The Puritan pepper and salt, if it looked like granite tasted like drama. It had two sides to it. Everything in Belfast had two sides.'[142] Rodgers was, according to Derek Mahon, 'a renegade Presbyterian minister with an all-Ireland perspective (he liked to say he had "a foot in both graves")'.[143] In a similar way John Hewitt argued that while he himself might have appeared 'Planter's Gothic', there was 'a round tower somewhere inside and needled through every sentence' he uttered.[144] Although 'now he is remembered as an idiosyncratic rhymester who started late and stopped early and produced at most five or six lyric poems of continuing interest', W.R. Rodgers, based as a producer with the BBC in London, was an influential voice in the literary circles of Belfast in this period.[145] In addition, he also published three important prose pieces on Northern Ireland: 'Conversation piece: an Ulster Protestant' in *The Bell* in 1942, 'Black north' for *New Statesman and Nation* in 1943, and *The Ulstermen and their country* for the British Council in 1946. For John Hewitt, Northern Ireland's 'most troublesome and deeply fissured problem' was 'the lack of integration of Ulster's peoples'.[146] In his 1942 article for *The Bell*, Rodgers explored that lack of integration: according to Rodgers, 'however admirable a Catholic may be, the Protestant feels that in a time of crisis each of them will be found on different sides of the fence'.[147] It was the 'racial difference' which Rodgers argued was fundamental to 'an understanding of Ulster':[148]

> In the same way the Catholic has an emotional sinuosity and fluency of expression which accommodates and contains the feelings of his hearer. The Protestant Ulsterman has halts and suppressions of feeling in his speech, is slow to communicate, reserved, self-conscious, inarticulate, and therefore makes his connections with other people through logic rather than emotion. That is why he is hardly understood by outsiders.[149]

In 'The Colony' Hewitt explored the nature of the relationship between the state and its catholic population:

> Teams of the tamer natives we employed
> to hew and draw, but did not call them slaves.
> Some say this was our error. Others claim
> we were too slow to make them citizens;
> we might have made them Caesar's bravest legions.[150]

Longley argues that Hewitt's attitude to catholicism in his poetry, 'the lifted hand between the mind and truth', shows 'how hard it is for an Ulster Protestant radical to tread the line between atheism or secularism and anti-Catholicism'.[151] Although, Tom Clyde suggests that:

> Hewitt's antipathy to Catholicism was based, not on Ulster Protestant bigotry, but on a blind spot common to most socialists of his generation, particularly those who had been involved with communism. Those born at the start of the century were the inheritors of 'scientific socialism', for whom the Catholic Church was the incarnation of mumbo-jumbo, witch doctors paid by the establishment to dazzle the proletariat with theatricals, and trick them into rejecting the class struggle in favour of humility,

pie in the sky and brute ignorance. Since this generation experienced first hand the Catholicism of the Lateran Treaty, of symbolic relationships with the dictatorships in Portugal and Spain and the anti-communist propaganda disseminated directly from the pulpit, their attitude was understandable, if a little simplistic.[152]

In comparison to W.R. Rodgers, then, Hewitt was less forthright in addressing the sectarian nature of the Northern Irish state. Rodgers argued that there were two groups of people in Northern Ireland, with a triple barrier between them:

> It is one of religion, of race, and of class, all coincident. It separates Catholic from Protestant, Gael from Scotch settler stock, poor from rich. It operates from birth to death . . . Men of one group go through life having as little to do as possible with men of the other group. Each segregates itself: in every Ulster town you will find a Catholic quarter, and always it is the poorer one.[153]

In this article he articulated the by-now traditional dichotomy – 'Ulstermen' were exclusively protestant, and 'Irishmen' catholic.[154] Here he echoed arguments familiar from the unionist histories of the 1920s, concluding his article with a reminder of the legacy of the plantations:

> The burning sores and breathing antagonisms of the Plantation persist in Ulster, bright and smoking as ever. They persist not in conscious terms of history but in the racial memories. They are conveyed from generation to generation not so much by words as by looks and attitudes and all the minute emotional expressions which a child gathers from its parents' faces.[155]

Duality, as John Wilson Foster has noted, pervaded all aspects of Rodgers's poetry.[156] He believed that the division not only existed between catholics and protestants, but also between protestants themselves.[157] This theme was to re-emerge in his *New Statesman* article, 'Black north', in 1943. In 1942 he argued that yet another barrier existed between Ulster protestants and the English, anticipating in this way Hewitt's point in 'The Colony' about the alienation of Northern Irish protestants from the English, of them being 'strangers in the capital':

> For the bias of our Protestant education is English. We learn English history, read English literature, are taught English traditions, acquiesce in English law, absorb the atmosphere of the English countryside – as if these things were our own . . . But as soon as we meet an Englishman in the flesh we revolt. We realise he is not of us, and his ways are not ours.[158]

In common with many unionist writers, then, Rodgers was critical of the British; England was for him 'a land with surface but with no emotional depth'.[159]

Rodgers had been ordained a presbyterian minister in 1935, but, by 1941, when his first book of poetry had been published, he was no longer satisfied with his ministry. In 1943 he took a leave of absence and moved to Oxford. It was while he was there that he was invited to submit an article on Northern Ireland to the *New Statesman and Nation*. 'Black north' appeared in November 1943, and became the basis for, and foundation of, future prose pieces by Rodgers on Northern Ireland, and Ireland in general. In this article he stereotyped both catholic and protestant; 'Catholic Ulstermen' he described as 'open in speech, sinuous and intuitive in mood', while the 'Ulster Protestant' was 'a logical, close person, deliberate, sarcastic, rational and far seeing in speech and action':

> A straight character, that will break rather than bend. Its virtue is in its stability. Its Puritanism comes from an opposition of mind and flesh, and its pitfall is that of hypocrisy. For always it hitches its wagon to the farthest star of profession, and often it ends by falling in the gutter of performance, knowing and loathing itself.

And he described the historical mindset of the 'Ulsterman':

> In Ulster the attitudes of invader and dispossessed persist. The memory of a peasant people, Protestant and Catholic, is not historical but emotional, and reason cannot reach its fears. An emotional memory is a timeless memory.

In Rodgers's earlier essay in *The Bell* and later piece for the British Council, these traits were largely confined to protestants. 'Black north' argued that Northern Ireland was politically independent from both Westminster and Dublin, and would never submit to the governments of either: 'in effect we have here the makings of a Protestant Nationalist state. But no Ulster loyalist would admit this':

> For he still depends on Great Britain for his social services; he still fears the opponent in his midst; and, not less important, Ulster is close enough geographically to England to be able daily to replenish its stores of loyalty. [160]

In relation to the position of the catholic population in the Northern Irish state, and more broadly to the Free State, Rodgers believed that 'to be just, and, much more, to be generous to an opponent one must have either security or humility . . . not till Ulster has a sense of security will she be able to approach her problems in a detached way'.[161] Asking, and answering, the question whether the Northern Irish government was 'fascist', Rodgers was vague, contending that to the 'Irishman' 'office without power' was meaningless. His portrait of Northern Irish society was more specific and less flattering. Industrial wealth, he maintained, was held in protestant hands, and as a result catholics were disadvantaged in terms of employment: 'Only [a] few [protestants] dare employ a Catholic without inviting disaffection among other employees. For the temper of the Protestant majority in Ulster is hostile to the Catholic.' He laid the blame for this state of affairs squarely at the door of the unionist government: 'In twenty years of office it has not sought for better relations between Protestant and Catholic, but has, without hesitation, used ill relations in order to keep power.'[162] This article was 'a witty, truthful and therefore inflammatory portrait of Catholic-Protestant divisions' according to John Hewitt,[163] and Rodgers's parishioners in Loughgall were not impressed. Hewitt wrote to him to say that he had been 'delighted to read in the article' that he offended 'both camps beautifully'.[164] Although he returned to Loughgall in 1944, by 1946 Rodgers had resigned his ministry and moved to the BBC in London.

Rodgers's 'Black north' article was the foundation of his more restrained 1946 British Council booklet, *The Ulstermen and their country*, as well as being culled for his introduction to *Ireland in colour* and his 1950s' radio script 'Return to Northern Ireland'. Although John Hewitt believed that *The Ulstermen and their country* was Rodgers's statement of his attitude to 'our background', in which he outlined his interpretation of Northern Irish history and 'Ulster', it is in fact 'Black north' which remains his most important, and revealing piece of prose.[165] In 1945 the British Council offered the commission for *The Ulstermen and their country* to Rodgers.[166] 'What we want', the British Council wrote, 'is a study of people as they are and not a history of Ulster. I doubt in any case whether you could do a history of Ulster for people who will never have heard of Cromwell or anybody else in English history'.[167] The series of booklets, which was to include England, Scotland and Wales, would, the British Council expected, make a 'valuable contribution' to their work overseas, 'including that in liberated Europe':

> Most of the space should be devoted to the national characteristics of the Ulstermen, though we realise that they cannot be explained without reference to topography, industry and so on, on which to a large extent the characteristics depend . . . Could you put yourself in the position of a Persian or a Costa Rican who can read normal English but has never been outside his own country and would like to know a little about this country called Ulster of which he has been told?[168]

One of the central themes of *The Ulstermen and their country* was that of community; the pattern of Ulster life according to Rodgers was centred around the community: 'It is not built round the individual but round the community: and it embraces not only the living but the dead, the past as well as the present'.[169] Rodgers reinforced the concept of the historical separateness of Northern Ireland from the rest of the island; 'but always' , he wrote, 'it was Ulster, the north of Ireland, that stood longest and strongest against the waves of invasion whether from sea or land': 'History is tenacious. That spirit of strong will and stubborn independence still marks the Ulsterman, and marks him off from the other people of Ireland'. 'If you visit Ulster today', he continued:

> You will at once note that this northern province – which is under the English Crown – has its own Government and also its own deliberate frontier fencing it from the South of Ireland. There is nothing new in

> this. For you may yet see the remains of the Black Pig's Dyke, a great wall
> built by Ulstermen in the 3rd century a. d. to keep out Southerners.[170]

What he euphemistically referred to as the 'opposition' between protestant
and catholic in the state was something, he argued, which appeared in all
countries: 'the indisputable fact is that some kind of tension or conflict is
inseparable from life itself and is inherent to it. One might say that life *is* the
struggle between opposites.'[171] Rodgers himself felt the book was 'somewhat
ham-strung', but that it had made a breakthrough; as he wrote to Dan Davin:
'All mention of politics was forbidden, and finally it was blue-pencilled by the
Ulster Government Office. Still it's the first time they've allowed the existence of a Catholic-Protestant problem.'[172] As the unionist histories of the
state had done previously, Rodgers testified that the 'Ulsterman' was steeped
in history, tradition, and the deeds of his ancestors. 'The peasant', he wrote,
'has history in his bones, and community in his loins'.[173] In this booklet
Rodgers reinforced the idea of 'Ulster' as a united and homogenous community, despite the 'oppositions': 'It is the diversity and interplay of opposites
that makes Ulster life such a rich and fascinating spectacle.'[174] Over ten years
later, drawing heavily on this British Council piece, Rodgers wrote the introduction to *Ireland in colour*.[175] In keeping with the book's theme, he spoke in
terms of the significance of colour in Ireland:

> To talk about the Irish scene without noting the considerable symbolism
> of Orange and Green would be to blind oneself to the character and
> history of the country for the last century and a half . . . The Orange Lily
> seems to me to represent very well the close, sultry, emotional character
> of the Ulsterman, just as the white and green Easter Lily – symbol of
> resurgence – has in it the clear cold air of hope that always inspired
> Nationalist Ireland. The two characters, however much opposed, are
> complementary . . . 'If there wasn't the one sort', as we say in Ireland,
> 'there wouldn't be the other'.[176]

It was a theme which he had highlighted in his radio script 'Return to
Northern Ireland', produced by Sam Hanna Bell for the *Third Programme* in
1950.[177] 'If you want to live and belong amongst them', wrote Rodgers, 'you
must do as they do, and say as they say. You must keep the same face.'[178] In a
phrase which Bell was to echo in *December bride*, Rodgers described Northern Ireland as a place which was as 'rounded as the belly of a pebble you'd
pick up on the seashore'.[179] 'Life isn't all tension in Northern Ireland', wrote
Rodgers. 'It has its place and its time, like the Twelfth of July, the fifteenth of
August. Outside that, things run in a very rounded and smooth way.'[180]

The 'Ulstermen' in Rodgers's narrative, and in keeping with past unionist
authors, were almost exclusively protestant: 'cautious, logical and far-seeing'
in speech and action, and distrustful of 'eloquence'.[181] He summed them up
in his unfinished poem 'Epilogue':

> I am Ulster, my people an abrupt people
> Who like the spiky consonants in speech
> And think the soft ones cissy; who dig

The *k* and *t* in orchestra, detect sin
In sinfonia, get a kick out of
Tin cans, fricatives, fornication, staccato talk,
Anything that gives or takes attack,
Like Micks, Tagues, tinkers' gets, Vatican,
An angular people, brusque and Protestant,
For whom the word is still a fighting word,
Who bristle into reticence at the sound
Of the round gift of the gab in Southern mouths.[182]

Even in 'Epilogue' Rodgers highlighted the Northern Irish protestants' distrust of southern Irish volubility, although Rodgers's own poetry was characterised itself by a degree of the same. The 'Ulsterman's' love of progress, a theme familiar from these histories, was, according to Rodgers, 'partly because there is in him a strain of the colonist who came to this corner of Ireland only three centuries ago, and so his traditions are still in the making: he is restless for the future, and not arrested by the past'.[183] The 'Ulsterman' was then 'remote enough [from Europe] to have preserved its own ancient human pattern, yet near enough to profit by the new industrial patterns of life'.[184] In *The Ulstermen and their country* he contributed to a common historical narrative, developing the concept to the point where the Ulsterman now embodied history. According to Rodgers the Northern Irish took no interest in the past 'for a peasant people is the past, so they have no need to dwell on it'.[185] In this direct identification of the people as history, Rodgers foreshortened time until the past and present became one, leaving the pattern of the future easily discernible:

The past is not 'mere history' to him, and he cannot be neutral about it. He 'puts himself into it', and it lives. Often I have listened to him talking about people and happenings of 150 years ago with as intimate a knowledge and as cunning a detail as if they had been his neighbours and contemporaries.[186]

He echoed this same concept in a letter to Dan Davin in 1956, but broadened it to include the whole of Ireland: 'I have started my Epilogue, meaning it to be a kind of requiem or "wake" for the dead of Ireland; and what else was Ireland ever, but her dead?'[187]

In February 1946 the British Council wrote to Rodgers about *The Ulstermen and their country*: 'Your manuscript for "The Ulstermen and their Country" has now been returned by the government of Northern Ireland Office, and I am glad to say that they like it very much indeed.'[188] Their relief that Rodgers's typescript had been approved is unsurprising given the list of authors which the Northern Irish government had previously rejected. Louis MacNeice, not Rodgers, had been the government's first choice. In April 1944, the Northern Irish Cabinet Publicity Committee noted that the British Council had arranged for the publication of a series of booklets on 'Peoples of the United Kingdom', including one on Ulster:

The booklets dealing with England, Wales and Scotland will be entitled 'England and the English', 'Wales and the Welsh', 'Scotland and the

Scottish'. It is suggested that the Ulster contribution should be headed 'Ulster and the Ulsterman'. The British Council do not favour St John Ervine as the author, and we have tentatively suggested that they should approach Louis MacNeice or Mr R.V. Williams.[189]

MacNeice was then considered as 'eminently suitable' for the commission by the Cabinet Publicity Committee.[190] The British Council approached MacNeice and Cyril Falls who submitted typescripts, which the Northern Irish government, through the Cabinet Publicity Committee, then vetted. Both submissions 'proved unacceptable'.[191] Louis MacNeice's article, 'Northern Ireland and her people', dealt with many of the themes touched on ultimately by Rodgers: general stereotypes of protestant and catholic 'Ulstermen', relations between both groups, and between Ulster protestants and the English, and so on. However, where MacNeice's script differed from Rodgers was in its directness in addressing, for instance, the question of violence in the Northern Irish state, and indeed the vexed issue of what constituted 'Northern Ireland':

> If you look at a map of Ireland you will find a small portion in the north-east (one-sixth of the island) cut off from the rest by an irregular border; this is 'Northern Ireland', otherwise known as the Six Counties or, sometimes, Ulster. It is to be noted however that this area excludes three counties of the old province of Ulster and, incidentally, the *most* northerly part of Ireland, which is in County Donegal. From a purely geographical point of view this partition looks odd. Those who visit the district however will find many things that at first sight seem still odder.[192]

MacNeice dealt blatantly with the question of violence in the state:

> As recently as 1935 there were serious shootings and burnings in Belfast between Protestant and Catholics (NB the political alignment in the country is all but identical with the religious alignment) . . . The fact remains that Northern Ireland has in our time had more experience of political violence than England, Scotland, or Wales. This is why her policemen, unlike those in the other three territories, always carry arms when on duty.[193]

Rodgers, meanwhile, in his article referred more euphemistically to the 'clash' between the 'two racial patterns' which he argued resulted in a 'wave' being thrown up between them, 'a creative wave of self-consciousness'.[194] In addition to these thorny issues, MacNeice focused on the position of catholics within the state:

> As one person out of three in Northern Ireland is a Catholic it will be understood why this minority, which can never either be submerged or come to power, is a frequent occasion of dissension.[195]

He took up Rodgers's point about the racial differences within the state; catholics were descended from 'that Catholic population which dominated this district before the plantations of English and Scottish settlers', while 'Northern Unionists' were the descendants of the planters. This, he argued was evident from the lack of Gaelic names among Ulster protestants, and he used the first Northern Irish government as proof.[196] He argued that political difference was reinforced by class difference: 'on the average the income per head and the standard of living, in Northern Ireland, are considerably lower among the Catholics'.[197] Orange Order parades, while seeming 'primitive', 'sinister', and 'smacking even of fascism', were, according to MacNeice 'an emotional safety-valve'.[198] He concluded the article with what was a particularly sensitive subject for the unionist government at this time, commenting on the recruits to the British forces during the Second World War from Northern Ireland and the Free State:

> In one famous North of Ireland regiment the recruits come about equally from north and south of the border and, of course, among the Northerners are many of the Catholic minority. It is a fact that these men, brought up in opposing camps, drop their mutual suspicion and latent hostility almost as soon as they get in the same unit; all that remain is badinage – 'Sing us one of your blank rebel songs', or 'Sing us one of your blank Orange ballads'.

Finally, MacNeice's article expressed the hope that people from all quarters in Northern Ireland would be able 'at last to sink their differences'.[199] 'Northern Ireland and her people' was examined by the Ulster Office in London in April 1944:

> We examined it carefully in consultation with the Council's representatives and have expressed strongly our view that the script is most unsatisfactory. The Council have agreed to ask the author to revise or rewrite it. If he declines, a new and more suitable author must be found.[200]

Helen Waddell was suggested as an alternative author, although the minister of education, Col. Hall-Thompson, had some doubts 'as to whether the political convictions of the author . . . would enable her to write the book from the right standpoint'.[201] In any event, Waddell refused the commission but recommended W.R. Rodgers, and the cabinet publicity committee agreed in May 1945 that he be invited to write the piece.[202]

In 1949 Rodgers and MacNeice were invited by Dan Davin of Oxford University Press to become one of the editors of *The character of Ireland*, the major publishing project of the era; 'one of those phantom Irish volumes, full of genius and fire, that never get written'.[203] Edited by Rodgers and MacNeice,[204] in response to the publication of *The character of England*, it never reached the presses.[205] Jon Stallworthy has dubbed it the book it took Rodgers and MacNeice the 'rest of their lives not to complete'.[206] All the commissioned articles were submitted, but the editors were both champion procrastinators, despite Dan Davin's constant haranguing for progress. The blame lies ultimately with them for the non-appearance of the book. From the extant essays for the book it is clear that *The character of Ireland*'s potential was immense. The line-up of authors for the book's articles reads like a who's who of commentators on Irish culture for the period.[207] Rodgers wrote to Sam Hanna Bell for advice on the project in 1955, but received a reply couched in very negative terms:

> Perhaps I'm tired and a little jaundiced, but not for the life of me could I give you a hundred intelligent words on the literary situation in Ulster. What we need, is for you to come back and write a hundred thousand angry explosive words on the situation – there's your literature! We have to live here.[208]

This accords with John Boyd's assessment that there was a general air of depression in the state at this time.[209] Of course it was not only 'Ulster' which drew negative remarks; *The character of Ireland*'s pieces on the Irish republic were no more optimistic. Arland Ussher, who was commissioned to write an article on 'the Irish rebel', wrote: 'The Irishman – incredible as it may sound – has ceased to be concerned with politics. The rebels like the saints, have retreated, almost, into his mythology; a new political movement seems as remote in Éire today as a new religion.' And he echoed Bell's despondency about the fate of literature in the 1950s in Northern Ireland: 'Irish writers – unpublished and unread, when not also censored and boycotted, in their homeland – know that a country's ideas, like its people can become inbred'.[210]

Throughout the 1940s and '50s protestant writers such as Hewitt, Bell, Rodgers, Shearman and MacNeice combined traditional unionist and protestant stereotyping with an alternative version – and vision – of Northern Irish identity and the Northern Ireland state. For Hewitt, Bell, Rodgers, MacNeice and even Shearman that state was not a homogenous enclave, but a place of diversity and disharmony. Unlike official unionism this was not problematic for them, and instead they subscribed to Bell's lament that it would be a matter for concern if everything in a diverse community was only open to one interpretation.[211] However, writers such as Rodgers (and Shearman) who accepted official commissions (such as that to write the British Council booklet) could adapt and adopt the traditional unionist line in order to produce the required tone – hence the contradiction between Rodgers's *New Statesman* articles and his official (tamer) pieces for the British Council or the BBC. Hewitt faced with the same dilemma chose not to continue in the BBC's series *Ulster Commentary* precisely because he could not say what he wanted to and still be considered for the directorship of the Ulster Museum. The implication of all this is that these creative writers felt constrained in Northern Ireland and were acutely aware of the difficulty of speaking freely, or criticising the contemporary political or broader social situation, although all did so on various occasions. Their alternative visions of Northern Ireland went against the ethos of official unionist thinking in the period which 'avoided thinking or rethinking'. 'Experience teaches', commented the *Belfast Telegraph* journalist, and contributer to *The character of Ireland*, Martin Wallace, 'that the old shibboleths are the best.'[212]

Notes and References

1   'For another, the Establishment (to use a currently vague but not necessarily abusive term) has since Plato's day been canny and careful about writers, who correspondingly have had to assert themselves. Symphonies, paintings, and sculpture are quite harmless in the present dispensation or in any dispensation, but ideas are not', W.R. Rodgers, 'Memorandum on literature and writers in Northern Ireland', 18 June 1965, D2833/G/15/1–2.

2   Tom Clyde, 'A stirring in the dry bones: John Hewitt's regionalism', in Gerald Dawe and John Wilson Foster (eds.), *The poet's place: Ulster literature and society. Essays in honour of John Hewitt, 1907–87* (Belfast, 1991), p. 249. Clyde is here referring to Rutherford Mayne and Richard Rowley.

3   According to John Wilson Foster: 'Ulster (Protestant and Catholic Ulster) was a community *in fact* but it remained, and remains, to be imagined by the majority of its inhabitants', *Colonial consequences, essays in Irish literature and culture* (Dublin, 1991), p. 281. 'Ulster', however, had been imagined by the unionist government, the BBC and unionist historians.

4   As Tom Clyde points out, the war also meant that more money was available to writers and artists given that the state was cut off from Britain. In addition, with Allied soldiers stationed in the state, there was an added demand for those who could entertain, with readings, drama and so on. Tom Clyde, 'A stirring of the dry bones', p. 251. This is contrary to Brian Barton who argues that the war caused a 'progressive narrowing of cultural life', 'The impact of World War II on Northern Ireland and on Belfast–London relations', *The Northern Ireland question in British politics* (London, 1996), p. 47.

5   Tom Clyde, 'A stirring of the dry bones', p. 251.

6   Louis MacNeice (1907–1963), born in Belfast; son of a church of Ireland clergyman; educated at Marlborough and Oxford; first book of poems, *Blind fireworks*, 1928; went to Spain in 1936; CBE 1958. 'Ireland appears in his early verse a country alienated from the real world, but emerged in his post-1945 work as a haven from what Yeats termed the "filthy modern tide"', R.F. Foster, *Modern Ireland, 1600–1972* (London, 1988) p. 168.

7   'Through entering the imaginative worlds provided by these poets, a reader can perhaps gain a sensitivity to the psychological dimensions of the Ulster problem', Terence Brown, *Northern voices: poets from Ulster* (Dublin, 1975), p. 2. In many ways MacNeice is a marginal figure in this context; during this period his contact with, and involvement in, Northern Ireland was minor and peripheral; it came mainly through return visits to watch Ireland play in international rugby matches, and via the BBC in London, where he was based, to contacts he had in the BBC in Belfast, such as Bell. See Jon Stallworthy, *Louis MacNeice* (London, 1995). The Hewitts appear to have had little contact with Louis MacNeice. On the only occasion recorded by Ruby Hewitt in her diary, MacNeice was drunk, RH 3 Dec.1949, D3838/4/6. Of course this did not mean that he did not comment on Northern Ireland, see for instance *Letters from Iceland*, with W.H. Auden (London, 1937).

8   In addition to protestant dissent, this period, particularly the later 1940s and early 1950s, saw the emergence of the northern catholic voice through the work of Michael McLaverty, Benedict Kiely, and Joseph Tomelty for instance.

9   Frank Ormsby, (ed.), *The collected John Hewitt* (Belfast, 1991), p. 1. Terence Brown argues that Hewitt 'especially as his later works come more fully into focus in relationship with what went before, is more than the chronicler of a people's identity crisis, more than the pastoral poet of an Ulster landscape that is read for sociological and regionalist ethos', 'John Hewitt: an Ulster of the

mind', *The poet's place*, p. 301. Although ironically Hewitt, according to Tom
Clyde, was not a typical Ulsterman: 'the bitterness, piety, tribal warmth and
understanding of revenge which number among most Ulster people's characteristics appeared in his poems, not in the man'. Tom Clyde, 'A stirring in the dry
bones', p. 258.

10   Ruby Hewitt referred to the discussions that took place among some Northern
      Irish writers about the region, or 'home': 'To Sam Hanna Bell's to meet W.B.
      Stanford and wife from Dublin. Jane and D Boyce there, Ursula Eason, John
      Boyd, Dennis Hanley, Joe Tomelty. Discussion on home and what should be
      written towards morning. Home 3 a.m', RH, 17 May 1948, D3838/4/6.

11   Script of BBC NI programme *Art in Ulster*, Nov. 1945, D3838/2/4A.

12   John Hewitt, 'Regionalism: the last chance', *Northman*, 1947. Tom Clyde, (ed.),
      Ancestral voices: the selected prose of John Hewitt (Belfast, 1987), p. 125.

13   'In truth, the Hewitt region did not extend beyond the familiar home counties of
      Antrim and Down', Roy McFadden, 'No Dusty Pioneer: a personal recollection of
      John Hewitt', *The poet's place*, p. 176.

14   'The Colony' (1950), *The selected John Hewitt*, edited with an introduction by
      Alan Warner (Belfast, 1981), p. 24.

15   John Hewitt, 'Regionalism: the last chance', *Northman*, 1947. Tom Clyde, (ed.),
      Ancestral Voices, p. 124.

16   John Wilson Foster, *Colonial consequences*, pp. 279, 280–1.

17   Frank Ormsby, *The collected poetry of John Hewitt*, p. li. Hewitt also did a
      master's dissertation on Ulster poets between 1800 and 1870: 'The weaver-
      poets' uprightness and sturdy independence of outlook were admired by John
      Hewitt, and it also pleased him that each was associated with a particular local-
      ity – Campbell of Ballynure, Herbison of Dunclug, and so on', Patricia Craig,
      'Assertors and protestors: John Hewitt as literary historian', *The poet's place*, p.
      226. According to Hewitt himself: 'And yet the Gaels came to Ireland three
      thousand years ago, we Saxon-Scots three hundred. It is only a matter of
      centuries, of perspective and scale'. 'The bitter gourd: some problems of the
      Ulster writer', *Lagan*, 1945.

18   From 'Conacre' (1943), *The selected John Hewitt*, p. 15.

19   John Wilson Foster, *Colonial consequences*, p. 158.

20   PEN stood for 'Playwrights, Poets, Editors, Essayists and Novelists'. 'Was it
      Hewitt or myself, or someone else, who declared that the initials P.E.N stood for
      Phoneys, Eccentrics and Neurotics?', Roy McFadden, 'No dusty pioneer', p. 173.

21   RH, 5 Nov. 1950, D3838/4/6. 'It is to be a monthly thing and they are talking
      about publication', RH, 1 Oct. 1950, D3838/4/6. This is probably the same as
      the group that Roy McFadden writes about in 'No dusty pioneer': 'he [Hewitt]
      proposed that a group of writers should meet for a meal every first or fourth
      Sunday and address a pre-arranged topic. But inevitably the conversation
      degenerated into the chat, and one anecdote borrowed another',. *The dusty
      pioneer*, p. 176.

22   In November 1948 John Hewitt was invited to meet George Barnes, programme
      head of the BBC: 'All the writers were there but J. found it a waste of time too
      many and too much drink and no conversation', RH, 10 Nov. 1948, D3838/4/6.
      The Hewitts were at the BBC reception for the station's twenty-fifth anniver-
      sary, which Sir William Haley, the BBC's director general, attended, RH, 22 Oct.
      1949.

23   Sam Hanna Bell, *The arts in Ulster* (London, 1951), p. 20.

24   In an article for the *Irish Press* Hewitt focused on PEN's international charter:
      'The first affirmation of which reads: "Literature, national though it be in origin,
      knows no frontiers"; and the fourth: "The P.E.N. stands for the principle of

unhampered transmission of thought within each nation and between all nations".' In the same article he discussed Gaelic literature: 'The Ulster writer of planter stock is not antipathetic to the value of Gaelic literature when he takes the trouble to discover it for himself in translation. He will, I am sure, find it easier to pluck nourishment from it than the olive trees of ancient Greece', *Irish Press*, 5 Mar. 1954, D3838/2/4B.

25   John Hewitt had also been chairman of PEN in 1945. The vice-chairman that year was D.A. Chart, D2833/C/2/7/11.

26   D1246/2B. This talk of Chart's was his chairman's address to PEN, 5 Jan. 1946. 'I said about someone "He's like Dr Chart – you know, like some you would look at and then roll up and put away"', RH, 14 Aug. 1950, D3838/4/6.

27   Roy McFadden, 'No dusty pioneer', p. 173.

28   RH, 7 May 1949, D3838/4/6.

29   RH, 16 May 1949, D3838/4/6. Denis Ireland (1894–1974) was a protestant republican.

30   Edna Longley, 'Progressive bookmen: politics and northern Protestant writers since the 1930s', *The Irish Review*, no. 1, 1986, p. 56.

31   Roy McFadden, 'No dusty pioneer', p. 170.

32   Patricia Craig, 'Assertors and protestors: John Hewitt as literary historian', *The poet's place*, p. 236.

33   John Hewitt, cited in Edna Longley, 'Progressive bookmen', *The living stream*, p. 118.

34   ibid. p. 112.

35   John Hewitt was already a unique feature in the Ulster Museum; he and the museum's carpenter were the only two in the museum 'to read the Statesman and Nation', RH, 9 Jan. 1952, D3838/4/7.

36   'I wrote in this diary that if it continued it might be read later when we are no more and fill in a part of the Belfast picture – I hope the worse [*sic*] thing in it would be my spelling', note in RH, nd, D3838/4/6. More importantly, Ruby Hewitt's diary provides another valuable view of this period in Northern Ireland's history, and the life of its literary citizens.

37   RH, 31Dec. 1951, D3838/4/7. In February 1950 Ruby Hewitt noted that John Boyd, a producer with BBC NI, had told John Hewitt that 'it was BBC policy not to have him on air too much', RH, 6 Feb. 1950, D3838/4/6.

38   RH, 23 Feb. 1949, D3838/4/6.

39   RH, 11 Mar. 1952, D3838/4/7.

40   'He would have liked it as he loves the Gallery and this Ulster . . . On Wed 23 J. got a phone call from a Councillor Holmes, who used to be in Labour Party and is now a Unionist he said some things were being said about J. that he thought he should know. They arranged to meet on King's Bridge at 3 o'c . . . He told J. that a Ms O'Malley an Eire Labour Party member had written to say she could not be at a Council Meeting but her support would go for John Hewitt. Mr Tucker, the Chairman of the Libraries and Museum and Art Gallery committee showed this letter round Unionist members and said J. was being backed by the Eire Labour Party and was therefore disloyal', RH, 8 Sept. 1952, D3838/4/7.

41   Edna Longley, 'John Hewitt, 1907–87', *Fortnight*, Sept. 1987.

42   Also in this letter he refers to Rodgers's article in the *New Statesman*: 'I was delighted to read the article you offend both camps delightfully. I suppose Savory will have a letter about it', John Hewitt to W.R. Rodgers, 26 Nov. 1943, D2833/C/1/8/1–10.

43   Patricia Craig, 'Assertors and protestors: John Hewitt as literary historian', p. 236.

44   John Hewitt, review of *Now in Ulster* (Belfast, 1944), in *Unity*, 14 Dec. 1944, D3838/2/4A.

45   Keidryan Rhys, review of Robert Greacen, *Northern harvest: anthology of Ulster writing* (Belfast, 1944), in the *Tribune*, 8 Sept. 1944, D3838/2/4A.

46   ibid.

47   In 'Regionalism: the last chance', Hewitt complained that 'Hugh Shearman in his officially sponsored brochure on Northern Ireland gave no name of artist or writer associated with our contemporary developments', *Northman*, 1947. Tom Clyde, *Ancestral Voices*, p. 125. He is referring to Shearman's *Northern Ireland: its history, resources and people* (HMSO, 1946).

48   In February 1949, John Hewitt had a letter published in the *New Statesman and Nation* responding to Hugh Shearman: 'it won't', Ruby Hewitt noted, 'be popular with Tories, Nationalists, or Labour people here . . . it is a true statement of now'. 'We are always in a war', Ruby complained, 'and I feel och it would be nice to be popular with someone for a while', RH, 9 Mar. 1949, D3838/4/6.

49   Jonathan Bardon, *A history of Ulster* (Belfast, 1992), pp. 600–1.

50   Hugh Shearman, 'Divided Ireland', *New Statesman and Nation*, 12 Feb. 1949.

51   W.R. Rodgers, 'Black north', *New Statesman and Nation*, 20 Nov. 1943.

52   Hugh Shearman, 'Divided Ireland', *New Statesman and Nation*, 12 Feb. 1949.

53   John Hewitt, 'Divided Ireland', *New Statesman and Nation*, 19 Feb. 1949.

54   Martin Wallace, 'Government in Northern Ireland', typescript for *The character of Ireland*, D2833/D/12/1/19.

55   John Hewitt, 'Divided Ireland', *New Statesman and Nation*, 19 Feb. 1949.

56   According to Kenneth Darwin, former deputy keeper of the PRONI, and a contemporary of Shearman's, 'the Unionists couldn't find anybody reasonably intelligent and literate to write anything for them, they were glad enough they had a tame Shearman to write'. Author's interview with Kenneth Darwin, deputy keeper of PRONI, 1955–69, Feb. 1995.

57   *Not an inch: a study of Northern Ireland and Lord Craigavon* (London, 1942), *Northern Ireland: its history, resources and people* (HMSO, 1946), *Ulster* (London, 1949), *How Northern Ireland is governed* (HMSO, 1951), *Modern Ireland* (London, 1952), *Northern Ireland, 1921–71* (HMSO, 1971).

58   Hugh Shearman to R.S. Brownell, Ministry of Education, 4 Aug. 1944, CAB 9F/123/18.

59   'Not an inch started as a couple of papers to the history society here at Queen's. A lot of the framework was carved out of that life, that two or three volume life of Carson by Colvin and someone else . . . I threw the thing together, it was a job journalism. It was just when I had started at Trinity that I discovered that Faber had taken up the thing', interview with Hugh Shearman, 26 Jan. 1995.

60   Hugh Shearman, *Not an inch*, p. 165.

61   ibid., p. 178.

62   He also suggested that prior to the Government of Ireland Act, the British administration had allowed Ireland 'to fall into a terrible state of disorder', ibid., p. 168.

63   Hugh Shearman, ibid., p. 5.

64   Interview with Hugh Shearman, 26 Jan. 1995.

65   Hugh Shearman, *Anglo-Irish relations* (London, 1948), p. 178. Shearman also had an interesting argument on the subject of the past: 'It is in the present that we must live and not in the past; but we cannot afford, in coping with the demands of the present, to dispense altogether with those larger and more accurate standards of reference and much long-range sightings with which history provided us', p. 9.

66   Of course, separate attention for the state's war effort found its ultimate manifestation in the publication of John Blake's *Northern Ireland in the Second World War* (Belfast, 1956). Hewitt's pride and identification with Ulster was an

inclusive act, and he saw himself as part of Ulster, Ireland, Britain and beyond. He explored the broader vista, while conversely Shearman adopted a narrowing vision centred exclusively around Northern Ireland.

67   Hugh Shearman, *Anglo-Irish relations*, p. 252.
68   ibid., p. 202.
69   Cited in Dennis Kennedy, *The widening gulf: northern attitudes to the independent Irish state, 1919–49* (Belfast, 1988), p. 239.
70   Hugh Shearman, 'Recent developments in Anglo-Irish relations', in *World Affairs*, Apr. 1949, p. 159.
71   ibid., p. 161.
72   'The Ireland Act of 1949 gives the Six Counties the right of self-determination; there can be no constitutional change without the approval of Stormont. Despite this, and despite each election's voting figures, the Unionists forever appear to be on the defensive – forever attempting to justify themselves', Martin Wallace, 'Government of Northern Ireland', D2833/D/12/1/19.
73   Hugh Shearman, *Anglo-Irish relations*, p. 274.
74   Hugh Shearman, *Ulster* (London, 1949), p. 260.
75   ibid., *Ulster*, p. 358.
76   CAB 9F/123/18.
77   From *Autumn Journal*, XVI. Jon Stallworthy, *Louis MacNeice*, p. 255.
78   Cabinet Publicity Minutes, 19 Apr. 1944, CAB 9F/123/18.
79   Northern Irish Ministry of Education memorandum on Shearman's draft, March 1944, CAB 9F/123/18.
80   W.R. Rodgers, 'Black north', *New Statesman and Nation*, 20 Nov. 1943. In February 1944 George Marshall's (director of BBC NI) monthly report for January also referred to this unusual state of affairs: '[D]uring a debate in the House of Commons, a member referred to the fact that an Orange Hall in Portrush was not being put to the use for which its founders intended and that instead it had been handed over to Roman Catholic members of the U.S. Forces, while another mentioned that Mass had been said in it on several occasions. The Minister of Home Affairs (Mr W. Lowry) was heard to remark by way of comment that he understood that the Hall was being fumigated and this naturally gave rise to an outburst from the Opposition and R.C. members, who demanded an immediate withdrawal and apology . . . The incident has now blown over, at least in the surface, but it has embarrassed the Prime Minister and not improved the relationship between Protestant and Catholic in NI', M.R, Northern Ireland Region, Feb. 1944, R34/748/1.
81   Robert Gransden to Cooper, 6 July 1944, CAB 9F/123/18. All the ministries had an opportunity to comment on the drafts Shearman submitted. In one memorandum from the parliamentary secretary, at the ministry of health and local government, it was asked whether it would be advisable 'to point out that at various periods in its history the number of counties in Ulster varied?' But some objections, such as that from the Ministry of Agriculture, concerned the accuracy of Shearman's work: the section on agriculture was 'so bad and gives such a completely misleading view of Northern Irish agriculture, if indeed it can be said to describe it in any way whatever, that I thought it impossible to amend'. At the end of this letter, a note that Robertson rewrote the section himself, Robertson to Knipe, 10 Oct. 1944, CAB 9F/123/114.
82   'The various excisions and adjustments proposed in the memorandum have been made, and also the general character of them has been taken as a guide in making other alterations', Hugh Shearman to R.S. Brownell, at the Ministry of Education, 4 Aug. 1944, CAB 9F/123/18.
83   Hugh Shearman to R.S. Brownell, 4 July 1944, CAB 9F/123/18.

84　Hugh Shearman to R.S. Brownell, 4 Aug. 1944, CAB 9F/123/18.

85　Cabinet Publicity Minutes, 22 May 1944. Memorandum from Col Hall-Thompson on Shearman's draft, CAB 9F/123/34.

86　W.R. Rodgers to Hewitt, 21 July 1946, D3838/3/17A. 'Shearman', wrote Hewitt to Rodgers in November 1946, 'is now whoring with articles in the *Telegraph*. His last was on the rich! variety of Literary activity during the decade in Ulster and how we just accept it. Novelists living round the corner, philosophers a tramride away', John Hewitt to W.R. Rodgers, 26 Nov. 1946, D2833/C/1/8/1–10.

87　See chapter 1 for a fuller discussion of Chart's text.

88　Author's interview with Hugh Shearman, 26 Jan. 1995.

89　The press officer continued: 'We are in touch with Mr R. Anderson, (one of the publishers), and have asked that the book should also be made available to education authorities and schools in Great Britain', CAB 9F/123/49.

90　Hugh Shearman, *The bishop's confession: being a memoir found among the papers of the late Right Reverend Percival MacPeake D.D. Lord Bishop of the United Diocese of Bangor, Dungannon, and Strabane* (London, 1943), *A bomb and a girl* (London, 1944).

91　Hugh Shearman, *The bishop's confession*, p. 5. In an interview Shearman gave the background to the writing of the novel: 'That arose [because] there was some bishop, I forget who he was, he wrote his autobiography, entitled *The Adventures of a Bishop*. My father and I were rather amused at this book, I said I can write a better bishop's biography than that. The basic plot was that the further the bishop rose in the church the more sceptical he became about the church . . . Apart from ecclesiastical matters, there was a boy, he had committed suicide with his father's home guard revolver, and I came to the conclusion that it was juvenile sex difficulties and his father's attitude towards him. I thought I'd give my bishop juvenile sex difficulties.' Author's interview with Hugh Shearman, 26 Jan. 1995. The book he refers to is Charles Frederick D'Arcy's *The adventures of a bishop: a phase of Irish life, a personal and historical narrative* (London, 1934).

92　Hugh Shearman, *The bishop's confession*, p. 200.

93　'Belfast has always had a sad, pleasant sobriety for me, but Dublin is still an alien place, with its gossip and dirt and public-houses and prostitutes', ibid., p. 113.

94　He describes the life: 'we were simply a group of lonely, mildly disillusioned, and rather uneasy men' ibid., p. 177.

95　ibid., p. 35.

96　ibid.

97　'Presbyterianism was not a proper religion for a gentleman, but it was quite a good religion for the lower classes who took it seriously', ibid., p. 36 and p. 89.

98　ibid., p. 100.

99　ibid., pp. 104–5.

100　ibid., p. 113. MacPeake goes as a curate to a working-class parish in east Belfast: 'I regarded mill girls as females of a lower class, and I was able to deal with them as calmly as I might have dealt with herd of cows', ibid., p. 127.

101　ibid., p. 186.

102　'Though I could not say so, I really meant by "much more suitable men" men who actually believed the doctrines of the Church and really regarded themselves as Christians, which I scarcely did'. ibid., p. 196, p. 234.

103　Hugh Shearman, *A bomb and a girl*, p. 8. He also points out that 'the police and their activities as described do not reflect the character, organization, methods or personnel of a real police force', p. 8.

104　ibid., p. 25.

105 Stanislas sees his desire for women as a weakness of character, and has the same expectations as MacPeake of not finding an equal in a woman but a pleasant and good-looking companion: 'external appearances must come first, so that the world might know the scale of the achievement of Stanislas'. His relationships with women are futile and full of frustration, and almost more dysfunctional than Bishop MacPeake's: 'the frequent sight of girls, all full of animal spirits, in bright colours, with bare sunburnt arms and legs, caused him to feel deep longings which were very painful to him when he knew his inability to satisfy them'. ibid., p. 45.

106 ibid., p. 31.

107 ibid., pp. 56–8.

108 ibid., p. 65.

109 ibid., p. 65.

110 'Professor Oliver, with his height of six feet three inches and his weight of seventeen stone was hardly less tremendous to meet as an individual than he was to behold and hear as a public speaker at the Ulster Unionist Council', op. cit., pp. 72–6.

111 ibid., p. 66.

112 ibid., pp. 90–114.

113 ibid., p. 139.

114 ibid., p. 145.

115 Or for that matter W.R. Rodgers, who was equally involved in writing publicity pieces on Northern Ireland in the same period.

116 Sam Hanna Bell described his younger self as 'a radical with a faint Nationalist colouration', and with a 'nostalgic hankering for 1798', cited in Edna Longley, 'Progressive bookmen: politics and northern Protestant writers since the 1930s', p. 55. He was also one-time editor of Labour Progress.

117 'So the first job of Ulster writers is to make a clearing: to satirize, to parody, and to ridicule all this sham stuff every time they read it or see it or hear it; to laugh at the persons who are responsible for it; and to explain exactly what is happening to the people on whom it is inflicted', John Boyd, Lagan, no. 1, 1943.

118 Sam Hanna Bell, 'The microphone in the countryside', The BBC in Northern Ireland, 1924–49 (Belfast, 1949), p. 10.

119 This bias is unsurprising given Rodgers's upbringing; his parents were 'good living', and barred Shakespeare, full-length mirrors and alcohol from their home, John Wilson Foster, Colonial consequences, pp. 128–9.

120 W.R. Rodgers, 'Conversation piece: an Ulster Protestant', The Bell, vol. 4, no. 5, August 1942, p. 308.

121 'Rodgers felt that Ulster Protestant men and women spoke without zest or style, and that this was an expression of their circumspect, calculating character'. Terence Brown 'W.R. Rodgers: romantic calvinist', Northern voices: poets from Ulster, p. 125.

122 John Wilson Foster, Colonial consequences, p. 115.

123 From 'The Colony' (1950), The selected John Hewitt, p. 24. According to Tom Clyde 'snigger' and 'breed like flies' undermine the speaker. Thus, while Hewitt was showing his understanding of the colonists/planters position, he was also revealing his ambivalence to some of their prejudices.

124 Cited in Douglas Carson 'Sam Hanna Bell, 1909–90', Honest Ulsterman, no. 89, Summer 1990, p. 48. Another of Bell's productions for radio was The Islandmen. A short piece from this was used for a collection of stories about Ulster customs and folklore which Bell published in 1956 called Erin's Orange Lily (London, 1956).

125 Sam Hanna Bell, Erin's Orange Lily, p. 8.

126 ibid., preface.

127 Although generally well received, December bride (Belfast, 1974) did come under the censor's axe in the Republic of Ireland.

128 Sam Hanna Bell, interview in the *Newtownards Chronicle*, 30 Dec. 1987.
129 *BT,* 19 July 1919.
130 John Wilson Foster, *Forces and themes in Ulster fiction* (London, 1974), p. 55.
131 John Hewitt to W.R. Rodgers, 9 July 1955, D2833/C/1/8.
132 Reflected in this novel is what Edna Longley has referred to as 'open and open-ended' regionalism, and not the 'crypto-Unionist genealogy of the planters' territorial claim', Edna Longley, 'Progressive bookmen: politics and northern Protestant writers since the 1930s', p. 56.
133 Sam Hanna Bell, *December bride*, p. 10.
134 Sam Hanna Bell, *The arts in Ulster*, p. 14.
135 Sam Hanna Bell, cited in Edna Longley, 'Progressive bookmen: politics and northern Protestant writers since the 1930s', p. 52. While opposed to unionism, Bell equally had little time for nationalism. He looked towards the presbyterian radicals involved in the United Irish Rising of 1798 whose ideology he saw as more attractive. Bell, in common with Hewitt, emphasised the 'proto-socialism of the northern rebellion much more than the patriotic adventure', Edna Longley, 'Progressive bookmen: politics and northern Protestant writers since the 1930s', p. 54.
136 Hugh Shearman, *How Northern Ireland is governed*, p. 36.
137 Edna Longley, 'Progressive bookmen: politics and northern Protestant writers since the 1930s', p. 56.
138 Sam Hanna Bell, *December bride*, p. 147.
139 ibid.
140 Sam Hanna Bell, *The arts in Ulster*, p. 14.
141 Douglas Carson, 'A Kist o' Whistles', *Fortnight*, Autumn 1990, p. 4.
142 Cited in D'Arcy O'Brien, *W.R. Rodgers* (Bucknell, 1970), p. 22.
143 Derek Mahon, reviewing Michael Longley (ed.), *Poems: W.R. Rodgers* (Meath, 1993), *Irish Times*, 15 Jan. 1994.
144 Edna Longley, 'John Hewitt, 1907–87'.
145 W.R. Rodgers: born in Belfast in 1909. He became a Presbyterian minister in 1935 and served in Loughgall, Co. Armagh, until 1946 when he joined the BBC and moved to London. He published two books of poetry *Awake! and other poems* (London, 1941) and *Europa and the bull and other poems* (London, 1952). He died in California in 1969. In addition, Tom Clyde has credited the success of Rodgers's first collection, *Awake! and other poems*, as acting as the catalyst for interest in Northern Ireland as a creative place and not just a cultural backwater, 'A stirring of the dry bones', p. 251. John Wilson Foster believes that Rodgers lacked political commitment, and this is certainly true when compared to Hewitt. Rodgers did however have his own particular vision of Ireland and was not without political opinion, *Colonial consequences*, p. 65.
146 John Hewitt, 'The bitter gourd: some problems of the Ulster writer', *Lagan*, no. 3, 1945.
147 'Yes, that difference remains, and it is, I maintain, a racial one. Its roots are hidden, and are hidden, more deeply every day, but they still nourish the tree', W.R. Rodgers, 'Conversation piece: an Ulster Protestant', p. 312.
148 ibid., p. 307.
149 'That is why his heart and soul went out to Carson (a Southerner) in whom he welcomed logic, and admitted eloquence', ibid., p. 309.
150 'The Colony' (1950), *The selected John Hewitt*, p. 21.
151 Edna Longley, 'Progressive bookmen: left-wing politics and Ulster Protestant writers', p. 115.
152 Tom Clyde in correspondence with the author, May 1996.
153 'Broadly speaking in the Ulster landscape the valley farms and the good lands

belong to the Protestants, the stony outcrops and the hilly places to the Catholics', W.R. Rodgers, 'Conversation piece: an Ulster Protestant', p. 307.

154 It is reminiscent of Lord Ernest Hamilton's argument in *The soul of Ulster*: 'The religion marks the race, so much so, in fact, that religion actually stands for nationality', *The soul of Ulster*, p. 14.

155 'It is impossible to convince an Ulster Protestant farmer that, in the event of an all-Ireland government being formed independent of Westminster, his farm will not be taken away from him and given to his Catholic neighbour. And, mark you, it is equally impossible to convince the Catholic neighbour that *he* will not be given the Protestant's farm', W.R. Rodgers, 'Conversation piece: an Ulster Protestant', pp. 131–314.

156 John Wilson Foster, *Colonial consequences*, p. 126.

157 Yet while Rodgers embraced the oppositions of life, he believed he could 'fashion oneness merely out of his love for Ireland and in the finitude of his poems', ibid., p. 125.

158 'We are really a "split" people, we Protestant Ulstermen. Our eyes are turned towards England but our hearts and feet are in Ulster', W.R. Rodgers, 'Conversation piece: an Ulster Protestant', p. 310.

159 ibid., p. 311.

160 W.R. Rodgers, 'Black north', *New Statesman and Nation*, 20 Nov. 1943.

161 ibid.

162 ibid.

163 John Hewitt to W.R. Rodgers, 26 Nov. 1943, D2833/C/1/8/1–10.

164 ibid.

165 John Hewitt to Marianne Rodgers, W.R. Rodgers's widow, 28 July 1970, D2833/G/37.

166 'Did not the Incas abandon writing because they thought it a black art and evolve a curious language of knots and symbols? I hope that the Ulstermen will not go as far as this because I have enjoyed reading your manuscript very much', British Council official (signature illegible) to W.R. Rodgers, 5 Feb. 1946, D2833/C/2/8/9.

167 British Council official (signature illegible) to W.R. Rodgers, 22 June 1945. D2833/C/2/7/19.

168 ibid.

169 W.R. Rodgers, *The Ulstermen and their country* (British Council, 1952), p. 14.

170 Both D.A. Chart and Hugh Shearman had made the argument for Ulster as historically a separate place, W.R. Rodgers, *The Ulstermen and their country*, p. 1.

171 W.R. Rodgers, ibid., p. 15.

172 W.R. Rodgers to Dan Davin, 3 Apr. 1949, OUP archives, 5561.

173 W.R. Rodgers, *The Ulstermen and their country*, p. 22.

174 ibid., p. 18.

175 In his portrait of the Twelfth of July parades he wrote in theatrical terms: 'It is all part of the serious drama of life, an outlet for religious and political feelings. To dramatise is to civilise; it is to work out one's salvation on a stage, and the Irishman has always preferred to work *out* his dilemma rather than to bleed inwardly with it. Conflict, friction, opposition, is the very stuff of drama'. W.R. Rodgers's draft introduction to *Ireland in colour* (London, 1957), D2833/D/10/11/1. Large parts of this introduction were adapted from the 1950 radio script 'Return to Northern Ireland'. In the radio script version Rodgers writes: 'Ulstermen say least when they mean most. They prefer to bleed inwardly, for they're a determined people, dramatic in their opposition', D2833/D/4/6.

176 W.R .Rodgers's draft introduction to *Ireland in colour*, D2833/D/10/11/1.

177 'In this programme W.R. Rodgers goes back to look at the face and mind of his native province, Northern Ireland', introduction to the programme, D2833/D/4/6.

'Every Ulster village and town has a Catholic quarter and a Protestant quarter. The Ulsterman, in fact, likes to have things distinct and separate, and opposite and *dramatic*. It's the only way he can get a detached view of life', W.R. Rodgers's script for 'Return to Northern Ireland', Sept. 1950, D2833/D/4/6.

178   W.R. Rodgers's script for 'Return to Northern Ireland', D2833/D/4/6. This accords with Martin Wallace's argument that individualism, political thinking, rethinking and self-criticism had suffered under the northern Irish state, in his article on Northern Ireland for *The character of Ireland*, D2833/D/12/1/19.

179   W.R. Rodgers's script 'Return to Northern Ireland', D2833/D/4/6. Sarah's lament that the parson in *December bride* wanted everything to be 'smooth from the outside', *December bride*, p. 147.

180   W.R. Rodgers's script 'Return to Northern Ireland', D2833/D/4/6.

181   W.R. Rodgers, *The Ulstermen and their country*, p. 15.

182   'Mine was not born with silver spoons in gob,
      Nor would they thank you for the gift of tongues;
      The dry riposte, the bitter repartees
      The Northman's bite and portion, his deep sup
      Is silence; though, still within his shell,
      He holds the old sea-roar and surge
      Of rhetoric and Holy Writ'.
      'Epilogue', *Poems: W.R. Rodgers*, pp. 106–7.

183   W.R. Rodgers, *The Ulstermen and their country*, p. 3. Estyn Evans on the future: 'But I am not a supporter of those who, indulging in sentimental regrets for a Celtic twilight of doubtful authenticity, find in the past a Golden Age to which they would have us return. Our view should be forward', *Irish heritage: the landscape, the people, and their work* (Dundalk, 1942), p. 3.

184   W.R. Rodgers, *The Ulstermen and their country*, p. 32.

185   ibid., p. 14. In 1926 W.A. Phillips, professor of modern history at TCD, argued in similar terms but with reference to the Irish natives: 'the memory of the Irish peasant is very long; he has no sense of historical perspective; the wrongs suffered by his ancestors centuries ago are to him as things of yesterday', *The revolution in Ireland, 1906–23* (London, 1926), p. 13.

186   W.R. Rodgers, *The Ulstermen and their country*, p. 14.

187   W.R. Rodgers to Dan Davin, August 1956, cited in Davin's introductory memoir to *Collected poems: W.R. Rodgers* (London, 1971).

188   British Council to W.R. Rodgers, 13 Feb. 1946.

189   Cabinet Publicity Committee Minutes, 11 Apr. 1944, CAB 9F/123/34.

190   ibid.

191   Cabinet Minutes, 3 May 1945, CAB 9F/123/34. Although there is no indication why Falls's piece was unacceptable.

192   Louis MacNeice, 'Northern Ireland and her people', in Alan Heuser (ed.), *Selected prose of Louis MacNeice* (Oxford, 1990), p. 142. In a footnote to this article Heuser notes that the publication of the article is untraced, but it is clearly that commissioned by the British Council for the Northern Irish government.

193   Louis MacNeice, 'Northern Ireland and her people', pp. 145–6.

194   W.R. Rodgers, *The Ulstermen and their country*, p. 18.

195   Louis MacNeice, 'Northern Ireland and her people', p. 147.

196   'The first Northern Ireland government (1921) consisted of ministers with the following names: Craig, Pollock, Bates, Andrews, Vane-Tempest-Stewart (the Marquis of Londonderry), Archdale. The telephone directory will prove to you at once the preponderance of a non-Gaelic stock', Louis MacNeice, 'Northern Ireland and her people', p. 147.

197 ibid.
198 ibid., pp. 148–9.
199 ibid., p. 153.
200 Letter from the Ulster Office, London, to the Cabinet Publicity Committee, April 1944, CAB 9F/123/34.
201 Cabinet Minutes, 3 May 1945, CAB 9F/123/34. Helen Jane Waddell (1889–1965), medieval scholar and translator, born in Tokyo, educated at Queen's University, Belfast. It is possible that Waddell's involvement in the cause of six Belfast youths condemned to capital punishment in August 1942 motivated government objections to her. See D. Felicitas Corrigan, *Helen Waddell. A biography* (London, 1990) pp. 310–13. I am grateful to Dr Jennifer Fitzgerald for this information.
202 In 1959 the Central Office of Information in London asked Rodgers to submit a proposal for a film on Northern Ireland as part of a series of films for Canada and Australia and 'directed at an audience generally unfamiliar with the characteristics of the countries of the United Kingdom'. 'We are not looking for "folksy" films featuring stove pipe hats or haggis (although if these are essential to create atmosphere they should not be excluded) but more for films which, whilst giving a representative picture of a country and its people, give an overall sense of unity within the United Kingdom', A.C. White, Central Office of Information to W.R. Rodgers, 13 Oct. 1959, D2833/G/18. Rodgers suggested in his proposal interviews with John Sayers of the *Belfast Telegraph*: 'An excellent speaker, known for his well-balanced views and progressive interests. He could give the visitor a bird's-eye-view of Northern Ireland in its administrative (he was one time secretary to Lord Craigavon) and social aspects, could remark the salient features of its economy, and will probably end up by saying that the next ten years will see such economic advances that many of the old problems, particularly political ones will cease to exist'; Estyn Evans: 'Author of "Irish Heritage", "Mourne Country" etc. is chairman of the NI Committee on Folklife and Traditions ("Nothing less than the whole of the past is needed to explain the present"). An able and varied talker, he knows more about the land and its people than anyone, and is particularly good on the factors – climatic, geological, geographical – that conditioned the character of people and industries'; and Sam Thompson, author of the controversial 'Across the Bridge': 'A Belfast shipyard worker, Thompson is Belfast-made from the feet up. Blunt, outspoken, with a pungent gift of phrase. Like many Ulstermen, he is versatile; has written plays and documentary broadcasts on shipyard life. He likes to have a pint in his hand', W.R. Rodgers's outline of proposed script, nd, D2833/G/18.
203 Honor Tracy to W.R. Rodgers, 21 Dec. 1955, D2833/D/12/5/80.
204 Writing about Louis MacNeice, Jon Stallworthy notes that: 'His political alignment, unlike that of many of his literary contemporaries, remained consistently left of centre, and it is clear that he was increasingly seen as subversive by the hierarchy of the BBC', Jon Stallworthy, *Louis MacNeice*, p. 457.
205 Ernest Barker (ed.), *The character of England* (Oxford, 1947). Dan Davin wrote to Rodgers in April 1949 suggesting the book: 'I fancy that I once raised with you the question of our producing a book to be called The Character of Ireland which would consist of a group of essays by various hands for us on various aspects of Ireland', Dan Davin to W.R. Rodgers, 1 Apr. 1949, D2833/D/12/5/3. Louis MacNeice had a harsh attitude to Northern Ireland, as 'Autumn Journal' (1938) illustrates:
       A city built upon mud;
       A culture built upon profit;
       Free speech nipped in the bud,
       The minority always guilty
       And I envy the intransigence of my own

Countrymen who shoot to kill and never
See the victim's face become their own
Or find his motive sabotage their motives.

Louis MacNeice: collected poems (London, 1979), p. 101. W.R. Rodgers wrote a poem 'Epilogue', which was unfinished, for the book and MacNeice the 'Prologue':

Yet at this phase
With her children either leaving or loosing Ireland
Or remaining there to lose themselves, we can still
Take stock before we are silenced. What can we offer
To still make sense or leave a grateful taste?
'The Character of Ireland'? Character?
A stage convention? A historical trap?
A geographical freak? Let us dump the rubbish
Of race and talk to the point: what is a nation?

Cited in Jon Stallworthy, *Louis MacNeice*, p. 488.

206 Jon Stallworthy, *Louis MacNeice*, p. 392.

207 These are the authors and titles: Estyn Evans 'The countryman', Geoffrey Taylor 'Natural history', Henry Wheeler 'Archaeology and pre-Georgian architecture', David Greene 'The Irish language and its literature', Elizabeth Bowen 'The big house', Arland Ussher 'The Irish rebel', John D. Stewart 'Wild geese and other migrants', and 'The Irish navy', Peadar O'Donnell 'The shuttle between emigrant and home', John Kelleher 'The American Irish', Brian Fitzpatrick 'The Irish in Australia', Dan Davin 'The Irish in New Zealand', J.M. Mogey 'Presbyterianism in Ireland', J.C. Beckett 'The church in Ireland', Brian Inglis 'Government of the Republic of Ireland', Martin Wallace 'Government of Northern Ireland', John Hewitt 'The visual arts in Ireland', Maurice James Craig 'Architecture in Ireland', Sean O'Boyle 'Folk music', Frank O'Connor 'Irish literature', Michael MacLiammoir 'Aspects of the Irish theatre', Maire Sweeney 'Irish folklore', J.G. Simms 'Ireland and her invaders'. Rodgers had wanted Sean O'Faolain to write an essay on the church in Ireland, to which O'Faolain responded: 'As for the f_____g [*sic*] church in Ireland – a million times no! I'll give you my new stetson hat or a copy of my stories or a loan of my Ella Fitzgerald records – anything dear Bertie but that!', Sean O'Faolain to W.R. Rodgers, 11 June 1958, D2833/D/12/5/171. Conor Cruise O'Brien had initially been asked to write this essay, on the proviso that he would remain anonymous as the author. In November 1957 he wrote to W.R. Rodgers to withdraw as author: 'I am now known to be the contributor of this section – and known by people who will use that knowledge, not for my good, when the book appears. So I would be a fool to go ahead. I suggest you ask someone who has nothing to loose but their chains – someone like Brendan Behan. Or else make better security arrangements next time', D2833/D/12/5/161.

208 'Our two most fertile writers are still Joe Tomelty and Ben Kiely . . . MacLaverty, Anne Crone, Stephen Gilbert are still at it, and one borrows their new works from the lending library. In the old days it was a point of honour to buy them. Nothing is bad here, every safe piece of trash will get its ill-written, ill-informed favourable review in one paper or another', Sam Hanna Bell to W.R. Rodgers, 13 July 1955, D2833/C/1/1. Jon Stallworthy cites Bell as one of the book's contributors but, although invited, he never was. He was considered for a piece on 'the six counties' but wrote to W.R. Rodgers explaining that: 'The fact is that after overcoming the inertia of a fresh start I've got my novel moving again. I gave it up three years ago for the very unrewarding task of writing Erin's Orange Lily for Dobson. When I came back to it, it looked so bad that I threw it away in

disgust. But I had 40,000 words written. I gave it to Martin to read and he convinced me that I had to go to the end of that novel', Sam Hanna Bell to W.R. Rodgers, 4 Apr. 1957, D2833/D/12/5/144.

209   John Boyd to W.R. Rodgers, 19 Feb. 1950, D2833/C/3/1/18.

210   Arland Ussher, 'The Irish rebel', D2833/D/12/1/7. Arland Ussher's *The face and mind of Ireland* was published in London in 1949.

211   Sam Hanna Bell, *The arts in Ulster*, p. 14.

212   Martin Wallace, 'Government of Northern Ireland', D2833/D/12/1/19.

Conclusion

In the period 1920 to 1960 the expression of Northern Irish identity was largely dominated by protestant élites – government officials, biographers, creative writers, the BBC, and journalists. Protestant writers who dealt with Northern Ireland did so for a variety of reasons. In the case of unionist historians it was to explain by means of a historical narrative the position of the state, and in doing so, legitimise it. For creative writers, the motive was to give expression to an alternative vision of Northern Ireland and the Northern Irish. All had a significant role in the imagining of Northern Ireland. By the late 1950s, unionists still equated Northern Irish protestants with the Northern Irish state, and represented protestant culture as the state's sole identity. But even within protestant circles there was substantial diversity and disharmony, witnessed by the Stormont government's repeated emphasis on the need for unity amongst protestants over forty years, and testified to in the writings of protestants from Hugh Shearman to John Hewitt. Religiously and culturally, at almost all levels of society, protestants and catholics remained dichotomised.[1] And, although there were some moves among senior unionists towards a more tolerant view of the minority, the majority of unionists continued to see catholics as potential traitors who could, at best, be tolerated. Brian Maginess, addressing Young Unionists at Portstewart, for instance, argued,

> To shed our parochialism is not to deny our inheritance. To broaden our outlook means no weakening of our faith. Toleration is not a sign of weakness, but proof of strength. This will require . . . considered words instead of clichés, reasoned arguments instead of slogans.[2]

On the other hand, 'for generations', Professor Thomas Wilson wrote in 1955,

> They [catholics] were the underdogs, the despised 'croppies', the adherents of a persecuted religion, who were kept out of public affairs by their Protestant conquerors. They were made to feel inferior, and to make

matters worse they often *were* inferior, if *only* in those personal qualities
that make for success in competitive economic life.[3]

Unionists, however, did not deny northern catholics so much as they
denied the diversity of the state they governed, and by extension then
marginalised not only catholics and nationalists, but anyone who strayed
from the official unionist line. What marked this period in particular was the
development of a Northern Irish identity dominated by protestant political
and literary élites. It was an identity which was split between that which
presented the Northern Irish as exclusively (and distinctively) protestant and
loyalist, and those protestants who acknowledged not only the catholics in
the state and their contribution to the nature of that society but who also
saw no threat in the diversity within protestant ranks. The state did not
contain a homogenous population, and the denial of that fact by many unionists suppressed problems which would eventually help to fuel the civil
disturbances of the later 1960s.

The creation of the image of the 'Ulsterman' had a stagnating effect on
government in Northern Ireland. As the unionist histories of the '20s and
'30s highlighted, clichéd stereotypes were canonised into what became a
central identity. Diversity within the north's protestant population was
glossed over, while non-protestants and non-unionists were written out of
the equation altogether. This is evident not only in the writings of unionist
historians but manifest in the commemorations for Edward Carson and the
celebration of the opening of Stormont. The rhetoric of unionism often
spoke of the 'people' and 'everyone', but it was an exclusive rather than an
inclusive generality. The fact remained that there was a sizeable minority of
disaffected and marginalised citizens in Northern Ireland, whose presence
was denied by omission or specifically sidelined, as during the Festival of
Britain, or in the policy of the BBC. Unionist rhetoric was, moreover, ultimately self-defeating in its nature. Throughout this period, unionists
clamoured for recognition as an integral and valuable part of the United
Kingdom. This was particularly the case during both world wars. Yet, paradoxically, by their very insistence, unionists appeared to be asserting
something that was not self-evident. Moreover, unionism was often couched
in anti-British, as much as anti-Irish, terms. Given this context, the cumu-
lative effect of unionist demands for recognition and inclusion acted to
demonstrate and psychologically perpetuate a lack of integration – this was
particularly noticeable, for instance, in the British response to the official
Northern Irish history of the Second World War.

Unionist culture and literature provide a rich context within which unionism and the northern Irish state, its institutions and behaviour, can be
explored and described. In this study, particular attention has been accorded
to the unionist histories of the 1920s, the royal and civic ceremonies which
recurred throughout the period 1920–55, the BBC and the alternative
protestant writings of the 1940s and 1950s. These manifestations of unionist
culture reveal some of unionism's key characteristics and concerns. And in
the variety of cultural expressions which intersected with political and social

developments, the complexity of unionism is apparent. This was not a simple case, as one writer has recently argued, of Ulster protestants 'in their outlook, their way of life, their loyalty, and their sense of history' being 'distinctively British'.[4] Indeed, on the contrary, many unionists were overtly anglophobic or were, at the very least, hostile towards the British government. Moreover, their sense of history was of a decidedly 'Ulster' variety, and throughout this period they argued for a history which was rooted in Ireland, as well as Britain, and specifically in Ulster, focusing on the uniqueness of Ulster and the 'Ulsterman'. In addition to the planter tradition, their connection with Britain was highlighted in terms of war contributions made by Northern Ireland in the First and Second World Wars. Yet while both allowed unionists to establish their separateness from southern Ireland, and their oneness with Britain, at the same time they represented their war-time experiences as unique within the United Kingdom. Their proclaimed 'Britishness', when it did arise, was often a reflection of political necessity which co-existed with a sense of being 'Ulster' and, to a lesser extent, 'Irish'. Unionist culture was thus at times repetitive and contradictory: it claimed distinctiveness and individuality within the United Kingdom, while at the same time it rejected the state's own unique local culture (particularly catholic) which it saw as a cover for an Irish national culture; and while it claimed unity with Britain, its culture simultaneously projected elements of anti-Englishness. Official unionist views of the state came in ceremonies such as the unveiling of the Carson statue, the Festival of Britain in Northern Ireland and the visits of monarchy to the state, in particular the coronation visit of Elizabeth II in 1953. Such ceremonies aimed at testifying to the permanent position of the state within the union, and the unity of the protestant population behind a number of symbols, particularly and repeatedly that of the monarchy. These ceremonies in tandem with official unionist literature testified to the continued survival of the state. But even in the most unexpected of places, in the novels of the unionist apologist Hugh Shearman for instance, there is a complexity and contradiction reflective of general tenets within unionism.

Unionist unity had developed over a thirty-year period prior to the establishment of the state, with an ethos and structure based on the resistance to home rule and centred around a protestant heritage which glossed over all divisions within the movement. In 1920 unionists had no constructive philosophy with which to govern the state they had been presented with, and having achieved their own parliament they found protestant unity hard to maintain.[5] In the early years of the state there was a need for unionists to find new political moorings, to create a state which would reflect the basic traits of unionist tradition and identity. The survival of the state depended upon unionists getting support from the protestant rank and file, and thus on their ability to create a state which in image and reality focused on protestant history and tradition and addressed an exclusively protestant audience. To cement the alliance of all protestants the unionist government structured the state to ensure that protestants would retain exclusive power. In addition, they created an identity and self-image of the state for unionists, based upon events and traditions peculiar to northern Irish protestants. Through civic and royal ceremonies the state was represented as a united protestant entity, endorsed by the monarchy, and by the ruling élites in the state.

Unionists' image of the state was exclusive, and one which alienated many, in particular, but not exclusively, catholics. In fact, the position or attitude of catholics in the state concerned unionists to a far lesser degree than the behaviour and response of protestants, who often dissented from the will of the government. It is clear from the working of the BBC in the state and from the writings of protestant writers such as John Hewitt, Sam Hanna Bell and Hugh Shearman that not only was there a great deal of diversity within the state but that this found particular expression within protestant circles themselves.[6]

Through the visits of royalty and affirming state ceremonies, such as the unveiling of the Carson statue, the Northern Irish state was reinforced and made tangible for unionists. While, at times (say the coronation visit of 1953) this was an expression of triumphalism, often it was a defensive response to a perceived threat – the opening of the Stormont parliament came directly after the return to triumphal catholicism with the Eucharistic Congress in the Free State. The primary audience for such unionist ceremonies were unionists and protestants in the state. In those areas where the unionist government did not dominate, again in the BBC and in the work of declared unionists such as St John Ervine, that diversity did come through, and displayed a rich and complex identity. The contradictions inherent within official unionism were compounded by the government and its representatives who simply glossed over any divisions within the state, fearful that the picture of Northern Ireland and the Northern Irish which they were trying to project would be complicated and confused by the acknowledgement of other images and alternative identities. It is a myth to talk of the monolith of unionism in general, or of the inarticulateness of unionists, given that up to the 1950s unionists aimed at representing and preserving protestant unity and power through elaborate and expressive royal and civic ceremonies. Thus, as one writer has noted, the decades which followed the establishment of the state were not 'silent years' but have, until now, been neglected ones.[7]

Martin Wallace, a journalist with the *Belfast Telegraph* and a contributor to the ill-fated *Character of Ireland*, wrote of Northern Ireland in 1956:

> Individualism has suffered; so have political thinking and rethinking, self-criticism, the democratisation of the party machinery, the evolution of a community less embittered by differences between the Protestant-Unionist majority and the Roman Catholic-Irish Nationalist minority.[8]

Unionists, Wallace argued, were characterised by defensiveness, 'forever attempting to justify themselves', and unduly sensitive to outside opinion. His astute article concluded that it was possible that there was no hope for a 'united community' in Northern Ireland, or an 'Ulster community whose differences would enrich much more than impoverish'. Six years later when unionists marked the fiftieth anniversary of the Solemn League and

Covenant, their election manifesto was launched under the heading 'This We Will Maintain'. Little progress in political terms seemed to have been made since the establishment of the state when James Craig declared that what protestants had they would hold.[9] According to Martin Wallace's assessment, John Hewitt's hopes of a decade earlier – that the sectarian divisions in Northern Ireland could be transcended – had come to nothing.[10] In the late 1950s, it appeared that the Northern Irish state was, to quote Hewitt, left once more 'precariously perched' upon a 'melting iceberg'.[11]

Notes and References

1   The most significant and illustrative text on the 1950s in Northern Ireland is Rosemary Harris's *Prejudice and tolerance in Northern Ireland: a study of neighbours and 'strangers' in a border community* (Manchester, 1972).

2   Jonathon Bardon, *A history of Ulster* (Belfast, 1992), p. 611.

3   T. Wilson, 'Devolution and partition', in T. Wilson (ed.), *Ulster under home rule* (Belfast, 1955), pp. 208–9.

4   For this argument see Bryan A. Follis, *A state under siege: the establishment of Northern Ireland, 1920–25* (Oxford, 1995), p. 187.

5   Patrick Buckland, *The factory of grievances: devolved government in Northern Ireland, 1921–39* (Dublin, 1979), p. 5.

6   Although equally they argued for a common, though not unproblematic, culture between Northern Irish catholics and protestants.

7   Séan McDougall, in Peter Catterall and Séan McDougall (eds.), *The Northern Ireland question in British politics* (London, 1996), p. 43.

8   Martin Wallace, 'Government of Northern Ireland', typescript of piece for *The character of Ireland*, D2833/D/12/1/19.

9   James Craig, cited in St John Ervine, *Craigavon: Ulsterman* (London, 1949), p. 489.

10   Martin Wallace, 'Government of Northern Ireland', typescript of piece for the *Character of Ireland*, D2833/D/12/1/19.

11   John Hewitt, 'Regionalism: the last chance', *Northman*, 1947.

Bibliography

Primary Material

(i) Manuscript sources – private

(a) *Public Records Office of Northern Ireland* (PRONI)
John Hewitt's papers: D3838.
Diary of Ruby Hewitt (RH): D3838/4/6.
W.R. Rodgers's papers: D2833.
Edward Carson's papers: D1507.

(b) *Sam Hanna Bell's papers* (SHBP) are held privately.

(ii) Government records

Public Records Office of Northern Ireland (PRONI)
Cabinet minutes.
Cabinet papers.
Ministry of finance papers.
Ministry of commerce papers.
Ministry of home affairs papers.
Local authority papers for Belfast.
Ulster Unionist Council papers.
Minutes of the Arts Council of Northern Ireland (formerly the Council for the Encouragement of Music and the Arts).

(iii) BBC Written Archive Centre, Reading, England

BBC Northern Ireland papers, including monthly reports by the controller of BBC Northern Ireland. These sources are identified with the prefixing letters 'R' and 'T' in the footnotes.

(iv) Newspaper sources (with abbreviations)

Belfast Newsletter (BNL).
Belfast Telegraph (BT).
Northern Whig (NW).

Belfast Weekly Newsletter (BWNL).
Belfast Weekly Telegraph (BWT).
Weekly Northern Whig (WNW).
Belfast Evening Telegraph (BET).

(v) Printed Sources

(a) *Northern Hansard.*
(b) *Ulster Yearbooks.*
(c) *BBC Yearbooks.*
(d) *Ulster To-day* (HMSO, November, 1945).
(e) Government of Northern Ireland. Ministry of Education list of Text Books in Reading, History, Citizenship, Economics and Irish 1926–1936.
(f) Council for the Encouragement of Music and the Arts (NI): First annual report 1.2.43–31.3.44.
(g) Listing of items from the Exhibition of Northern Ireland Books and Manuscripts, Festival of Britain in Northern Ireland, 1951.
(h) *Ulster for Your Holidays*, issued by the Ulster Tourist Development Assoc. Ltd (Belfast, 1929).
(i) Report on the Festival of Britain in Northern Ireland by CEMA, 1951.
(j) *The dictionary of national biography, 1922–30* (London, 1937).

(vi) Contemporary printed material

Armour, W.S.	*Armour of Ballymoney* (London, 1934).
	Facing the Irish question (London, 1935).
	Barker, E. (ed.) *The character of England* (Oxford, 1947).
Bates, Jean Victor	*Sir Edward Carson: Ulster leader* (London, 1921).
Bell, Sam Hanna and John Hewitt and Nesca Robb (eds.),	
	The arts in Ulster (London, 1951).
Bell, Sam Hanna	*December bride* (Belfast, 1951).
	Erin's Orange Lily (London, 1956).
	The hollow ball (Belfast, 1961).
	Within our province: a miscellany of Ulster writing (Belfast, 1972).
	A man flourishing (Belfast, 1973).
	Across the narrow sea (Belfast, 1987).
Blake, John	*Northern Ireland in the Second World War* (Belfast, 1956).
Camblin, Gilbert	*The town in Ulster* (Belfast,1951).
Campbell, Arthur and Campbell,George (eds.)	
	Now in Ulster (Belfast, 1944).
Campbell, T.J.	*Fifty years of Ulster, 1890–1940* (Belfast, *Irish News*, 1941).
Carty, J.	*A class-book of Irish history* (London, 1929).
	A junior history of Ireland, part 1 & 2 (London, 1932).
Chart, D.A.	*Ireland from Union to Catholic Emancipation* (London, 1910).
	A history of Northern Ireland (Belfast, 1927).
Colvin, Ian	*The life of Lord Carson*, vol. ii (London, 1934).
	The life of Lord Carson, vol. iii (London, 1936).
Crozier, F.P.	*Ireland for ever* (London, 1932).

Ervine, St John   *Sir Edward Carson and the Ulster movement* (Dublin, 1915).
                   Ulster (Ulster Tourist Development Association, 1926).
                   'Is liberty lost?', *Post-War Questions No. 8* (The Individualist
                      Bookshop Ltd, London, 1941).
                   Craigavon: Ulsterman (London, 1949).
Evans, E.E.   *Irish heritage: the landscape, the people and their work*
                      (Dundalk,1942).
                   *Northern Ireland: a new guide book with an introduction by
                      E. Estyn Evans* (London, 1951).
                   Northern Ireland – a portrait (Published for the Festival of
                      Britain in 1951).
Falls, Cyril   *The history of the 36th (Ulster) Division* (Belfast, 1922).
                   *The history of the first seven battallions: the Royal Irish
                      Rifles* (Aldershot, 1925).
                   The birth of Ulster (London, 1936).
                   *The place of war in history: an inaugural lecture delivered
                      before the University of Oxford on 22 November 1946*
                      (Oxford, 1947).
                   The Second World War: a short history (London, 1948).
                   'Northern Ireland and the defence of the British Isles', in
                      T.Wilson (ed.), *Ulster under Home Rule* (London, 1958).
                   The Great War (Toronto, 1959).
Greacen, Robert   *Northern harvest: anthology of Ulster writing* (Belfast,
                      1944).
Green, A.S.   *The old Irish world* (Dublin, 1912).
Guthrie, Tyrone   *The BBC in Northern Ireland, 1924–49* (Belfast, 1949).
Hamilton, Lord Ernest
                   The first seven divisions (London, 1916).
                   The soul of Ulster (London, 1917).
                   The Irish rebellion of 1641 (London, 1920).
Hayden, M. and Moonan, G.A.
                   *A short history of the Irish people: from earliest times to
                      1920* (London, 1921).
Hayward, Richard   *In praise of Ulster* (Belfast, 1938).
                   Belfast through the ages (Dundalk, 1952).
Hewitt, John   'Regionalism: the last chance', *Northman*, 1947.
Hyde, Montgomery   *Carson* (London, 1953).
Ireland, Denis   *Ulster to-day and to-morrow: her part in a gaelic civilisation,
                      a study in political re-evolution* (London, 1931).
                   Six counties in search of a nation (Belfast, 1947).
Johnstone, T.M.   *Ulstermen: their fight for fortune, faith and freedom* (Belfast,
                      1914).
Kerr-Smiley, P.   *The peril of home rule* (London, 1911).
Kiely, Benedict   *Modern Irish fiction* (Dublin, 1950).
Logan, James   *Ulster in the x-rays* (London, 1923).
Macardle, D.   *The Irish republic* (London, 1937).
MacKnight, Thomas *Ulster as it is* (2 vols, London, 1896).
MacKnight, W.A.   *Ireland and the Ulster legend or the truth about Ulster*
                      (London, 1921).
MacNeill, E.   *Celtic Ireland* (Dublin, 1921).

McNeill, Ronald   *Ulster's stand for union* (London, 1922).
Marjoribanks, Edward
                     The life of Lord Carson, vol. i (London, 1932).
Maxwell Henry   *Ulster was right* (London, 1934).
Mogey, J.M.   *Rural life in Northern Ireland* (Oxford, 1947).
                     Northern Ireland: A Pictorial Survey (Belfast, 1952).
Morrison, H.S.   *Modern Ulster: its character, customs, politics and industries*
                     (London, 1920).
Phillips, W.A.   *The revolution in Ireland, 1906–23* (London, 1926).
Rodgers, W.R.   'Conversation piece: an Ulster protestant', *The Bell*, vol. 4,
                     no. 5, Aug. 1942.
                     'Black north', *New Statesman and Nation*, 20 Nov. 1943.
                     The Ulstermen and their country (London, 1947).
                     Collected poems (London 1971) with an introduction by Dan
                     Davin.
                     Irish literary portraits (London, 1972).
Shearman, Hugh   *Not an inch: a study of Northern Ireland and Lord Craigavon*
                     (London, 1942).
                     *The bishop's confession: being a memoir found among the
                     papers of the late Right Reverend Percival MacPeake,
                     D.D., Lord Bishop of the United Diocese of Bangor,
                     Dungannon, and Strabane* (London, 1943).
                     A bomb and a girl (London, 1944).
                     Northern Ireland: its history, resources and people (HMSO,
                     1946).
                     'Divided Ireland', *New Statesman and Nation*, 12 Feb. 1949.
                     'Recent developments in Anglo-Irish relations', *World Affairs*,
                     Apr. 1949.
                     Ulster (London, 1949).
                     How Northern Ireland is governed (HMSO, 1951).
                     Modern Ireland (London, 1952).
                     Northern Ireland, 1921–71 (HMSO, 1971).

Secondary Sources

Akenson, D.H.   *Education and enmity: the control of schooling in Northern
                    Ireland, 1920–50* (New York, 1973).
Banham, M. and Hillier, B.
                    A tonic to the nation: the Festival of Britain 1951 (London,
                    1976).
Bardon, Jonathon   *A history of Ulster* (Belfast, 1992).
Barthes, Roland   *Mythologies* (London, 1983).
Barton, Brian   *The blitz, Belfast in the war years* (Belfast, 1989).
                    'The impact of World War II on Northern Ireland and on
                    Belfast-London relations', in Peter Catterall and Séan
                    McDougall (eds.), *The Northern Ireland question in British
                    politics* (London, 1996).
Beadle, Gerald   *Television: a critical review* (London, 1963).
Beckett, J.C.   'Carson – unionist and rebel', in F.X. Martin (ed.), *Leaders and
                    men of the Easter Rising: Dublin 1916* (London, 1978).

Ben-David, Joseph and Terry Nichols-Clark (eds.)
    Culture and its creators: essays in honor of Edward Shils (Chicago and London, 1977).
Benjamin, Walter   *Illuminations* (London, 1988).
Bennett, T., Martin, G., Mercer, C., and Woollacott, J.
    Culture, ideology and social process (London, 1981).
Bew, Paul, Gibbon, Peter and Patterson, Henry (eds.)
    The state in Northern Ireland, 1921–72: political forces and social classes (Manchester, 1979).
Boyce, D.G.   *Englishmen and Irish troubles* (London, 1972).
    '"The marginal Britons": the Irish', in R. Colls and P. Dodd (eds.), *Englishness: culture and politics* (Beckenham, 1986).
    The Irish question and British politics, 1868–1986 (London, 1988).
    'Edward Carson (1854–1935) and Irish unionism', in Ciaran Brady (ed.), *Worsted in the game: losers in Irish history* (Dublin, 1989).
    Nineteenth century Ireland: the search for stability (Dublin, 1990).
and Robert Eccleshall and Vincent Geoghegan (eds.)
    Political thought in Ireland since the seventeenth century (London, 1993).
and Alan O'Day (eds.)
    The making of modern Irish history: revisionism and the revisionist controversy (London, 1996).
Boyd, J.   *The middle of my journey* (Belfast, 1990).
Bradley, A.   'Literature and culture in the north of Ireland', in M. Kenneally, (ed.), *Cultural contexts and literary idioms in contemporary Irish literature* (Bucks., 1988).
Brady, Ciaran (ed.) *Ideology and the historians* (Dublin, 1991).
Briggs, Asa   *The history of broadcasting in the United Kingdom* (5 vols, London, 1961–95).
Brown, Terence   'W.R. Rodgers: romantic calvinist', in T. Brown, *Northern voices: poets from Ulster* (Dublin, 1975).
    Ireland: a social and cultural history, 1922–85 (London, 1985).
    The whole protestant community: the making of a historical myth (Derry, 1985).
Buckland, Patrick *Irish unionism, 1885–1923: a documentary history* (HMSO, 1973).
    The factory of grievances: devolved government in Northern Ireland, 1921–39 (Dublin, 1979).
    James Craig (Dublin, 1980).
    A history of Northern Ireland (Dublin, 1981).
Buckley, A.D.   *History and ethnicity* (London, 1989).
Budge, I. and O'Leary, C.
    Belfast: approach to crisis (London, 1975).
Bushaway, Bob   'Name upon name: the Great War and remembrance', in R. Porter (ed.), *Myths of the English* (Cambridge, 1992).

Canetti, Elias   *Crowds and power* (Harmondsworth, 1973).
Cannadine, David   and Simon Price (eds.), *Rituals of royalty: power and ceremonial in traditional societies* (Cambridge, 1987).
Canning, P.   *British policy towards Ireland, 1921–41* (Oxford, 1985).
Cardiff, David with Paddy Scannell
                    'Broadcasting and national unity', in James Curran, Anthony Smith and Pauline Wingate (eds.), *Impacts and influences: essays on media power in the twentieth century* (London, 1987).
Carroll, Joseph   *Ireland in the war years* (Newton Abbot, 1975).
Cathcart, Rex   *The most contrary region, the BBC in Northern Ireland, 1924–84* (Belfast, 1984).
Catterall, Peter and McDougall, Seán (eds.)
                    The Northern Ireland question in British politics (London, 1996).
Chaney, David   'Fictions in mass entertainment', in James Curran, Michael Gurevitch, Janet Woolacott (eds.), *Mass communication and society* (London, 1977).
                    Fictions and ceremonies: representations of popular experience (London, 1979).
                    'A symbolic mirror of ourselves: civic ritual in mass society', in R. Collins et al. (eds.), *Media, culture and society: a critical reader* (London, 1986).
Clark, Jon, Heinemann, M. Margolies, D. and Snee, C. (eds.)
                    Culture and crisis in Britain in the thirties (London, 1979).
Clifford, B.   *Ireland in the Great War: the Irish insurrection of 1916 set in its context of the world war* (Belfast, 1992).
Clyde, Tom (ed.)   *Ancestral voices: the selected prose of John Hewitt* (Belfast, 1987).
                    'A stirring in the dry bones: John Hewitt's regionalism', in Gerald Dawe and John Wilson Foster (eds.), *The poet's place: Ulster literature and society. Essays in honour of John Hewitt, 1907–87* (Belfast, 1991).
Collins, R., Curran, J., Garnham, N., Scannell, P., Schlesinger and Sparks, C. (eds.)
                    Media, culture and society: a critical reader (London, 1986).
Cosgrove, D. and Daniels, S. (eds.)
                    The iconography of landscape: essays on the symbolic representation, design and use of past environments (Cambridge, 1988).
Craig, Patricia   'Assertors and protestors: John Hewitt as literary historian', in Gerald Dawe and John Wilson Foster (eds.), *The poet's place: Ulster literature and society. Essays in honour of John Hewitt, 1907–87* (Belfast, 1991).
Cronin, J.   'Prose', in M. Longley (ed.), *Causeway – the arts in Ulster* (Belfast, 1971).
Curran, James and Seaton, Jean Power
                    Power without responsibility: the press and broadcasting in Britain (St Ives, 1991).
Curran, James, Gurevitch, Michael and Woolacott, Janet (eds.)
                    Mass communication and society (London, 1977).

Curran, James, Smith, Anthony and Wingate, Pauline (eds.)
　　　　　　　Impacts and influences: essays on media power in the twentieth century (London, 1987).
Dangerfield, George　*The strange death of Liberal England* (London, 1936).
Davin, D.　　　　　*Closing time* (Oxford, 1975).
Dawe, Gerald with John Wilson Foster (eds.)
　　　　　　　The poet's place: Ulster literature and society. Essays in honour of John Hewitt, 1907–87 (Belfast, 1991).
Dickson, David, Keogh, Daire and Whelan, Kevin (eds.)
　　　　　　　The United Irishmen: republicanism, radicalism and rebellion (Dublin, 1993).
Dilthey, William　'The understanding of other persons and their life-expressions', in Patrick Gardiner (ed.), *Theories of history* (New York, 1959).
Dunn, D. (ed.)　　*Two decades of Irish writing* (Cheshire, 1975).
Dunne, Tom (ed.)　*The writer as witness* (Cork, 1987).
Eksteins, Modris　*Rites of spring: the Great War and the birth of the modern age* (London, 1990).
Farrell, M.　　　*Arming the protestants: the formation of the Ulster special constabulary, 1920–27* (Dingle and London, 1983).
Ferro, Marc　　　*The use and abuse of history: or how the past is taught* (London, 1981).
Fisk, Robert　　　*In time of war: Ireland, Ulster and the price of neutrality* (London, 1983).
Follis, Bryan A.　*A state under siege: the establishment of Northern Ireland 1920–25* (Oxford, 1995).
Foster, J.W.　　　*Forces and themes in Ulster fiction* (London, 1974).
　　　　　　　Colonial consequences (Dublin, 1991).
Foster, R.F.　　　*Modern Ireland, 1600–1972* (London, 1988).
　　　　　　　Paddy and Mr Punch, connections in Irish and English history (London, 1993).
　　　　　　　The story of Ireland: an inaugural lecture delivered before the University of Oxford on 1 December 1994 (Oxford, 1995).
Frayn, M.　　　'Festival', in Michael Sissons and Philip French (eds.), *Age of austerity: 1945–51* (Oxford, 1986).
Freedman, L. (ed.)　*War* (Oxford, 1994).
Fussell, Paul　　*The Great War and modern memory* (Oxford, 1975).
　　　　　　　Wartime: understanding and behaviour in WWII (Oxford, 1989).
　　　　　　　(ed.) *The bloody game, an anthology of modern war* (London, 1991).
Gardiner, Patrick (ed.)
　　　　　　　Theories of history (New York, 1959).
Geertz, Clifford　*The interpretation of cultures: selected essays* (New York, 1973).
Gerth, Hans and C. Wright Mills
　　　　　　　Character and social structure: the psychology of social institutions (London, 1954).
Gibbon, P.　　　*The origins of Ulster unionism* (Manchester, 1975).

Goffman, Erving   *Frame analysis* (Norwich, 1974).

Gorham, M.   *Forty years of Irish broadcasting* (Dublin, 1967).

Grana, Cesar   *Fact and symbol: essays in the sociology of art and literature* (Oxford, 1971).

Harbinson, J.W.   *The Ulster unionist party 1882–1973: its development and organisation* (Belfast, 1973).

Harkness, David   *Northern Ireland since 1920* (Dublin, 1983).

Harris, M.   *The catholic church and the foundation of the northern Irish state* (Cork, 1993).

Harvey, A.D.   *Collision of empires: Britain in three world wars, 1793–1945* (London, 1992).

Heaney, Seamus   (ed.), *Collected short stories: Michael McLaverty* (Dublin, 1978).

An open letter (Derry, 1983).

Hempton, D. and Hill, M.

Evangelical protestantism in Ulster society (London, 1992).

Heuser, Alan (ed.)   *Selected prose of Louis MacNeice* (Oxford, 1990).

Hewison, R.   *In anger: culture in the cold war, 1945–60* (London, 1981).

The heritage industry (London, 1987).

Homberger, E. and Charmley, J.

The troubled face of biography (London, 1988).

Jackson, P.   *Maps of meaning: an introduction to cultural geography* (London, 1989).

Jackson, A.   *The Ulster Party: Irish unionists in the House of Commons, 1884–1911* (Oxford, 1989).

Sir Edward Carson (Dundalk, 1993).

'Irish unionism', in D.G. Boyce and Alan O'Day (eds.), *The making of modern Irish history: revisionism and the revisionist controversy* (London, 1996).

'Irish unionism and the empire, 1880–1920: classes and masses', in Keith Jeffery (ed.), *'An Irish empire?' Aspects of Ireland and the British Empire* (Manchester, 1996).

Jeffery, Keith   *The British army and the crisis of empire, 1918–22* (Manchester, 1984).

(ed.), *'An Irish empire?' Aspects of Ireland and the British Empire* (Manchester, 1996).

Johnson, D.   *The interwar economy in Ireland* (Dublin, 1985).

Johnston, R.   *Orders and desecrations* (Dublin, 1992).

Johnstone, T.   *Orange, green and khaki: the story of the Irish regiments in the Great War, 1914–18* (Dublin, 1992).

Jusdanis, G.   *Belated modernity and aesthetic culture: inventing national literature* (Theory and History of Literature, vol. 81, 1991).

Kelly, James   *Bonfires on the hillside, an eyewitness account of political upheaval in Northern Ireland* (Belfast, 1995).

Kenneally, M. (ed.)   *Cultural contexts and literary idioms in contemporary Irish literature* (Bucks., 1988).

Kennedy, Dennis   *The widening gulf: northern attitudes to the independent Irish state, 1919–49* (Belfast, 1988).

Kern, Stephen   *The culture of time and space, 1880–1918* (Mass., 1988).

Kingsley-Ward, G.   *Courage remembered: the story behind the construction and maintenance of the commonwealth's military cemeteries and memorials of the wars of 1914–18 and 1939–45* (London, 1995).

Klapp, O.E.   *Symbolic leaders: public dramas and public men* (Chicago, 1964).

Klein, Holger (ed.)   *The second world war in fiction* (London, 1984).

Kritzman, Lawrence D. (ed.)
Foucault: politics, philosophy, culture. Interviews and other writings 1977–84 (London, 1988).

Laffan, Michael   *The partition of Ireland, 1911–25* (Dundalk, 1983).

Lee, J.J.   'Some aspects of modern Irish historiography', in E. Schulin (ed.), *Gedenkschrift Martin Gohring: studien zur europaischen geschichte* (Wiesbaden, 1968).

Ireland 1912–85: politics and society (Cambridge, 1989).

Longley, Edna   'The writer and Belfast', in M. Harman (ed.), *The Irish writer and the city* (Gerrards Cross, 1984).

'"When did you last see your father?": perceptions of the past in Northern Irish writing, 1965-85', in M. Kenneally (ed.), *Cultural contexts and literary idioms in contemporary Irish literature* (Bucks., 1988).

'The Rising, the Somme, and Irish memory', in M. Ní Dhonnchadh and T. Dorgan (eds.), *Revising the Rising* (Derry, 1991).

The living stream: literature and revisionism in Ireland (Newcastle-upon-Tyne, 1994).

Longley, Michael (ed.)
Causeway: the arts in Ulster (Belfast, 1971).
Poems: W.R. Rodgers (Meath, 1993).

Loughlin, James   *Ulster unionism and British identity* (London, 1995).

Lukes, Steven   *Power: a radical view* (London, 1974).
Essays in social theory (London, 1977).

Lyons, F.S.L.   *Ireland since the famine* (London, 1971).
Culture and anarchy in Ireland, 1880–1939 (Oxford, 1980).

Lyons, J.B.   *The enigma of Tom Kettle: Irish patriot, essayist, poet, British soldier, 1880–1916* (Dublin, 1983).

Mansergh, Nicholas   'The influence of the past', in D. Watt (ed.), *The constitution of Northern Ireland* (London, 1981).

The unresolved question, the Anglo-Irish settlement and its undoing, 1912–72 (London, 1991).

Marwick, A.   (ed.), *The arts, literature and society* (London, 1990).
Culture in Britain since 1945 (London, 1991).

Meinig, D.W. (ed.)   *The interpretation of ordinary landscapes* (Oxford, 1979).

MacDonagh, Oliver   *States of mind* (London, 1983).

McFadden, Roy   'No dusty pioneer: a personal recollection of John Hewitt', in Gerald Dawe and John Wilson Foster (eds.), *The poet's place: Ulster literature and society. Essays in honour of John Hewitt, 1907–87* (Belfast, 1991).

McGuinness, Frank   *Observe the sons of Ulster marching towards the Somme* (London, 1986).

McIntosh, Gillian   'Acts of "national communion": the centenary of Catholic Emancipation 1929 as a forerunner of the Eucharistic Congress 1932' in Joost Augusteijn (ed.), *Ireland in the 1930s* (Dublin 1999).

McLoone, Martin (ed.)
   Broadcasting in a divided community, seventy years of the BBC in Northern Ireland (Belfast, 1996).

McMahon, Deirdre   *Republicans and imperialists: Anglo-Irish relations in the 1930s* (Yale University, 1984).

Miller, D.W.   *Queen's rebels: Ulster loyalism in historical perspective* (Dublin, 1978).

Moloney, Ed, with Andy Pollak
   Paisley (Dublin, 1986).

Moody, T.W. and Beckett, J.C. (eds.)
   Ulster since 1800: a political and economic survey (London, 1955).
   Queen's Belfast, 1845–1949, the history of a university, 2 vols (London, 1959).

Morgan, K.O.   *The Oxford history of Britain* (Oxford, 1993).

Moss, G.L.   *Fallen soldiers: reshaping the memory of the world wars* (Oxford, 1990).

O'Brien, D.   *W.R. Rodgers* (Lewisburg, 1970).

Ó Buachalla, Breandan
   I mBeal Feirste Cois Cuain (Dublin, 1968).

O'D. Hanna, Denis   *The face of Ulster* (London, 1952).

O'Faoláin, S.   *The Irish* (Harmondsworth, 1962).

O'Halloran, Clare   *Partition and the limits of Irish nationalism* (Dublin, 1987).

Ormsby, Frank (ed.) *The collected John Hewitt* (Belfast, 1991).

Orr, Phillip   *The road to the Somme: men of the Ulster division tell their story* (Belfast, 1987).

Orwell, George   *The road to Wigan Pier* (London, 1937).
   Collected essays (London, 1961).

Paulin, Tom   *Ireland and the English crisis* (Newcastle-upon-Tyne, 1984).
   Minotaur: poetry and the nation state (London, 1993).

Phillip, Alan B.   *The Welsh question: nationalism in Welsh politics, 1945–70* (Cardiff, 1975).

Phoenix, E.   *Northern nationalism: nationalist politics, partition, and the catholic minority in Northern Ireland 1890–1940* (Belfast, 1994).

Reid, Betty   'The Left Book Club in the "thirties"', in Jon Clark, Margot Heinemann, David Margolies and Carole Snee (eds.), *Culture and crisis in Britain in the 'thirties* (London, 1979).

Rickman, H.P.   *Understanding and the human studies* (London, 1967).

Ricoeur, Paul   *A Ricoeur reader: reflection and imagination* (Hemel Hempstead, 1991).

Rolston, Bill   *An oral history of Belfast in the 1930s* (Belfast, 1987).

Scannell, Paddy   'Broadcasting and the politics of unemployment, 1930–35', in R.Collins et al. (eds.), *Media, culture and society: a critical reader* (London, 1986).

and David Cardiff   *A social history of British broadcasting: serving the nation,*
1922–39, vol. i (Oxford, 1991).

Seton-Watson, Hugh
Nations and states: an enquiry into the origins of nations
and the politics of nationalism (London, 1977).

Shea, P.   *Voices and the sound of drums: an Irish autobiography*
(Belfast, 1981).

Short, John Rennie *Imagined country: society, culture and environment*
(London, 1991).

Siepmann, Charles *Radio, television and society* (Oxford, 1950).

Sissons, Michael and French, Philip (eds.)
Age of austerity: 1945–51 (Oxford, 1986).

Smith, A.C.H., Immirzi, E., Blackwell, T.
Paper voices: the popular press and social change, 1935–65
(London, 1975).

Stallworthy, Jon   *Louis MacNeice* (London, 1995).

Steedman, Carolyn *Landscape for a good woman: a story of two lives* (London,
1986).

Stevenson, John, and Cook, Chris
The slump: society and politics during the depression
(London, 1977).

Stewart, A.T.Q.   *The Ulster crisis* (London, 1967).
The narrow ground: aspects of Ulster, 1609–1969 (London,
1977).
Sir Edward Carson (Dublin, 1981).

Taylor, A.J.P.   *English history, 1914–45* (Oxford, 1965).

Taylor, P.M.   *The projection of Britain: British overseas publicity and*
propaganda 1919–39 (Cambridge, 1981).

Terraine, J.   *The smoke and the fire: myths and anti-myths of war*
1861–1945 (London, 1980).

Thomas, Hugh (ed.) *The establishment: a symposium* (London, 1959).

Thompson, E.P.   *Customs in common* (London, 1991).

Todd, Jennifer   'Unionist political thought, 1920–72', in D.G. Boyce, Robert
Eccleshall, Vincent Geoghegan (eds.), *Political thought*
in Ireland since the seventeenth century (London,
1993).

Turner, John (ed.) *Britain and the first world war* (London, 1988).

Vance, Norman   *Irish literature: a social history. Tradition, identity and*
difference (Oxford, 1990).

Vincent, John (ed.) *The Crawford papers, the journals of David Lindsay twenty-*
seventh earl of Crawford and tenth Earl of Balcarres,
1871–1940, during the years 1892–1940 (Manchester,
1984).

Waites, B., Bennett, T., Martin, G. (eds.)
Popular culture: past and present (London, 1982).

Wallace, M.   *Northern Ireland: 50 years of self-government* (Newton
Abbot, 1971).

Warner, Alan (ed.) *The selected John Hewitt* (Belfast, 1981).

Watt, D. (ed.)   *The constitution of Northern Ireland* (London, 1981).

Welch, Robert (ed.) *The Oxford companion to Irish literature* (Oxford, 1996).

White, Hayden   *Tropics of discourse: essays in cultural criticism* (London, 1978).
Whyte, J.H.   'How much discrimination was there under the unionist regime, 1921–68', in T.Gallagher and J O'Connell (eds.), *Contemporary Irish studies* (Manchester, 1983).
                       Interpreting Northern Ireland (Oxford, 1990).
Wichert, Sabine   *Northern Ireland since 1945* (London, 1991).
Willener, A.   *The action-image of society: on cultural politicization* (London, 1970).
Williams, Raymond   *Culture and Society* (Harmondsworth, 1961).
                       The long revolution (London, 1961).
                       'The analysis of culture', in T. Bennett, G. Martin, C. Mercer, J. Woolacott (eds.), *Culture, ideology and social process* (London, 1981).
                       Television: technology and cultural form (London, 1990).
Wilson, A.N.   *C.S. Lewis: a biography* (London, 1990).
Wilson, Thomas   *Ulster under home rule* (Oxford, 1955).
Wolff, Janet   *The social production of art* (London, 1981).

Articles

Blumler, J.G., Brown, J.R., Ewbank, A.J., and Nossiter, T. J.
                       'Attitudes to the monarchy: their structure and development during a ceremonial occasion', *Political Studies*, vol. xix, no. 2 (1971), pp. 149–71.
Carson, Douglas   'A Kist o' Whistles', *Fortnight* (Autumn, 1990).
                       'Sam Hanna Bell, 1909–90', *The Honest Ulsterman*, no. 89 (Summer, 1990), pp. 43–52.
                       'The pursuit of the fancy man: Sam Hanna Bell and W.R. Rodgers, 1952–55', in *The Honest Ulsterman*, no. 92 (Winter, 1991), pp. 18–25.
Cathcart, Rex   'BBC Northern Ireland: 50 years old', *Listener*, vol. 92, no. 2372, 12 Sept. 1974.
Clyde, Tom   'W.R. Rodgers: 1909–69', *The Honest Ulsterman*, no. 92 (Winter, 1991), pp. 3–8.
Cronin, Seán   'Nation building and the Irish language revival movement', *Éire-Ireland*, vol. xiii (Spring 1978), pp. 7–14.
Dawe, Gerald   'The parochial idyll', *The Honest Ulsterman*, no. 92 (Winter, 1991), pp. 9–12.
Fanning, Ronan   'The response of the London and Belfast governments to the declaration of the Republic of Ireland, 1948–49', *International Affairs*, vol. 58, no. I (1981–2), pp. 95–114.
Foster, R.F.   'History and the Irish question', *Transactions of the Royal Historical Society*, 5th series, vol. 33 (1983), pp. 169–92.
Gailey, Andrew   'King Carson: and essay on the invention of leadership', *IHS*, vol. xxx, no. 117 (May 1996) pp. 66–87.
Greer, Alan   'Sir James Criag and the construction of Parliament Buildings at Stormont', *IHS*, vol. xxxi, no. 123, May 1999.

Hammerton, Elizabeth and David Cannadine
'Conflict and consensus on a ceremonial occasion: the Diamond Jubilee in Cambridge in 1897', *The Historical Journal*, vol. 24, no. 1 (1981), pp. 111–46.

Jackson, A.   'Unionist history, 1', *Irish Review*, no. 7 (Autumn 1989), pp. 58–66.

'Unionist history, 2', *Irish Review*, no. 8 (Spring 1990), pp. 62–9.

'Unionist politics and protestant society in Edwardian Ireland', *The Historical Journal*, 33 (1990), pp. 839–66.

'Unionist myths, 1912–85', *Past and Present* (August, 1992), pp. 164–85.

Longley, Edna   'John Hewitt, 1907–87', *Fortnight*, September 1987.

'Progressive bookmen: politics and northern protestant writers since the 1930s', *Irish Review*, no. 1 (1986), pp. 50–57.

Loughlin, James   'Northern Ireland and British fascism in the inter-war years', *IHS*, vol. xxix, no. 116 (Nov. 1995) pp. 535–52.

MacDonald, Peter   '"The fate of identity": John Hewitt, W.R. Rodgers and Louis MacNeice', *Irish Review*, no. 12 (Spring/Summer, 1992).

Nutt, Kathleen   'Irish identity and the writing of history', *Éire-Ireland*, vol. xxix, no. 2 (Summer 1994), pp. 160–72.

O'Neill, Michael   'W.R. Rodgers's revolutionary theology', *The Honest Ulsterman*, no. 92 (Winter 1991), pp. 13–17.

Rodner, W.S.   'Leaguers, covenanters, moderates: British support for Ulster, 1913–14', *Éire-Ireland*, vol. xvii, no. 3 (1982), pp. 68–85.

Ward, A.J.   'Lloyd George and the 1918 Irish conscription crisis', *The Historical Journal*, vol. xvii, no. I, 1974, pp. 107–29.

Theses

Armour, D.A.N.   'W.S. Armour at the *Northern Whig*', unpublished MA dissertation, Sept. 1995, Queen's University Belfast.

Callan, P.   'Voluntary recruitment for the British army in Ireland during the First World War', unpublished Ph.D thesis, 1984, University College Dublin.

Canny, Liam P.   'Recruiting in the Irish Free State and Northern Ireland for the British armed forces during the 1939–1945 war', unpublished MA dissertation, Sept. 1995, Queen's University Belfast.

McIntosh, G.   'Politics as theatre: the popular culture of Ulster unionism', unpublished MA, Sept. 1992, University College Cork.

Index

239